THE FIRST
FEMALE PHARAOH

"With his customary flair for unearthing the secrets of the ancient world, Andrew Collins's study of the little-known female Egyptian pharaoh Sobekneferu is destined to become a classic. Her life and place in Egyptian history is presented engagingly and forensically, while the author's own passion for the subject is clear on every page. This is an important book."

LYNN PICKNETT AND CLIVE PRINCE, AUTHORS OF
*WHEN GOD HAD A WIFE: THE FALL AND RISE OF
THE SACRED FEMININE IN THE JUDEO-CHRISTIAN TRADITION*

"This new book by Andrew Collins, who I've known for more than forty years, deals with the story of the first female ruler in history. Sobekneferu was the last ruler of the Twelfth Dynasty in Egyptian history. More than two centuries later Hatshepsut became the second Egyptian queen. As always, Andrew Collins uses his historical knowledge, along with his deep imagination, to bring the story of Sobekneferu to life."

AHMED OSMAN, AUTHOR OF *THE EGYPTIAN ORIGINS OF
KING DAVID AND THE TEMPLE OF SOLOMON* AND
THE LOST CITY OF THE EXODUS

"Finally, a long-overdue opus honoring one of history's most enigmatic women—Sobekneferu. Andrew Collins has scoured historical records, archaeological discoveries, and scattered images of this mysterious yet powerful female ruler of Upper and Lower Egypt to piece together this first major overview of her Twelfth Dynasty reign as a queen and pharaoh."

ANI WILLIAMS, HARPIST, SINGER, SONGWRITER, AUTHOR,
SOUND THERAPIST, AND PILGRIMAGE GUIDE

THE FIRST
FEMALE PHARAOH

Sobekneferu, Goddess of
the Seven Stars

ANDREW COLLINS

Bear & Company
Rochester, Vermont

Bear & Company
One Park Street
Rochester, Vermont 05767
www.BearandCompanyBooks.com

Bear & Company is a division of Inner Traditions International

Cataloging-in-Publication Data for this title is available from the Library of Congress

ISBN 978-1-59143-445-0 (print)
ISBN 978-1-59143-446-7 (ebook)

Printed and bound in China by Reliance Printing Co., Ltd.

10 9 8 7 6 5 4 3 2 1

Text design by Kenleigh Manseau and layout by Debbie Glogover
This book was typeset in Garamond Premier Pro with Gill Sans MT Pro,
The Bartender and Trenda used as display typefaces

Image Credits
Dieter Arnold, fig. 33.6; Brooklyn Museum, Charles Edwin Wilbour Fund (creative
commons), fig. 6.4; Nick Burton, front matter hieroglyphics, figs. 2.2, 4.2, 7.1, 8.4, 33.3;
Andrew Collins, figs. 9.1, 21.1, 22.1, 38.2, pls. 1, 3, 13, 14, 15, 16; Creative Commons
Agreement 2022, figs. 1.4 (by Postdlf), 18.1 (by Vassil), 18.5 (by Rama), 30.2 (by Franck
Monnier), 33.5 (by Heshbi), pls. 12 (by Tekisch), 17 (by Graeme Churchard), 24 (by
Ahmed Mosaad); Google Earth, figs. 2.3, 5.1, 7.4, 8.1, 19.1, 30.1, 34.1; Rodney Hale,
figs. 6.3 (reconstruction), 35.4; Russell M. Hossain, preface image, figs. 7.3, 11.2, 20.2;
Meretseger Books, pls. 5–8; Metropolitan Museum of Art, New York (public domain),
figs. 6.1, 6.2, 6.3, 12.3, pl. 4; Starfire Publishing, fig. 38.1, pl. 25; Stellarium, 37.1; Ani
Williams, figs. 32.1, 32.2; pls. 9–10, 18–23.

All other illustrations and plate pictures are in the public domain. Original sources of
noncopyright images are indicated in the caption. Every attempt has been made by the
author to clarify the ownership of illustrations used in this book. Any oversights or
omissions will be corrected in future editions.

To send correspondence to the author of this book, mail a first-class letter to the author
c/o Inner Traditions • Bear & Company, One Park Street, Rochester, VT 05767, and we will
forward the communication, or contact the author directly at **www.andrewcollins.com**.

To the memory of Storm Constantine (1956–2021),
a true priestess of the ancient goddesses of Egypt

Contents

History Is Made of Discoveries

By Jan Summers Duffy

Tutankhamen's highly acclaimed tomb, KV62 (King's Valley 62), and what we have discovered from it—including the artifacts it contains—are in many ways comparable to the enigma of Sobekneferu (Sobekkara). A lifetime of research and work in Egypt on tomb missions including KV62's artifacts; KV63, the fascinating storage chamber found next to Tutankhamun's tomb in 2005; the "lost tomb" TT223 (Theban Tomb 223) at Qurnet Murai, south Assasif, on the west bank of the Nile opposite to Luxor; as well as my work with Penn State at the Mendes Delta site, have all convinced me of one assurance. This is that there is a great deal more to be discovered from further research and exploration just as there was before Tutankhamun's tomb was found. Whether a hidden burial location, artifacts belonging to family members, or political intrigue, these all tell us new things about the past.

Before the discovery in 1922 of his tomb in Egypt's Valley of the Kings by Howard Carter, the young boy king Nebkheperure Tutankhamun (1333 BCE–1323 BCE) was unknown. Previously, Carter had discovered minor artifacts that were relevant to his tomb, and this was enough to encourage the British archaeologist to continue digging, knowing that there must be more to be found. Finally, 10 years later, determination led him to Tutankhamen's final resting place. This important discovery has revealed to us surprising information about ancient Egyptian royal life, culture, art, death, religion, mummification, and the belief in the afterlife. Nevertheless, KV62 may still be hiding some of the secrets even after 100 years. For this reason, we continue working and doing research on ancient Egypt to confirm one thing—there is more to be discovered.

Sobekneferu, the subject of this book, was a strong Egyptian woman destined for the throne of ancient Egypt. Thrust into the forefront, she must have had an absolute determination and destiny to govern the Two Lands as a pharaoh. She lived in the Twelfth Dynasty during the Middle Kingdom (MK) approximately around 1800 BCE. From what we can surmise it was an era of strict rule of a country in transition, and at a time when a female ruler faced many hurdles. With only a few known artifacts and statuettes attested to her name, some of which are available to view in museums today, we know little of Sobekneferu. All that is truly known is that she was significant and the first woman in ancient Egypt to wear the crowns of both Upper and Lower Egypt. She was as central to her time as other female pharaohs were to theirs. This includes Hatshepsut (1479/1473–1458/57 BCE), Nefertiti (circa 1340–1335 BCE), and Cleopatra VII (51–30 BCE).

Sobekneferu is today being brought out of the darkness and into the light, just as the discovery of KV62 did for Tutankhamun in 1922. Like Tutankhamun, Sobekneferu was undoubtedly involved in political intrigues and uncertainties in taking the throne, especially for a woman. Yet little is really known of her life or her burial, a matter now addressed by the author of this present book. Andrew Collins has been able to piece together the life of Sobekneferu, and the monarch's relationship to her immediate family, by bringing together all available information known about her, not only from contemporary sources, but also from apparent echoes of her memory preserved in Greek, Hebrew, and Arab-Islamic tradition. This can now help us flesh out her world in this first ever biography of Egypt's first female pharaoh.

As archaeologists, Egyptologists, and students, we strive to find details through archaeological evidence, which can then be published to enhance further research. We know it's important to find out more. By following this, we enrich everyone's knowledge of the past and of those who existed in a time when there were no records to survive.

By further exploration of Egypt, we can begin to uncover the secrets of lost pharaohs like Sobekneferu, who played a big role in Egyptian history, but whose history has almost entirely been forgotten.

JAN SUMMERS DUFFY

JAN SUMMERS DUFFY, A.A.S.B.A. archaeology/Egyptology, M.Sc. Classical archaeology, Ph.D. (in progress), is an archaeologist/curator and Egyptologist who divides her time between New York, Idaho, and Egypt. She is with the College of Idaho, formerly with the New York State facility at historic Iona Island's Native American Collection. Before that, she excavated with New York State Archaeology Association (NYSAA) at Dutchess Quarry Caves, a significant mastodon site in the Northeast United States. In Idaho, she is the discoverer of the Warm Springs Site (10AA-612), an obsidian cache that may be linked to the Western Idaho Burial complex.

In Egypt, Summers has worked at several important sites including Mendes in the Nile Delta with Penn State, Theban tomb 223 (TT223), and several other tombs in the Luxor area. Her specific research is Egyptian funerary objects from KV62. Jan is the editor of a journal published on the KV62 headrests from Tutankhamun's tomb. In 2020 she consulted for the Tutankhamun exhibit at Boise, Idaho, and she serves as advisor and contributor for several groups and magazines.

Acknowledgments

First I want to thank Richard Ward and Debbie Cartwright for the many think tank sessions that helped inspire the reconstruction of Sobekneferu's life as presented in this book. I thank also Nick Burton and Russell M. Hossain for their illustrations, time, and patience; Caroline Wise and Michael Staley for their advice on the material contained in the final part of this book and for their pictures from the Kenneth Grant collection; Jan Summers for her foreword and for her careful reading of the manuscript to check Egyptological facts; Rodney Hale for overseeing technical aspects of this project; Greg Little for his continued help and support; Ani Williams for her thoughtful insights and for photographing the Fayum on my behalf; François Olivier and Meretseger Books for the use of images; Kara Cooney and Claire Malleson for their Egyptological advice; and Dieter Arnold and Franck Monnier for their correspondence and help.

My thanks also go out to Maria Louise, Hugh Newman, J. J. Ainsworth, Jacqui Maroun, Lora Little, Lisa Weaver, Kerry Ann Dar, Yuri Leitch, Paolo Sammut, Paul Weston, Rob Macbeth, Leela Bunce, Buster Todd, Abbie Todd, Darcie Todd, Joan Hale, Catherine Hale, Yvan Cartwright, Graham Phillips, Renee Goulet, Miriam Miller, Angela Saxton, Catja de Lorenzo, Özgecan Berdibek, Jim Hibbert, Eileen Buchanan, Danielle Lainton, Roma Harding, Melissa Tittl, Ioannis Syrigos, Joanna Gillen, Melissa Thiringer, and, finally, Alicia McDermott for the part they have played in this extraordinary quest of discovery. My additional thanks go out also to all those at my publisher, Inner Traditions. Thank you for continuing to believe in me.

Last, my thoughts are with my dear departed friend Storm Constantine. She was a wonderful sister, colleague, and priestess, whose legacy lives on in her many books and in Immanion Press, the publishing house she helped create (immanion-press.com). They have now published a unique memorium volume in celebration of Storm's life titled *Pashterina's Peacocks*. It has contributions from, among many others, Neil Gaiman, Michael Moorcock, and myself. This book is dedicated to her.

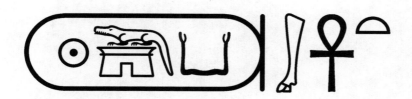

Sobekkara, may she live again

Artist's impression of Sobekkara Sobekneferu, ruler of the Two Lands, by artist Russell M. Hossain. It is based on the reconstruction of the now lost Berlin bust from a surviving photograph (see chapter 4 and plate 3).

The Knowing of Sobekneferu

The date is around 1800 BCE and the location the royal palace attached to the temple of the crocodile god Sobek at Shedet in the midst of Ta-she, the Land of the Lake (modern-day Fayum in central Egypt). Having walked slowly through the stone corridors in the company of two of her most trusted advisors, Sobekkara Sobekneferu, ruler of Upper and Lower Egypt, slowly climbed the flight of stairs that would take her to the Window of Appearance overlooking the large open courtyard below.

Some three dozen Egyptians and some Aamu (Asiatic) advisers had assembled to hear the monarch's regular address to those who ran the country. Among them were courtiers, officials, priests from key temples, some governors of provinces, as well as a few permitted members of their families. No matter who they might be, those present, whether ally or foe, now held sway over her future destiny.

With stern gaze Sobekneferu looked out over the crowd before preparing to welcome them to the royal palace. Her sheer presence was enough to tell all present that she remained firmly in control of the Two Lands, which she had ruled with an iron fist for just over three and a half years. All feared her, but she was also respected by those who remained faithful to her justified cause.

She knew very well, however, that her strict political strategies had not been greeted kindly by some members of the Egyptian population, in Lower Egypt in particular, while the leaders of the highly influential Aamu communities in the Nile Delta saw her actions as highly disfavorable to their presence in the country. But always her decisions had been made to keep the country united as one so that all might live in *ma'at*—"truth, justice and cosmic harmony"—thus ensuring the continuance of creation in the outside world.

There was, of course, a certain amount of remorse on her part about all that had passed to ensure her own place on the throne. Her will, however, had always been blessed by the gods and her coronation legitimized by the goddess Hathor herself. Gazing out over the audience assembled before her, the monarch knew that among them were those who had carried out her wishes in full, whether this be in public or in private.

That said, there were those among the crowd whom she could not trust, their motives either unclear or downright contrary to the political decisions she had made to strengthen her rule of the Two Lands. These individuals and their advisors were there to spy on her and plot their strategies against her place on the throne. For the time being, all she could do was accept that her orders would continue to be carried out by those who had remained loyal and acknowledge the fact that the majority of Egyptians still supported her. Despite this comfort she sensed that she was not long for this world.

What she had achieved had brought her great satisfaction as well as a personal feeling of immense gratitude for the opportunities that life had given her. In the eyes of her supporters, she would hopefully be long remembered. Her path to sovereignty had, however, been treacherous and at times had appeared like an impossible course to navigate. This had seemed especially so since her half-sister Neferuptah and full brother Maakherure Amenemhat had been bestowed the full rights of kingship ahead of her by their father, the great king Nimaatre Amenemhat.

Like Hathor, who had swallowed the seven cobras to gain the power of the *heka*-magic, she too had invoked this same power to ensure the outcome of her own future destiny, and through this act had risen to become the first woman ever to wear the double crown of Upper and Lower Egypt.

Now, however, the tides were turning. Forces were moving against her and there were those who would do anything to show that she was failing in her duties to protect the fertility of the Two Lands. Dissenting priests had spread false rumors that the gods were angry, citing the low floodwaters brought about by the actions of Hapy, the god who brings new life to the great Iteru (the River Nile) each year. They make it clear to all who have ears to listen that this means the seeds cannot be properly sown in the fields and that a poor harvest will spell the beginning of another great famine like those that plagued the early years of her father's reign.

They say that Hapy is disfavoring the people because Sobekneferu has made the divine crocodile the one true spirit of every god and insists that the priesthoods from every nome (district) come to Ta-she to pay homage to Sobek; a falsehood that will bring only ruin to the Two Lands.

Her political strategies, no matter how harsh some of the people might see them, would remain. As monarch she would change nothing. Those moving against her would be resisted until the very end. Until, that is, they did come for her. This she knew would happen soon enough. She could feel it, and those she most trusted had warned her of dark clouds looming heavily on the eastern horizon.

When the time was right she would remove herself from the path of humiliation and surrender to the gods in her own way. It would then be up to her followers, her devotees, and her chosen successors in the new dynasty to continue what she and her father had begun. Her own fate now was very firmly in the hands of the gods, and what awaited her in death she would readily embrace to ensure the future destiny of Egypt.

This is an imaginary scenario based on what we know of the events surrounding the life of Sobekkara Sobekneferu, the first woman to wear the crowns both of Upper Egypt and of Lower Egypt. So who exactly was Sobekneferu? How did she emerge from a predominantly patriarchal society to become monarch of the Two Lands? What did she believe in? What monuments has she left behind? How did she die, and what lasting impact has she had on the world around us?

As we shall see, Sobekneferu's life, played out toward the end of the Twelfth Dynasty of Egyptian history, was remarkable in so many different ways. During her early years she would appear to have taken a spiritual path, being linked perhaps with a temple somewhere in Egypt. Two siblings—her half sister Neferuptah and her full brother Amenemhat IV—stood to inherit the throne in front of her. What is more, their father the king, Amenemhat III, had chosen them to rule the country jointly, even allowing Neferuptah to bear her name within the royal cartouche, the first woman ever to be given this unique privilege. Any offspring she and her half-brother produced would have been next in line to inherit the throne.

Then tragedy struck. Just before this arranged marriage could occur, Neferuptah—still just a teenager—died mysteriously, leaving Amenemhat IV to ascend to the throne on his own, seemingly now with his full sister Sobekneferu by his side. What happened to Neferuptah? Did she die of natural causes or was she murdered?

Thereafter Sobekneferu was able to engineer her own accession to the throne and rule the country in a concerted effort to keep Egypt together as a single nation. It was something she ably managed to achieve, but in doing so the monarch would appear to have made enemies of one of Egypt's most powerful priesthoods, and this would ultimately cost her not only her place on the throne, but also, it would seem, her life.

That a woman, who was not the first or even the second in line for the throne, should rise to become the first female monarch of the Two Lands of Egypt is an extraordinary realization. Yet without her absolute belief and conviction in the fact that she was destined to take the throne of Egypt, her intentions could never have been fulfilled. In this book we find tentative evidence that Sobekneferu took part in unorthodox religious ceremonies to help ensure her future destiny, something that made her believe in herself, and as a consequence believe that it was her divine right to rule the kingdom.

Her strict policies, some of which might well be viewed as contrary to modern progressive attitudes today, enabled those who followed in her footsteps to carry forward the torch of Egyptian sovereignty across the next two and a half centuries. The concerted efforts of these ruling houses, remembered as the Thirteenth and Seventeenth dynasties of Egyptian history, would help ensure the kingdom's survival through one of its darkest hours, that of the Second Intermediate Period. Their actions would eventually lead to the vanquishing of the Hyksos, the Asiatic warlords who had taken control of the north of the country around 1675 BCE and had ruled from their capital Avaris in the Nile Delta for the next 125 years. In doing so, Kamose, the final king of the Seventeenth Dynasty, and his brother Ahmose, the first king of the Eighteenth Dynasty, would initiate the foundation of one of the most powerful and most successful periods of Egyptian history, the New Kingdom, which opened with the Eighteenth Dynasty, circa 1550 BCE.

STRUCK FROM EXISTENCE

History itself, however, has not been kind to Sobekneferu. Even though she was deified in death, later generations would seem to have wrongly blamed her for the events leading up to the Hyksos invasion. Sobekneferu's name would appear to have been ignored by some later king lists. The Fayum, her power base, would also seem to have suffered afterward because of its affiliations with the crocodile god Sobek, who in later dynastic history would come to be seen as a vehicle of the evil god Seth (also written Set). On top of this, her place of burial was lost and her achievements absorbed into those of her more successful father, Amenemhat III, whom she herself had deified.

We learn how Sobekneferu's memory survived, how she was portrayed by Egyptologists during the nineteenth century, and how she has arisen as an important pop icon through her role as Bram Stoker's ruler of the Two Lands who returns from the dead in his Egyptian novel *The Jewel of Seven Stars*. It was through this fortutituous association with gothic fiction that the female monarch came to be seen as the initiator of potent occult traditions that continue to thrive today. For the first time ever we learn the story of this remarkable woman and how she came to control one of the most powerful nations of the ancient world, and how when her adversaries did finally come for her she found a way to ensure that Egypt's future destiny was indeed secured.

"I say a great thing; listen!
I will teach you the nature of the Eternal One."

SEHOTEP-AB-RA
(BRUGSCH 1881,
2ND EDITION, VOL. I, 197)

PART I

DISCOVERING SOBEKNEFERU

1

Female Pharaohs

Cleopatra. Nefertiti. Hatshepsut. All of them are ancient Egyptian female rulers, immortalized in films, in books, and on television. They celebrate the great achievements of powerful women in history who rose above predominantly patriarchal societies to become leaders of what was arguably the greatest empire of the ancient world. Each bore royal titles signifying their dominion over both Upper and Lower Egypt, a vast kingdom that at times stretched from the Mediterranean Sea in the north to the limits of Palestine-Syria in the east and ancient Nubia, modern-day Sudan, in the south.

THE CHARACTER OF CLEOPATRA

Very few people will not know the story of Cleopatra (fig. 1.1), with her charismatic and highly intellectual personality, her penchant for entertainment, and the political ingenuity and cunning she displayed in her dealings with the mighty empire of Rome. In addition to this she spoke as many as a dozen languages and studied astronomy, mathematics, and philosophy, as well as the art of persuasive public speaking.

Cleopatra is most remembered, however, for her controversial relationship with the Roman dictator and general Julius Caesar, along with her later love for the Roman military commander and administrator Mark Antony. As we are informed by the classical writers, it was after the defeat of a joint Roman and Egyptian fleet at the battle of Actium in 31 BCE that Antony and Cleopatra both committed suicide, which in her case was effected, it is said, by the bite of a poisonous snake (a matter explored in chapter 20).

Fig. 1.1. First-century CE portrait of Cleopatra from Herculaneum in Italy. Painted posthumously, the original shows the monarch with red hair and realistic features, wearing a diadem and pearl-studded hairpins.

Much of what we know about Cleopatra from classical writers is perhaps based on some variation of the truth according to which sources are consulted. For better or worse, however, these stories admirably reflect the manner in which this extraordinary woman ruled Egypt for 22 years, between 51 and 30 BCE.

ENTRY INTO ROME

Of all the tales told about Cleopatra VII (she was the seventh Ptolemaic queen to bear this name, but the only one to become outright ruler of the country), it is her dramatic entry into Rome to present her son, the future king Ptolemy XV Caesarion, to his father Julius Caesar that might be seen as the most triumphant. Whenever one thinks of this monumental event it is difficult not to picture its spectacular cinematic portrayal in the 1963 film *Cleopatra,* directed by Joseph L. Mankiewicz. Starring Elizabeth Taylor as the iconic Queen of Egypt, it was the film that not only helped Cleopatra become a household name but also created the stereotypical view we have today of ancient Egyptian royal women. This, most assuredly, was down to Taylor's charismatic performance, with her future husband Richard Burton starring opposite her as Mark Antony and Rex Harrison as Julius Caesar.

When we think of a Queen of Egypt some part of us will always unconsciously picture Elizabeth Taylor in her role as Cleopatra complete with her signature black wigs, beautiful gold jewelry, dazzling costumes, period-perfect makeup, and stylized kohl eyeliner. It is a stereotypical image that remains strong, despite being gradually replaced by a more inclusive and realistic portrayal of ancient Egyptian royal women in both fictional and nonfictional settings.

THE BEAUTY OF NEFERTITI

When we think of Queen Nefertiti it is *that* stucco-painted limestone bust that comes to mind. Found during excavations in 1912 in an artist's workshop at Tell el-Amarna in Middle Egypt, where Nefertiti's husband and co-regent Akhenaten had created a new capital city, it was removed to Germany, where it has since had a checkered history. Today it attracts around

Fig. 1.2. The famous bust of Nefertiti found at Tell el-Amarna in 1912 and on display today in the Egyptian Museum of Berlin (from Breasted 1936, pl. 130).

half a million visitors a year as a central exhibit at the Egyptian Museum in Berlin. Everyone who has ever gazed into the eyes of this iconic bust (one of which was left unfinished by the artist—see fig. 1.2) cannot help but be mesmerized by the stunning features of this iconic woman who thrived in a troubled world some 3,350 years ago.

Like Cleopatra, the life of Nefertiti has also been portrayed in films, in books, and on television. Most often she is cast as the devoted wife and queen of the pharaoh Akhenaten and as the mother of their many children. His main claim to fame was outlawing the kingdom's many gods in favor of a single, omnipotent deity called the Aten. This was the nourishing force of the sun represented in art as a golden sun disk from which emerged rays of light in the form of arms, each ending in hands that hold an *ankh,* the Egyptian symbol of life.

The story of Akhenaten and Nefertiti, and how together they attempted to change the art, religion, and lifestyle of the ancient Egyptian world is well known, and need not be recounted here. Suffice to say that Akhenaten's explosive 17-year reign, circa 1351–1334 BCE,* managed to stir considerable outrage among the existing priesthoods, particularly that of Amun, the patron god of Thebes (modern Luxor) in the south of the country. In the end this caused the collapse of Akhenaten's regime, which in turn led, inevitably, to the return of the old gods. Not only was Akhenetan's new capital at Tell el-Amarna destroyed, but all memory of his name and that of his dreaded Aten faith was chiseled out of every possible monument and inscription. Akhenaten was, in effect, unpersoned, his wife and consort Nefertiti suffering a similar fate simply by association.

With the old gods back in their rightful place, the newly reinstated Amun priesthood under the control of the military genius Horemheb, himself a future pharaoh, attempted to restore order and stability in the country by engineering the election to the throne of Akhenaten's young son Tutankhaten. His name would quickly be changed to the more acceptable Tutankhamun, honoring Amun's time-honored relationship with kingship in Egypt.

---

*All dates of Egyptian chronology featured in this book are derived, unless otherwise stated, from the UCL website "Digital Egypt for Universities," created in 2000–2003 and managed by Stephen Quirke.

THE EMERGENCE OF NEFERNEFERUATEN

What is less well known about Egypt's Amarna age is that Nefertiti not only ruled Egypt alongside her husband before his death, but that she might also have risen to become monarch herself, taking the name Neferneferuaten, meaning "beautiful are the beauties of the god Aten."[1] If correct, then her brief reign must have preceded that of the boy king Tutankhamun, who reigned for 10 years circa 1333–1323 BCE and died at the age of 18. (See fig. 1.3 for a breakdown of Egyptian royal kingdoms, dynasties, and individual rulers.)

Some scholars think Neferneferuaten was not Nefertiti at all, but Akhenaten's eldest daughter Meritaten,[2] the elder queen having disappeared or died before this time. Whether or not this was the case, the tantalizing possibility that Nefertiti might have worn the double crown of Upper and Lower Egypt is a thought-provoking idea at the very least. She was not, however, the first queen who rose to become outright ruler of Egypt. There had been others before her including her husband Akhenaten's great ancestor Hatshepsut.

THE ACHIEVEMENTS OF HATSHEPSUT

As the daughter of king Thutmose I, who ruled circa 1504–1492 BCE, Hatshepsut became queen of Egypt after marrying her half-brother, Thutmose II, when he was just 12 years old. After his death around 1479 BCE, Hatshepsut assumed the role of regent on behalf of her stepson. This was the infant Thutmose III, the son of Thutmose II (circa 1492–1479 BCE) and his secondary wife or concubine Iset. Through the immense power Hatshepsut now wielded and the manner she conveyed herself in public, the queen would quickly rise to assume the position of sole ruler of the country wearing the all-important double crown of Upper and Lower Egypt.

Now, as a fully-fledged pharaoh, Hatshepsut was able to motivate the kingdom in a number of different ways. During her six-year reign, circa 1479/1473–1458/1457 BCE, Hatshepsut extended foreign trade into distant lands like Punt, an exotic country located at the southern end of the Red Sea, while at the same time overseeing a large number of ambitious building projects. They included the creation of sanctuaries and obelisks at Karnak,

Date	Egyptian Period	Selected Dynasties
3200–3100 BCE	Pre-Dynastic Age	
3100–2686	Early Dynastic Age	
2686–2181	Old Kingdom	Dynasty 3 (2686–2600 BCE) Dynasty 4 (2600–2450) Dynasty 5 (2450–2300) Dynasty 6 (2300–2181)
2181–2025	First Intermediate Period	
2025–1794/3 or 2025–1700	Middle Kingdom	Dynasty 11 (2046–1976) Dynasty 12 (1976–1794/3)
1794/3–1550	Second Intermediate Period	Dynasty 13 (1794/3–c. 1640/39) Dynasty 14 (1794/3–c. 1675) Dynasty 15 (c. 1675–1550) Dynasty 16 (??) Dynasty 17 (1650–1550)
1550–1069	New Kingdom	Dynasty 18 (1550–1292) Dynasty 19 (1292–1185)
1069–664	Third Intermediate Period	
664–525	Late Period	Dynasty 26 (664–525)
525–404	First Persian Period	
404–343	Late Dynastic Period	
343–332	Second Persian Period	
332–305	Macedonian Period	
323–30	Ptolemaic Period	
30 BCE–640 AD	Roman Period	
640–1517	Islamic Period	

Fig. 1.3. Chronology of ancient Egypt showing dates, periods, and dynasties featured in this book (from the University College London website). Dates for the Second Intermediate Period are approximate.

Fig. 1.4. Red granite sphinx of Hatshepshut found at Deir el-Bahri, West Thebes, and today housed in the Metropolitan Museum of Art, New York. Note that the monarch wears a false beard as a sign of sovereignty. Photo by Postdlf.

the sprawling religious center serving the city of Thebes, as well as the construction of a breathtaking terraced mortuary temple on the western side of the Nile River at a site known today as Deir el-Bahri (you can read more about this important religious location in chapter 5). Hatshepsut's extraordinary complex is famous not only for its striking aesthetics, built as it is into a natural rockface, but also for the fact that within its interior is a frieze celebrating a remarkable trading expedition to the land of Punt that took place during the monarch's reign.

What's so important about Hatshepsut is that she not only assumed the double crown of Upper and Lower Egypt, but she also deliberately went out of her way to depict herself as male in public statues. Along with the familiar *nemes*-headdress of kings, she would be seen wearing a false beard, which was an important symbol of kingship (see fig. 1.4). Being portrayed as a male was, very clearly, something she saw as important in a highly patriarchal world unlikely to accept her for the way she was; that is, as a king who was a woman. For a while her strategy worked. Hatshepsut was accepted as rightful pharaoh, trusted by the royal court, by the priesthoods, and, most important of all, by her subjects.

HATSHEPSUT'S FALL

Following her death, however, circa 1458/1457 BCE, everything changed. Her successor, the now fully grown Thutmose III, went out of his way to extinguish all trace of his mother's reign. Monuments were defaced or destroyed, and her royal name was chiseled out of cartouches. These were the ornate oval-shaped frames used to contain the names of kings as well as some royal women. Worse still, all evidence of Hapshepsut's rule was expunged from official records with her architectural achievements now credited to Thutmose III.

Hatshepsut's legacy was thereafter forgotten until the nineteenth century when explorations by pioneering Egyptologists at various sites along the Nile started to uncover indisputable evidence of her reign. This was followed by the discovery in 1902 of her tomb during excavations in the Valley of the Kings under the leadership of British archaeologist Howard Carter (1874–1939). He, of course, would go on to discover Tutankhamun's tomb in the same valley exactly 20 years later in 1922. Very gradually a much clearer picture of who Hatshepsut was and what she achieved was finally obtained, allowing her place in Egypt's long history to be rightfully restored.

These are the stories behind ancient Egypt's most well-known female rulers, their legacies having persisted down through the ages, despite concerted attempts to eradicate all memory of their achievements by those who followed them. Through both serendipity and the accomplishments of Egyptological exploration across the past two centuries these remarkable women have been able to speak to us across the millennia, allowing them to become household names throughout the western world. More than this, in the cases of Cleopatra and Nefertiti at least, they have risen to become icons of modern pop culture.

OTHER FEMALE RULERS

There were, of course, other women in ancient Egypt's 3,000-year dynastic history who rose to become rulers of its people. The earliest of these was Queen Merneith (also written Merit-neith or Meryt-neith, and meaning "beloved of the goddess Neith"). She lived during Egypt's Early Dynastic Period (circa 3100–2686 BCE) and is thought to have been the great wife of a king named Djet and the mother and regent of his successor, Den.

For her achievements in life Merneith was granted a tomb in a royal cemetery usually reserved for male rulers. Some believe the manner she was treated in death warrants her being classified as Egypt's first female ruler. At Naqada in southern Egypt, a seal was found showing Merneith's name within a *serekh* exactly in the same manner that the names of male rulers were written.[3] Not enough, however, is known about her life and achievements to confirm whether or not this was the case.

Then there is Khentkhawes I, a powerful royal mother and queen of Egypt's highly influential Fourth Dynasty of kings. (Circa 2600–2450 BCE, the Fourth Dynasty formed part of Egypt's Old Kingdom period, which embraced dynasties Three to Six circa 2686–2181 BCE.) As the daughter of Menkaure, the builder of Giza's Third Pyramid, Khentkhawes I is thought to have been the royal wife of two kings, Shepseskaf, the last ruler of the Fourth Dynasty, and Userkaf, the first king of the Fifth Dynasty (circa 2450–2300 BCE). She may also have been the mother of two kings of the Fifth Dynasty, Sahure and Neferirkare.

For all that she achieved in life Khentkhawes I was honored with an extraordinary monument at Giza often referred to as the Fourth Pyramid or, occasionally, the "false pyramid."[4] Located within the plateau's main cemetery, a little east of the Third Pyramid and southwest of the Great Sphinx, its upper portion was constructed of limestone blocks while its lower half was carved directly out of the existing bedrock. It is within this monument that her shaft tomb can be found.

According to Egyptologist archaeologist Selim Hassan (1886–1961) an inscription noted on a granite doorjamb in the chapel attached to Khentkawes's tomb appeared to refer to her under such titles as "Mother of the King of Upper and Lower Egypt," "Daughter of the god," and, more controversially, "King of Upper and Lower Egypt."[5] This suggested to Hassan that she had risen to become sovereign herself,[6] a conclusion supported by German archaeologist Hermann Junker (1877–1962).[7] If correct, then Khentkawes I should be honored as Egypt's first female ruler of Upper and Lower Egypt, especially since she is shown in one bas-relief seated on a chair, holding a flail, and wearing a ritual beard. Against the idea of Khentkawes I's outright sovereignty, however, is the fact that her name is never seen contained in a cartouche, a prerequisite of any crowned ruler, nor is she featured in any contemporary king list.

So, did Khentkawes I really rule Egypt immediately after powerful Fourth Dynasty kings such as Khufu, Khafre, and Menkaure, the builders of the three main pyramids at Giza? The matter would appear to have been resolved in the 1970s when a Czech archaeological team working at the pyramid field of Abusir, about 6 miles (10 kilometers) south of Giza, excavated a small pyramid complex belonging to Khentkawes II, a queen who lived a generation after the aforementioned Khentkawes I. Remarkably, this second Khentkawes bore the same royal titles as her predecessor.[8] This showed clearly that Selim Hassan had wrongly interpreted the original inscription at Giza, which when understood in full referred not to the fact that she had been "king of Upper and Lower Egypt," only that Khentkawes I had been *mother* to two "kings of Upper and Lower Egypt," her royal titles honoring this achievement.[9]

Another queen who produced two future kings of Egypt was Ahhotep I. Toward the end of the Seventeenth Dynasty (circa 1580–1550 BCE) she would come to rule the country on behalf of her eldest son Kamose. Ahhotep is thought to have been the sister and wife of the Seventeenth Dynasty king Seqenenre Tao.

It was Kamose, the last king of the dynasty, and his brother Ahmose, the first king of the Eighteenth Dynasty, who following in the footsteps of their father, brought together an army to drive out of Egypt the Asiatic peoples known as the Hyksos or Shepherd Kings. They had controlled most of the country for around 125 years from their capital at Avaris in the Nile Delta circa 1675–1550 BCE. While Kamose was engaged in these military campaigns, his mother, Ahhotep I, acted as ruler, although she was never given any official title to this effect.

Then there is the story of Twosret or Tausret, the last known ruler of the Nineteenth Dynasty (1194/93–1186/85 BCE). She was the wife of king Seti II, and when he died she became regent for their son Siptah, heir to the Egyptian throne. In this manner Twosret reigned the country for around two years before Egypt was suddenly plunged into a civil war that only ended with her demise and the foundation of the next dynasty, the Twentieth, by a king named Setnakht (1186/85–1183/82 BCE).

The Egyptian priest and historian Manetho, who somewhere between 300–250 BCE compiled a definitive history of the kings of Egypt (see chapter 12), refers to Twosret under the name Thouoris, whom he accredits a reign of seven years, although this includes that of her predecessor Siptah who ruled circa 1194/93–1186/85 BCE. She is missing from some king lists, meaning that at the time she was not recognized as a legitimate pharaoh.

Just two female rulers of Egypt remain to be mentioned, the first being the legendary, although somewhat nebulous, Nitocris. Manetho lists her as the last ruler of the Sixth Dynasty (circa 2300–2181 BCE),[10] but no hard evidence of her existence, never mind her reign, has ever been found. It is a mystery that needs more than just a few lines to explore in any detail, and since the stories of Nitocris will turn out to become extremely relevant to our own quest of discovery, I shall say no more about her until chapter 16.

ENTER SOBEKNEFERU

The only other notable female ruler that carved out her mark during Egypt's dynastic age is the highly enigmatic and quite mysterious Sobekneferu (pronounced *sob-bek-nef-frew*). She remains the country's first fully attested female ruler to wear the crowns of both Upper and Lower Egypt, her reign lasting for just under four years circa 1798/7–1794/3 BCE. Despite this, she remains relatively unknown outside of Egyptological circles. Sobekneferu has simply not received the same type of mass exposure that her later compatriots Cleopatra, Nefertiti, and Hatshepsut have received.

Sobekneferu exists like a ghost in the darkness, her story ever hidden behind a veil of mystery and imagination. Remarkably, however, the ominous lack of clarity surrounding her short but unquestionably eventful reign has, for better or worse, permitted Sobekneferu to become an unwitting icon of modern pop culture. Not, however, in the same manner as her better-known female compatriots.

Sobekneferu's fame, admittedly quite anonymously for the most part, derives from 150 years of speculation regarding the somewhat bold nature of her little-understood religious revolution. It is an extraordinary journey of discovery that, for me, began with a very memorable visit to one of the world's most renowned public institutions in the study of ancient history— London's British Museum.

2

Ruler of the Two Lands

The year is 1990. With the sound of car horns, black taxis, and red buses filling the air I passed through the visitor's gate into the grounds of one of London's most iconic institutions, the British Museum. Walking alongside groups of mostly foreign tourists I made my way toward the magnificent flight of stone steps that leads up to the building's huge colonnaded entrance.

I had visited the museum on many occasions before, usually focusing my attention on its Egyptian and Mesopotamian rooms filled with thousands of exhibits of all shapes and sizes. Here you can find everything from small gold rings bearing inscriptions in the name of Akhenaten and his family to the monolithic Neo-Assyrian winged bulls from the palace of Khorsabad in Iran. This, however, was not my reason for being there that day. I had come to see a single object—one that was an obvious start in any quest to truly understand the life of Sobekneferu, Egypt's first official female ruler. A formal request to examine and photograph the object in question had duly been granted by the Museum's Trustees on behalf of its Department of Egyptian and Mesopotamian Antiquities. All I had to do was present myself at its entrance door and someone would go and fetch the item for my inspection. I hoped this would permit me a much clearer idea of Sobekneferu's status both as a female pharaoh and as a woman of royal blood living in Egypt around 3,800 years ago.

Having arrived early, I awaited the appearance of my colleague Caroline Wise. Being an authority on ancient Egyptian goddess cults and religions she had agreed to join me for the meeting.

13

Standing between the building's entrance columns, I gazed out over the rooftops of the pubs, cafes, shops, and residential buildings of central London and thought about how the life of Sobekneferu had become important to me. It was not simply because of my avid interest in the mysteries of ancient Egypt. What intrigued me more was the manner in which this female monarch had captivated the imaginations of those interested in everything gothic and occult, even though so little was really known about her. It intrigued me why her story had become of such interest to a whole new following in the modern age through her supposed religious revolution and her fictional representation in horror films. Who was she really, and what could be learned about the real person behind the few vague references we have of her from contemporary inscriptions and ancient king lists? What do we really know about where she lived, how she lived her life, and what became of her? Only by examining every known relic from her reign could we learn more.

Caroline soon arrived, and together we entered the museum's Entrance Hall, alive as always with the sound of echoing voices speaking in an assortment of languages. We edged our way past the crowds of visitors and headed first into the Assyrian Transept, where we paused momentarily to examine the aforementioned Assyrian winged bulls, before passing through into the Egyptian Gallery. Here it is very easy to get waylaid examining one or another of the hundreds of exhibits on display, such as the room's exquisite life-sized statues of the lioness-headed goddess Sekhmet from Karnak in southern Egypt. On this occasion, however, we allowed ourselves just a few moments to acknowledge their presence before moving toward the rear exit. Beyond the Egyptian Hall a staircase took us up to the entrance of the Department of Egyptian and Assyrian Antiquities, today renamed the Department of Egypt and Sudan.

Ever since the museum opened its "Mummy Room" as far back as 1837, allowing visitors to inspect its large collection of mummies and countless other related antiquities for the first time, its Egyptological Department has played host to some of the great names of Egyptology. They have included Sir Edgar Wallis Budge, Henry Reginald Hall, I. E. S. Edwards, and T. G. H. James, the last of whom I had had cause to correspond with some years earlier. All of them made massive contributions to our understanding of ancient Egyptian history, and we were now about to walk in the footsteps of these great luminaries, a humbling experience if ever there was one.

After pressing the bell to announce our arrival, we were finally met by an assistant who ushered us through a long corridor into a fair-sized side room overlooking the City of London. A large table occupied its central area where, we quickly realized, any contact would take place between us and whatever it was we were there to see.

Following a brief wait, the door opened and into the room came a man in his mid-thirties with beard, glasses, and tweed jacket. He held before him a slim wooden tray that under any other circumstance might have been used to serve biscuits.

"Mr. Collins?" the man said casually as he moved toward our position by the table. I said yes, and once satisfied we were who we said we were, the Egyptological assistant introduced himself and affirmed that he was there to show us the item we had requested.

At this the tray was placed down on the table before us. What it contained was a fair-sized cylinder seal carved from a type of stone known as white schist.* It had been glazed with faience so that its inscribed hieroglyphs stood out in turquoise against a much paler background. Sizewise it is recorded as being 1.7 inches (4.4 centimeters) in length with a diameter of 0.61 inches (1.55 centimeters), somewhat larger than most cylinder seals of this type. It had been drilled longitudinally so that it could be strung from a cord and worn perhaps around the neck.

THE ROYAL TITULARY

Having been given permission to pick up this precious object, I turned it over to examine its carved hieroglyphs. They were arranged in a series of columns, which when holding the cylinder seal were to be read from top to bottom and from left to right (see fig. 2.1 on page 16 and also plate 1). The inscription listed four out of five of Sobekneferu's royal titulary, the titles adopted by every ruler of Upper and Lower Egypt on ascending the throne; only one of which, the so-called *nomen,* or personal name, being borne from

---

*See Petrie 1894, vol. 1: 196–97, which states the cylinder seal is made of white schist. Some sources, such as the seal's description within its British Museum entry (EA16581, registration number 1868,1102.230), say it is made of steatite (see the British Museum website). Steatite is a green/grey/brown form of metamorphic rock made from talc-schist.

Fig. 2.1. The British Museum cylinder seal showing the royal titles and titulary of Sobekneferu (from Habachi 1954, XIII, B).

birth. Each title relates to the monarch's royal status with respect to the country's oldest religious institutions, which were tied to the veneration of specific deities associated with rites of kingship.

First up on the cylinder seal was an honorary title, no doubt chosen by the monarch herself, which was "Beloved [*meryt*] of Sobek Shedety." It was a reference to her devotion to the crocodile god Sobek and his principal cult center of Shedet in the Fayum. This was followed by the first of the titulary titles, her so-called Horus name, honoring the fact that in life the pharaoh was seen as an incarnation of the hawk or falcon god Horus. It was a role that, in theory, a pharaoh was destined to fulfill from birth, something Sobekneferu must have come to accept was her rightful destiny. The Horus name is usually contained inside what is known as a *serekh,* a tall rectangular box, signifying the niched or gated façade of a palace, on top of which the god Horus is shown as a bird. In Sobekneferu's case her Horus name was Meryt-Ra, meaning "Beloved of the sun god Ra." (For Sobekneferu's full royal titulary see fig. 2.2.)

Nomen or personal name
Sobek neferu (nfrw-sbk)
"Beauties of Sobek of Shedet"

Horus name
Meryt Ra (mri-t-r^c)
"Beloved of Ra"

Two Ladies or Nebty name
Sat sekhem nebet tawy (s3t-shm-nbt-t3wi)
"Daughter of power,
mistress/golden one of the Two Lands"

Golden Horus name
Djedet khau (ddt-h^{c}w)
"Stable is she in rites of kingship"

Praenomen or Throne name
Sobek ka Ra (sbk-k3-r^c)
"Sobek is the ka of Ra"

Fig. 2.2. Complete royal titulary of Sobekneferu
(from "Neferusobek," Pharaoh.se website). Illustration by Nick Burton.

Interestingly, the hieroglyph for the Horus bird on top of the serekh had been changed from its original male form (*Hr,* the root of Horus) by the addition of a small symbol, like a small semi-circle (the hieroglyph for the letter "t"), creating a feminized form of the name reading something like *Hrt, Heret,* or even *Horusette* as Egyptologist Kara Cooney has proposed.[1] This then was just one of the many ways that, as we shall see, Sobekneferu attempted to make a male-dominated world of kingship fall in line with her own brand of female masculinity, in other words masculinity that was not male in nature.[2]

Sobekneferu's Horus name can be seen to honor the sun god Ra (also spelt Re, and pronounced something like "rar," as in "car"). This name was chosen not simply to appease the Ra priesthood, whose cult center was at Heliopolis, somewhere lost today beneath the sprawling suburbs of northeastern Cairo. The monarch's dedication to Ra was associated very strongly with the religious beliefs and practices attached to the Fayum depression, a huge

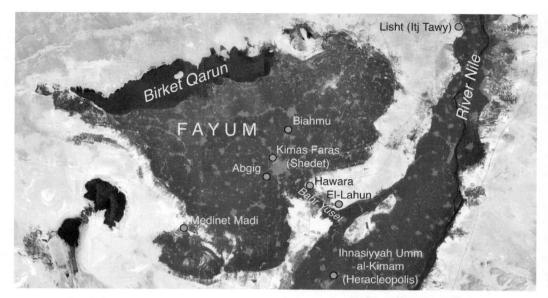

Fig. 2.3. Map of the Fayum region showing key sites featured in this book.

fertile oasis situated around 62 miles (100 kilometers) south-southwest of Heliopolis. It was the center of worship of the crocodile god Sobek of Shedet, with Shedet (the Greek city of Crocodilopolis) being the name of the region's main cultus place during dynastic times. It lay around 6 miles (10 kilometers) northwest of the massive Twelfth-Dynasty necropolis at Hawara, the two locations probably having once been connected by a processional avenue of some sort. Today all that's left of Shedet is a neglected area of disturbed ground and scattered remains at a site known as Kiman Faras, located at the northwestern edge of the modern city of Medinet Fayum (see fig. 2.3), the capital of the Fayum region. In addition to a major temple of Sobek, Shedet also housed a royal palace that contemporary documents indicate formed part of the same complex, the two linked perhaps by a central court.[3]

DAUGHTER OF SEKHEM AND MISTRESS OF THE TWO LANDS

Next up on the British Museum's cylinder seal was the queen regnant's Nebty or Two Ladies name, with the ladies in question being the vulture goddess Nekhbet and the snake goddess Wadjet. Each one guarantees the reigning monarch divine protection, which stemmed from Nekhbet and Wadjet's cult centers in, respectively, Upper Egypt in the south and Lower Egypt in the north. Sobekneferu's Nebty name was Sat-sekhem-nebet-tawy, which means something like "Daughter of power [*sat sekhem*], mistress of the Two Lands [*nebet tawy*]."

This choice of name on Sobekneferu's part would have reflected the fact that the monarch was considered to rule from the place where the Two Lands, that is Upper and Lower Egypt, were seen to come together or meet. Usually this was deemed to exist at a latitude corresponding with Memphis, the ancient city known as "White Walls," which acted as the capital of Lower Egypt. One of its titles was Ankh-tawy, meaning "life [*ankh*] of the Two Lands [*tawy*]." Sobekneferu, however, and her immediate ancestors saw the demarcation between Upper and Lower Egypt as existing farther south, coincident to the Fayum region. This was where she and her immediate predecessors had ruled the Two Lands from their capital Itj-tawy, meaning "Seizer of the Two Lands."

Itj-tawy is thought to have been located close to a Twelfth Dynasty necropolis at Lisht in the Nile Valley.[4] (See fig. 2.3 for the location of Itj-Tawy in relation to the Fayum region.) It acted both as the place of coming together of the Two Lands *and* as the ruling seat of the kings of the Twelfth Dynasty and subsequent Thirteenth Dynasty.[5] It would have been the official seat of Sobekneferu's rule, although due to her devotion to the crocodile god Sobek she would no doubt have shared her time between Itj-tway and the royal palace at Shedet.

Reigning pharaohs (and some queens) would wear the symbols of the Two Ladies, the vulture and snake, as part of a headdress or diadem, showing that they ruled Upper and Lower Egypt under Nekhbet and Wadjet's divine patronage. As we see in chapter 6, Sobekneferu found a very unique way of incorporating the vulture and snake into a highly stylized form of royal headdress.

The Golden Horus

Turning the cylinder seal still further revealed Sobekneferu's Golden Horus name, which usually appears in association with the hieroglyph for the divine falcon either perched on or next to the symbol for gold (*nebu*). The term *Golden Horus* was a very ancient name for the Pharaoh, although during the

Middle Kingdom the hieroglyph for gold was shown alongside another that symbolized the word *goddess,* feminizing the title and associating it with the goddess Hathor who was a divine protector both of kingship and of queenship. In Sobekneferu's case, her Golden Horus name was Djedet khau (*ddt-h'w*), which meant something like "Stable is she [*djedet*] in rites of kingship [*khau*]." The *djed*-pillar was a major symbol of stability in ancient Egypt, and was identified with the backbone of Osiris, the god of the underworld and of the dead.

The Beauties of Sobek

The monarch's Golden Horus name is followed on the cylinder seal by her more familiar personal name (or *nomen*) Sobekneferu (or Neferusobek as it can also be written*). It means "the beauties [*neferu*] of the god Sobek," the patron god of the Fayum region. The name is yet another indication that the monarch held a special interest in the Fayum's crocodile god, and that she truly was "beloved of Sobek of Shedet" as the British Museum's cylinder seal makes clear. This was a familiar expression used not only by Sobekneferu, but also by various of her predecessors, including her father Amenemhat III (1853–1806/05 BCE), who was responsible for construction work both at the Shedet temple complex and also at its royal palace.[6] In this manner Sobek of Shedet rose to become one of the most important and also one of the most interesting gods in the whole of Egypt.[7]

Not only was Sobek of Shedet seen as the vehicle of important gods such as Horus and Ra, both of which the pharaoh was identified with in life, but during the reign of Amenemhat III the crocodile god also came to be associated with the right of kings to rule,[8] something that had previously only been the case with other more obvious cult centers such as that of Ra at Heliopolis. Following in the footsteps of her father Amenemhet III, Sobekneferu, as her name suggests, was quite literally born to serve the god Sobek and in doing so support its extremely powerful priesthood.

---

*For a full study on the order of the components of Sobekneferu/Neferusobek's *nomen,* and also that of her *prenomen* Sobekkara/Kasobekre, see Canhão 2020, 2–5. Although he argues that Neferusobek and Kasobekre, and not Sobekneferu and Sobekkara (or Sobekkare), are the correct English transliterations of the original hieroglyphic names, the choice of use remains with the individual writer. I have chosen to use the more time-honored Sobekneferu for the monarch's nomen and Sobekkara for her prenomen. In this respect I follow the lead of Stefania Pignattari (see Pignattari 2018, 12 n. 91).

The one royal title missing from the British Museum's cylinder seal providing Sobekneferu's titulary was her prenomen or throne name, which is usually headed by the *nswt-bjtj,* which means "of the Sedge and Bee." Shown as the hieroglyphs for the sedge plant and bee, these two signs were ancient symbols of kingship going back to Egypt's First Dynasty (circa 3100 BCE). They would normally be seen above Sobekneferu's throne name, which was Sobekkara, meaning "Sobek is the soul [*ka*] of Ra," although on the cylinder seal the sedge and bee signs appear above the monarch's personal name. The hieroglyphic elements of her prenomen can also be rearranged to spell Kasobekra, although I have chosen to remain with the more recognizable Sobekkara. (For a full explanation of the usage of English transliterations of Sobekneferu/ Neferusobek and Sobekkara/Kasobekra see the previous footnote.)

Sobekneferu's throne name appears to reflect the close association that existed between Sobek and the sun god Ra, which in Fayumic tradition was seen to take the form of the crocodile god to pass through the waters of the region's great lake at night before rising anew on the eastern horizon at dawn the following morning.[9] Although this tradition is only recorded during the Graeco-Roman period (it being contained in an important hieroglyphic text known as the Book of the Fayum explored in detail later in this book), there is every reason to believe that this myth cycle involving the sun's nightly journey through the waters of the lake formed part of the cult of Sobek of Shedet at its greatest stage of development under Amenemhat III and his daughter Sobekneferu, thus explaining the female monarch's adoption of the throne name Sobekkara.

A pharaoh's fivefold titulary expressed his or her right to ascend to the throne of Egypt and rule the country in a manner begun as early as 3100 BCE with Menes, the legendary first king to unite the Two Lands and wear the double crown of Upper and Lower Egypt. Pharaonic kingship was seen as a divine institution bestowed on the rightful candidate by gods such as Horus, Ra, and, during the age of Sobekneferu, by Sobek of Shedet. It was this age-old tradition, already as much as 1,300 years old by Sobekneferu's time, that she embraced when she succeeded to the throne of the Two Lands.

Sobekneferu, however, wanted to establish new precedents in her own interpretation of kingship, which she and her father saw as exclusively associated with the cult of Sobek of Shedet.[10] For instance, in the case of both her nomen and prenomen, instead of using hieroglyphs to spell out

"Sobek" the monarch used the theophoric form of the god's name, which was a pictorial hieroglyph showing a recumbent crocodile on a boxlike shrine.[11] In this way she was able to emphasize the importance of the god (and his cult center) every time either her personal name or throne name was included within an inscription. Not only was this use of the crocodile sign a break from existing tradition, but it also showed that she aligned herself with a highly dangerous and very fierce male deity, an action that was unquestionably meant to instill fear in everyone who gazed upon her name.

In adopting Sobek as her principal deity, and promoting him as a symbol of kingship, Sobekneferu was moving away from the religious affiliations established by her own direct ancestors. Prior to her reign every pharaoh of the Twelfth Dynasty had borne names honoring either the god Amun, patron of the city of Thebes in southern Egypt, or Wosret, Amun's consort who was the tutelary goddess of the same city.

Sobekneferu's clear political allegiance to the cult of Sobek with its powerful priesthood was yet another sign that she was attempting to achieve something quite different, both for herself as Egypt's first official female ruler and for the royal dynasty, the Twelfth, which was arguably one of the most successful to date. As we shall see, however, all this was short lived for there were dark clouds looming on the horizon not just for her but also for the future destiny of the country.

A SECOND CYLINDER SEAL

The British Museum cylinder seal is important because it is the only object from Sobekneferu's reign to tell us the monarch's Nebty/Two Ladies and Golden Horus names.[12] Nowhere else have they been found. Having said this, it is not the only known cylinder seal bearing her royal titulary. Another housed in the Egyptian Museum, Cairo,[13] shows her throne name Sobekkara preceded by the title *Sa-Ra,* "Son of Ra."[14] What's interesting about this is that the form of the epithet used is very clearly masculine, since it does not have the additional semicircle or "t" hieroglyph, which both feminizes the word and changes it to *Sat-Ra* instead of Sa-Ra (also written Sa-Re). This is in contradiction to other documents and inscriptions bearing Sobekneferu's throne name, which do show it in its feminine form. In addition to this, on the Cairo cylinder seal the monarch's Horus (or *Horusette*) name, written Meryt-Ra, "beloved of Ra," on the British Museum cylinder seal, is here spelled Mery-Ra, its *male* form (that is, without the inclusion of the feminizing letter "t").[15]

How did so much confusion come about regarding the genderization of Sobekneferu's royal names? Did the queen regnant gradually transform her names from their original feminine form into their male equivalents, or did this happen in reverse—male forms of her name being gradually feminized? Or can these sharply contrasting spellings of her names and titles be put down simply to inconsistencies on the part of royal scribes who didn't know whether to address her as a man or as a woman?

Frustratingly, there are no hard answers to this enigma. There is simply not enough evidence to say one way or another. What we can say, however, is that similar problems dogged Hatshepsut when, some 350 years later, she too attempted, very successfully it must be added, to introduce the concept of female masculinity into the long-held male dominated rites of kingship during Egypt's New Kingdom.

Hatshepsut's own inspiration had unquestionably been Sobekneferu, whose own introduction of a form of female masculinity into ancient Egyptian kingship she both embraced and developed in her own unique way. This has been something recognized by a number of scholars who have noted strong similarities between the reigns of the two female monarchs.[16]

In adopting male aspects of kingship it would have helped convince the priesthoods, courtiers, officials, as well as the Egyptian population as a whole, that even though Sobekneferu was a woman she was strong enough to rule the country with an iron rod, something that would have been necessary to ensure a long lasting status quo not only on a sociopolitical level, but also on a religious level as well. Perhaps more crucially, it would have helped convince detractors that, as an embodiment of the god Horus, Sobekneferu had the divine right to wear the double crown of Upper and Lower Egypt and also bear a full royal titulary, the first woman ever to do so.

THE ROBERT JAMES HAY COLLECTION

As for the British Museum cylinder seal (which bears the item number BM16581), it was acquired in 1868 having previously formed part of a large collection of antiquities belonging to a famous Scottish traveler, antiquarian, and draftsman named Robert James Hay (1799–1863). In 1818 he visited

Egypt's capital, Alexandria, while in the British Navy. He would later return to the country staying there between November 1824 and 1828, and again between 1829 and 1834. During these visits Hay would routinely record details of any temples or monuments he came across, making copies of the inscriptions they bore. He also made a series of architectural plans, which are today housed in the British Library, London. Following his death in 1863, Hay's extensive collection of antiquities was sold partly to the British Museum and partly to the Boston Museum of Fine Arts.[17]

Tracing where Hay might have acquired the cylinder seal bearing Sobekneferu's royal titulary has, unfortunately, proved difficult. It probably came from the Fayum, where the Egyptian Museum's own cylinder seal also most likely came from.

PERCY NEWBERRY'S DISCOVERY

For completion, it is perhaps important to mention that British Egyptologist Percy E. Newberry (1869–1949) recorded the existence of a third cylinder seal bearing Sobekneferu's throne name. It was found, he says, at a mound site named Kom el-Aqarib, close to the site of the ancient city of Heracleopolis Magna (Egyptian *Hemen-nesw*), situated around 9 miles (14 kilometers) south-southwest of the entrance to the Fayum depression.

Newberry chanced upon the slightly damaged cylinder seal in a "dealer's shop" in Cairo, where he was permitted to make a copy of its hieroglyphic inscription (see fig. 2.4). It included the line, "Sobekkara, beloved of Shedet," with the word "beloved," *mery,* written in its masculine form (that is, without the added "t" hieroglyph).[18] Presumably the storeowner in Cairo was able to tell him where it had been found. What happened to the cylinder seal after this time is not recorded. As we shall see in chapter 26, the Kom el-Aqarib mound, which lies close to the modern town of Ehnasya el-Medina, will be found to have other connections to Sobekneferu and her reign.

A FOURTH CYLINDER SEAL

In addition to the cylinder seals mentioned already, a "bead" recorded by Egyptian Egyptologist Labib Habachi (1906–1984) also gave Sobekneferu's

Fig. 2.4. Hieroglyphs on the cylinder seal seen in a "dealer's shop" in Cairo by Percy E. Newberry. It was apparently found at the site of Heracleopolis Magna just outside the Fayum (from Newberry 1943a, 75). They read "Sobekkara, beloved of Shedet," with the word "beloved," *mery,* written in its masculine form.

throne name, Sobekkara, along with the fact that she was "Lord of Shedet, residing in the palace."[19] Habachi suspected that the bead was owned by King Faraok, and described it as 1.8 inches (4.5 centimeters) long, and made of green faience so pale the whole thing was almost white. It had the appearance of an elongated cylinder "resembling the known perfume vases [of ancient Egypt]" and was said to have come from the Fayum.[20] The unique nature of this bead, and the fact that it bore an inscription in Sobekneferu's name, makes it likely that it was once a personal possession of the monarch, perhaps forming part of a necklace or bracelet.

So did the British Museum's own cylinder seal also once belong to Sobekneferu? Had it been worn around her neck at some point? Although we shall probably never know I was humbled by the thought that it was one of the few surviving items from her reign that had almost certainly passed through her hands.

Just holding this small cylindrical object connected me not just with her world, but also with her as a person—this remarkable woman who virtually wrote the book on female empowerment in ancient Egypt. In one way or another Hatshepsut, Nefertiti, and maybe even Cleopatra, might all have been inspired by Sobekneferu's achievements. But who exactly was she? What do we know about the age in which she lived, and, more pressingly, what became of her? It is these questions that we start to look at next.

3

Sobekneferu—The Story As We Know It

Sobekneferu was the last ruler of Egypt's Twelfth Dynasty, which spanned a period of approximately 182 or 183 years circa 1976–1794/3 BCE. During this time the country had gained its greatest stability since the Pyramid Age several hundred years earlier. In all it saw a total of eight kings, all of whom, except for its last, Sobekneferu, were called either Amenemhat, "Amun is in front," or Senusret (also written Senwosret or Usertesen) meaning "Man of the Goddess Wosret." Both names showed the dynasty's strong alliance to the Theban god Amun and his consort Wosret, who acted as divine patrons of the city of Thebes. It was an affiliation the Twelfth Dynasty kings had inherited from the outgoing Eleventh Dynasty (circa 2046–1976 BCE), which had established a close bond with the cult of Amun and its priesthood.[1]

Sobekneferu was almost certainly the daughter of one of those Amenemhat kings, the third, whose reign lasted for at least 45 years, circa 1853–1806/05 BCE (see fig. 3.1). Toward the end of his life, he is thought to have entered into a co-regency, or co-rule, with the next king, Amenemhat IV,[2] whom the Turin Canon says ruled the country for 9 years, 3 months, and 27 days (circa 1807/06–1798/97).[3] How long this co-regency lasted is unclear, although in all likelihood it was no more than one to two years, after which time the new king ruled on his own.[4]

According to Manetho, Amenemhat IV—whom he calls "Ammenemes" and says reigned "8 years"—was replaced by a ruler named Skemiophris.[5]

Fig. 3.1. Head of Amenemhat III in granite housed in the Egyptian Museum (from Breasted 1936, pl. 103).

This is unquestionably Sobekneferu, since Skemiophris (from the original Greek Σκεμιοφρις) is probably just a corrupted form of the monarch's personal name. She, Manetho writes, was Ammenemes's "sister," adding that she ruled for "4 years."[6] Whether or not Sobekneferu was a full sister of Amenemhat IV is something we'll explore in chapter 12, when we look more closely into the familial relationship between these various different royal individuals. In the Turin Canon, written in Egyptian hieratic script during the Nineteenth Dynasty (1292–1185 BCE), we find an entry for Sobekneferu stating she ruled for 3 years, 10 months, and 24 days.[7] This figure corresponds very well with the four-year reign of Skemiophris offered by Manetho.

It is not known whether Amenemhat IV entered into a co-regency with Sobekneferu. No inscriptions or monuments suggest as much,[8] although some scholars have proposed this possibility.[9] Equally, nothing has been found indicating that Sobekneferu might have been Amenemhat IV's royal wife during his reign.[10] In fact, other than a statue base found at Tel Gezer in what is today Israel,[11] and a black granite offering bowl found close to the pyramid of her great ancestor Senusret I at Lisht,[12] which bears an inscription in Sobekneferu's name from when she was still a princess (see chapter 7), almost nothing is known about her until she succeeds to the throne following the assumed death of her brother in around 1798/1797 BCE.

Some scholars have proposed a co-regency between Sobekneferu and her father, Amenemhat III, based on the discovery of certain reliefs showing their two names side-by-side found in his funerary complex at Hawara.[13] Although an interesting proposition, knowledge that the crown passed from her father to her brother Amenemhat tells us that any kind of co-regency between father and daughter makes no sense at all.

The fact, however, that Sobekneferu was, according to Manetho, Amenemhat IV's "sister" does suggest a close bond existed between the two siblings, meaning that there is every chance she *did* become his royal wife and queen before she herself assumed control of the country.[14] Under what circumstances all this came about remains unclear, although it is a topic we shall return to later on in this book.

COLLAPSE OF THE DYNASTY

What we do know is that Sobekneferu's brief reign brought to a close not only the Twelfth Dynasty of ancient Egyptian history, but also, according to some scholars, the entire Middle Kingdom, which up until that time had spanned a period of almost 250 years (circa 2046–1794/3 BCE). Some Egyptologists today extend the Middle Kingdom beyond the Twelfth Dynasty to embrace the Thirteenth Dynasty, thought to have lasted for approximately 154 years. This is because the Thirteenth Dynasty can be seen as a basic continuation of the Twelfth Dynasty.[15]

What is clear, however, is that the Middle Kingdom gave way to what is referred to as the Second Intermediate Period (circa 1794/1793–1550 BCE), within which we shall include the Thirteenth Dynasty for this present study. It would be marked, according to Manetho, by five dynasties ruled in many cases by faceless and often weak princes. It seems possible that these dynasties either partially or completely overlapped with each other, their kings ruling from different locations in the country.

The first of these dynasties, the Thirteenth, consisted of a series of rulers whose exact relationship with their predecessors of the Twelfth Dynasty remains unclear. As many as seven of them bore names honoring Sobek, showing a close association with the religious affiliations of Amenemhat III and his daughter Sobekneferu. Both pharaohs would appear to have been deified after their deaths, Amenemhat III during the reign of his daughter[16] and Sobekneferu at the beginning of the Thirteenth Dynasty.[17] The Thirteenth Dynasty was shadowed by the Fourteenth Dynasty, the two almost certainly having run parallel with each other.[18]

Like the Twelfth Dynasty, the incoming Thirteenth Dynasty was ruled from the existing capital of Itj-tawy, or to give it its correct name Amenemhat-itj-tawy, which means "Amenemhat, Seizer of the Two Lands." As previously mentioned, this was located at Lisht, east-northeast of the Fayum on the edge of the Nile Valley. (See fig. 3.2 for a map of Egypt showing key sites featured in this book.)

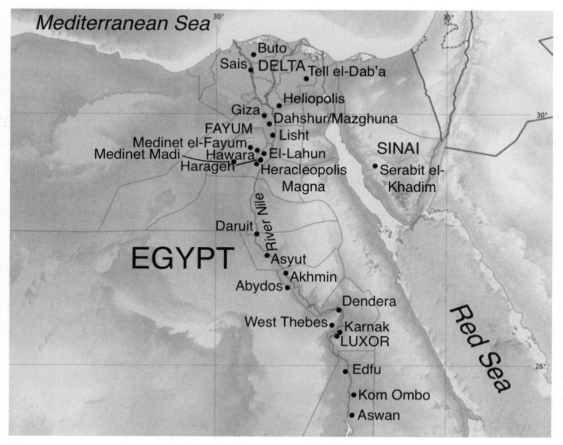

Fig. 3.2. Map of Egypt showing key sites featured in this book.

The kings of the Thirteenth Dynasty also reestablished a dynastic relationship with Thebes and its cult of the god Amun, making the city their secondary seat of power. This reaffirmation of the importance to kingship of the cult of Amun with its powerful priesthood is displayed in the fact that some of the Thirteenth Dynasty kings continued the tradition of calling themselves Amenemhat, meaning "Amun is in front."

ASIATIC IMMIGRANTS

In contrast, the main seat of power of the Fourteenth Dynasty was probably the city of Avaris (modern Tell el-Dab'a) in the eastern Nile Delta.[19] This is despite the fact that Manetho tells us they ruled for a period of 184 years from Xois (modern Sakha) in the central-northern part of the Delta.[20]* Its kings had close ties with the region's western Asiatic population, which had emerged in the Nile Delta during the reign of Amenemhat III,[21] and arguably even earlier during the reign of his father Senusret III.[22] This incoming population, which spoke a West Semitic language similar to Arabic and possessed its own distinctive material culture, originated in the Levant, and is remembered under names such as the Aamu—meaning "Asiatics"—and the Retjenu, which simply means "highlanders," in other words the people from the highlands of Palestine and Syria.[23]

The Asiatic population of the Nile Delta would go on to adopt an Egyptian lifestyle and create its own royal dynasty—the Fifteenth—before a new Egyptian dynasty, the Seventeenth, based in Thebes, would eventually rise up against these foreigners who are remembered in Jewish and classical sources as the Hyksos or Shepherd Kings. (Note: A lack of firm information regarding Egypt's Sixteenth Dynasty makes it impossible to tell for certain what its affilitions were.)

The Egyptian army, led by Kamose, the last king of the Seventeenth Dynasty, embarked on a fierce military campaign against the Hyksos warlords, their final banishment being accomplished by Kamose's brother, Ahmose (or Aahmes). He was the first king of the incoming Eighteenth

---

*The Armenian version of Eusebius says that the kings of the Fourteenth Dynasty ruled for 484 years, but this is clearly a scribal error (Manetho, fr. 41a, Armenian version of Eusebius. See Waddell [1940] 1964, 74–75).

Dynasty (circa 1550–1292 BCE), which also marked the commencement of the country's New Kingdom (circa 1550–1069 BCE). It was during this period that dynastic Egypt rose to become one of the most powerful and successful empires of the ancient world.

Factored somewhere into these tumultuous events in the history of ancient Egypt is Sobekneferu's brief reign. That she was the first female ruler to wear the double crown of Upper and Lower Egypt, something that was supposed to bring order and stability to the Two Lands, must have had some impact on why both the Twelfth Dynasty and the country's Middle Kingdom collapsed soon after her death in circa 1794/1793 BCE. Its fall could simply be down to the fact that neither Sobekneferu nor her predecessor Amenemhat IV produced an heir to continue the dynasty. Even if this was the case, and certainly as we shall see there is some evidence to suggest that the first kings of the incoming Thirteenth Dynasty were the natural successors to Amenemhat IV, it has occasionally been proposed that Sobekneferu's reign was a major contributory factor in the demise of the dynasty.[24]

AN ABNORMAL REIGN

Scholars such as Nicolas Grimal have concluded that Sobekneferu's rule ended in violence,[25] while Alan Gardiner (1879–1963) wrote that her reign was "so abnormal" it was a situation that by its nature contained the "seed of disaster."[26] What would not have helped is the fact that graffiti inscribed on a rock face above the banks of the River Nile, at Kumma (or Semna East) immediately south of the Second Cataract and close to Egypt's border with Sudan (ancient Nubia), records that in Year Three of Sobekneferu's reign the floodwaters at the time of the annual inundation had reached a height of just 6 feet (1.83 meters) above the average water level of today. This was considerably lower than in previous years.[27] (Note: The Cataracts of the Nile are areas of the river that are impassable due to a series of whitewater rapids caused by countless boulders and stones either jutting out of the water or present just below the surface. They occur between Khartoum in Sudan and Aswan in southern Egypt.)

It was a situation that might well have spelled disaster for Egypt since the country relied heavily on the arrival of these surging waters produced each summer by the arrival of the monsoon rains in the Ethiopian highlands. They would flow into Egypt via the River Nile and flood the low-lying agricultural lands of the Nile Valley and Fayum depression leaving behind not only water for irrigation but also a nutrient-rich alluvial deposit that was essential for the successful planting of seeds the following season. Without a good inundation, famine and drought could result, along with any number of other economic difficulties.[28]

In a superstitious world of the past, natural calamities of this sort would have been blamed both on the inability of the monarch to properly rule coupled with the belief that such actions were the result of gods who had been angered in some way. What would not have helped is that Sobekneferu's patron god, Sobek, was intimately linked not only with rites of kingship, but also with the Nile and its floodwaters.[29] So Sobekneferu, with her close association with the god, could very easily have been blamed for what happened in Egypt as a result of this particularly low inundation during Year 3 of her reign.[30] Unfortunately, no similar graffiti exists for the rest of her reign, so we have no idea whether the annual inundation was high or low for these years.[31]

What might have happened to Sobekneferu to cause her untimely death after just four years on the throne of Egypt should be understood in the knowledge that some of the female pharaohs who came after her ended their reigns under quite tragic circumstances. Hatshepsut's reign, as we saw in chapter 1, was erased from all official records and her achievements suppressed by her successor Thutmose III. Nefertiti's reign was also expunged from the official records as the Amarna age collapsed into chaos, while the reign of Twosret or Tausret, the last ruler of the Nineteenth Dynasty, ignited a civil war that only ended with her violent death. Lastly, Cleopatra's reign collapsed when both she and her partner, the Roman general Mark Antony, committed suicide following the defeat of a joint Roman-Egyptian naval fleet at the Battle of Actium in 31 BCE.

Of course, the exact circumstances behind all these tragic demises of female pharaohs were probably quite different, although unfortunately in a heavily patriarchal world the fact that they were women will have played at least some small part in how their reigns came to an end. In this knowledge one could be forgiven for not at least considering the possibility that Sobekneferu herself might have succumbed to an untimely death. So is this correct? Did she die of natural causes, or did something untoward happen to her?

The answer to these questions will require examining every last piece of information we have, not only on her reign, but also those of her father Amenemhat III and her brother Amenemhat IV. Only then might we be able to come to a better understanding of what truly happened to her and even where she might have been buried, for that too remains unclear. Before getting into that, however, it is important to learn more about the woman behind the pharaoh, and for this we shall start by looking at her known statuary, some of which is on display in museums, while other examples, sadly, are today lost to the world. Examining these can hopefully tell us something about Sobekneferu's character, her motivations in life, and, possibly, what she might have looked like.

4

The Woman behind the Pharaoh

Only a handful of monuments remain from Sobekneferu's reign. There are some reliefs and inscriptions mentioning her that were found either at the site of the Labyrinth at Hawara or elsewhere in Egypt, and these we look at shortly. Other than that, there are just a few pieces of statuary that can help us to learn something about her character, her intentions, and perhaps even the way she wanted to portray herself to her subjects.

THE PARIS STATUE

The best attested statue of Sobekneferu is that found in the Louvre Museum, Paris.[1] It was acquired in 1973, although its prior history and place of discovery remains unknown. Made of quartzite, it is today headless with the lower half of the statue completely missing (see plate 2). It is life-size, being currently 19 inches (48 centimeters) in length with a suggested original height of the entire statue in the range of 5 feet 2 inches (1.6 meters).[2]

Very clearly the statue's present state is highly suggestive of iconoclastic activity in that it was deliberately smashed at some point in its history. This might have occurred in the wake of Sobekneferu's tumultuous reign by those opposed to her memory. Equally, these destructive actions could have occurred much later, arguably even in post-dynastic times. We simply don't know.

Despite its fragmented condition we can see that Sobekneferu is wearing the familiar *nemes*-headdress, the pleated lappets of which rest on each shoulder. This is essentially the same royal headdress present on the Great Sphinx at Giza and on the gold death mask of Tutankhamun. Until Sobekneferu's reign the *nemes*-headdress had been a symbol of kingship reserved for the country's male rulers alone. However, in the Paris statue we see this female pharaoh sporting the royal regalia of a man, confirming to all who gaze upon her form that she is unequivocally ruler both of Upper and Lower Egypt.

Having established this fact there is little question that the rest of Sobekneferu's attire is a curious mix of male and female features. For instance, she can be seen wearing a high-waisted, diaphanous shift dress held in place by a double strap across the shoulders. Over this, however, is a masculine *shndyt*-kilt and kilt knot that includes a starched triangular panel. Once again, this shows Sobekneferu's desire to be portrayed in male form. The belt of the kilt is unusually high, ending just below her breast line, a deliberate attempt perhaps to emphasize her femininity. It is on the kilt's belt buckle that we find an inscription identifying the monarch, since this reads: "The daughter of his body, Sobekneferu, may she live like Ra forever."[3] So there can be no question that the statue is of her.

Around the monarch's neck is a pendant on a long cord. It has been identified as a stylized representation of a "pierced heart,"[4] which could symbolize the *ab,* meaning "heart," which was one of the many aspects of the human soul in ancient Egyptian tradition. This same type of pendant, maybe even the same one, was worn by her grandfather Senusret III, and perhaps even by her father, and so there is a possibility that the pierced heart was an identifying mark of the royal dynasty.[5]

One last point about the Louvre statue is the fact that the queen seems to have flattened breasts, which might well suggest another deliberate attempt at masculinizing her female form in statuary. This is something we saw also in connection with the manner in which her royal names and titles were occasionally shown in their male form, that is, without the feminizing "t" hieroglyph.

Kelly-Anne Diamond of Villanova University, Pennsylvania, argues that with the Paris statue we see Sobekneferu's bold attempt at introducing a previously unseen form of female masculinity, one that included the adoption of male regalia and dress, while at the same time attempting to keep some of her more obvious feminine traits.[6]

As evidence of this Diamond cites the observations of Vivienne Gae Callender of the Charles University in Prague, one of the world's foremost authorities on the reign of Sobekneferu. In Callender's opinion, the Louvre statue "represents the first experimental stage by sculptors to accommodate the female form in pharaonic guise, and that it is reminiscent of Hatshepsut's early statuary."[7] As we see shortly, there is little question that Hatshepsut may have stylized at least some of her statues after those representing Sobekneferu.

THE BERLIN BUST

Another statue of Sobekneferu, this one with its head, was housed in the Egyptian Museum, Berlin, until it was either lost or destroyed in an Allied bombing raid during World War II; its exact fate having never been determined. Luckily, however, official photos of the bust do exist (see fig. 4.1),[8]

Fig. 4.1. Front and three quarters view of the Berlin bust showing the only known likeness of Sobekneferu (from Fechheimer [1914] 1920, pl. 57 and 58. See plate 3).

as does a mold taken from the bust in 1905.[9] From these and from official records we know the bust was 5.5 inches (14 centimeters) in height, with a width of 3.5 inches (9 centimeters) and a depth of 2.4 inches (6.2 centimeters). Everything below the hips is missing, and from the position of the break it is clear the bust once formed part of a seated statue, a fact stunningly confirmed quite recently, as we shall see shortly.

Bequeathed to the Berlin Museum in 1899 by Dr. Deibel and given the acquisition number 14475,[10] the statue has been fashioned from greywacke, a hard, dark grey stone commonly used for statuary and architectural features during the reign of Amenemhat III.[11] The appearance of this royal woman is quite striking, showing an individual with high cheekbones, powerful eyes, and an expression that exudes a strong sense of knowledge and power. The impression offered by her features is of a woman in her early thirties, a fact that has suggested to some that this was Sobekneferu's age when she succeeded to the throne.[12]

Like the Louvre statue of Sobekneferu, the Berlin bust is seen wearing a *nemes*-headdress, although in style it has the appearance of a tripartite, braided wig. Starting at her upper forehead it sweeps backward across her scalp before splitting into three parts—one section that rests flat on her back and two tubular plaits that wrap around her ears and come to rest just above her breasts.

The Berlin statue's twin plaits were deliberately positioned so as to expose Sobekneferu's rather large ears. Their unusual size and angle, perpendicular to the head, probably doesn't reflect the monarch's actual physiognomy. Large exposed ears in Middle Kingdom statuary were common. Why? The answer is twofold. Firstly, large ears would allow the monarch to hear all prayers, chants, and words of power spoken in his or her presence. Secondly, such ears on a statue helped instill the belief that the king as the living Horus could hear any and all dissent being spoken in his or her presence, even the faintest whisper![13]

Present also on the Berlin bust we see on each shoulder the straps of a shift dress, like that found also on the Paris statue. It is pulled up to just below the breasts, which have not been flattened this time. Such inconsistencies do suggest that during Sobekneferu's reign there were differences of opinion on how a female monarch should be portrayed in visual terms, echoing, once again, the way in which Sobekneferu's royal titles were sometimes expressed in male form and at other times in their female form.

The Bottom Half Found!

So how do we know the Berlin bust shows Sobekneferu? It was always assumed that it could represent the monarch simply because its style showed it to be from the latter part of the Twelfth Dynasty, and only one woman ruled at this time and that was Sobekneferu. However, there was never any confirmation of this fact until by an incredible stroke of good fortune the lower half of the statue was realized to be in the possession of Boston's Museum of Fine Arts![14]* This shows the hips and legs of a royal woman seated on a throne.

The item was found during routine excavations conducted during the 1920s by American Egyptologist George A. Reisner (1867–1942) at the Nubian fortress of Semna in modern-day Sudan.[14] Since the fort dates from the reigns of the Twelfth Dynasty kings Senusret III and his successor Amenemhat III, who built there a temple and, quite possibly, an artificial dam to control the Nile flood waters,[15] the likelihood is that the statue was taken to Semna by officials during Sobekneferu's reign.

THE NEFERUSOBEK PROJECT

Confirmation that the two statue fragments do indeed derive from the same art piece has come from the inspired work of the Neferusobek Project, headed by American Egyptologist Biri Fay, who lives in Berlin, Germany. She and her team were able to digitally match up the two halves by comparing the fracture of the Boston statue base with high quality photographs of the Berlin bust as well as the plaster cast made in 1905.[16]

It is now Biri Fay and her colleagues' intention to create two complete statues, one of which will be presented to the Boston Museum of Fine Arts and the other to the Egyptian Museum in Berlin.[17] In Biri Fay's words, "The reconstruction is the first complete statue of this female pharaoh and finally provides a face that can with certainty be associated with her name."[18] So having these in museums, complete with the backstory behind their creation,

---

*Boston Museum of Fine Arts accession number 24.742. See "Lower Body Fragment of a Female Statue Seated on a Throne" 2019. It was found at Semna in Sudan in 1924 and was excavated by the Harvard University–Boston Museum of Fine Arts Expedition. Unlike the Berlin bust, which is said to have been greywacke, this item is described as steatite. Since greywacke and steatite are often difficult to tell apart, I see no problem with this discrepancy.

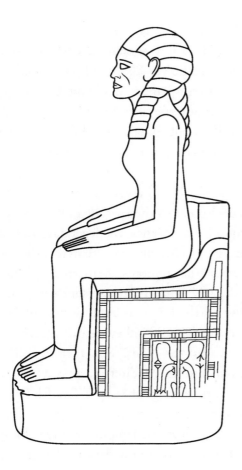

Fig. 4.2. Side view of the Berlin bust reunited with its base showing the sema-tawy symbol of kingship. Illustration by Nick Burton.

will no doubt increase peoples' awareness of the life and reign of Egypt's first female pharaoh.

How then can we be certain that this reconstructed statue is truly a representation of Sobekneferu? The answer is that on each side of the throne base is a symbolic motif usually only found on the statues of ruling pharaohs. Since there was just the one female ruler who reigned during the whole of the Middle Kingdom this means we have to be gazing into the eyes of Sobekneferu when we look at pictures of the Berlin bust.

The motif in question is what is known as the *sema-tawy,* meaning "uniter (*sema*) of the Two Lands (*tawy*)."[19] It is composed of two plants, the reed and the papyrus, knotted together around an upright pole with what looks like wings at its base (see fig. 4.2). This strange device is an abstract representation of either a human trachea and lungs or, alternately, the spine and hipbone of an individual. Which of the two explanations is correct remains unclear, although what we do know is that this highly stylized motif signified the union of Upper and Lower Egypt, with the reed plant representing Upper Egypt and the papyrus plant symbolizing Lower Egypt. The purpose of including the *sema-tawy* on the sides of thrones signified the manner that the ruling pharaoh unified both Upper and Lower Egypt in a state known as *ma'at,* a term implying the concepts of truth, balance, and cosmic order.

The place of coming together of the Two Lands was, as mentioned in chapter 2, originally thought to correspond to the latitude of Memphis, the ancient capital of Lower Egypt founded by Menes, the legendary first pharaoh of a united Upper and Lower Egypt.[20] Memphis is situated at the southern edge of Lower Egypt, exactly where the country's northern kingdom met its southern counterpart, Upper Egypt. "Upper" meant south in dynastic times, while "lower" referred to the north. This was because the Nile River, the main source of life and fertility in the Nile Valley basin, entered Egypt in the south and flowed northward into the Nile Delta. Here it split into several branches before emptying out into the Mediterranean Sea.

As we also saw in chapter 2, the earliest kings of Egypt's Twelfth Dynasty would appear to have made a concerted attempt to move the place of meeting between the Two Lands from its old seat at Memphis to a new location some 19 miles (30 kilometers) farther south corresponding to the latitude of their new capital Itj-tawy.[21] This is thought to have been situated somewhere in the vicinity of the Middle Kingdom cemeteries at Lisht on the edge of the Nile Valley, close to the pyramids of two Twelfth Dynasty kings, those of Amenemhat I (1976–1947 BCE) and Senusret I (1956–1911/10 BCE). Since the entire necropolis was reserved exclusively for the burial of royalty and elite individuals then the capital must have been close by.[22]

Why exactly Lisht was chosen as the point of demarcation between Upper and Lower Egypt remains a mystery. Most probably its line of latitude at around 29 degrees 35 minutes was deemed important in its own right, especially since at a distance of around 31 miles (50 kilometers) west of Lisht are sites in the northern Fayum region associated with the great ancestors of the Twelfth Dynasty kings, a matter explored in chapter 32.

Finally, we must ask ourselves whether or not the newly reconstructed statue of Sobekneferu composed of the Berlin bust and the throne base and legs recently rediscovered in Boston's Museum of Fine Arts really does provide a true likeness of Egypt's first female pharaoh. As much as we would all like this to be so, there are, however, some obstacles to overcome.

During the second half of the Twelfth Dynasty a deliberate policy was employed whereby the reigning monarch was no longer shown as youthful with realistic features reflecting their true age. Instead they were often portrayed in statuary as mature in age with stern, somber faces.[23] The reason for this change in art style was so that the statues could convey a sense of absolute power and divine authority.

This same manner of representation of a monarch's physical features is probably behind the physiognomy seen in connection with the Berlin bust. The artist created the impression of a powerful female who is pretty terrifying to behold, the effect it was no doubt meant to convey to the beholder. Very clearly this is how Sobekneferu wanted herself to be portrayed as a woman and as a ruler—someone who was to be feared but also respected by her subjects. We can't say for certain that the Berlin bust shows the monarch's true physiognomy, although if it does then it really does provide us with her only true likeness.

It was with this thought in mind that I attempted to "repair" the bust's broken nose using a digital program. The result is stunning as can be seen from plate 3. As Kara Cooney, the author of *When Women Ruled the World,* commented on first seeing this reconstruction, "With the nose, she really does come to life!"[24] Indeed, she does, and there can be little doubt that Sobekneferu was not only a woman of quite striking appearance, but also one of deep knowledge and wisdom. As terrifying as she might have wanted to come across to her subjects, there is still in this bust a sense of humanity that shows not only her character, but also her personality. (See also Russell M. Hossain's stunning artist's impression of Sobekneferu based on the reconstructed Berlin bust on page xviii.)

For the first time ever we can connect with Sobekneferu as an individual. Behind the mask, however, is still the sense that she was unquestionably a force to be reckoned with and that if anyone crossed her they did so at their own peril! As throwaway as these observations might seem, we shall see that this deliberately fierce attitude on the monarch's part might well have been a key factor in the way she was able to both ascend to the throne and remain the country's sovereign for those all-important four years of her reign.

5

The Cult of Sobekneferu

Further representations of Sobekneferu from her brief reign provide us with an even greater insight into her personality, her background, and her achievements in life. They include three near life-size basalt statues of the monarch found at Tell el-Dab'a in Egypt's Nile Delta, fairly close to the border with Palestine.[1] The entire district marked the former site of the ancient Egyptian city of Avaris, the future capital of the Hyksos kings, whose forerunners had begun occupying northern Egypt around 1700 BCE, this being about a century after Sobekneferu's death.

Archaeological exploration of the ancient city had begun in 1885 under the direction of Swiss Egyptologist and Bible scholar Édouard Naville (1844–1926) working on behalf of the Egypt Exploration Fund. Then in 1928 Egyptian Egyptologist Mahmoud Hamza turned his attention to an area north of Tell el-Dab'a known as Qantir (see fig. 5.1 for a map showing the area in question), which he was convinced could be identified with the city of Piramesse, a major Delta residence during the Nineteenth Dynasty mentioned in the Hebrew Bible under the name Raamses or Rameses. This would eventually prove to be correct, although it was something that was not confirmed for many decades. Much earlier, however, this had been the location of Avaris, the stronghold of the Hyksos, a fact established through extensive excavations at the site under the leadership of Austrian archaeologist Manfred Bietak (1940–).[2]

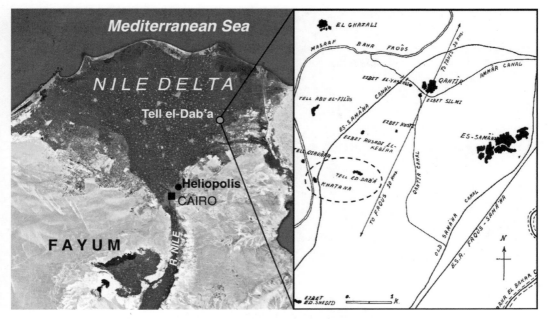

Fig. 5.1. Map of the Egyptian Nile Delta complete with, *right,*
the original map of the Tell el-Dab'a area by Labib Habachi
(from Habachi, *Annales du Service des Antiquités de l'Egypte* 52, 1954, pl. I).

HABACHI'S DISCOVERY

In 1938 Egyptian Egyptologist Labib Habachi was appointed Chief Inspector of the Delta. Shortly after his arrival at Tell el-Dab'a he was informed of the discovery nearby of five life-size statues. These he investigated in 1941 in an attempt to establish their true age and archaeological context. All of them, he determined, had been associated with a building made of thick mud brick walls, which appeared to have been a sanctuary, shrine, or temple of some kind. In addition to evidence of burnt bone offerings Habachi found a number of portable objects, which he dated to the late Twelfth Dynasty and subsequent Thirteenth Dynasty.[3] Due to the presence of this nearby building he concluded that the statues, which in every case were lower sections devoid of their upper halves, had remained basically in situ since the time of its construction (see fig. 5.2 on page 44). This seemed verified by the fact that four out of five of the statues bore inscriptions from this same epoch; the fifth example was devoid of any inscriptions.

Fig. 5.2. Statue bases of Sobekneferu and Hetepibrê' Iamu-Sahornedjheriotef
found at Tell el-Dab'a and investigated by Labib Habachi in 1941
(from Habachi 1954, pl. VI).

Two of the statues, which were little more than oversized feet on pedestals, appeared to show a Thirteenth Dynasty king by the name of Hetepibrê'
Iamu-Sahornedjheriotef (also just written Hornedjheryotef), this being evidenced from an inscription on one of the two fragments.[4] The one with the
inscription was made of schist while the other was made of basalt, a hard
volcanic rock that is usually grey-black in color.[5]

The other three statues, all of which were made of basalt, dated from
the reign of Sobekneferu. Two showed the monarch seated, although only
her legs, the throne, and evidence of a dorsal support pillar remained
(see fig. 5.3). They bore inscriptions giving Sobekneferu's Horus name
Meryt-Ra and her throne name Sobekkara, along with the proclamation
that she was: "beloved of Sobk the Fayumite [Shedety], the Horus residing
in the Fayyum in peace, Sobk who is in. . . . "[6] The hieroglyphic text was
missing beyond this point, although one of the statues bore a more complete inscription that allowed Habachi to read the next line as ". . . Sobk
who is in Khentishe-en-pera' . . ."[7] (see fig. 5.4).

This curious term, *Khentishe-en-pera'*, translated as meaning "the Garden
of the Palace," Habachi identified as very likely a place of residence of the

Fig. 5.3. Statue base of
Sobekneferu from Tell el-Dab'a
showing the monarch seated
on a throne (from Habachi
1954, pl. VIII).

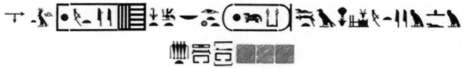

Fig. 5.4. Hieroglyphs from one of the statue bases from Tell el-Dab'a showing
Sobekneferu seated on a throne. They read "The Female Horus Meritre,
the king of Upper and Lower Egypt, master of ceremonies 'Sobkkare,
[beloved of] Sobk of the Fayum, the Horus residing in Fayum in peace,
Sobk who is in Khentishe-en-per'a . . ." (from Habachi 1954, 460).

crocodile god Sobek in the Tell el-Dab'a area. Noting that the old name for
the area where the statues had been found was Tell el-Birka, meaning the
"Mound of the Pools," Habachi suspected that this was the former site of
a Sobek temple, built most probably during Sobekneferu's reign, which had
continued in use through the Thirteenth Dynasty.[8] He even noted the fact
that a pool had once existed at the location, which might possibly have been
the one alluded to in the local place-name.[9]

These findings allowed Habachi to speculate on the possibility that
Sobekneferu could have had some special relationship with Tell el-Dab'a,

somewhere known to have been patronized by her own immediate ancestors. For example, a monumental gateway bearing inscriptions in the names of Sobekneferu's grandfather Senusret III, as well as the founder of the Twelfth Dynasty, Amenemhat I, was located just a short distance away from the statues investigated by Habachi.*

SOBEKNEFERU—THE PRIESTESS?

The third and final statue of Sobekneferu found at Tell el-Daba showed the monarch in a kneeling position on a rectangular pedestal (see fig. 5.5).[10]

Fig. 5.5. Statue base of Sobekneferu from Tell el-Dab'a showing the monarch kneeling in a prayer position (from Habachi 1954, pl. VII, B).

---

*See Habachi 1954, 448–58. Swiss Egyptologist Édouard Naville had earlier noted the presence at nearby Khatana of a large red granite lintel-stone of a doorway, possibly leading into a temple. It was found to bear an inscription in the name Amenemhat I. On excavating fragments of the pillars that held up this lintel they were found to have an inscription bearing the names of Senusret III and, seemingly, Amenemhat III (see Naville 1887, 22). This was presumably the monumental gateway subsequently noted by Habachi.

The upper part of the body was, once again, completely missing with the remaining portion rising only to a height of 33 inches (85 centimeters). Habachi recorded its inscription as follows:

> May live the king of Upper and Lower Egypt Sobkkare, beloved of Sobk the Fayumite, the Horus residing in the Fayum, the one of Khentische-en-pera', may she live.[11]

Often, when a statue shows the person in a kneeling position they usually hold out in each hand a *nw*-pot. These were small, spherically-shaped vessels usually made of stone with a lip and opening at the top to allow the entry of liquids.[12] They were used to make libations to a deity or divine ancestor, implying that the subject of the statue, in this case Sobekneferu, was being shown performing a priestly duty.

It was these facts that led Kelly-Anne Diamond of Villanova University to propose that the gesture of the Tell el-Dab'a statue "arouses ideas of gratitude, blessedness and intended communication, in that Sobekneferu sought wisdom and council from the gods to help her rule according to *m3't*, [*ma'at*, truth, balance and cosmic harmony]." She goes on to say: "It also illustrated that she was the intermediary between her people and the gods and could nurture the fragile, but reciprocal, relationship between the two."[13]

Since only the king was able to fulfill the role as intermediary between the world of the living and the realm of the gods, this "privileged kneeling gesture" adopted by Sobekneferu in the Tell el-Dab'a statue, she suspects, "designated her as the only performer of the cult and as one with an ability to function outside the confines of the physical world."[14] These are perceptive observations indeed, suggesting that on occasions at least Sobekneferu acted in the role of a priestess making offerings either to the gods or to her divine ancestors.

What's interesting in this respect is that Sobekneferu's Horus name, Meryt-Ra, "Beloved of Ra," was often used in the Twelfth Dynasty as a title for priestesses. This was noted by Kara Cooney, who observed: "With this name, Neferusobek [that is, Sobekneferu] and her supporters seem to be claiming both that she was beloved of the sun god himself and that one of her foundations of power was her priestly affiliation before she took the kingship."[15]

So both in the kneeling statue of Sobekneferu found at Tell el-Dab'a and in her Horus name Meryt-Ra there is evidence to suggest that the monarch acted in the capacity of a priestess. So before she rose to become sole ruler of Egypt in the wake of her brother's death, had she been a priestess? This much seems possible, although did she fulfill similar duties even after her accession to the throne?

Another interesting fact raised by the discovery of the kneeling statue of Sobekneferu from Tell el-Dab'a is just how similar it is to ten life-size red granite statues of Hatshepsut that once adorned the monarch's terraced mortuary temple at Deir el-Bahri in West Thebes, two of which are today in New York's Metropolitan Museum of Art.[16]

During the reign of her father Thutmosis I, Hatshepsut would have become the highest-ranking priest in the cult of Amun at Karnak. Was it possible, therefore, that Hatshepsut deliberately chose to depict herself in the kneeling position of an individual carrying out priestly duties after seeing one or more statues of Sobekneferu in exactly the same pose?

That a similarity exists between the statuary of Hatshepsut and that of Sobekneferu has been a conclusion reached by various Egyptologists who have examined the life of this Twelfth Dynasty female ruler.[17] The question then becomes why? Why did Hatshepsut want to mimic the achievements of her predecessor? Did she look up to her as an inspiration? Did she see her as one of her great ancestors? Or was Sobekneferu simply one of Hatshepsut's personal heroes? We might never know for sure.

SOBEKNEFERU AS A SPHINX

Returning now to Tell el-Dab'a we find that the three statues of the monarch investigated by Labib Habachi were not Sobekneferu's only material presence in ancient Avaris. A short distance to the east of their place of discovery Swiss Egyptologist Édouard Naville had in 1885 recorded the presence of a "black granite" sphinx, minus its head, "on the top of the highest mound" in the nearby village of Khatana.[18] (See fig. 5.1 on page 43 for a map of the area.) It was apparently fairly large (although no actual size is given by Naville) and bore a "much erased inscription" between its forepaws that, like the Tell el-Dab'a statues, included Sobekneferu's throne name Sobekkara (see fig. 5.6). This huge monument was, seemingly, found in situ having

Fig. 5.6. Partial inscription from the black granite Sphinx of Sobekneferu found at Khatana by Édouard Naville showing the monarch's throne name Sobekkara (from Habachi 1954, pl. II, C).

most likely been in the same position since the end of the Twelfth Dynasty. Habachi recorded that local women would go to the sphinx to deliberately smash water vases on its stone surface in the belief that it would help them become pregnant.[19] Whether or not this monument was exposed to the air when Naville first came across it is unclear.

During his excavations at the site, Naville had dug around the base of the sphinx to a depth of some 10 feet (3 meters) and come across a number of what appeared to be deliberately placed burial deposits.[20] They included "large oval urns containing ashes, pieces of charcoal, and bones," some of which were those of animals while others, he wrote, were quite possibly human.[21] Alongside these were "small pots of red and black earthenware," as well as an assortment of "small cups and saucers," all of which he felt were made to contain "oil and perfumes." He also retrieved some scarabs, along with two bronze knives and several small items.[22]

The red and black earthenware pots were of an entirely unfamiliar type not seen before during excavations, although the "ware" itself was of a style already known from Thirteenth Dynasty tombs excavated at Abydos in southern Egypt.[23] One of the scarabs found bore the name of a king "of that period," confirming that the burials and deposits were indeed from the Thirteenth Dynasty.[24] In conclusion, Naville wrote: "We have thus a burial-place of the Thirteenth Dynasty, which corresponds with the name I deciphered on the sphinx [that is, Sobekneferu's throne name], and is consequently anterior to the time of the Hyksos kings."[25]

THE CULT OF SOBEKNEFERU

Naville's statement that the offerings found next to the large Sphinx found at Khatana were *anterior* to the time of the Hyksos kings is very important since it is clear evidence of a presumably local cult existing there during the reign of the female monarch. If correct then it implies that following her death Sobekneferu was being venerated in the future capital of the Hyksos as a deified pharaoh. An inscription on a limestone stela found at Abydos in southern Egypt during the nineteenth century and housed today at the Mediterranean Archaeology Museum in Marseilles, France (with the catalogue number Marseilles no. 223), seems to confirm this surmise.[26] Dating from the Thirteenth Dynasty, its inscription speaks of a cult existing at this time in the name of Sobekneferu.[27]

Further evidence of a cult in Sobekneferu's name comes from "tourist" graffiti in the chapel attached to the tomb of a woman named Senat, who was buried alongside her husband or son, whose name was Antefoqer. He was vizier to Amenemhat I, the founder of the Twelfth Dynasty, and afterward to his son Senusret I. It is not known whether this Senat was Antefoqer's mother or wife, since nothing is made clear in surviving inscriptions.

What we do know is that Senat was a priestess of the goddess Hathor[28] and was honored with a beautifully decorated tomb on a hillside at Sheikh Abd el-Qurna, part of the greater necropolis at western Thebes in southern Egypt (the tomb's number is TT60).[29] The site has the largest concentration of private tombs on the Theban West Bank (which includes the world famous Valley of the Kings), although what makes Senat's tomb special is that it is the only example from the Middle Kingdom constructed there specifically for a woman.

It was arguably because of its uniqueness that the tomb of Senat would receive visitors during the New Kingdom (1550–1069 BCE), who would enter its funerary chapel to pay their respects to the deceased's *ka,* the part of the soul that remained close to the place of interment.

Some of the tomb's "tourists" have left behind inscriptions in a hieratic script on the walls mainly of the shaft, although some are visible also in the chapel.[30] (Note: Hieratic script was a writing system that developed from the much earlier hieroglyphic system used from the fourth millennium BCE onward. It continued to be used through the Greco-Roman period, circa 332 BCE–395 CE, although by this time it had mostly been replaced by a more basic version of the Egyptian written language known as demotic.)

Much of the graffiti seen inside the tomb of Senat simply includes the name of the visitor and what they thought of the tomb. Some tourists, however, were going there for a quite specific reason. This can be determined from two inscriptions (see fig. 5.7), and arguably still more, that make it clear that Senat's tomb was being venerated as the final resting place of Sobekneferu. One reads, "The scribe . . . came [to see] this tomb of Sobeknefer[u]. He found it like heaven in its interior."[31] A second example, using very similar terminology, reads, "The scribe Bak (came) to see (this) tomb of the time(?) of Sobekneferu. He found it like heaven in its interior."[32]

Other inscriptions speak in similar terms, although who or what they came to see was no longer legible when, around the time of World War One, the graffiti was copied by British Egyptologist, linguist, and philologist Alan H. Gardiner (1879–1963) and his colleagues Norman de Garis Davies (1865–1941) and his wife Nina M. Davies (1881–1965). Their findings were published in 1920 as part of a monograph titled *The Tomb of Antefoker. Vizier of Sesostris I, and of His Wife, Senet (No. 60).*[33]

Fig. 5.7. Graffiti from the tomb of Senat and Antefoqer at Sheikh Abd el-Qurna near Deir el-Bahri on the Theban West Bank left by tourists who had come to pay their respects to Sobekneferu (from Davies, Gardiner, and Davies 1920, pl. XXXV, A2 and A3).

Gardiner, in his introduction to the graffiti,[34] wrote that in his opinion most of it derived from the reign of Thutmosis I, circa 1504–1492 BCE. It should be recalled that he was Hatshepsut's father, and that during this time she would have visited both the city of Thebes (modern Luxor) and the nearby temple of Amun at Karnak in her capacity as the highest-ranking priest of Amun. So, might Hatshepsut have come to hear about how some of the tourists visiting the tomb of Senat believed it to be the final resting place of Sobekneferu? It seems very possible indeed. So how exactly did this tomb, so far away from the Fayum and the Twelfth Dynasty's capital city of Itj-tawy at Lisht in the Nile Valley, come to be identified with Sobekneferu?

Sobekneferu's true final resting place has never been found.[35] Nobody would seem to have officially recorded what happened to her at the end of her short reign. Having said this, there are solid contextual grounds to suspect that one of two pyramids at Mazghuna, a site just beyond the Nile Valley just 1.6 miles (2.6 kilometers) south of the main pyramid field at Dahshur, *might* have been intended as her final resting place, a subject explored in chapter 30.

THE POWERFUL SOBEKNEFERU— THE HARAGEH LETTER

What can be said is that a reference exists to what appears to have been the funerary complex of Sobekneferu. It is mentioned in a near contemporary document found at Harageh at the entrance to the Fayum, close to an important Twelfth Dynasty site named El-Lahun, noted as the location of the pyramid complex of Senusret II (1882–1872 BCE). In 1913 and 1914 British Egyptologist and engineer Reginald Engelbach (1888–1946) excavated a number of dynastic cemeteries there.[36]

Among the finds was a papyrus letter dating from the Thirteenth Dynasty (Papyrus Harageh no. 6, UCL 32778), which speaks of a place called Sekhem-Sobekneferu.[37] The text is damaged, so the exact context of the toponym is unclear, but it does seem to indicate the existence of a place that was seen to be the monarch's funerary complex.[38] If correct, then where exactly was Sekhem-Sobekferu, and was Sobekneferu actually buried there? Unfortunately, no one knows. It could refer to one of the pyramids at Mazghuna, or equally it could refer to somewhere that came to be seen as her final resting place.

Whatever the answer, the existence of the Harageh letter with its reference to Sekhem-Sobekneferu, the "Powerful (place) of Sobekneferu," is yet further evidence of a cult existing in Sobekneferu's name long after her death.[39] This, along with the stela from Abydos, the sphinx venerated in ancient and more modern times at Khantana in the Delta, and the "tourist" graffiti from the tomb of Senat in West Thebes, are all clear indications that Sobekneferu was still considered a powerful force well into the Second Intermediate Period and arguably even beyond that in the New Kingdom.

With these considerations in mind, the fact that during the early to middle Eighteenth Dynasty people were visiting Senat's tomb in the belief that it was the resting place of Sobekneferu makes it clear that by this time the monarch's exact whereabouts were almost certainly lost, certainly to the general population at least. This undue interest in the tomb of Senat is something that would surely have become known to Hatshepsut if, as many scholars believe, she was herself inspired by the achievements of the Twelfth Dynasty monarch. Did Hatshepsut herself visit the tomb of Senat to inspect its interior and perhaps gain some insight into her own future destiny? We probably will never know, although it is worth noting that the Sheikh Abd el-Qurna hillside, where Senat's tomb can be found, is just under half a mile (600 meters) south of Hatshepsut's spectacular mortuary temple at Deir el-Bahri.

How long a cult in the name of Sobekneferu might have continued is unknown. Did it really have dedicated followers that continued to venerate her through the New Kingdom and even into much later times? If so, why would she have been seen as particularly special, over and above any other past ruling monarch in Egypt? As we see next, further clues can be gleaned from other items left behind from the time of her reign.

6

Sobekneferu and the Heb Sed Mystery

The statues of Sobekneferu from the Louvre and from Berlin, as well as those found at Tell el-Dabʻa in the Nile Delta, help us to better understand how the monarch wanted to be perceived by those who gazed upon her living form. They do not, however, provide us with a clear impression of what exactly was going on during her reign, or how she came to wear the double crown of Upper and Lower Egypt. So can any clues be gleaned from other statues thought to be representations of her?

THE METROPOLITAN'S HEB SED STATUE

One piece of statuary that might just offer us a better idea of Sobekneferu's reign is held by New York's Metropolitan Museum of Art.[1] It is a small figurine of a royal woman made of dark green schist. It is 6.4 inches (16.3 centimeters) in height, 4.3 inches (11 centimeters) wide, with a depth of 2.9 inches (7.5 centimeters). Nothing remains of the statue below the waistline, although it is clear the figure is in a seated position (see fig. 6.1 and plate 4).

Although the statuette bears no inscription, the museum is confident that it belongs to the late Twelfth Dynasty or early Thirteenth Dynasty, "circa 1825–1750 BCE."[2] Whether this statuette does in fact show Sobekneferu remains a matter of debate among Egyptologists. Gae Callender, an acknowledged expert on the reign of Sobekneferu, says yes, it is her.[3] Other scholars

Fig. 6.1. Twelfth Dynasty statuette housed at the Metropolitan Museum of Art, New York, showing a royal female of the late Twelfth Dynasty thought to be Sobekneferu. Note that she uncharacteristically wears the Heb Sed cloak. Courtesy of the Rogers Fund, 1965. See plate 4.

concur with this view,[4] while the Metropolitan Museum prefers to keep an open mind.[5] As we shall see, there is good reason to suspect that it really does show Sobekneferu, although in a highly unorthodox manner.

The royal female in question wears a thick, high-collared cloak, from which her left hand emerges to connect with her right breast. Her garment is that which would have been worn by a ruling monarch following his or her completion of the Heb Sed festival, also known as the Sed festival. This would take place around the thirtieth year of a monarch's reign and involve a series of rigorous tasks and trials, which, if undertaken successfully, proved sufficiently to onlookers, and to the gods themselves, that the monarch remained of sound body and mind and thus was able to continue ruling the Two Lands.

The problem concerning the Metropolitan Museum's figurine, however, is that Sobekneferu ruled Egypt for just under four years, meaning there can be no good reason why she should have been depicted wearing the Heb Sed garment, so this is a matter that will need to be addressed.

The individual wears on her head a globular wig with horizontal striations that, in common with the wig or headdress seen on the Berlin bust,

Fig. 6.2 Overhead of the Metropolitan Museum of Art statuette that could be Sobekneferu showing the unique snake and double vulture headdress over her globular wig. Courtesy of the Rogers Fund, 1965.

is wrapped firmly behind the individual's ears (a common theme in almost all royal statuary from the Middle Kingdom). Where the wig parts at the center of the forehead is the remnants of a raised cobra representing the *uraeus*-snake, the sacred symbol of royal protection. The rest of the creature's body curls its way across the top of the figure's scalp as incised parallel lines. Either side of the snake, spread across the entire scalp, are two incised vultures with their wings outstretched. The tips of their wings meet together at the rear of the head to create the impression of a unique decorative crown or circlet (see fig. 6.2).[6]

The vulture and *uraeus*-snake represent, respectively, the power of the goddess Nekhbet, who presided over Upper Egypt, and the power of the goddess Wadjet, protector of Lower Egypt. The presence of this crown tells us that the woman in question is under the protection of these deities, the "Two Ladies," and is thus almost certainly a female monarch, with only Sobekneferu being in the right place at the right time. It was through her Nebty or Two Ladies name Sat-sekhem-nebet-tawy, meaning "Daughter of power [*sat sekhem*], mistress of the Two Lands [*nebet tawy*]," that the protection of Nekhbet and Wadjet would have been bestowed upon her at the time of her coronation. This then is further confirmation that the figurine does indeed show a female ruler that can really only be Sobekneferu.

Fig. 6.3. The Metropolitan Museum of Art statuette with its face and nose restored. Courtesy of the Rogers Fund, 1965. Digital restoration by Rodney Hale.

Unfortunately the right side of the woman's face including her jaw and nose is completely missing (as is part of the figure's back) making it difficult to assess her full physical appearance. When an attempt, however, is made to try and restore her features (something undertaken at my request by chartered engineer Rodney Hale—see fig. 6.3), the individual emerges as a fairly youthful woman in the prime of her life. Although the shape of the face is more rounded than that of the Berlin bust, the high cheekbones, slightly extended jaw, and deep-set eyes all indicate that the two statues are indeed representations of the same royal woman.

Gae Callender believes that if the figurine does show Sobekneferu then the *uraeus*-snake and double vulture circlet worn by the monarch was entirely unique to her reign.[7] In other words, it was likely something of her own creation. Callender further notes that in this statue the monarch is shown in the role she embraced at the time of her coronation, a crucial realization, as we shall see.[8]

Whereas it is indeed possible that the figurine shows Sobekneferu at her coronation, the use of the Heb Sed cloak might well imply that she was trying to convey the fact that she herself had undergone special trials *comparable* with those of the Heb Sed festival. What these trials might have involved we can only but guess, although they must have been of a type that would have been recognized not just by her courtiers, but also, more importantly, by the powerful priesthoods involved with rites of kingship. These would have included the priests of Sobek of Shedet from the Kiman Faras temple complex, the priests of the cult of Ra at Heliopolis, and the priests of Amun at Thebes in southern Egypt. All of them would have needed to be convinced that whatever trials Sobekneferu claimed to have undergone were not only legitimate but also gave her the divine right to rule Upper and Lower Egypt.

As to how old Sobekneferu might have been when she ascended the throne remains a matter of debate. The Metropolitan figurine seems to show a person in her twenties, while the Berlin bust appears to show a woman in her early- to mid-thirties. So which is right? If we accept that she was 16 years old when her brother entered into a brief one- to two-year co-regency with her father, after which the younger king went on to rule for the rest of his nine-year reign, then she would have been around 25 when she became ruler of Egypt. If she was, say, 25 when her brother entered into a co-regency with her father, then Sobekneferu would have been around 34 at the time of her accession. We simply do not know which solution makes better sense, although from what we do know about her familial background it is the current author's suspicion that Sobekneferu was probably no more than 30 years old when she became Egypt's first female pharaoh.

THE BROOKLYN SPHINX HEAD

One other possible representation of Sobekneferu is a carved head of a sphinx on display in the Brooklyn Museum, New York.[9] Made of green chlorite, it is 15.7 × 13.2 × 14 inches (40 × 33.5 × 35.5 centimeters) in size, and weighs 124.5 pounds (56.5 kilograms). What we see is the head of a youthful woman of quite striking appearance (see fig. 6.4). Museum specialists are of the opinion that it dates from the Twelfth Dynasty.[10] As to its provenance, the Brooklyn Museum's website suggests it came originally from the site of the ancient city of Heliopolis in Lower Egypt, and that for a while it had languished in the Emperor Hadrian's Villa in Rome.[11]

The woman wears a centrally parted wig curled behind her ears. On her forehead are the remnants of a *uraeus*-snake that emerges from beneath the wig to show that it forms part of a headband. As is the case with so many of the statues from this age the nose is missing. Noses were probably broken off

Fig. 6.4. Late Twelfth Dynasty sphinx head housed at the Brooklyn Museum, New York. Some believe it shows Sobekneferu. Courtesy of the Brooklyn Museum, Charles Edwin Wilbour Fund.

statues in the belief that the head embodied the spirit of the individual and that by defacing them their soul would be unable to breath in the hereafter. Nose breaking was thus a deliberate act of iconoclasm done by those who opposed the continuing influence of an outgoing reign or royal dynasty.

Unlike the somewhat more mature face of the Berlin bust, the individual represented by the Brooklyn sphinx head exudes what can only be described as a glowing warmth; there is even the faint hint of a smile. The royal female in question displays the same high cheekbones and general head shape as the Berlin bust and the Hed Sed figurine in the possession of the Metropolitan Museum of Art in New York. Having said this, knowledge that the eyes, lips, and chin were repaired in the eighteenth century CE means that the woman's physical features could have been altered from their original form.

The big question is who exactly does the head represent? During the Middle Kingdom both kings and queens started to be shown as stone sphinxes; indeed, we explored the example found at Khatana in the eastern Delta inscribed with Sobekneferu's name in a previous chapter. Since, however, the Brooklyn sphinx head is devoid of any inscriptions there is no way of knowing exactly who it shows. The presence on the forehead of the *uraeus*-snake is also unhelpful as not only kings, but also royal woman wore headbands bearing this protective symbol. The Brooklyn sphinx head *could* represent Sobekneferu, but equally it could show any one of the many royal women from the second half of the Twelfth Dynasty. Despite this there is a common belief, on the internet especially, that the head does indeed date from Sobekneferu's reign,[12] a conclusion that remains unconfirmed at this time.

To complete our understanding of Sobekneferu based solely on her associated statuary, we turn our attention to a highly important statue fragment found not in Egypt, but in the ancient land of Canaan, a clue that will now take us on the female monarch's previously unexplored road to destiny.

PART 2

ROAD TO DESTINY

7

Sobekneferu in Canaan

Tel Gezer is a large occupational mound straddling two adjoining hills in the Aijalon Valley, midway between Jerusalem and Tel Aviv in modern-day Israel. Here, in 1971, during routine excavations conducted by American archaeologist William G. Dever (1933–)—working on behalf of The Hebrew Union College Biblical and Archaeological School, the Jewish Institute of Religion, and the Harvard Semitic Museum—a quite unexpected statue fragment was unearthed. It shows the feet of an Egyptian royal woman standing on a heavy rectangular pedestal (see fig. 7.1).

Despite the statue fragment being found in secondary use within a Late Bronze Age wall, there seems little question that it dates from the site's Middle Bronze Age IIA (MB IIA) period, circa 1950–1740 BCE.* (See fig. 7.2 for a comparison between Bronze Age dates from the Levant and those of Egyptian royal dynasties.) This assumption fits well with its hieroglyphic inscription. (The same statement appears on both sides of the statue's feet, although because only part of the base remains, the hieroglyphs on the left-hand side were found to be almost entirely missing.) It reads:

. . . The King's Daughter of his body, Sobekneferu, may she live.[1]

---

*Weinstein (1974, 53) suggests that the Sobekneferu statue dates from Tel Gezer's MB IIB phase since during the MB IIA phase just a few seminomadic peoples occupied the mound. However, this is now known to be false as recent excavations undertaken by the New Orleans Baptist Theological Seminary uncovered evidence that a major water system and gate complex, as well as various significant finds (see Warner and Yanni 2016), all date to the MB IIA, removing any objections to the statue's arrival at Tel Gezer during this earlier phase of building activity.

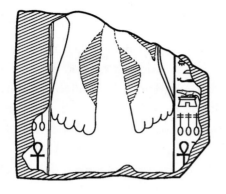

Fig. 7.1. The statue base of Sobekneferu found in 1971 at Tel Gezer in modern-day Israel (from Weinstein 1974, 50). Illustration by Nick Burton.

Bronze Age in the Levant	Egyptian Dynasties
Early Bronze Age (EBA)	
3300–3000: EBA I	
3000–2700: EBA II	Dynasty 3 (2686–2600 BCE)
2700–2200: EBA III	Dynasty 4 (2600–2450 BCE) Dynasty 5 (2450–2300 BCE)
2200–2100: EBA IV	Dynasty 6 (2300–2181 BCE)
Middle Bronze Age (MBA)	
2100–2000: MBA I	Dynasty 11
2000–1750: MBA II A	Dynasty 12
1750–1650: MBA II B	Dynasty 13 (1794/3–c. 1640/39 BCE) Dynasty 14 (1794/3–c. 1675 BCE) Dynasty 15 (c. 1675–1550 BCE) Dynasty 16 (??)
1650–1550: MBA II C	Dynasty 17 (1650–1550 BCE)
Late Bronze Age (LBA)	
1550–1400: LBA I	Dynasty 18 (1550–1292 BCE)
1400–1300: LBA II A	
1300–1200: LBA II B	Dynasty 19 (1292–1185 BCE)

Fig. 7.2. Bronze Age dates in the Levant shown alongside corresponding Egyptian dynasties featured in this book.

WHICH SOBEKNEFERU?

James M. Weinstein of Cornell University, in a paper written three years after the statue base's discovery, stated that the identity of the Sobekneferu mentioned in the inscription could not be confirmed. Although the statue did indeed date back to the Twelfth Dynasty of Egyptian history, he said that its inscription could allude to one of two women named Sobekneferu—the first being the queen regnant of this name, who was the daughter of Amenemhat III, while the other was the daughter of King Senusret I, the second king of the Twelfth Dynasty, who also bore the same name.[2]

Evidence of this other Sobekneferu comes from a single black granite (possibly syenite) bowl fragment forming part of an offering stand, which was found among discarded funerary rubbish next to the mortuary temple belonging to Senusret I's pyramid complex at Lisht.[3] On its polished exterior was a damaged hieroglyphic inscription that read *s3t-n(jswt) Sbk-///,* "King's daughter, Sobek [Neferu]"* (see fig. 7.3).

If it can be argued that the inscription on the bowl fragment refers, not to some previously unrecorded daughter of Senusret I, but to Sobekneferu, the daughter of Amenemhat III[4]—the offering stand having been left

Fig. 7.3. Fragment of a black granite or syenite bowl found close to the pyramid of Senusret I at Lisht along with its partial inscription showing the name of Sobekneferu without a cartouche. Illustration by Russell M. Hossain.

---

*This is according to Arnold 1992, 58, item no. 23. Some slight evidence of the neferu hieroglyph is present, although its cross "T" is missing.

behind following some kind of special ceremony to her great ancestor—then there seems no reason why the Tel Gezer statue fragment should also not be seen as a representation of this same Sobekneferu. It is certainly an opinion shared by others who have looked into this matter.[5]

Confirmation that the Tel Gezer statue fragment does belong to Sobekneferu, the last ruler of the Twelfth Dynasty, would make its existence highly significant indeed. Not only would it provide evidence of Sobekneferu's influence outside of Egypt, but it is also one of the few pieces of statuary relating to her life from *before* she succeeded to the throne. We can say this for in similar with the bowl fragment found at Lisht the inscriptions seen on either side of the feet of the Tel Gezer statue show the name Sobekneferu *without* the use of an oval cartouche, which would have been present if she had already succeeded to the throne. So when the inscription on the Tel Gezer statue base was carved Sobekneferu was still a princess, her future as ruler of Egypt still ahead of her. (A third item bearing Sobekneferu's name without the presence of a cartouche is discussed in chapter 33.)

Another important feature concerning the Tel Gezer statue is that it constitutes one of only a handful of examples of statuary from Egypt's late Middle Kingdom to be found in the former land of Canaan, historical Syria-Palestine; another being a sphinx of Amenemhat IV found much farther north in Beirut, Lebanon.[6] Thus the sheer presence of Sobekneferu's statue at Tel Gezer could help tell us something about the political situation existing between Egypt and Canaan immediately prior to her accession.

THE HIGH PLACE

Tel Gezer was an important Canaanite stronghold and ancient city, as well as a major cultic center. Located in the foothills of the Judean Mountains, overlooking the southern coastal plain, its earliest building phases date to the Middle Bronze Age IIA (MB IIA) period, circa 2000–1750 BCE, with continued occupation through the Late Bronze Age (circa 1550–1200 BCE) into the Iron Age (King Solomon, for instance, is said to have rebuilt the city around 1000 BCE).[7] A certain amount of activity from the Early Bronze Age (circa 3300–2100 BCE) and even the Chalcolithic or Copper Age (circa 4000–3300 BCE) has also been recorded at the site.[8]

A central focus of the city and fortress was a religious shrine, still in place today, known as the "High Place" (Hebrew: *bamah*). It consisted of a straight course of ten huge megaliths, the largest being around 10 feet (3 meters) in height.* These unhewn standing pillars, known in Hebrew as *masseboth* (singular *massebah*), are aligned almost precisely north-south, suggesting that they once held a cosmological significance to the Canaanite inhabitants of the region.

We don't know what deities were venerated at Tel Gezer during the Middle Bronze age IIA period. The recent discovery, however, of large deposits of gold and silver votive offerings, alongside figurines showing a Canaanite form of Ishtar, the Akkadian goddess of fertility, love, sex, and war, as well as the moon god Sin, all of which appear to date to the Middle Bronze age IIB era, would tend to suggest that these deities at least were important there.[9]

What then was a life-size statue of Sobekneferu doing at a Canaanite cult center well outside of Egypt? It could be argued that the statue was removed to the location by the retreating Hyksos armies following their expulsion from Egypt at the end of the Second Intermediate Period. The same solution has been proposed for the presence of the statues of Sobekneferu at Tell el-Dab'a, which, it is suggested, could have been transported there from the Fayum during the reign of one of the Hyksos kings.[10] This was not, however, the conclusion of Labib Habachi, the person who excavated the site. He felt inclined to accept that the statues were more or less in situ when discovered.[11] Other scholars agree with him. They see the presence at Tell el-Dab'a of the statues— which, unfortunately, are today lost—as evidence for the migration into the region of the cult of Sobek of Shedet toward the end of the Twelfth Dynasty.[12]

If this was the case, then equally there seems to be no need to assume that the statue of Sobekneferu found at Tel Gezer was simply removed from Egypt by the Hyksos as they retreated from Egypt. Evidence of this comes from the fact that by this time, circa 1550 BCE, Canaan had moved into the Middle Bronze age IIB period, whereas the Sobekneferu statue almost certainly reached the site during the Middle Bronze age IIA period, which coincided with Egypt's Twelfth Dynasty.

---

*Although it has long been accepted that Tel Gezer's High Place dates to the MB IIC period and even the Iron Age, a reevaluation of the archaeological evidence from the shrine site shows it must have existed as early as MB IIA, and arguably during the Early Bronze Age, circa 3300–1950 BC. See Ben-Ami 2008, 26–27.

DIPLOMATIC MISSION
AND MILITARY CAMPAIGNS

Is it possible that the statue of Sobekneferu was given as a gift or tribute to the governor of Tel Gezer as part of some kind of diplomatic mission on behalf of the ruler of Egypt? The purpose of such missions would have been to affirm existing trading links with the Canaanite city state, while at the same time making it clear that any attempt to upset Egypt's foreign policies would be considered an act of aggression and met with immediate military force.[13] This had happened during the reign of Senusret III, Sobekneferu's grandfather, who had led a fierce military campaign against the inhabitants of Canaan as is recorded on the stela of Sobekkhu found in 1901 at Abydos in southern Egypt by British archaeologist John Garstang (1876–1956).[14]

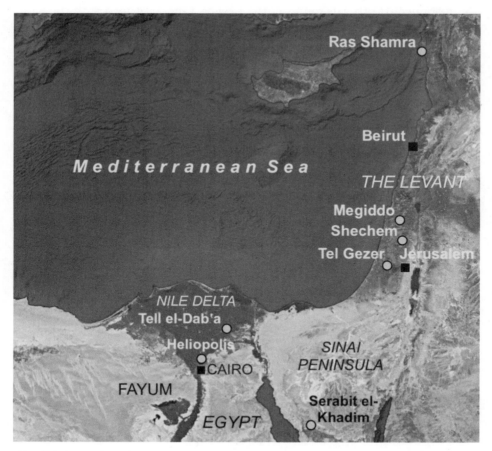

Fig. 7.4. Map of the Levant and northern Egypt showing sites featured in this book.

The stela speaks of Senusret III conquering the dreaded Retjenu, "highlanders," everywhere he went until he reached a place called Sekmem, where he halted his advance. Sekmem (*skmm*) was almost certainly the ancient biblical city of Shechem, identified as the archaeological site of Tell Balata in what is today the city of Nablus in the Palestinian West Bank, some 31 miles (50 kilometers) north of Jerusalem. (See fig. 7.4 for a map of sites in the Levant mentioned in this book.) The city played a crucial role in the establishment of the Jewish nation from the age of Abraham, the great patriarch of the Hebrew Bible, through until the conquest of Canaan by Joshua and the Israelite tribes, a matter dealt with elsewhere by the present author.[15]

Diplomatic missions into Canaan during the reigns of Twelfth Dynasty kings could well explain the presence of statues of two important Middle Kingdom court officials found in the Levant. One, inscribed with the name of a vizier named Senusret-Ankh, was found at Ras Shamra, the location of the former city of Ugarit in northern Syria.[16] The other statue, bearing an inscription in the name Djehuty-hotep, a powerful *nomarch* (governor) of Egypt's Hare *nome* in the southern part of the country,[17] was found at Megiddo in northern Israel.[18]

Djehuty-hotep thrived during the reigns of three Twelfth Dynasty kings, Amenemhat II (1914–1879/76 BC), Senusret II (1882–1872 BC), and Senusret III, while Senusret-Ankh lived at the end of the Twelfth Dynasty, circa 1800 BCE.[19] (Note: *Nome* was the ancient Greek name for an administrative district or division of land in ancient Egypt—the Egyptian hieroglyphic term being *sepat*. There were 22 nomes in Upper Egypt and 20 nomes in Lower Egypt.)

Both of these important Egyptian officials would have reported directly to the king, so did they also act as foreign envoys on behalf of their country? Could this explain the presence of their statues so far away from their homeland? This was certainly the conclusion of John van Seters (1935–), a Canadian scholar of the Hebrew Bible and Ancient Near Eastern studies, in an important study of Egypt's relations with its Asiatic neighbors during the Middle Kingdom and Second Intermediate Period. He suspects that both officials acted as foreign envoys sent into Syria-Palestine on diplomatic missions, which if correct explains the presence of their statues in this foreign land.[20]

THE EXPEDITION OF KHNUMHOTEP

Evidence of a similar diplomatic mission into Canaan comes from a columnar stela of a "high steward" and vizier named Khnumhotep found in association with his mastaba tomb at Dahshur in northern Egypt.[21] It alludes to a maritime expedition undertaken by the owner who is given the title "overseer of an expedition of sailors."[22] He departs from Egypt with several ships with the purpose of obtaining cedar wood from the land of the Retjenu. The fleet's destination is given as the port of Ullaza, which is reached following a stopover at nearby Byblos in what is today Lebanon. There they enlist the help of the city's ruler (*malku*), who sends his own ships as an advance guard along with a battalion of soldiers that moves overland.[23]

Khnumhotep's expedition takes place during the reign of Senusret III, and perhaps coincides with the military campaign undertaken by the king into Canaan recorded on the Sobekkhu stela mentioned above.[24] Trading expeditions to Byblos were seemingly fairly common during the Twelfth Dynasty, explaining perhaps the presence of the sphinx of Amenemhat IV found in nearby Beirut.[25]

Khnumhotep was probably chosen to lead the expedition into the land of the Retjenu because he and his family possessed some knowledge both of the geography and the inhabitants of Syria-Palestine. I say this since at Beni

Fig. 7.5. Aamu dignatory arriving at the court of Senusret II seen on the wall of Khnumhotep's tomb at Beni Hassan (from Newberry 1893, pl. 28).

Fig. 7.6. Aamu visitors to the court of Senusret II seen on the wall of the tomb of Khnumhotep at Beni Hasan (from Newberry 1893, pl. 31).

Hasan in southern Egypt, in the tomb of Khnumhotep's father (designated Tomb no. 3), who also bore the name Khnumhotep, there is a well-known wall scene showing a caravan of western Asiatic foreigners arriving at the court of Senusret II (circa 1882–1872 BC) bearing gifts (see figs. 7.5 and 7.6).

The peoples shown are referred to as Aamu,[26] a name simply meaning Asiatic foreigners, while the leader, who can be seen presenting as a gift a Nubian ibex, is named as Abisha the Hyksos, this being the ancient Greek rendition of the original Egyptian term, which was *Heqa-kasut,* meaning something like "rulers of foreign countries."[27] This is the earliest known reference to the Hyksos, or Shepherd Kings, who during the Second Intermediate Period would come to occupy Egypt for a period of around 150 years circa 1700–1550 BCE.

Remarkably, the son of the tomb's owner, Khnumhotep the Younger as we might call him, is shown with these Asiatic foreigners alongside an inscription that reads, "Asiatics that the high official's son Khnumhotep brought on account of galena [a lead ore]," in Regnal Year 6 of the king's reign.[28] In a separate inscription from the tomb we hear that the younger Khnumhotep is the "one who gets what is useful for its owner [that is, Senusret II], and doorway of foreign lands."[29] These facts, along with further textual evidence from a stela found at a place named Wadi Gasus on the Red Sea,[30] all hint strongly that Khnumhotep the Younger had some special connection with the land of the Retjenu and its inhabitants. Moreover, that this personal interest was one of the reasons why his father recorded the arrival of the Aamu at the royal court of Senusret II in the famous scene found in his tomb.

Khnumhotep the Younger's achievements during his life were manifold. For instance, an inscription in his mastaba at Dahshur mentions a pyramid named "Perfect one of Amenemhat," which is likely a reference to that of Amenemhat III located close by. As Egyptologist James P. Allen makes clear, "This indicates that his [Khnumhotep's] career lasted some three decades, from at least the first Regnal Year of Senwosret II (ca. 1887 B.C.) and into the reign of Amenemhat III," which began ca. 1850 B.C.[31]

The political, military, and diplomatic relationship between Egypt and Canaan during the second half of the Twelfth Dynasty is crucial in understanding not only how a statue of Sobekneferu could have reached Tel Gezer, but also what might have been happening in Egypt around this time. Could Sobekneferu, as the daughter of Amenemhat III, have acted as a foreign envoy on behalf of her father or brother, the statue having been presented to the Canaanite stronghold and religious center during a diplomatic mission similar to those described above? It is a fanciful notion, although it is one that does fit the facts as they stand. However, if this really was the case then what circumstances might have led to the princess making such an expedition?

CANAANITE CONTACT

During the second half of the Twelfth Dynasty a bond of mutual cooperation slowly began to build between Egypt and its neighbors over the border in Syria-Palestine. This must have started around the same time as the appearance of the well-known wall scene in Khnumhotep the Elder's tomb at Beni Hasan showing the arrival of the Aamu at the royal court of Senusret II.

Back then such visits would have been infrequent and an oddity enough for them to be recorded in the manner we see in this tomb. However, these visits would have slowly increased during the reign of Senusret III, despite his military campaign against the Retjenu, until by the reigns of Amenemhat III and Amenemhat IV we find overwhelming evidence of large numbers of Semitic-speaking Asiatic peoples settling in Egypt's Nile Delta, as well as in the Nile Valley itself.[32] We even find some of them in the role of high-ranking officials.[33] Others would have become mercenaries in the Egyptian army, sailors in the Egyptian navy, or they would have sought manual work of some kind. Those remaining close to Egypt's eastern border with Palestine would have been responsible for organizing caravans departing Egypt for the Sinai Peninsula and the Levant as a whole. These caravans would have followed age-old routes long controlled by indigenous Asiatic peoples from the regions in question.[34]

It is also highly possible that members of Egypt's growing western Asiatic population were employed in the construction of Senusret III's pyramid complex at Dahshur. This knowledge comes from the discovery inside one of the pyramid's passages of graffiti showing the profiles of individuals

Fig. 7.7. Graffiti from the pyramid of Senusret III at Dahshur
highly suggestive of the presence during its construction of western Asiatic
peoples (from Morgan 1903, fig. 137).

who match very well the style of the Aamu pictured inside Khumnhotep the Elder's tomb at Beni Hasan (see fig. 7.7).[35]

Since Senusret III's pyramid complex is located in the same general vicinity as Khnumhotep the Younger's mastaba tomb, I cannot help but think there must be a connection between the presence of these Asiatic peoples at Dahshur and the official's celebrated maritime expedition to the land of the Retjenu.

Was Khnumhotep the Younger responsible for inviting into Egypt Asiatic peoples who were already craftsmen skilled in stonemasonry, building construction, and engineering work? Did these people introduce into Egypt new ideas that would be carried forward from the reign of Senusret III into those of his successors, Amenemhat III and Amenemhat IV? I am deliberately leaving out Sobekneferu's name for reasons that will become apparent in due course.

Among the Asiatic peoples who did come to settle in Egypt were those classed as slaves. Many were assigned to private individuals or temples. Some would go on to attain positions of responsibility and honor. Many of them were women, the spoils perhaps of Senusret III's military raids into the land of the Retjenu. Many of these slaves would, however, go on to intermarry with Egyptians.[36]

GREAT CHANGES IN EGYPT

At the same time all this was happening Senusret III made the decision to divide Egypt into three separate geopolitical zones, whereas in the past there had been just two—Upper and Lower Egypt. Henceforth the southern part of the country would be controlled from Thebes, the middle part from the capital Itj-tawy, while the northern part of the country would come under the governmental administration of a new center in the eastern Nile Delta, close to the border with Palestine.[37] Almost certainly the Delta's center of governmental control was the slowly emerging city of Tell el-Dab'a and its environs, the future Avaris, which from around 1700 BCE would start to become a stronghold for the incoming Hyksos warlords.

The relationship between Egypt and its neighbors in the Levant, the land of the Retjenu, is something that might at first seem unconnected with the suspected interest Sobekneferu would appear to have shown in these same foreign territories, as appears evident from the presence of her statue at Tel Gezer. Matters become clearer, however, when we begin to focus our attention on an important cult center in the Egyptian Sinai, where the goddess Hathor was venerated both by Amenemhat III and by his successor Amenemhat IV. As we see next, it is a connection that will increase our understanding not only of Sobekneferu's belief that she was destined to assume the throne of Egypt, but also in what happened when she took control of one of the most powerful kingdoms of the ancient world.

8

The Vengeful Goddess

Sobekneferu, as we saw in chapter 5, had deliberately decided to represent herself as a large stone sphinx right in the heart of the Nile Delta's administrative center at what would soon become Avaris, the capital of the Hyksos kings. They would come to control large parts of Egypt from around 1675 BCE onward for around 125 years. Why did she do this? Why represent yourself as a terrifying sphinx and place it so close to the border with neighboring Palestine?

The trend in queens, and some kings, being shown as sphinxes— human-headed recumbent lions—gained momentum during the second half of the Twelfth Dynasty.[1] By taking on this leonine form the king or queen was embodying the powerful, and also the quite vengeful, aspect of the goddess Hathor, who in this guise bore the name Sekhmet. It is a name derived from the Egyptian word *sekhem*—"divine might," "great strength," or even "absolute power," leading to the general opinion that the name Sekhmet meant something like, "The Powerful One."

Sekhmet was thus the vengeful and quite terrifying aspect of Hathor, embodied in sphinxes like the one set up at Khatana by Sobekneferu as a symbol of her absolute dominion over its population. This rather stern message sent out by the female monarch was directed not simply toward her Egyptian subjects, but also toward the incoming western Asiatic peoples who were beginning to settle in the region en masse.

How these actions relate to Sobekneferu's reign, as well as the statue of her as a princess found at Tel Gezer in modern-day Israel, now becomes crucial in our understanding not only of how she rose to power, but also what happened to her at the end of her brief reign. For this we must temporarily transfer our attention to what was going on in the Sinai, for it was there during the reigns of Amenemhat III and Amenemhat IV that native Egyptians and western Asiatic peoples would work together in the extraction and subsequent transportation of turquoise, malachite, and copper ore from mines located in the southwestern part of the peninsula.[2]

THE CULT CENTER OF SERABIT EL-KHADIM

Close to one turquoise mine was an important religious center named Serabit el-Khadim. Situated on a small mountain plateau, elevated above the desert terrain (see fig. 8.1 for a map of the region), it was dedicated primarily to the goddess Hathor (its other affiliation was to Sopdu, a god of the sky who was seen as "lord of the east"). Her temple there contained a cave shrine, which had almost certainly existed as a natural fissure in the rock prior to any dynastic activity at the location.

Hathor was seen as the mother and sometimes even the consort of the falcon god Horus the Elder (not to be confused with Horus the Younger, who was the offspring of Osiris, god of the underworld, and his sister-wife Isis). The name Hathor means the "house of Horus," a reference to the goddess's womb as the place of gestation of the god, who was thought to be born within every child destined to rule the Two Lands.[3] It was this relationship between Hathor and Horus that linked the goddess with the perceived legitimacy of a pharaoh's reign.

In addition to being shown in her vengeful form as Sekhmet, who was represented usually as a lioness-headed human figure, Hathor was personified in the night sky as a celestial cow, the animal's four legs acting as supports for the vault of heaven. When not being depicted as a bovine in reliefs and statuary, Hathor was shown as a woman with cow ears, inturned cow horns that supported a solar or lunar disk, and a wig that rested on her shoulders as two distinctive plaits curled outward into neat spirals (see fig. 8.2).

Hathor was seen also as the divine personification of human acts such as love, joy, sex, dancing, music, merriment, poetry, and motherhood; in fact, almost every aspect of femininity and motherhood came under her patronage. The goddess also received human souls as they entered the afterlife—their thirst quenched with water poured by the goddess from her sacred tree, the sycamore.

Fig. 8.1. Map of Egypt and the Sinai Peninsula showing the location of the turquoise mining area of Serabit el-Khadim.

Fig. 8.2. Hathor heads found at Serabit el-Khadim in the Sinai peninsula. They date from the reign of Thutmosis III and thus the age of Hatshepsut (from Petrie 1906, pls. 103 and 104).

Lady of Turquoise

In addition to these attributes, Hathor presided over the success of the mining operations taking place in the Sinai, a role that gained her the title Lady of Mafkat; with *mafkat* being the ancient Egyptian name for turquoise.[4] This was a reference to the greatly prized green imperial turquoise found

Fig. 8.3. Stelae on the approach route to the cult center
at Serabit el-Khadim in the Sinai (from Petrie 1906, pl. 100).

in the vicinity of the Serabit el-Khadim cult center established during the reign of Amenemhat I, the first king of the Twelfth Dynasty.[5] So important was turquoise to the triangular-shaped peninsula situated between the Mediterranean Sea, Red Sea, and Gulf of Aqaba that the Sinai even became known as the "land" or "country of Mafkat."

Later kings of the same dynasty also patronized Serabit el-Khadim with royal expeditions leaving behind offerings of statues and carved inscriptions giving thanks to the goddess Hathor (see fig. 8.3). Each added new architectural features and erected round-topped commemorative stelae in the temple's open court and approach route, many of which remain in situ today. This royal patronage continued through to the reigns of Amenemhat III and Amenemhat IV, whose presence is recorded in various inscriptions found at the site.[6]

Hathor as Cat Goddess

Hathor was also venerated at Serabit el-Khadim in the form of a wild cat. Many small figurines and flat tablets with figures of cats, which served as votive objects, were found during excavations there in 1904–1905 by renowned British archaeologist and Egyptologist W. M. Flinders Petrie (1853–1942).[7] The species represented was sometimes a cheetah and at other times a serval,[8] an animal usually associated with the land of Nubia beyond Egypt's southern border in what is today Sudan. As a mythical creature the Nubian cat was an aspect of Hathor in her vengeful aspect both as Sekhmet and also as the so-called Eye of Ra, an epithet additionally applied to other feline goddesses such as Bastet and Tefnut.

As to the function of the cult shrine at Serabit el-Khadim, from the discovery of a large number of small stone cells both in a temple area and in the surrounding landscape, Petrie suspected that visitors went there for the purposes of dream incubation in that they would go to sleep in the belief that the goddess would speak to them through dreams.[9]

Hathor was patron not only of the copper and turquoise mines of Sinai, but also mineral extraction in general. For example, she bore the epithet Lady of Amethyst in her role as guardian of the amethyst mines at a site named Wadi el-Hudi,[10] situated between Aswan and Egypt's Red Sea coast. Amethyst was directly connected with the goddess in her role as guardian protector of dreams of the sort that visitors to Serabit el-Khadim could expect to experience when there.[11] Hathor was also known as Lady of Silver[12]—a title alluding to her guardianship of Egypt's silver mines in Syria—as well as "The Gold"[13] or the "Golden One,"[14] a reference perhaps to the country's sources of gold in Ethiopia.

HATHOR AND AMENEMHAT III

Amenemhat III is known to have had a very close relationship with Hathor, not just through his own patronage of her temple and cave shrine at Serabit el-Khadim, but also because of the discovery at the Labyrinth—that is, his mortuary complex at Hawara in the Fayum, a subject fully explored in part 6 of this book—of various statue fragments representing the goddess.[15] Moreover, one statue of the king found there shows him wearing the leopard skin garment of a priest with a pendant around his neck that has been identified as the *menit,* a symbol special to the goddess.[16]

In addition to this, there seems good evidence to suggest that Amenemhat III's eldest daughter, Neferuptah, Sobekneferu's older sister, was considered a priestess of Hathor. In the Twelfth Dynasty temple at Medinet Madi (which was called Dja by the ancient Egyptians and Narmuthis by the Ptolemaic Greeks), situated around 15 miles (24 kilometers) southwest of Shedet (modern-day Kiman Faras) and dedicated primarily to the snake goddess Renenutet (Greek: Thermouthis), Neferuptah is shown holding a sistrum, an instrument sacred to Hathor. This she shakes toward a carved relief of the snake-headed deity as her father stands behind her (see fig. 8.4; see the full panel in plate 9).[17] Further links between Neferuptah and the cult of Hathor come from a contemporary papyrus fragment from the goddess's main cult center at Dendera in southern Egypt, although this evidence is disputed.*

There is also a strong hint that Sobekneferu followed in the footsteps of her father and her elder sister and was herself a devotee of Hathor. This information comes not only from the manner in which she is portrayed as a sphinx at Khatana in the Nile Delta, but also from the fact that she was

---

*The Neferuptah in question could well have been a daughter of Senusret I, since the Dendera papyrus fragment states she is in Khenemet-swt (*hnmt-swt*), the "pyramid temple," a term used for the king's pyramid at Lisht. See Farag and Iskander 1971, 104–5 and Pignattari 2018, 8.

Fig. 8.4. Neferuptah (center) in the temple of Renenutet at Medinet Madi in the southern Fayum. The princess holds an oversized sistrum sacred to the goddess Hathor. As shown in plate 9, to her left is her father Amenemhat III and to her right is the snake goddess Renenutet. Illustration by Nick Burton.

responsible for completing the Labyrinth at Hawara. The various statue fragments of the goddess found at the site almost certainly indicate the presence there of an important chapel or shrine dedicated to Hathor, one that would have been active during Sobekneferu's reign.[18] So did the female monarch have a particular interest in this goddess? If so then what did Hathor mean to her?

Hathor was seen as guardian of Deir el-Bahri in West Thebes where she was known as "Lady of the West," since she presided over Egypt's western desert, which forms part of the much greater Libyan Desert. Indeed, Deir el-Bahri featured in the Valley Festival, where the goddess would be specifically honored.[19] It was also, as we have seen, the chosen site of Hatshepsut's magnificent mortuary temple, which included a fairly substantial chapel dedicated to Hathor. So, there is every reason to believe that Hatshepsut bore a strong devotion to the goddess since she is thought to have added architectural features to the existing temple at Serabit el-Khadim.[20]

As previously noted, immediately south of Hatshepsut's mortuary temple at Deir el-Bahri is the Twelfth Dynasty tomb of Senat, a priestess of Hathor.[21] It was probably because of her close association with the goddess that Senat was interred in a cemetery usually only reserved for men.

Senat's tomb, as we saw in chapter 5, had by the reign of Hatshepsut's father, Thutmosis I, come to be seen as the tomb of Sobekneferu. Her association with the location was almost certainly due to the fact that Senat and Sobekneferu not only lived during the same dynasty, but that they were also both seen as avatars of Hathor.

The existence of a Hathor shrine in the Labyrinth at Hawara, along with the presence of a large stone sphinx of Sobekneferu in the city of Avaris in the Nile Delta, can certainly be considered evidence of the monarch's devotion to the goddess. Is there anything else from Sobekneferu's reign that can help validate this supposition? The answer would appear to be yes as we now delve into why at her coronation the monarch made the unprecedented decision to wear the ceremonial cloak usually only worn by kings who had successfully undergone the Heb Sed festival. As we see next, it was very likely a decision made by Sobekneferu not only because of her firm belief that Hathor could legitimize her right to rule the Two Lands, but also because of her absolute conviction that this was her one and only true destiny.

9

Divine Right to Rule

The goddess Hathor, as previously noted, governed over the legitimacy of a king's right to rule through her role as the provider of the "house," or womb, from which the god Horus would be born into this world. The god's spirit was thought to incarnate within any child truly destined to rule the Two Lands, something that must have been considered preordained even before the child's conception. This, we must assume, is something that Sobekneferu would have been very much aware of and would have needed to wholeheartedly embrace not just during her early life but also in the lead up to her coronation.

To try to better understand Sobekneferu's own unwavering belief that she would one day rule Egypt as the incarnate Horus we need to return to the green schist figurine of a late Twelfth Dynasty royal female dressed in a Heb Sed cloak housed in New York's Metropolitan Museum of Art. Since the identity of the woman shown can really only be Sobekneferu, her wearing of this unique ceremonial garment makes no logical sense whatsoever. The Heb Sed garment was usually worn by kings only after they had successfully completed their first Heb Sed festival, which involved them participating in a series of quite strenuous physical tasks and trials to determine whether they were capable of continuing to rule the country. The problem is that this event would only usually take place after the monarch had reigned for a period of 30 years. Thereafter it would be repeated every third or fourth year through until the end of their life.

Why then does the Metropolitan Museum of Art's figurine show Sobekneferu wearing the Heb Sed cloak? Is it possible that she herself underwent certain trials, perhaps ritualistic in nature, that in her mind gave her the *right* to wear the Heb Sed cloak at her coronation ceremony?[1]

If such a rite did occur, then what it entailed and who might have performed it may never be known, although there are grounds to believe it *could* have been conducted under the patronage of the goddess Hathor. I say this for Hathor presided not only over the legitimacy of a monarch's reign, but also, by virtue of this, his or her continued right to rule following the completion of the Heb Sed festival.

THE MENKAURE TRIADS

The connection between the goddess Hathor and a king's right to rule is seen in the case of the so-called triad panels found in 1908 by American Egyptologist George A. Reisner in the valley temple of the Fourth Dynasty king Menkaure at Giza. These magnificent pieces of sculpture are around 4,450 years old. Four remain: three in the Egyptian Museum, Cairo, and one in Boston's Museum of Fine Arts. Fragments of at least another three triads exist, bringing the total known to seven. Each slightly undersized sculpture is made of greywacke and shows the king in the company of two divinities—one is always Hathor, while the other is either a male or female figure representing the *genius loci* ("spirit of a place") of an individual *nome* or district, each being identified by the nome's standard on their head (see fig. 9.1). Of those triads remaining only Upper Egypt is represented (Thebes, Diospolis Parva, Hermopolis, and Cynopolis), although other examples that have not survived would presumably have signified nomes in Lower Egypt.

There are two types of triad. Type 1, of which three good examples remain, shows the king striding forward wearing the crown of Upper Egypt and flanked by Hathor on his right and the nome representative on his left. Type 2 shows Hathor in the center seated or enthroned with the king standing on her left-hand side with the nome representative on her right-hand side. Behind them are back slabs, which although indicative that they might have been intended to slot into wall spaces does not ever seem to have been the case. They were meant, it would seem, to have been freestanding within the king's valley temple, which was made of mudbrick.

The reason why Hathor is always the principal deity represented in these

Fig. 9.1. Two examples of the triad panels found in the valley temple of Menkaure at Giza. Hathor stands on the left with the king center and the nome representative on his right. Note that the standard borne by the nome figure in the example seen on the right-hand side denotes one of the estates of Hathor. Both triad panels are on display in the Egyptian Museum.

triad panels is that during the Old Kingdom (2686–2181 BCE) the goddess was seen both as the mother as well as the divine wife of the pharaoh. In addition to this, we know that a cult in her name existed in the Memphis area, arguably at Giza itself, where she bore the title Mistress of the Southern Sycamore.[2]

In addition to Hathor's familial relationship to Menkaure as his divine mother, her presence in the triads, and the way she embraces the king, relates to the legitimacy of his kingship. As Florence Dunn Friedman of Brown University makes clear following her own extensive study of the symbolism and purpose of the triads, "Legitimation is the first visible theme of the triads."[3]

Friedman proposes that the triads were designed and placed within Menkaure's valley temple to reflect multidirectionality with each one serving to connect with Hathor's estates in the nomes in question. More specifically they exist as affirmations of the goddess's role in the Heb Sed festival. This is confirmed in one of the triads, which shows Menkaure holding in his left hand the *mks*—the leather document given to the king by the gods following the successful completion of the festival.[4]

The importance being conveyed by the triads, Friedman writes, is the king's legitimization not only in life, but also in the hereafter, where the sustenance produced by the goddess's estates will nourish him in death.[5] In summary Friedman lays out the clear connection between the Heb Sed festival and the importance of the cult of Hathor to Menkaure by saying:

> Hathor is the key to understanding the triads. She provides the king, in the context of the heb sed, with legitimation, provisioning and sed confirmation, as well as with multi-directionality, a royal benefit that while not new, is for the first time shown to have Hathor as its source. The relationship of Menkaure to his divine mother is emphasized in each triad. He is the beloved of Hathor in her preeminent Memphite cult and in "all her cult places"—cult places that he and former kings endowed. And as he endows a cult place for her, she cares for him.[6]

SOBEKNEFERU AND LEGITIMIZATION OF KINGSHIP

If Friedman is correct then the Heb Sed festival's affirmation of a king's right to rule was something recognized by the goddess Hathor, who was herself seen as legitimizing kingship in her capacity as divine mother of each and every rightful king. However, if the Heb Sed festival was performed only after a monarch had reigned for 30 years, why then did Sobekneferu dare to go against 1,200 years of religious and cultural tradition by being portrayed wearing the Heb Sed cloak at what appears to have been her coronation? The key seems to be in the fact that, as Friedman writes, "Heb sed confirmation is not shown as coming from multiple gods; it comes solely from Hathor."[7]

So did Sobekneferu participate in some variation of the Heb Sed ritual, done perhaps under the patronage of Hathor, the only goddess who could confirm her divine right to rule the country? If so, then any such rite is unlikely to have been seen as truly legitimate in the eyes of Egypt's powerful priesthoods like those of Amun, Ra, or even Sobek of Shedet. Indeed, with her brother Amenemhat IV on the throne before her, any kind of rite of passage ensuring her own legitimacy as future ruler would surely have had to have been done in private at one of the goddess's cult centers, such as at Dendera in what is today Middle Egypt, or even at Deir el-Bahri in West Thebes.

It is even possible that any such rite had to be conducted outside of Egypt's Nile Valley, perhaps even at Serabit el-Khadim in the Sinai. Not only was this an important cult site for the goddess, but it was also patronized heavily both by Sobekneferu's father Amenemhat III and by her brother Amenemhat IV. Beyond this everything is pure speculation, although the likelihood of such a rite of kingship affirming the female monarch's right of legitimacy to the throne could explain why she might have decided to so boldly wear the Heb Sed cloak at the time of her coronation.

THE DEATH OF HER BROTHER

When Amenemhat IV died after a reign of 9 years 3 months and 27 days, according to his entry in the Turin Canon, Sobekneferu was ready and waiting to take the throne of Egypt. Almost certainly her accession was not, however, something thrust on her simply because she was the last person standing in her royal dynasty. This we can surmise in the knowledge that the first two kings of the incoming Thirteenth Dynasty, Sobekhotep I and Sonbef, used Amenemhat as a personal name indicating, according to Egyptologist Kim Ryholt, that they were sons of Amenemhat IV.[8]

It could even be proposed that Sobekhotep and Sonbef were the offspring of Amenemhat IV and Sobekneferu, born during the former's reign. This remains a distinct possibility, although if this was the case then in theory one or other of them should have taken the throne following the death of their father, arguably with Sobekneferu as regent.

There is no confirmation of any of these facts from the contemporary evidence available to us. Despite this frustrating situation, Ryholt addresses the circumstances regarding Sobekneferu's succession to the throne in the following manner: "The royal status of Nofrusobk [that is, Sobekneferu] does not in itself explain her accession, as her father had designated Amenemhat IV as his successor, and the latter had sons of his own. . . . It would seem therefore that Nofrusobk usurped the throne from the heirs of Amenemhat IV."[9] Once again, this is possible, yet remains unproven.

Ryholt's additional belief that Amenemhat IV was of nonroyal blood and had been chosen to be king by the aging Amenemhat III ahead of his own daughter, Sobekneferu, resulting in a "dynastic struggle" toward the end of the Twelfth Dynasty,[10] is something we'll look at more closely in part 3 of this book.

During the reign of her brother, Sobekneferu would appear to have known exactly what she wanted and how to achieve it. That she portrayed herself clothed in the Heb Sed cloak at the time of her coronation was probably done to send out a clear message to all her potential detractors. She wanted to tell them she was the offspring of Hathor, the divine mother of the incarnate Horus. Not only did she have the divine right to rule, but the legitimacy and recognition of this fact had been affirmed by the goddess herself.

How exactly then did Sobekneferu come to be in this very powerful and also very privileged position in the first place? Whom might she have had to supplicate or, alternately, eradicate to reach her true destiny as ruler of the Two Lands? What possible role did her father play in her future destiny, and what was her relationship with the outgoing king Amenemhat IV, to whom she was "sister" according to Manetho?

Once again we find ourselves asking the question: Who exactly was Sobekneferu? We know who her father was as she is addressed as "king's daughter" on items from when she was still just a princess. But what about her mother? Who was she? And what was Sobekneferu's relationship with her sister, Neferuptah, someone who, as we see next, was very clearly being groomed to become a future royal wife either for her father, Amenemhat III, or his successor, Amenemhat IV. It is these matters that we start to address in the next part of the book, beginning with everything we know about Neferuptah.

PART 3

SEEDS OF DESTRUCTION

10

The Sister of Sobekneferu

It was in 1936 while making soundings at Hawara South around 1.2 miles (2 kilometers) southwest of the site of the Labyrinth that Egyptian Egyptologist Labib Habachi uncovered evidence of a previously unrecorded mudbrick structure of some considerable size. Since, however, he was shortly afterward appointed head of excavations in the Nile Delta he was unable to take the investigations any further.

The existence of the unexplored mudbrick structure was not, however, forgotten and in 1955 Nagib Farag, the Fayum's inspector of antiquities, was finally able to investigate the site. He found it to contain a rectangular chamber roofed over by seven enormous limestone blocks placed side by side.[1] The structure, he determined, had once formed the sepulcher of a fair-sized pyramid constructed of mudbrick and probably overlaid with limestone casing blocks.[2] All this, however, had long since disappeared having probably been destroyed in antiquity.

The following year, 1956, Farag, along with his colleague Zaky Iskander, lifted six out of seven of the huge roofing blocks and descended into the tomb chamber below. Very quickly they realized they had found the undisturbed tomb of Neferuptah,[3] a known daughter of Amenemhat III.[4] Knowledge of her place in history had previously come from the discovery in the late nineteenth century of a rather strange makeshift sarcophagus constructed alongside that of her father in his pyramid at Hawara. (See fig. 10.1 for a map of the Hawara area.)

Farag and Iskander found that the sepulcher's rather cramped interior had been divided into two separate compartments through the placement of

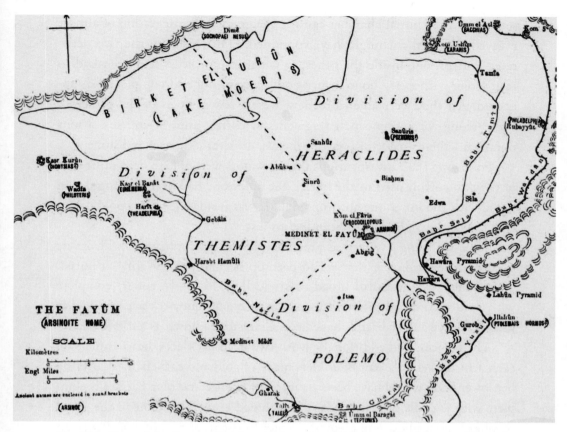

Fig. 10.1. Map of the Fayum showing the location of Hawara, the Hawara Channel, the Bahr Yusef waterway, Kiman Faras (ancient Shedat and Crocodilopolis), and the Birket Qarun lake (ancient Lake Moeris) (from Grenfell et al. 1900, pl. XVIII).

a large upright slab. On one side of this partition, its north side, they found an enormous red granite sarcophagus over 9.8 feet (3 meters) in length (see plate 5),[5] while in the other smaller compartment they came across a scattering of funerary objects. Curiously, the burial vault bore no access door, meaning that the sarcophagus must have been put in place and the princess interred while the pyramid was still under construction.[6]

AN UNFORTUNATE FIND

One unfortunate problem that Farag and Iskander soon realized after they removed the lid of the sarcophagus was that groundwater had regularly seeped into the burial chamber causing the gradual disintegration of almost everything organic it might have contained.[7] This included the two decorated coffins, one inside the other, in which the princess had been laid to rest; along with every bone in her body, everything had completely disappeared. All they were able to retrieve were a few samples of the princess's skin,[8] along with some small fragments of coffin, and, of course, various nonorganic items made of precious metals, minerals, faience, and stone.

Following their investigations the excavators were able to determine that of the two coffins used in the burial, the outer one had been rectangular in shape with the inner one anthropoidal.[9] It was inside the anthropoid coffin that the princess's body had been laid to rest.

Some stunning jewelry was present inside the sarcophagus, and from its position it seemed clear that it had been on her body at the time of burial. This included a beautiful broad collar (called the *wsekh*-collar) complete with beaded cord and counterpoise along with a unique necklace that had as its centerpiece a large barrel-shaped carnelian stone known as a *sweret*-bead.[10]

The princess had additionally worn two bead necklaces, bead armlets on each arm, as well as a pair of anklets made of gold and carnelian.[11] Covering her lower body would have been an apron of faience and blue frit beads complete with a girdle of disc beads that included a small pendant in the shape of a hawk or swallow (see plate 6). (Note: Blue frit, also known as Egyptian blue, was a substance used for decoration and jewelry. It was made from quartz and lime, along with a copper compound and an alkali. Finished items were heated to a temperature of between 1562 and 1832 degrees Fahrenheit [850 and 1000 degrees centigrade]. It also came in a green color.)

In addition to these remarkable treasures Farag and Iskander found in the tomb three beautiful silver vases (see plate 8),[12] along with an alabaster jar and an assortment of other items. They included a flail made of carnelian stones and faience (see plate 7), as well as a black granite offering table inscribed with the princess's name.[13] Indeed, her sarcophagus as well as several other objects found in the tomb bore inscriptions with her name enclosed in a royal cartouche.[14] Repeatedly, Neferuptah is referred to either as "king's daughter" or as "beloved king's daughter of his body,"[15] the king in question being, of course, her father Amenemhat III. When mentioned in an inscription it was his throne name Nimaatre (Ni-ma'at-Ra) that was used, and not his *nomen* or personal name, Amenemhat.[16]

THE MYSTERY OF THE MAGICAL FORMULAE

One of the most curious features about Neferuptah's tomb—and there are several—concerns the discovery of bands of gold leaf that had once adorned the rectangular coffin. These bore hieroglyphic spells meant to help the deceased pass successfully into the hereafter.[17] Although the use of these magic formulae was fairly common for royal burials during the Middle Kingdom, the manner of composition of those found in Neferuptah's tomb was quite unique and would not be seen again until the New Kingdom some 350 years later.[18]

It is a mystery that has intrigued German archaeologist Wolfram Grajetzki, a leading expert on the Middle Kingdom and in particular its funerary culture. He noted that the same arrangement of magic spells seen on Neferuptah's middle coffin was present also on the sarcophagus prepared for Hatshepsut before she rose to become sole ruler of the country.[19] So what was going on? How might this have come about, especially since Neferuptah's tomb had clearly not been disturbed since the time of its construction?

In 2005 Grajetzki wrote the following on the matter: "Two of these texts [from Neferuptah's rectangular coffin] can be paralleled with certainty on the sarcophagus of Hatshepsut, while one other text provides a possible third parallel." He further added that, "it is clear that Hatshepsut as 'great king's wife' copied for her sarcophagus the form and the textual programme of one or more coffins of the late Middle Kingdom."[20] In 2014, Grajetzki took the matter even further, stating:

> Even though no other Middle Kingdom coffins with such texts are known, it seems most likely that this is due to a gap in the archaeological record. It seems impossible that New Kingdom coffin designers would have seen the coffin of Neferuptah. Maybe there were other examples accessible to them, or they had access to papyri showing Middle Kingdom coffin designs.[21]

It is certainly possible that in the New Kingdom surviving papyri from the Middle Kingdom contained details of the magical formulae uniquely used in the tomb of Neferuptah. Possible, although as yet unproven, begging the question of how Hatshepsut really did come across this very specific set of magical formulae? Unfortunately, there are no hard and fast answers at this time.

The greater mystery, however, is why Hatshepsut should have wanted to use the same sequence of magical formulae as a member of the royal family living at the end of the Twelfth Dynasty. Just one answer makes sense: the monarch was deliberately attempting to align herself with the owner of the coffin or sarcophagus the magical spells had come from. Since this person is unlikely to have been Neferuptah the chances are the magical formulae came from a tomb belonging to someone else in the same family.

We have no idea who that might have been, although in some ways it doesn't matter. What *is* important is that Hatshepsut may well have deliberately sought out and used this specific set of magical formulae for her sarcophagus in which her soul would begin its journey into the afterlife. Is it possible that she was attempting to align herself not so much with Neferuptah, but more specifically with her sister Sobekneferu? I think this is a very plausible explanation, and one that backs up the growing awareness that Hatshepsut was greatly inspired by Sobekneferu, and so wanted to associate herself with her forerunner, not just in life *but also in death*.[22] As far reaching as this statement might seem, Hatshepsut's personal interest in Sobekneferu and her family deserves fuller attention in the future.

All these facts prompt us to look more closely into who exactly Neferuptah was, and what her relationship might have been with her sister, Sobekneferu. Were they *actual* sisters? Did they get along with each other? And how did the fate of one sister impact on the other?

THE LIFE OF NEFERUPTAH

Neferuptah means "beauties of (the god) Ptah." It is a name constructed in the same manner as Sobekneferu, which as we know means "beauties of (the god) Sobek." It is a name that, as we have seen, can equally be written Neferusobek. Most Egyptological sources chose to write Neferuptah's name with its two main elements, *neferu* and *ptah,* this way around, although it can equally be written Ptahneferu. Even though the princess's personal name might suggest a connection with the god Ptah, whose main temple was at Memphis, Neferuptah's religious interests probably lay elsewhere.

As previously mentioned, we find Neferuptah shown in carved relief on a wall within the temple of Renenutet at Medinet Madi in the southwestern part of the Fayum. There her name is seen within the royal cartouche and, just like in her pyramid tomb, she is described as "king's daughter of his body."[23] Standing behind her is her father, Amenemhat III (see plate 9). Both he and Neferuptah face toward the snake-headed goddess suggesting that they are there to address Renenutet as part of a religious ritual.

The Medinet Madi temple was constructed by Amenemhat III toward the end of his reign and completed most likely during his brief co-regency with Amenemhat IV (see plate 10).[24] Thus there is every reason to suspect that the relief showing Neferuptah and her father in the presence of Renenutet was put in place when Amenemhat III was still alive.

NEFERUPTAH AND THE MEDINET MADI TEMPLE

Neferuptah is shown at the Medinet Madi temple as a young princess wearing a diadem with plumes similar to that worn in death by princess Sithathoriunet ("Daughter of Hathor of Dendera"), her name, of course, honoring the goddess Hathor.[25] She was a probable daughter of Senusret II, making sense of why her tomb was found next to the pharaoh's pyramid complex at El-Lahun. Neferuptah is seen holding out toward the snake goddess a wooden instrument known as a sistrum, which she clenches with both hands. (See fig. 8.4 on page 81 and plate 9 to see the carved relief of Neferuptah from the temple at Medinet Madi.)

The sistrum was an instrument sacred to Hathor, something emphasized in the relief of Neferuptah at Medinet Madi, since the instrument's particularly large head is shaped like a cow's face and has inturned horns, both recognizable symbols of the goddess. Between the two horns are strung the horizontal struts that would have held the tiny cymbals, so that when shaken the instrument would have made a pleasant melodic sound. Curiously enough, monks and priests of the Ethiopian Church even today use sistrums that are very similar to those that featured in religious ceremonies in ancient Egypt. The Medinet Madi relief is the earliest known depiction of a sistrum being used by a member of an ancient Egyptian royal family.[26] The princess's apparent association with Hathor would probably have been essential in the lead up to her becoming a royal wife. As an incarnation of the goddess she would have been expected to give birth to the next living Horus, that is the rightful heir to the throne.

So who exactly was Neferuptah being lined up to marry? One theory is that she was to become the next royal wife of her father, Amenemhat III,[27] although whether or not this actually took place is unclear. There is a much greater chance that she was to become the wife and consort of her father's chosen successor Amenemhat IV, although not simply as a queen but, as we see next, *as his co-ruler,* a situation that would definitely have been of great interest to her sister Sobekneferu.[28]

11

The King's Daughters

Evidence that Neferuptah was being groomed to become Egypt's next ruler comes from the unprecedented fact that her name appears inside a royal cartouche, the first woman in Egyptian history to be given this honor.[1] Not only do we see the royal cartouche with her name alongside the relief of the princess at Medinet Madi, but, as mentioned earlier, it is also present on various items found inside her pyramid tomb at Hawara South.

That Amenemhat III honored his daughter Neferuptah in such a unique manner reveals something else of incredible importance to this story. Although both Amenemhat III and his successor Amenemhat IV are shown in reliefs within the Medinet Madi temple, nowhere do we see Sobekneferu. She is completely missing. This is despite the fact that Manetho states that Sobekneferu, whom he calls Skemiophris,[2] was "sister" to the previous ruler "Ammenemes,"[3] that is Amenemhat IV.[4]

So we have to assume that Sobekneferu formed an integral part of the royal dynasty (Manetho states she was the seventh and final ruler of the Twelfth Dynasty,[5] even though there were in fact eight rulers in this dynasty). This seems confirmed from the inscription on the statue base found at Tel Gezer, which tells us that Sobekneferu was "the King's Daughter of his body,"[6] the very same title given to Neferuptah in inscriptions relating to her. Sobekneferu is also named as "king's daughter" on the black granite bowl found near the pyramid of her great ancestor Senusret I at Lisht.[7] What is more, Sobekneferu directly associates herself with Amenemhat III within inscriptions found at the site of the Labyrinth, where she is again referred to as "king's daughter."[8] In addition to this, a block of granite from the Labyrinth bears an inscription that ends "her monument to her father living forever," very clearly inferring that she is his daughter.[9]

All this points to the fact that Sobekneferu was not only a daughter of Amenemhat III, but also that she was of the same familial status as Neferuptah. The only difference between the two princesses from contemporary sources is that Sobekneferu's name is never shown inside a royal cartouche before her accession. That privilege was reserved for Neferuptah alone.

So where's Sobekneferu?

The fact that Sobekneferu is *not* mentioned anywhere in the Medinet Madi temple makes it clear that her father's chosen successor was Neferuptah. There seems little doubt about this at all. Sobekneferu, it would seem, formed no part in the dynasty's future plans.

What the evidence both from the Medinet Madi temple and from Neferuptah's pyramid tomb at Hawara South additionally tells us, however, is that Amenemhat III was fully disposed to the idea of a *female* ruler of Egypt, a new progressive attitude to kingship that might just have paved the way for Sobekneferu's own eventual reign. Of course, this choice of female successor could simply have been because Neferuptah was the king's eldest surviving daughter, and thus the natural heir to the throne. This makes sense, although we also now have to factor in Amenemhat IV, whom we know was the *historical* successor of Amenemet III and was no doubt being primed for this role even as Neferuptah's relief was being carved on the wall of the Medinet Madi temple. So who exactly was Amenemhat IV, and how did he fit into the royal family?

In all likelihood, before his brief, possibly one- to two-year co-regency with Amenemhat III,[10] Amenemhat IV was himself being groomed to become the next ruler of Egypt. Most likely he was to have had Neferuptah by his side as co-ruler, although what official title she would have been given on succeeding to the throne is unclear. This makes sense of the evidence, but as we shall see the story is far more complex than this rather convenient solution. I say this, for the immediate questions that arise from evoking such a carefully orchestrated dynastic arrangement are: What became of Neferuptah? Why is she never seen again after the construction of the Medinet Madi temple? Why has no mention of her been found in connection with the reign of Amenemhat IV? Was she even alive at this time?

THE FATE OF NEFERUPTAH

The sad but obvious answer is that Neferuptah must have died at a fairly young age most likely before her father's own death.[11] If she had been chosen to rule alongside Amenemhat IV, then her demise must have thrown the royal dynasty not only into a period of mourning, but also into a certain amount of turmoil. Such a crisis would have required the immediate implementation of a plan B—one that might not have been anticipated or even discussed prior to this unfortunate and presumably unexpected tragedy. That plan B would appear to have involved Amenemhat IV ruling on his own, a decision that makes complete sense if he was being lined up to rule alongside Neferuptah.

How old Neferuptah might have been when she died and what the circumstances were behind her death are important to establish if we are to better understand how this tragedy came about and what impact this would have had on Amenemhat IV's own accession. Unfortunately her age can only be guessed at since her physical remains were completely dissolved by groundwater seeping into her pyramid tomb. What happened to the skin samples found in her tomb remains unclear, the chances being that they were either lost or destroyed.

What we can say is that the princess's sarcophagus was huge, almost 10 feet (3 meters) in length, although its purpose, of course, was to contain two full-sized coffins, one inside the other. Farag and Iskander, the excavators of Neferuptah's tomb, estimated the size of the inner anthropoid coffin as 5 feet 10 inches (178 centimeters).[12] Assuming that its thickness was no more than 2 inches (5 centimeters) at either end,* and taking into account the fact that the princess's body would have been wrapped in bandages extending the mummy's size by approximately 2 inches (5 centimeters) above her head and below her feet,† tells us that when she died Neferuptah was

---

*Based on a general assessment of the thicknesses of two Twelfth Dynasty coffins listed in Dodson 2015: MM 11399 at 1.7 inches (4.4 centimeters) and MM 10233 at 1.4 inches (3.6 centimeters).

†Based on the digital unwrapping of Amenhotep I. See Saleem and Hawass 2021, which has the thickness of the wrappings at the front of the body at a thickness of 3.1–4.4 inches (78–112 millimeters) and at the back with a thickness of 0.8–1.6 inches (21–40 millimeters). The mean average of all these dimensions would be 2.49 inches (63.25 millimeters). In case the amount was slightly less than the average thickness determined, I have used 2 inches (or 50 millimeters) for the purposes of any calculations.

probably around 5 feet 1.5 inches (156 centimeters) in height (see fig. 11.1).*

Can we find any confirmation of this conclusion? Indeed we can, in the relief of Neferuptah at Medinet Madi. This shows her small in comparison to her father who stands behind her (see plate 9). On its own, however, this tells us very little since it was standard practice in ancient Egypt to show the monarch larger than other members of the royal family, particularly sons and daughters. That said some very basic information can be gleaned from the proportions of the princess as shown in the wall relief. For instance, if the long pole-like handle of the sistrum held in both hands by the princess was approximately 24 to 27 inches (60 to 70 centimeters) in length then it would mean that the maximum height she could have been at the time the relief was carved is around 4 feet 7 inches to 4 feet 11 inches (140–150 centimeters). This is a little below that of the height determined for the princess based on the suspected size of her inner coffin.

Since the average height of men in ancient Egypt was approximately 5 feet 2.5 inches (159 centimeters) and that of women somewhere around 5 feet (153 centimeters),[13] it suggests that at the time of construction of the Medinet Madi temple Neferuptah had not yet reached full adulthood.

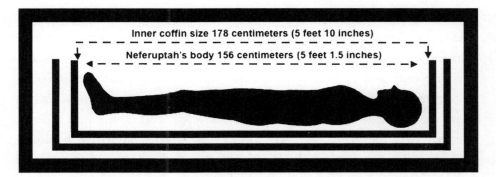

Inner coffin size 178 centimeters (5 feet 10 inches)

Neferuptah's body 156 centimeters (5 feet 1.5 inches)

Fig. 11.1. Neferuptah's body size based on the estimated dimensions of her inner coffin and mummy wrappings. (Please note that this illustration is not based on the actual shape of the sarcophagus and coffins. For this please see Farag and Iskander 1971, fig. 29.)

---

*This figure is derived from the anthropoid coffin's estimated size of 70.1 inches (178 centimeters) less 0.79 × 1.97 inches (2 × 5 centimeters) for its thickness at either end, 0.79 × 1.97 inches (2 × 5 centimeters) for the wrappings at the head and foot, and 0.79 × 0.39 inches (2 × 1 centimeter) for the suspected space between the coffin and mummy. Together this provides a total of 61.4 inches (156 centimeters).

Indeed, a rough guess would place her age at this time at around fifteen to sixteen. It is conceivable she was younger still, although her role at Medinet Madi as a priestess of Hathor pacifying the goddess Renenutet would tend to indicate that this was not the case. So if Neferuptah had died just a few years after this time, then from her estimated height based on the size of her coffins then it seems likely she was no more than eighteen to twenty years old when this occurred.

This is a particularly young age to die. Did she succumb to an illness perhaps, or could she have been involved in a tragic accident? Alternately, there may have been more sinister motivations behind her death. Indeed, there is every chance that she died of unnatural causes. As the princess was almost certainly being lined up to succeed her father to the throne of Egypt, then the possibility that she was murdered has to be considered. If this really was the case, then what circumstances might have led to this eventual outcome? More pressingly, what part might Amenemhat IV and Sobekneferu have played in this story?

If Neferuptah really was the rightful heir to the throne of Egypt, as seems likely, then we have to assume she was the most eligible daughter of Amenemhat III. There were, for instance, other daughters. We know of a Nubhotepet from a fragment of canopic jar found in Amenemhat III's pyramid at Dahshur,[14] a Sithathor who was buried "in a cutting in the entrance staircase of the king's pyramid at Dahshur,"[15] as well as a Hathorhetepet, who is also known only from a single fragment of canopic jar found in the same pyramid.[16] All are thought to have been daughters of Amenemhat III. What happened to them, however, is unknown. All we can say is that they are unlikely to have been alive when Neferuptah was chosen by her father to become the next ruler of Egypt.

THE IDENTITY OF SOBEKNEFERU

So who then was Sobekneferu? Other than the Tel Gezer statue, the black granite bowl from Senusret I's pyramid complex at Lisht, and one other small item we discuss in chapter 33, we hear nothing about her until her own succession to the throne. If Neferuptah and Amenemhat IV really were being lined up to become joint rulers of Egypt then there is every reason to assume that Sobekneferu was being overlooked for some reason, particularly if she

Fig. 11.2. Artists's impression of a young Sobekneferu at prayer
by Russell M. Hossain.

was of equal status to Neferuptah before this time. Why exactly she might have been sidelined is important to try to understand. One realistic possibility is that Sobekneferu was younger than Neferuptah and so would not have been seen as the natural heir to the throne on the death of her father.

Knowing she was not first in line for the throne, Sobekneferu could have taken a different course in life, devoting her time perhaps to magico-religious activities. As we saw in chapter 5, one of the Tell el-Dabʻa statues shows her kneeling in a manner indicative of her holding spherical *nw*-pots. This devotional attitude seen in ancient Egyptian statuary can suggest that the individual was religious in nature.[17] Then there is her Horus name, Meryt-Ra, "Beloved of Ra," which Kara Cooney says was common among priestesses during the Middle Kingdom, leading her to speculate that, "With this name, Neferusobek and her supporters seem to be claiming both that she was beloved of the sun god himself and that one of her foundations of power was her priestly affiliation before she took the kingship."[18] This does make sense and adds to the theory that Sobekneferu did indeed have very specific spiritual leanings, perhaps in connection with the cult of Hathor (see fig. 11.2).

Even if Sobekneferu *had* devoted her time to magico-religious practices during her early life there is no reason to assume that this was contributory to her being overlooked in favor of her sister Neferuptah as the next ruler of Egypt. Her age might well have been a greater factor. Just as important was Sobekneferu's maternal background, for whereas the two sisters might have shared the same father they were *almost certainly the offspring of two different mothers*. This, as we see next, is quite possibly crucial in understanding the true relationship between the two siblings.

12

Fate of the Dynasty

Amenemhat III's principal royal wife, who was presumably also his queen for much of his reign, was Aat, whose name means "The Great One."[1] Sadly, we know next to nothing about her life, but in death she was laid to rest in a specially prepared tomb chamber located directly beneath her husband's pyramid at Dahshur. Since we know that the king chose not to use this pyramid as his primary place of burial, either due to structural problems[2] or the fact that it was never intended to contain his tomb in the first place,[3] it seems logical to assume that Aat died before the completion of the monarch's later pyramid complex at Hawara. This is important as it helps us understand the timeline of events surrounding the better-known daughters of Amenemhat III—Neferuptah and Sobekneferu.

EXPLORATION OF THE BLACK PYRAMID

Today Amenemhat III's pyramid at Dahshur is known as the Black Pyramid. This is due to the fact that the removal in antiquity of the monument's limestone casing blocks exposed its grey mudbrick superstructure to the elements (see plate 12). Today it looks like a dark crumbling Tower of Babel jutting up above the treeline at the very edge of the Nile's fertile basin, hence its rather ominous name.

Exploration of the Black Pyramid began in the late nineteenth century under the direction of French mining expert, geologist, and archaeologist Jean-Jacques de Morgan (1857–1924). During two seasons, in 1894 and 1895, he explored the subterranean world located within the bowels of this enormous monument.[4] Although he failed to reach the tomb of Aat he did find some items bearing her name. They included part of a false stone door along with a fragment of an offering table.[5] Their presence convinced him that somewhere nearby was the queen's final resting place.[6]

It would not be until the German archaeologist Dieter Arnold (1936–) was able to fully investigate the pyramid across eight seasons between 1976 and 1984 that Aat's tomb would finally be found deep inside the southern part of its subterranean maze of tunnels and chambers.[7] On entering its interior he saw before him a large sarcophagus. Various pieces of funerary equipment were scattered about the place including a broken canopic chest or coffer, a complete canopic jar, seven alabaster cases in the form of ducks, and an alabaster unguent jar. He was also able to retrieve an assortment of scattered pieces of jewelry.

From the inscription on the false door it appeared that Aat had borne the titles "King's wife" and "United with the White Crown [of Upper Egypt],"[8] while an examination of her remains revealed that she had been around 35 years old at the time of death.[9] Aat had clearly been an important royal wife and was no doubt the mother of one or more of the king's children. Yet whether or not she was the mother of Neferuptah or Sobekneferu remains unclear. If, however, Neferuptah was the elder of the two daughters then Aat was almost certainly her mother.

Confusing the matter is the fact that Dieter Arnold, while exploring the depths of the Black Pyramid, uncovered the tomb of a second royal wife of Amenemhat III. Remarkably, her sepulcher was located almost next to that of his other royal wife Aat. The identity of this second royal wife has, however, been lost, and all that is really known about her is that her remains suggest she was around 25 years old when she died.[10] So did this royal wife also provide Amenemhat III with children? Almost certainly she did, although who they were we simply cannot say for sure.

The only other clue regarding the parentage of the children of Amenemhat III is something important recorded in the temple of Renenutet at Medinet Madi. Quite separate to the relief showing Neferuptah using a sistrum to pacify the snake goddess is another relief showing Amenemhat IV alongside a woman named Hetepti, who is referred to as the "king's mother."[11] So is Hetepti the identity of the unknown royal wife buried in Amenemhat III's pyramid at Dahshur? Since Manetho tells us that

Sobekneferu was Amenemhat IV's "sister," does this imply that Hetepti was not only Amenemhat IV's mother, but also Sobekneferu's mother as well?

AMENEMHAT IV'S NON-ROYAL BLOOD?

Once again this raises the question of whether or not Sobekneferu and Amenemhat IV really were brother and sister, or whether Manetho might have got it wrong and there was no direct familial link between the two rulers of Egypt. On this matter Kim Ryholt argues that Amenemhat IV was *not* in fact the son of Amenemhat III, and a panel from the Medinet Madi temple where the younger king calls the older king his father is, he suspects, simply honorary.[12] Neferuptah, he proposes, was the rightful inheritor of the throne through her outright legitimacy as Amenemhat III's true heir, even though it is not known whether she was given the official title of "royal wife." Amenemhat IV was then picked to be the country's male ruler, despite his nonroyal blood, with Neferuptah ruling by his side. She, however, died before her father, meaning that Amenemhat IV was left to become sole ruler of the country.[13]

Ryholt advances the theory that Amenemhat IV was related to a court official named Ankhew, who bore the title "Overseer of Fields."[14] As evidence of this relationship he cites the fact that Ankhew's mother was a woman named Merestekhi, who was posthumously given the title "king's sister."[15] This has to mean, Ryholt suspects, that her brother, Ankhew's uncle, must have become king for her to have been given this title. During her life Merestekhi bore no royal titles, so she and her family had to have been of nonroyal birth.

Ankhew's own career had begun as a temple scribe under king Senusret III. When still just a young prince he had become a retainer to Amenemhat III. Later Ankhew acquired the honorary title of "god's father" suggesting that he was retainer to the son of a king, although which king is not stated. Ryholt argues it was Amenemhat IV.[16] As we saw in chapter 9, Ryholt also suggests that two early kings of the Thirteenth Dynasty were most likely the sons of Amenemhat IV. These were Sobekhotep I and Sonbef, both of whom bore the secondary name Amenemhat showing their close relationship with this king and, presumably, the Twelfth Dynasty as a whole.[17]

Fig. 12.1. Panel from the Labyrinth showing the Horus names of (*left*) Amenemhat III and (*right*) Sobekneferu; the hawk of the former is offering the latter the symbols for life and stability (from Habachi 1954, pl. XV, A).

Ryholt goes on to propose that Sobekneferu was indeed the daughter of Amenemhat III, which is why in the Labyrinth she had commissioned various inscriptions and carved panels linking herself directly with her father. These included the Horus panel, which showed both Amenemhat III and Sobekneferu as falcons above serekhs containing their Horus names.[18] The bird representing her father as the god Horus is shown offering Sobekneferu's Horus bird the symbol of stability (the *djed*-pillar) along with the symbol of life (the ankh) (see fig. 12.1).[19]

The manner in which Amenemhat III is depicted in this panel strongly indicates that he is being shown as a deified ancestor, a living god—one now able to convey his divine blessings on his true living successor, his daughter Sobekneferu.[20] Clearly, by portraying herself in this manner she was attempting to legitimize her own rule through this direct association with her father.

The fact that nowhere in the Labyrinth, or indeed on any monument, does Sobekneferu link herself with Amenemhat IV has raised suspicions that she either fell out with her brother and/or that she did not recognize the legitimacy of his rule and the right of his sons to rule after him.[21] Ryholt sees this as additional evidence that Amenemhat IV was of nonroyal parentage and was brought into the royal family simply to pair up with the king's preferred daughter, Neferuptah.[22]

It should be pointed out also that Amenemhat IV's name does not appear in the Labyrinth, which, we should recall, included Amenemhat III's mortuary complex. Usually, it was the new king's respectful duty to complete the funerary complex of his predecessor, but this doesn't seem to have been the case with Amenemhat IV (see plate 13). This said, blocks from the valley temple attached to Amenemhat III's pyramid at Dahshur *do* bear his successor's name.[23] However, this work could easily have been carried out when Amenemhat III was still alive, arguably during the two kings' brief co-regency. Plus Amenemhat IV might have chosen to finish construction work at this site because his mother Hetepti was one of the royal wives buried beneath the pyramid.

Such disregard for Amenemhat III's final resting place at Hawara is curious and could suggest that, unlike Sobekneferu, Amenemhat IV had no need to prove his legitimacy to the throne, so made the choice to ignore the old king's funerary complex.[24] She, on the other hand, being a woman as well as the last choice for an heir to the dynasty (bearing in mind Ryholt's theory that Sobekneferu usurped the throne from Amenemhat IV's two sons), caused her to overemphasize her direct paternal relationship with Amenemhat III.[25]

SOBEKNEFERU AS SKEMIOPHRIS— MANETHO'S STATEMENTS QUERIED

Then we come to Manetho's statement that Skemiophris, that is Sobekneferu,* was the "sister" of the previous ruler Ammenemes, that is

---

*Skemiophris (Σκεμιοφρις) is thought to be a Greek rendition of the name Sobekneferu derived from ιοφρις = *(n)ofris,* from the Egyptian *neferu* or *nofru,* "beauties," and σκεμ = *skem,* a corruption of Sobek. However, one other possibility is that σκεμ could derive from the Egyptian *sḫm* or *skhm* = "power," "might," or "strength," meaning that Skemiophris could in fact be a Hellenization of the name Sekhem-neferu, meaning something like "beauties of the power" or "beauties of the strength." It could even have included the name Sekhmet, the goddess Hathor in her vengeful form, making it into "Beauties of (the goddess) Sekhmet." It should be recalled that Sobekneferu's Nebty name was Sat-sekhem-nebet-tawy, meaning something like "Daughter of power [*sat sekhem*], mistress of the Two Lands [*nebet tawy*]," while her funerary complex would appear to have borne the name Sekhem-Sobekneferu. Both are indicative of the importance Sobekneferu placed on the concept of sekhem and its personification as the goddess Sekhmet.

Amenemhat IV.[26] Surely this is powerful evidence that both Amenemhat IV *and* Sobekneferu, being related to each other by blood, were both legitimate heirs to the throne. Ryholt tackles this sticking point to his own theories by insisting that of the two versions of Manetho's *Aegyptiaca* ("History of Egypt") the statement about Sobekneferu being Amenemhat IV's sister is made only in one of them, this being of relatively late composition. Thus Manetho's claim that the two rulers were brother and sister was probably just an interpolation introduced by some later redactor of the original text. The other, older version, says nothing of this brother-sister relationship supporting Ryholt's suspicions.[27]

Africanus vs. Eusebius

At face value Ryholt's assessment of the evidence regarding Skemiophris's sisterly relationship with Ammenemes as presented by Manetho seems convincing. To get a fuller picture, however, we need to better understand how the two different versions of Manetho came about. The one with the statement in question derives from the chronicles of Sextus Julius Africanus (circa 160–240 CE). He was a Christian traveler and historian who thrived in the late second and early third centuries CE. His chronicle of events from biblical times through to his own age, within which Manetho's *Aegyptiaca* appears, has not survived. Luckily, however, some fragments of Africanus's work written in Greek were preserved in the writings of one George Syncellus, a Byzantine chronicler and ecclesiastic, who died around 810 CE. It is from him that Africanus's version of Manetho has come down to us.[28]

The other version of Manetho's *Aegyptiaca* was preserved originally in the writings of Eusebius of Caesarea (circa 260/265–339/340 CE). He was a Christian polemicist and historian of Christianity, who in about 314 CE became bishop of Caesarea Maritima on the Mediterranean coast of what is today Israel. His version of Manetho, written in Greek and published in his now lost work titled *Chronicle,* was also thankfully preserved by Syncellus, who realizing it to be at variance to Africanus's own version of the same text put them side by side in his *Ecloga Chronographica.*[29]

For completion, it should be noted that a separate version of Eusebius's *Chronicle* was preserved in the Armenian language; this dates to the fifth century CE.[30] It must be pointed out, however, that all the remaining versions of Manetho's *Aegyptiaca* are but *epitomai* (singular *epitome*), that is summaries of the original text compiled sometime after the author's death.

Kim Ryholt is correct in asserting that the entry in Manetho for Skemiophris reigning for four years and being "his [that is, Ammenemes's] sister" appears only in Africanus's version of the Epitome of Manetho[31] and does not appear in Eusebius's version of the same text.[32] This, however, does not decrease the value of Africanus's statement for a cursory reading of Eusebius's version of Manetho shows that it severely abbreviates and even misplaces some of its entries for the different Egyptian dynasties. This can be seen, for instance, in the fact that Eusebius's version of the Epitome abbreviates its entry for Egypt's Fifteenth Dynasty, transposing the list of kings Africanus gives into its entry for the Seventeenth Dynasty, which is entirely wrong. This and other discrepancies make it clear that Africanus's version of the Epitome of Manetho is not only more accurate but also contains additional information not found in Eusebius's version. The same conclusion was reached by the translator of the most definitive English language edition of Manetho, W. G. Waddell. In his opinion, "Of the two chronographers, the founder of Christian chronography, Sextus Julius Africanus . . . transmits the Epitome in a more accurate form; while Eusebius . . . is responsible for unwarranted alterations of the original text of Manetho."[33]

If this is the case then there can be no reason to doubt Manetho's statement that Skemiophris/Sobekneferu was the sister of Ammenemes/Amenemhat IV. Ryholt does try to address this potential eventuality by suggesting that Africanus's statement could simply refer to the fact that Sobekneferu was Amenemhat IV's stepsister.[34] But as we have seen there is no need to disregard or downgrade Manetho's assertation that Skemiophris/Sobekneferu was indeed "his [that is, Ammenemes's] sister." This was obviously a tradition that had been handed down to Manetho like so many other of the idiosyncratic statements he makes about certain rulers from the age of Menes down to the arrival in Egypt of Alexander the Great in 332 BCE.

In addition to this, Ryholt's proposal that Amenemhat IV was of nonroyal blood, the son of a woman named Merestekhi, who was posthumously given the title "king's sister," has recently been called into question. Since there is no certainty which king is being referred to in connection with this title it could just as easily allude to Amenemhat III, whose own lineage is in no way certain with some suggestion that he was not the son of the previous king Senusret III.[35] If correct, this would mean that Merestekhi was the sister, whether honorary or otherwise, of Amenemhat III and *not* of his successor Amenemhat IV.[36]

SIBLING RIVALRY

If we can accept that Amenemhat IV and Sobekneferu were indeed brother and sister it places a completely different spin on the dynastic situation toward the end of the Twelfth Dynasty. Both siblings were probably the offspring of Hetepti, who is shown in the company of Amenemhat IV in the Medinet Madi temple. Whether or not Sobekneferu was older or younger than her brother might never be known, although there are grounds to suspect there was little difference between their ages. Since Neferuptah was the chosen heir to the throne, this does imply that she was the oldest of the siblings and that both Amenemhat IV and Sobekneferu were younger than her. It is evident, however, that it was Amenemhat IV who was chosen in front of Sobekneferu to become the next ruler because with Neferuptah as his consort and co-ruler he had every likelihood of producing future heirs to the throne.[37]

It is worth pointing out that very little statuary showing Amenemhat IV has been preserved, so we do not have much to go on when it comes to his age at the time of his accession. In the British Museum there is a gneiss sphinx on a plinth showing the head of the king wearing the standard *nemes*-headdress.[38] Found in Beirut, Lebanon (see fig. 12.2 on page 112), it is 23 inches (58.5 centimeters) in length and on its breast between the forelegs there is an inscription that reads, "Maa-kheru-Ra [Amenemhat IV's throne name], living forever, beloved of (the god) Atum, Lord of Heliopolis."[39] Unfortunately, however, its face was remodeled in Ptolemaic times so this offers us little if any evidence regarding the king's true features. What it does do is provide an important link not only between the king and the creator god Atum, but also between Hatshepsut and the family of Sobekneferu.

I say this, for the sphinx (minus the headdress) was described by the British Museum in 1928 as being "exactly like that of the female sphinx at Rome attributed to Queen Hatshepsut . . . but which is certainly of the XIIth Dynasty and, except that it is larger, seems a feminine counterpart of

Fig. 12.2. Sphinx of Amenemhat IV found in Beirut, Lebanon. It bears an inscription in the name of Atum, Lord of Heliopolis (from Hall 1928, pl. LVIII, a).

our acquisition."[40] Since it is unlikely that Hatshepsut ever saw this particular sphinx found in Beirut it seems likely she saw another similar one linked in some way to Sobekneferu and so had herself represented in exactly the same manner.

One other representation of Amenemhat IV does exist. It is the head of a pharaoh, thought to be that of the king, housed in the Metropolitan Museum of Art, New York.[41] The king sports the *nemes*-headdress complete with a *uraeus*-snake seen immediately above his forehead. Made of limestone, the head stands 5.5 inches (14 centimeters) in height and clearly formed part of a much larger piece of statuary. It was found in 1907/1908 at Lisht North in debris to the west of the pyramid of Amenemhat I; Lisht, of course, being the site of Itj-tawy, the capital of Egypt during the Twelfth and Thirteenth dynasties. Also among the debris pile was a lintel from a limestone shrine bearing an inscription in the name of Amenemhat IV.[42] This, along with the fact that the head resembles other kings from the late Twelfth Dynasty,

Fig. 12.3. Head of Amenemhat IV found in 1907/1908 at Lisht
North currently housed at the Metropolitan Museum of Art,
New York. Courtesy of the Rogers Fund, 1908.

early Thirteenth Dynasty, has led to the conclusion that it shows the shrine's
builder Amenemhat IV. If correct, then this is a very revealing discovery since
the head is clearly that of a youth of no more than eighteen to twenty years
of age (see fig. 12.3).

Aside from these two items there is a copper alley bust and head of a
standing Twelfth Dynasty king wearing the *nemes*-headdress and *uraeus*-
snake above his forehead who could be Amenemhat IV. It was found in the
Fayum region and currently forms part of the George Ortiz collection in
Switzerland.[43] It shows an assertive individual who appears to be a young
adult. The problem with this item, however, is that its provenance is unclear,
its exact find spot being unrecorded. What is more, the face closely resembles that of Amenemhat III. Indeed, most usually the bust is attributed to
the older king, even on the George Ortiz website.[44]

Of the three art objects described above only the head housed in the Metropolitan Museum of Art perhaps provides a true likeness of Amenemhat IV, which if correct tells us that at the time of his accession he was probably no more than 18 to 20 years old. This is the same suspected age of Neferuptah at the time of her death, which probably occurred just prior to Amenemhat IV succeeding to the throne. It is even possible that Neferuptah was a year or so his senior, the reason why she was chosen by her father to become the next ruler in advance of him.

It *is* possible that Amenemhat IV was older than both Sobekneferu and Neferuptah, although if this was the case then there would have been no need to put so much emphasis on Neferuptah's greater importance, which, as we have seen, included the unprecedented honor of having her name contained within a royal cartouche. From all the evidence gathered this decision was made for two reasons: first, she was Amenemhat IV's senior, by a year or so at least, and, second, she was born of a different mother, Aat, who was probably Amenemhat III's queen and royal wife before Hetepti, the mother of Amenemhat IV and seemingly Sobekneferu, who rose to assume a similar role.

For these reasons Neferuptah was given priority over accession to the throne. Sobekneferu, on the other hand, was almost certainly a little younger than Neferuptah, and not being born to Amenemhat III's main queen and consort, Aat, and also being female, she was not considered a natural successor to the throne of Egypt. This is something she would have challenged in every way possible having quite obviously come to believe that she herself was destined to rule the Two Lands.

As we have seen, Sobekneferu's conviction that it was her divine right and true destiny to become the *first* woman to wear the double crown of Upper and Lower Egypt had probably been legitimized, in her mind at least, by the goddess Hathor in her role as the divine mother of the incarnate Horus. Very likely this conviction had been strengthened through one or more factions telling the princess this was the case and pledging their allegiance to her cause should she become ruler.

Whoever these people were they are unlikely to have been part of the country's orthodox priesthoods such as those of Sobek of Shedet or Amun of Thebes since they would have been loyal to the wishes of her father Amenemhat III, certainly before her own accession, that is. More likely is that any faction supporting Sobekneferu's claim to the throne would have been obscure in nature and, as such, might well have been responsible for arranging any initiatory rite that Sobekneferu would have seen as substituting for the traditional Heb Sed festival—the reason she deemed it right to wear the Heb Sed cloak at her coronation.

If correct then whatever faction or factions were supporting Sobekneferu behind the scenes would perhaps have had strong magico-religious allegiances and would have stood to benefit if she took the throne. It was probably these same individuals who convinced Sobekneferu that it was her birthright and destiny to rule Egypt—a prophecy that would have been fulfilled when, against all odds, she succeeded to the throne following the death of her brother.

A MURDER MYSTERY?

If all this becomes a plausible scenario based on the evidence available, then to better understand Sobekneferu's position as potential ruler of Egypt we have to now consider what her reaction would have been when it was made known that following the death of her father, Amenemhat III, her half-sister would rule the country jointly with her own brother. How might Sobekneferu—having become convinced that she herself was destined to ascend the throne—have reacted to this decision, especially since any children produced by the royal couple would by birthright become the natural heirs to the throne? Is it possible she intervened in some manner to change the course of history?

Was Sobekneferu either directly or indirectly responsible for the death of her sister, the woman whose shoes she would step into immediately upon the accession of Amenemhat IV? No one can say for sure, but if we look at who stood to benefit the most from Neferuptah's death there is only one answer—Sobekneferu. So whether Neferuptah was murdered or not, her death paved the way for the rise of Sobekneferu, who might never have been given the opportunity to rule the Two Lands were it not for this unfortunate tragedy.

It should be remembered too that shortly after the death of Neferuptah her father also died after a long reign lasting at least 45 years. Most obviously his cause of death was old age, although we can never be certain what happened to him. All we can say for sure is that he was interred in the pyramid prepared for him at Hawara, well away from his other pyramid at Dahshur where at least two of his royal wives—Aat and another who was possibly Hetepti, the mother of Amenemhat IV (and thus Sobekneferu)—would eventually be interred.

THE STRANGE CASE OF
THE MAKESHIFT SARCOPHAGUS

There is, however, another mystery to be unraveled before we can go any further. In addition to the pyramid tomb built for Neferuptah at Hawara South, another "makeshift" sarcophagus was prepared for her in her father's pyramid at Hawara. This was made by placing two upright slabs of stone parallel to each other between each end of her father's sarcophagus and the nearby wall of the burial chamber. Doing this created ample space for a coffin to be interred over which a large rectangular slab had been placed in position, this having been twisted askew in antiquity.[45]

When the pyramid was first excavated in 1888, the chief excavator, Flinders Petrie, came across certain funerary items bearing the name of Neferuptah that had been thrown down a well chamber in the same area as the makeshift tomb. This included an alabaster offering table similar in style to the black granite example found in the princess's pyramid tomb.[46] None showed the princess's name in a royal cartouche, even though her father's throne name, Ni-ma'at-Ra, usually written Nimaatre, was found to be present in the inscriptions.[47]

Petrie also found fragments of nine to ten dishes of differing sizes in the shape of ducks[48] as well as fragments from two large jars. These also bore the princess's name, although once again without the use of a cartouche.[49] The fact that none of the items retrieved from the sepulcher showed the princess's name in a cartouche tells us they were made before she was chosen to become a future ruler of the country.

TWO PLACES OF BURIAL

So what exactly was going on? Why had Neferuptah been given two places of burial? The discovery in Amenemhat III's pyramid at Hawara of the makeshift tomb and funerary items in Neferuptah's name convinced Petrie that it had been there that the princess's body had been lain to rest as an afterthought after construction was completed.[50] In his opinion: "She seems to have died young, before her father, and to have been buried side by side with him in his pyramid."[51]

It is important to remember that at this time the existence of Neferuptah's pyramid tomb at Hawara South was unknown, this only being discovered many years later. So what Petrie says strongly supports the idea that the princess died suddenly and unexpectedly and so had been temporarily interred inside her father's pyramid until construction work on her own pyramid could be completed.[52] Thereafter her body was transferred to its new place of burial and sealed in for all eternity. This must have coincided to some degree with the death of her father who was likewise interred in the Hawara pyramid just 1.2 miles (2 kilometers) away from her final resting place at Hawara South.

That this was the sequence of events is confirmed by the fact that only in the princess's pyramid tomb do we find funerary items with her name in a cartouche. This shows that her second interment now honored the fact that she had been chosen to become the future ruler of the country. Everything found in association with her makeshift sarcophagus inside Amenemhat III's own sepulcher had clearly been made before this announcement and so were used simply because there had not been enough time to prepare new funerary items. This seems evident, for example, from the existence of the two offering tables. The alabaster example found in association with her makeshift tomb bore her name without the use of a cartouche, while the black granite example from her pyramid tomb shows her name inside a cartouche. Of course, there were some items found in her pyramid tomb without the use of the cartouche, but these were probably used simply because they already existed and, once the tomb was sealed shut, would be forgotten about anyway: a case of out of sight, out of mind.

Other theories on why the princess was given a second place of interment do exist, of course, and they could easily have some merit. One proposal is that her makeshift sarcophagus constituted a dummy or symbolic burial, perhaps for her spirit double or *ka* to inhabit.[53] During the Middle Kingdom several members of the royal family including various kings had two burial places, making this proposition a valid one.

The whole idea, however, of Neferuptah being given her own pyramid tomb following her initial interment inside her father's pyramid is curious in itself. Who decided she should have a second place of burial when her remains could quite easily have stayed where they had been laid to rest in the first place? Why did her pyramid not have any entrance or exit passageway, something that in pyramid construction was seen as essential to enable the person's spirit to commence its journey to the afterlife? All pyramids had an entrance shaft, usually directed toward the north. So instead of being given an obvious rite of passage into the place of the afterlife Neferuptah was instead interred from above and sealed into the tomb through the placement of seven large blocks laid side by side to form the sepulcher's roof.

Farag and Iskander removed six out of seven of these slabs to permit them access to the tomb. Seven is a highly symbolic number that crops up many times in ancient Egyptian religious traditions including the fact that there were thought to be seven forms of Hathor (see chapter 33). Did the number of blocks chosen to seal in the tomb of Neferuptah have some special meaning either to the internee or to the person or persons responsible for creating her tomb?

Maybe there are no mysteries here, and we are seeing too much into the simple design of a late Twelfth Dynasty pyramid tomb prepared as the final resting place of a princess. However, there remains the possibility that something more was going on at this time that does indeed hint at personal agendas being played out in the wake of Neferuptah's apparently sudden and unexpected death.

Another point to mention is that although inscriptions from the princess's pyramid tomb include the name of her father, there is no mention anywhere of her half-brother and chosen co-ruler Amenemhat IV or of her half-sister Sobekneferu.

Once again there may be no mystery behind this fact, although it is certainly worth noting. What we can say is that Neferuptah was interred inside two beautifully inlaid coffins contained within a large red granite sarcophagus. She was also given a full set of magical formulae that were meant to aid her journey into the hereafter. It was this unique combination of magical spells that Hatshepsut would go on to use for her own purposes, quite possibly to align herself with her personal inspiration, Sobekneferu.

So what more was going on at this time? How exactly did Sobekneferu attain the throne herself? More importantly, what was the relationship between brother and sister after he became king of Egypt? It is these subjects of intrigue we look at next.

13

Sibling Rivalry

With Neferuptah now out of the picture the death of Amenemhat III saw the accession to the throne of Amenemhat IV, the son of Hetepti. According to the Turin Canon he would go on to reign for 9 years, 3 months, and 27 days, the first year or two forming part of a co-regency with his father. Some scholars believe that Sobekneferu married her brother and became his royal wife,[1] and that together they entered into a kind of co-rulership similar to that intended for Amenemhat IV and Neferuptah.[2] There are, however, no contemporary records confirming this took place.

Having said this, the fact that Sobekneferu did go on to become ruling monarch following the death of Amenemhat IV does suggest that both siblings did indeed rule the country together, although whether or not this was officially sanctioned with her becoming his queen or royal wife is unclear. This conclusion makes sense for if she had *not* helped rule the country alongside her brother then there would have been very little support for her own succession to the throne upon his death. Neither the royal court, the priesthoods, or the country as a whole are likely to have sided with her in favor of any other claimant, and as we see shortly there would appear to have been some support for her cause.

FEAR AND RESPECT

If Sobekneferu really had been a complete outsider who just happened to take the throne because she was the last person left standing in the royal dynasty, then there would have been no way she could have achieved what she did when she herself became sole ruler of the country. This is something that can only have come about through the fear and respect she had commanded during the reign of her brother. What is more she must have successfully fought off any challenges to her reign through the sheer determination instilled in her unwavering belief that, while she was alive, it was her destiny and nobody else's to rule the country. If she had not possessed such a powerful conviction there is no way she could have succeeded in becoming Egypt's first official female ruler of the Two Lands.

That said we must ask ourselves what exactly Sobekneferu's relationship was with her brother. Were they close? Did they get along with each other? Was their assumed co-regency, whether imagined or otherwise, simply an act of convenience suiting them both, or was she perhaps the more powerful of the two siblings ruling the country in the manner she had wanted even before the accession of her brother? Very clearly there are many different avenues that one can go down in attempting to answer these questions and, as we shall see, the evidence at hand initially presents a certain amount of conflicting information especially in the manner that Sobekneferu and her brother viewed each other.

Kim Ryholt offers some hint of Sobekneferu's attitude toward her brother. He sees their relationship, particularly at the end of his reign, as somewhat disharmonious, observing:

> It would seem therefore that Nofrusobek [that is, Sobekneferu] usurped the throne from the heirs of Amenemhat IV [in other words, his proposed sons, Sobekhotep I and Sonbef, who would go on to become the first two kings of the Thirteenth Dynasty]. This may reflect a dissatisfaction on her behalf with the adoption as coregent of a man who was not part of her family, especially if Amenemhat IV had forced himself upon Amenemhat III.[3]

This last statement stems, of course, from Ryholt's belief that Amenemhat IV was of nonroyal blood, and so at best was simply a stepbrother to Sobekneferu.[4] As we have seen this is unlikely to have been the case with Manetho's clear statement that she was his brother being not only valid, but also important in chronicling the fact that the line of succession went from brother to sister in that order.

Thus the very real "dissatisfaction" experienced by Sobekneferu that Ryholt feels came from the fact that Amenemhat IV was of nonroyal blood could have derived from somewhere else together. What then might this have been? One possibility is that it stemmed from the fact that Sobekneferu's half sister, Neferuptah, had been chosen above her to rule the Two Lands alongside her own brother, a problem that, as we have seen, would eventually go away of its own accord. In other words any dissatisfaction between the two siblings during Amenemhat IV's reign must have related to an altogether different matter, one that ended, so Ryholt suspects, with her usurping the throne from any "true" heirs of her brother at the time of his death. So what then was their relationship? If she did become his queen and royal wife then there would seem to have been no obvious problems at the commencement of his almost ten-year reign.

THE MAZGHUNA PYRAMIDS

Indeed, there is every chance that at this time Amenemhat IV, either on his own or in concert with his sister Sobekneferu, commissioned the building of two fair-sized pyramids at Mazghuna on the edge of the Nile valley basin, just 1.5 miles (2.5 kilometers) south of Amenemhat III's pyramid complex at Dahshur.* Interestingly, the location is well outside the Fayum being around 37 miles (60 kilometers) north-northeast of Shedet (modern Kiman Faras) and a similar distance away from Amenemhat III's pyramid at Hawara.

Before proceeding any further it is important to point out that both Mazghuna pyramids—which lie around 0.25 miles (400 meters) distance from each other and are known today as Mazghuna North and Mazghuna South—were destroyed in antiquity with the only evidence of their presence being two immensely complex substructures carved into the bedrock; neither of which are visible today.[5]

British archaeologist Ernest Mackay, who investigated the two Mazghuna pyramids in 1910,[6] concluded that due to structural similarities with the pyramid of Amenemhat III at Hawara,[7] they were almost certainly built

---

*The two Mazghuna pyramids were named after the train station of Mazghuna in the Nile Valley, this being despite the fact that, technically speaking, they lie closer to the village of Dahshur than almost all the monuments in that pyramid field (see Mackay 1912, 49).

for the kings that followed him and ended the Twelfth Dynasty, namely Amenemhat IV and his sister Sobekneferu.[8]

If, as seems probable, these two pyramids were indeed destined to be the burial places of Amenemhat IV and Sobekneferu, then we have every reason to suspect that at the time of their construction both siblings were not only close, but also intended to rule the country together as one unifying force. So even though she strove to link herself solely with her father during her own reign, her loyalty to her brother during his reign seems clear with the construction of the Mazghuna pyramids, sending out a clear message that in death as in life they would be together in every respect.

All this makes sense of the evidence presented by the Mazghuna pyramids. However, these were most likely begun at the *beginning* of Amenemhat IV's reign when it was important that brother and sister should be seen as united in their joint rule of the country. However, there is clear circumstantial evidence that their relationship must have soured very quickly and that by the end of his reign they were in opposition to each other on several different levels. This sentiment echoes exactly Ryholt's statement about Sobekneferu's dissatisfaction of Amenemhat IV following his accession and her final usurpation of the throne upon his death.

Yet what might that "dissatisfaction" have been? Why might Sobekneferu have fallen out with her brother sometime after he succeeded to the throne? As we see next, by far her greatest concern was what was going on in the country at this time, and the simple fact that, as king, her brother was doing nothing about it.

14

Flawed Visions

Some Egyptologists well versed on the political situation during the reigns of Amenemhat IV and his sister Sobekneferu have offered some distressing realizations about the state of the country at this time. Kim Ryholt, for instance, has written that the nature of the political differences existing between the two monarchs reached back to the age of their father Amenemhat III and centered around the constant influx into the country of western Asiatic peoples from both Syria and Palestine.[1]

As we saw in chapter 7 those groups known to the Egyptians as the Aamu and Retjenu had begun to settle in areas of the Nile Delta as manual workers, caravan drivers, mercenaries, sailors, and even as skilled craftsmen during the reign of Senusret III. This influx of western Asiatic peoples arriving in Egypt continued into the reign of his successor Amenemhat III with some individuals achieving positions of authority and power.[2]

EGYPT'S ECONOMIC AND POLITICAL PROBLEMS

By the time that Amenemhat IV took the throne, Egypt's western Asiatic population had become heavily Egyptianized, having established themselves in large communities mostly in the north of the country. They had also become practically independent and autonomous, while at the same time gaining more and more power and influence.[3]

Crucially, and as Kim Ryholt points out himself, Amenemhat IV would appear to have actively supported Egypt's open border policies, while at the same time extending a certain amount of good will to Semitic-speaking princes.[4] Unfortunately, this situation would appear to have led to a weakening of control in the eastern Delta due to this steadily growing influx of western Asiatic peoples into the region.[5] What is more, all this coincided with a gradual worsening economic and political situation in Egypt, something that was beginning to destabilize the country and would eventually lead to a great recession.[6] In part this was due to Amenemhat IV's liberal policies and complete openness toward what was happening in the north of the country.[7]

Coinciding with this situation was a sharp decline in monumental building construction with the last big "pyramid city" being that of Amenemhat III at Hawara.[8] Included within this complex was, of course, the Labyrinth, which was begun by Amenemhat III and finished during the reign of Sobekneferu.[9] Amemenhet IV would seem to have had little if anything to do with any activities at the site.[*]

This last statement about Amenemhat IV avoiding the Labyrinth goes hand in hand with another realization about his reign, and this was the noticeable shift in interest away from the Fayum, the seat of the cult of Sobek of Shedet.[10] This was something that would be overturned by Sobekneferu, who during her reign would once again make the Fayum the dynasty's principal seat of power after the capital Itj-tawy.

THE CULT CENTER OF HELIOPOLIS

As for Amenemhat IV he had begun patronizing religious cults in regions heavily occupied by Semitic-speaking peoples, something noted by Italian Egyptologist Stephania Pignattari.[11] She points out that the king would appear to have taken a great interest in the cult center of Heliopolis (Egyptian *Innu,* or *Anu,* and the Hebrew *On*), home of the creator god Atum, a form of Ra, the sun god, who throughout the Eleventh and Twelfth Dynasties had been sidelined somewhat in favor of honoring the god Amun, patron of the city of Thebes in the south of the country.[12]

---

[*]One possible statue of Amenemhat III and Amenemhat IV was found in the naoi of the Labyrinth, although these identifications remain a matter of conjecture. It is not enough evidence to suggest that the latter king was engaged in any building construction at the site. See Zecchi 2010, 59–60. Regarding inscriptions found at the site, several exist for Sobekneferu, but none for Amenemhat IV. See Canhão 2019/2020, 10.

Heliopolis became a place of considerable interest to the Hyksos during their time in Egypt.[13] Aside from the Egyptian god Seth or Sutekh, which they adopted as their principal god at Avaris, John van Setters writes that its kings "built a close association with the worship of Re Har-akhi, the chief deity of Heliopolis," while in contemporary accounts the Hyksos king Apophis is referred to as "beloved son of Re" and "the living image of Re on earth."[14] Geographically, Heliopolis was located at the southern terminus of at least two major branches of the Nile as well as one major overland caravan route, all of which acted as important arteries linking northern Egypt with both Palestine and the Sinai Peninsula. This made Heliopolis a perfect place of settlement for Asiatic peoples arriving from the Levant.

Amenemhat IV's interest in the god Atum can be seen, for instance, in the gneiss sphinx of the king found in Beirut, Lebanon.[15] An inscription on its breast between the forelegs reads "Maa-kheru-Ra [Amenemhat IV's throne name], living forever, beloved of Atum, Lord of Heliopolis."[16] That the king should prioritize Atum above any other god is very telling indeed and confirms that he bore very little interest in the Sobek-based spiritual ethos developed in the Fayum during the reign of his father Amenemhat III.

In addition to the veneration of Atum, Amenemhat IV would appear to have paid particular interest in the god Khenty-Khety.[17] His principal cult center was Athribis (Tell Atrib), situated on the Damietta branch of the Nile in the southern part of the central Delta region. Khenty-Khety was depicted either as a crocodile or as a crocodile-headed man, although in much later times he would be shown as a hawk-headed individual.

As Stephania Pignattari makes clear, Amenemhat IV's choice to patronize Khenty-Khety was not simply down to some random act of devotion. As a border town, Athribis was a "leaping point" into the Sinai, making Khenty-Khety a "border god" that would have been venerated both by Egyptians living or stationed in the eastern Delta as well as by western Asiatic peoples who had settled in the region.[18] In this way Amenemhat IV was trying to appeal to the multicultural inhabitants living in the north of the country, while at the same time deliberately distancing himself from many of the political and religious values held by his father during his reign and upheld by his sister during his own reign.

A NEW KINGDOM

Stephania Pignattari speculates that in the Sinai, at Serabit el-Khadim in particular, Amenemhat IV was attempting to create his own "celebratory place" within a brand-new kingdom he was carving out for himself as part of some utopic vision of a new Egypt both in a material and in a cosmological sense.[19]

It seems no coincidence that this new kingdom being created by Amenemhat IV was in a region familiar to many of the Semitic-speaking peoples who had come to settle in northern Egypt. They, of course, included the Aamu and Retjenu, some of whom were no doubt trusted court officials during Amenemhat IV's reign.[20] Very likely some of these individuals were beginning to influence the king's political and theological decisions.

SOBEKNEFERU AND THE WESTERN ASIATIC SITUATION

Sobekneferu's attitude toward Egypt's western Asiatic population during her own reign would seem to have been greatly at variance to that of her brother. We can see this from the fact that all mining operations in the Sinai "suddenly ceased" in Year Nine of Amenemhat IV's reign.[21] This was his penultimate year of rule meaning that these crucial activities vital to the country's economy must have stopped around the time that Sobekneferu succeeded to the throne, a very telling fact indeed. It suggests a complete change in policy regarding the cooperation extended up until this time to the western Asiatic population in the north of the country, some of whom would have organized the caravans running on a regular basis between Egypt's northeastern border and both Palestine and the Sinai Peninsula.[22]

John van Seters in his important study of the events leading up to Hyksos rule in Egypt makes it clear that this severence of "good relations" between Egypt and its Asiatic neighbors came about *following* Amenemhat IV's reign. It then continued into the Thirteenth Dynasty where "the increasing number of Asiatic slaves in Egypt" and even open hostilities with Syria-Palestine seems to bear out the fact that severe changes had taken place at the commencement of Sobekneferu's reign.[23]

Understanding why exactly Sobekneferu might have wanted to sever relationships with the Asiatic population is crucial to better understand not only the final disintegration of the Twelfth Dynasty, but also, as we see next, the rise of two rivaling dynasties—one supporting Sobekneferu and the other the result of the progressive policies adopted by her brother.

15

The Fall of Egypt

The kings of the Thirteenth Dynasty stayed loyal to the memory of their immediate predecessors Sobekneferu and her father Amenemhat III. They kept Itj-tawy as the capital, while at the same time tightening their relations with the cult of Amun, making Thebes their second capital. Its kings also continued to see Sobek of Shedet as one of their most important deities with no less than seven of its rulers bearing the name Sobekhotep, meaning "Sobek is satisfied" or "Sobek is contented."

It was also no doubt because of this devotion both to Sobek of Shedet and also to Sobekneferu, the cult's greatest patron, that in death the female monarch was deified and a cult established in her name.[1] This no doubt continued into the New Kingdom and probably survived beyond this time in some more abstract form.

The fact that the kings of the Thirteenth Dynasty adhered to Sobekneferu's political and economic policies concerning the western Asiatic groups both in the Nile Delta and also in Sinai tells us that its kings must have been very supportive of the female monarch's own response to the country's troubling political situation. For this reason it seems certain that the emergence of the Thirteenth Dynasty had its roots in an influential group or faction whose main concern was the continued unification of Egypt.

THE INCOMING HYKSOS ELITE AND THE RISE OF EGYPT'S CANAANITE DYNASTY

What might have been going on in Egypt to prompt this concern on the part of the incoming Thirteenth Dynasty of kings is explained by Kim Ryholt. In his opinion the evidence suggests that the migration of Canaanite peoples from Canaan into Egypt during the reigns of Amenemhat III and Amenemhat IV not only led to the collapse of the Twelfth Dynasty, but also the establishment of a Semitic-speaking western Asiatic dynasty in the eastern Delta.[2] This Canaanite-led dynasty, Ryholt surmises, had proclaimed its own king by the reign of Sobekneferu, having attained its independence and autonomy, very possibly through the progressive political ideologies of Amenemhat IV.[3]

Ryholt is not talking here about the Thirteenth Dynasty. Far from it. He is referring to the rise of the Fourteenth Dynasty, which would go on to run concurrently with the Thirteenth Dynasty. This rivaling Canaanite dynasty would establish itself in the eastern Delta, taking Tell el-Dab'a/Avaris as its chief city and in so doing pave the way for its eventual role as the capital of the incoming Hyksos elite, who had begun settling in northern Egypt by around 1700 BCE.[4] During this dynasty, Manetho tells us, "76 kings" would come to govern the north of the country from their seat at Xois (modern Sakha) in the central-northern part of the Delta for a period of "184 years."[5] More likely, however, is that Xois was simply a stronghold of the kings of the Fourteenth Dynasty with Tell el-Dab'a/Avaris being their true administrative and spiritual capital.

So while the Thirteenth Dynasty kings ruled from Itj-tawy in the middle of the country, and also from their second seat at Thebes in the south, the kings of the Fourteenth Dynasty would rule from their royal seat in the Nile Delta. Ryholt states that the relationship between the two dynasties was certainly not a peaceful one. The kings of the Thirteenth Dynasty did not accept the presence of this separate Canaanite dynasty—not at first at least, but eventually agreements were reached with each allowing the other safe passage through its territories for trading, diplomatic, and possibly even religious purposes.[6]

Toward the end of the approximately 125-year period of Hyksos rule in Egypt, circa 1675–1550 BCE, the Thirteenth Dynasty would pass on the torch of Egyptian nationalism to the incoming Seventeenth Dynasty. Its kings were, for the most part, subservient to the rule of the Hyksos warlords of the north. Having had enough of foreign suppression, the final kings of the Seventeenth Dynasty rose up against their enemies, sending them back to their homeland in Syria-Palestine. Thereafter began Egypt's New Kingdom starting with the Eighteenth Dynasty (1550–1292 BCE), when a fully reunited Egypt was able to go on to become one of the greatest empires of the ancient world with reigns from several very powerful pharaohs including Hatshepsut, Thutmose III, Amenhotep III, Seti I, Rameses II, and Rameses III. Had the last kings of the Seventeenth Dynasty along with Ahmose, the first king of the Eighteenth Dynasty, not managed to rout the Hyksos then the future destiny of Egypt might have been very different indeed.

THE RISE OF EGYPTIAN NATIONALISM

This entire sequence of events had begun, seemingly, with the establishment of the Canaanite-inspired Fourteenth Dynasty either during the reign of Amenemhat IV or shortly afterward during the reign of his sister Sobekneferu.[7] If this is correct it is highly likely that many Egyptians were starting to see Amenemhat IV's progressive approach toward the settlement of western Asiatic peoples in the north of the country as a potential threat to Egypt's stability on both a political and economic level.

One possibility is that during the reign of Amenemhat IV Egyptian nationalists turned to Sobekneferu for support asking her to bring about an end to what they saw as an ever-worsening situation that if left unchecked would eventually lead to the disintegration of Egypt as a unified country. In exchange for her cooperation these individuals would no doubt have pledged their full loyalty to the queen should she rise to become sole ruler of the country. It is even possible they offered Sobekneferu their help in ensuring that she did succeed to the throne—the price being that she agree to change Egypt's open border policy while at the same time clamping down on the expansion of the country's western Asiatic population.

Who these nationalists might have been is unclear, although in the knowledge that some of them would go on to establish the country's Thirteenth Dynasty it seems logical to conclude that they were connected in some way with one or more of the country's powerful and highly influential priesthoods, most obviously that of Sobek of Shedet, which would seem to have been sidelined during the reign of Amenemhat IV.

Since Sobekneferu was almost certainly chief patron of the cult of Sobek, this increased allegiance toward her cause actually makes sense, and will do still further when we come to examine the principal functions of the Labyrinth. That said, there would undoubtedly have been other nationalist groups involved in any plot to remove Amenemhat IV and these might well have included certain court officials. All these groups and individuals would have been united in a single cause—attempting to stop the rising influence of northern Egypt's Canaanite dynasty, a very real threat to Egypt's stability since we know that in just a few short generations the Hyksos warlords would come to dominate much of the country.

Even before Sobekneferu might have entered into an alliance with one or more of these nationalist groups there seems every chance that she had already clashed with not only her brother over his progressive ideologies, but also those individuals who were by now beginning to influence his political and economic decisions regarding the future of the country. We should remember that Amenemhat IV was still just a young man at this time, so could easily have been influenced by court officials who had served under his father and had remained loyal to the new king on his accession. Amenemhat IV's growing affiliation with the cult of Atum at Heliopolis might additionally have provided a new source of influence, especially since its age-old priesthood had been very slowly losing its importance both to the cult of Amun at Thebes and, more importantly, to the cult of Sobek of Shedet in the Fayum.

It is even possible that some of the advisors to the king were representatives of the country's western Asiatic community who had earlier gained the trust and respect of Amenemhat III during his reign. What is more there is every reason to suspect that they would have had the support of the priests at Heliopolis, which we know would go on to perform rites of kingship on behalf of the Hyksos kings.

Whoever these advisors to Amenemhat IV were, they were almost certainly influencing his political decisions regarding the future of the Nile Delta's western Asiatic population. These individuals would also have supported the king's plans of expansion into the Sinai to create a new kingdom, one that was clearly intended to eclipse the achievements of his immediate predecessors in the Fayum.

THE WORSENING BROTHER-SISTER RELATIONSHIP

I think it is safe to say the "advisors" working alongside Amenemhat IV would not have been on the same page as Sobekneferu. As potential co-ruler, whether in an official capacity or otherwise, she would have expected to be consulted regarding any policy decisions, particularly if they related to the future of the country. This was clearly not happening and we can understand her growing concerns in this respect, especially since she would have seen it as her birthright to not only rule the Two Lands, but also to uphold the principles of ma'at—truth, justice, and cosmic harmony.

With Sobekneferu perhaps being persuaded by Egyptian nationalists to change the country's open border policy and tackle the rising influence of its western Asiatic population, there seems every reason to conclude that the relationship between brother and sister eventually broke down irreparably. When exactly this took place is unclear, although the cessation of mining operations in the Sinai Peninsula after Year 9 of Amenemhat IV's reign tells us it must have occurred around this time.

With Sobekneferu believing that it was her destiny to wear the double crown of Upper and Lower Egypt there is good reason to suspect she was now siding with Egyptian nationalists plotting to overthrow her brother. Any such plot would surely have involved her succeeding to the throne upon his removal.

Others, we might suspect, would have become aware of the king's now vulnerable situation and advised him accordingly. What happened next according to Kim Ryholt is that, "It would seem therefore that Nofrusobek usurped the throne from the heirs of Amenemhat IV."[8] So if Sobekneferu really did usurp the throne from her brother, and arguably even his young sons Sobekhotep I and Sonbef according to Ryholt,[9] what might this have involved and how exactly was it executed? More importantly, what really did happen to Amenemhat IV?

Nowhere is it recorded whether Amenemhat IV experienced a natural or unnatural death. If it was the latter then it would almost certainly have been an act of regicide. This is the slaying of a monarch or sovereign usually for the purposes of the usurpation of power, something often carried out either by another member of the same family or by a rival dynasty.

As I will attempt to demonstrate in part 4 of this book there is compelling evidence that Amenemhat IV's death really was an act of regicide. This information, however, comes not from contemporary Egyptian sources, but from a Greek historical narrative that up until now has never been linked with the close brother-sister relationship that existed between Amenemhat IV and Sobekneferu. I speak here of the story of a legendary female monarch named Nitocris and her brother the king preserved in the writings of the Greek writer Herodotus, who heard the story when traveling through Egypt in 454 BCE.

The reason the connection has never been made between Nitocris and Sobekneferu, despite so many similarities linking their worlds, is because Manetho speaks of Nitocris as being the last ruler of Egypt's *Sixth* Dynasty, circa 2200–2180 BCE, and not its Twelfth Dynasty, when Amenemhat IV and his sister Sobekneferu ruled the country. However, and as we shall see next, there are firm grounds to believe that Manetho's Nitocris never existed while Herodotus's account of Nitocris records, albeit in an abstract manner, the murder of Amenemhat IV and, in the wake of this tragedy, the death of Sobekneferu.

PART 4

REGICIDE

16

The Mystery of Queen Nitocris

Born in 484 BCE in the ancient Greek city of Halicarnassus, modern-day Bodrum in Turkey, Herodotus would grow up to become a writer, geographer, and arguably the greatest of all the historians of the Greek classical world (see fig. 16.1). His principal work, titled *The Histories,* divided

Fig. 16.1. Bust of Herodotus. Stone sculpture from the second century CE.

into two books, provides a fascinating insight into the main players of the Greco-Persian Wars, which had taken place immediately prior to his time. The methodical and often witty manner he handles such complex matters prompted the Roman narrator Cicero to refer to Herodotus as the "The Father of History."[1]

The Histories explores the life of many great Greek, Persian, and Assyrian kings, along with the battles they fought, the political intrigues surrounding their royal courts, and the colorful characters met along the way. Herodotus has an eye for detail that provides the reader with a fascinating insight into ancient cultures, regional geographies, and royal dynasties, which is a joy to read.

Herodotus also traveled extensively to learn about some of the countries he would come to write about. It was in this spirit that he traveled to Egypt in the year 454 BCE with one of his purposes being to learn what he could about the achievement of its kings and the manners and customs of the Egyptians. To ensure that he gained the best information about Egypt's past, Herodotus consulted the priests at the temples he visited, particularly those of the temple of Hephaestus at Memphis. "Hephaestus" was the Greek name for the Egyptian god Ptah, the two deities having been seen as divine craftsmen.

THE EGYPTIAN CHRONICLES

The priests at the Memphis temple informed Herodotus that the "Egyptian chronicles" speak of the country's first king as being Min (or Menes, circa 3100 BCE), adding that he "separated Memphis from the Nile by a dam." It was for this reason that the river had once flowed on the side of Libya, and that he was responsible for the first temple to Hephaestus.[2] The Nile today flows well to the east of the village of Mit Rahina, the former site of Memphis, but in the past one of its branches ran to the west of the city making it into an island. The priests next tell Herodotus a story of tragedy, murder, and revenge, which they apparently saw as an integral part of Egypt's long history. It is included in book II of *The Histories*:

> After him [Min] came three hundred and thirty kings, whose names the
> priests recited from a papyrus roll. In all these many generations there

were eighteen Ethiopian kings, and one queen, native to the country; the rest were all Egyptian men. The name of the queen was the same as that of the Babylonian princess, Nitocris. She, to avenge her brother (he was king of Egypt and was slain by his subjects, who then gave Nitocris the sovereignty) put many of the Egyptians to death by guile. She built a spacious underground chamber; then, with the pretence of handselling it, but with far other intent in her mind, she gave a great feast, inviting to it those Egyptians whom she knew to have been most concerned in her brother's murder; and while they feasted she let the river in upon them by a great and secret channel. This was all that the priests told of her, save that also when she had done this she cast herself into a chamber full of hot ashes, thereby to escape vengeance.[3]

WHO WAS NITOCRIS?

This account is the earliest reference we have to a female sovereign named Nitocris who following the death of "her brother, the king"[4] committed suicide. So who exactly was Nitocris and how does she fit into the known history of ancient Egypt? These are questions that have been asked many times, although usually they are only ever answered from the perspective of what Manetho has to say about a certain sovereign of the same name, Nitocris, whom he lists as the sixth and final ruler of the Sixth Dynasty. This is what is said about her in the Epitome of Africanus:

Nitocris, the noblest and loveliest of the women of her time, of fair complexion, the builder of the third pyramid, reigned for 12 years.[5]

The entry for the same sovereign in the Epitome of Eusebius is equally puzzling:

There was a queen Nitocris, braver than all the men of her time, the most beautiful of all the women, fair-skinned with red cheeks. By her, it is said, the third pyramid was reared, with the aspect of a mountain.[6]

Unlike Africanus, Eusebius provides no list of kings for this dynasty, the statement on Nitocris's beauty and the fact she built the Third Pyramid (explained below) being the only facts deemed necessary to record. Aside from Manetho the only other place Nitocris is listed is within an ancient chronicle of Egyptian kings left behind by the Greek polymath, geographer, astronomer, mathematician, and poet Eratosthenes (circa 276–194 BCE).

Of the 38 Egyptian kings Eratosthenes records Nitocris is listed as the twenty-second in line. Not much is said about her other than ΝΙΤΩΚΡΙΣ ΓΥΝΗ ΑΝΤΙ ΤΟΥ ΑΝΔΡΟΣ ("Nitocris [was] a woman instead of a man"), and that her reign lasted for six years.[7] He adds only that her name means "ΝΙΚΗΦΟΡΟΣ" ("Bringer of Victory"),[8] this being an epithet of Athena, the Greek goddess of wisdom, handicraft, and warfare. Here Eratosthenes is linking Nitocris with the Egyptian goddess Neith, whose Greek equivalent was Athena. Nitocris's name is usually said to mean "Neith is victorious,"[9] a title honoring the goddess, who was thought to have a fierce warlike aspect. (The Roman writer Dio Cassius (155–235 CE) also refers to a Nitocris who ruled over "burden-bearing Egyptians," although nothing more is said about her. She features as part of a reported address that the ancient British warrior queen Boudicea gave, "woman speaking to woman," to the goddess Andraste before her final battle against the Romans.)[10]

So, once again, we have to ask the question: who exactly was Nitocris, and what is her true place in ancient Egyptian history? I say this since very clearly the account of her and her brother as given by Herodotus seems at complete variance to the one offered by Manetho.

Scottish language scholar W. D. Waddell (1884–1945), whose definitive English translation of Manetho was published in 1940, notes in connection with the queen's origins: "Nitocris is doubtless the Neit-okre(t) of the Turin Papyrus: the name means 'Neith is Excellent,' and was a favourite name under the Saite Dynasty (Dyn. XXVI.), which was devoted to the worship of Neith. A queen's reign ending the Dynasty is followed by a period of confusion, just as after Dyn. XII. when Queen Scemiophris (Sebeknofrurè') closes the line."[11]

THE TURIN CANON

The reference here to Sobekneferu and the close of the Twelfth Dynasty is telling and something we'll return to in due course. It is, however, Waddell's statement about Nitocris appearing in the Turin Papyrus, otherwise known as the Turin Canon, that needs examining first. This ancient text, written in Egyptian hieratic script, was found at Luxor in southern Egypt in 1820 by the Italian traveler Bernardino Drovetti (1776–1852). It was eventually acquired by the Egyptian Museum in Turin, Italy, but on being unpacked the fragile papyrus was found to have disintegrated into 50 or more separate pieces. Putting them back together has not been easy and there is debate even today on their exact order and arrangement.[12]

The papyrus itself dates from the reign of the Nineteenth Dynasty king Rameses II (1279–1213 BCE). It takes the form of a canon of Egyptian monarchs starting with the reign of the gods and the emergence of the First Dynasty (circa 3100 BCE) and continuing through to the end of the Seventeenth Dynasty (circa 1550 BCE).[13]

The Turin Canon is divided into eleven columns and in column 5 is the listing of kings who ruled during Egypt's Sixth Dynasty (2300-2181 BCE). The last of these is given as Neitiqerty, this being the translation of the text's original hieratic name, which is *nt-ikr.ti*.[14] The Egyptian name Neitiqerty was rendered into Greek as Νίτωκρις, the English Nitocris.

Since the Nitocris of Manetho and the Neitiqerty of the Turin Canon are both said to have reigned at the end of the Sixth Dynasty it was long ago concluded they must be one and the same person, which in the minds of many Egyptologists confirms the existence of a female sovereign bearing this name.[15] It is for this reason that W. D. Waddell in the notes accompanying his translation of Manetho asserts that "Nitocris is doubtless the Neit-okre(t) of the Turin Canon," with "Neit-okre(t)" being another way of writing Neitiqerty. Note, however, how Waddell adds in brackets an assumptive letter "t" feminizing the name's original masculine form, something that is not present in the Turin Canon.

THE NONEXISTENCE OF NITOCRIS

That the Neitiqerty of the Turin Canon corresponds with the Nitocris of Manetho continued to be accepted until the year 2000 when this theory finally fell apart. This happened following a fresh examination of the papyrus's relevant fragments by Kim Ryholt—a renowned expert on the Turin Canon and someone who is already familiar to the pages of this book. In a paper published that year he demonstrated that a microscopic analysis of the fibers of two adjoining fragments, these being fragments 40 and 43 from Column #5, shows that Neitiqerty is the king's *prenomen* or throne name, while his *nomen* or personal name can now be read as Siptah.[16] As simple as this realization might seem it has huge implications since Siptah, meaning "son of (the god) Ptah" is a male name, *and only a male name,* showing that the historical candidate behind Manetho's Nitocris *was a man.*[17]

In addition to this Ryholt noted that the name Neitiqerty as given in the Turin Canon is in fact a corruption of the name of the same king given in the king list carved in relief in the temple of Seti I at Abydos in southern Egypt.[18] Here the king's throne name is given as Netjerkare, derived from the original hieratic *ntr-ka-r',*[19] which means something like "deified [*ntr*] soul [*ka*] of Ra." This takes away still further the connection between this particular king of the Sixth Dynasty and a female sovereign of the name Nitocris since the first element of his name is clearly derived from the word *netjer,* or *neter,* meaning "god" or "deified," as opposed to *net* or *nit* meaning the goddess Neith.[20]

Ryholt acknowledges that it was the German Egyptologist Ludwig Stern (1846–1911), as far back as 1883, who first proposed that Manetho's Nitocris was a mistranslation of Netjetkare, the last king of the Sixth Dynasty as given in the Abydos king list.[21] Now it seems he was right in this identification, something confirmed by Ryholt's reexamination of fragments 40 and 43 of the Turin Canon.

So in summary it would seem that Nitocris's listing in the Sixth Dynasty of kings as presented by Manetho stems from a false association with a king named Netjerkare whose name in the Turin Canon is miswritten as Neitiqerty. Whether this error came from a consultation of the textual source used to create the Turin Canon or from the Turin Canon itself is difficult to say, but this now seems the most parsimonious explanation behind Manetho's introduction of a female sovereign named Nitocris in his chronicle of the kings of Egypt.

As a consequence of this realization Kim Ryholt makes it clear that "the supposed ruler Nitocris can be shown to be nonexistent."[22] As such there seems every reason to doubt even the existence of a female sovereign of this name who ruled in Egypt's Sixth Dynasty, something that many Egyptologists still find difficult to accept, searching instead for alternative explanations behind the presence of the name Neitiqerty, the Egyptian form of Nitocris, in the Turin Canon.*

THE SAITIC KINGS

What we *can* say about the Egyptian name Neitiqerty is that it became popular during Egypt's Twenty-sixth Dynasty, which had as its capital the city of Sais in the Nile Delta. One of its kings, Psamtik I (664–610 BCE), not only patronized the temple of Neith in Sais (modern Sa el-Hagar), but also had a daughter named Neitiqerty (see fig. 16.2), whose name is often written in its Greek form

Fig. 16.2. Funerary bust of Neitiqerty, the daughter of king Psamtik I, in vitreous enamel housed today in the Musée d'Art et d'Histoire, Geneva, Switzerland.

---

*See, for instance, the appendix to Ryholt 2000, by James Allen, who suspects that the transition from the Abydos king list's *ntr-ka-re* (vocalized as *natrikari'a*) to the Turin Canon's *nt-jkrtj* (vocalized as *nitaqrati*) is too great for a simple corruption through time. Instead he proposes that the name in the Turin Canon might originally have been *jkrtj-nt* "He of Neith's *jkrt*-serpent," making sense of its Hellenization into Nitocris. Allen does, however, accept that the king in question was male. See Ryholt 2000, 99–100.

as Nitocris. Her father famously sent her to Thebes where she adopted the role of high priest and was installed as the "wife" of the god Amun.[23]

It is a story told in the Nitocris Adoption Stela dating to circa 656 BCE and found in the forecourt of the temple of Amun at Karnak in 1897 by the French Egyptologist Georges Legrain (1865–1917).[24] Thus it seems possible that the religious devotions of Psamtik I's celebrated daughter might have helped popularize existing stories of a mythical queen of the same name who thrived during some more formative period of Egyptian history.[25*]

NITOCRIS AND THE MYSTERY OF THE THIRD PYRAMID

Adding further confusion to Manetho's account of Nitocris is the statement from the Epitome of Africanus to the effect that this queen was "the builder of the third pyramid."[26] The same basic statement is found also in the Epitome of Eusebius, which reads: "By her, it is said, the third pyramid was reared, with the aspect of a mountain."[27]

By "third pyramid" there can be little doubt that this alludes to the pyramid of Menkaure (Greek: Mycerinus), built at Giza following those of Khufu (Greek: Cheops) and Khafre (Greek: Chephren). All three kings belonged to Egypt's Fourth Dynasty (2600–2450 BCE), and the stories of their exploits including the pyramids they constructed are recorded in various classical sources, most notably in Herodotus' *The Histories,* who correctly lists each builder under their Greek name.[28]

W. D. Waddell, in the notes accompanying his translation of Manetho, proposes that Nitocris's connection with the "third pyramid" alludes not to Menkaure's pyramid itself, but to the monument erected to his daughter

---

*British Egyptologist Percy E. Newberry mentions a "Queen Nitocris" who lived during the reign of Amenemhat III. See Newberry 1943b, 51 n. 8. She is known from a small red sandstone statue found at Serabit el-Khadim where she is described as "Her beloved daughter. The hereditary princess, great in favour, great in charm, priestess of Hathor, lady of the turquoise, Neit-okret, true of voice, possessing honour." See Gardiner and Peet 1917, no. 98, Ammenemes III, table IV, pl. xxix; Černý 1955, no. 98. Ammenemes III, 104–5. As a royal female she might well have been a daughter of the king, although not enough is known about her to properly place her within the royal house of the late Twelfth Dynasty. It seems unlikely that she would have been living when Neferuptah and Sobekneferu reached adulthood.

Khentkawes I.[29] This was the enormous pyramid-like tomb built for her a little to the east of the Third Pyramid, which is occasionally referred to as the "fourth" or "false" pyramid.

Khentkawes I, whom we met with in chapter 1, has been considered by some scholars as a ruler in her own right. It is a claim, however, that has today been largely discredited in the knowledge that Egyptologist Selim Hassan misinterpreted one of the titles given to the queen when he first explored her tomb in 1932.[30] Despite this Khentkawes I's potential connection with Nitocris should not be dismissed out of hand. As Hassan reports, the popularity of Khentkawes I would seem to have lingered through to Greco-Roman times particularly in association with the Third Pyramid.

Indeed, it was Hassan's opinion that Khentkhawes I was herself Nitocris, which if correct added strength, he said, "to the conclusion that the report of Manetho concerning the pyramid of the queen, has a nucleus of reality. It was only by the assimilation of names and the misplacement of monuments that the contradictions were brought about. Khent-kawes (Nitokris) was thus made the builder of the Third Pyramid."[31]

Years earlier, however, British archaeologist and Egyptologist Flinders Petrie had offered his own ingenious solution as to how Manetho's Nitocris came to be associated with Giza's Third Pyramid. He pointed out that the king that ruled after the Netjetkare of the Abydos king list (he calls him Neterkara) is recorded as "Men-ka-ra," a name phonetically and linguistically the same as Menkaure, the builder of the Third Pyramid. Petrie suspected that this "queen Men-ka-ra" and the Neitiqerty of the Turin Canon (and thus Manetho's Nitocris) were one and the same person, explaining at least to his satisfaction how Manetho came to accredit Nitocris with the building of the Third Pyramid.[32] The problem, of course, is that the Men-ka-ra in question was male not female.[32]

Adding still further to the confusion, however, is the fact that first Herodotus,[33] and then later two further writers, the Greek geographer Strabo[34] (64/63 BCE–23 CE) and the Greek historian Diodorus Siculus (circa 90 BCE–30 BCE),[35] speak of the Third Pyramid as having been constructed for a woman named Rhodopis. So who was Rhodopis and how does she relate to Nitocris?

According to Herodotus, Rhodopis grew up in Thrace (a former kingdom geographically located in what is today Bulgaria), and having been kidnapped from her home she was sold as a slave in Egypt, where she was made to ply her trade as a prostitute.[36] After gaining her freedom Rhodopis's apparent beauty helped her become a courtesan (Greek *hetaira*) in the city of Naucratis, although eventually, however, she would rise to become queen of Egypt. It is the Roman author and teacher Aelian (175–235 CE) who tells us how this great transition took place:

> For whilest she was washing, and her Maids look'd to her clothes, an Eagle stooping down, snatched up one of her Shoes, and carried it away to Memphis, where [the king] Psammetichus was sitting in Judgement, and let the Shoe fall into his lap. Psammetichus wondring at the shape of the Shoe, and neatness of the work, and the action of the Bird, sent throughout Ægypt to find out the Woman to whom the shoe belonged; and having found her out, married her.[37]

The king in question in this Cinderella-like story is given as Psammetichus, the Greek rendering of Psamtik I, the ruler of the Twenty-sixth Dynasty whose own daughter was named Nitocris. In contrast to Aelian, however, Herodotus in *The Histories* tells us that the king who reigned when Rhodopis was brought to Egypt as a slave was Amasis, the penultimate king of the Twenty-sixth Dynasty and the last great ruler of the country prior to Persian rule.[38] Amasis was the Greek name for the king who in contemporary Egyptian sources is named as Ahmose Khnemibre. He reigned circa 570–526 BCE.

The connection once again between Rhodopis, the Third Pyramid, and the kings of the Twenty-sixth dynasty should not be overlooked. Not only did they reinvigorate the cult of Neith in the city of Sais, but they also single-handedly revived an interest in the Fourth Dynasty kings of Giza elevating them into culture heroes. So popular did Khufu, Khafre, and Menkaure become during the Twenty-sixth Dynasty that many elite members of society insisted on being buried in shaft tombs near those of these celebrated kings.*

---

*Percy E. Newberry proposed that the "third pyramid" of the Nitocris story must relate not to Giza's Third Pyramid but to one of the royal tombs of the kings of the Twenty-sixth Dynasty of Sais. He further proposed that Nitocris was in fact Queen Neith, the mother of King Pepi II, the first king of the Sixth Dynasty (see Newberry 1943b, 53–54).

NITOCRIS AND RHODOPIS

It seems plausible that it was during the reigns of kings such as Psamtik I (Psammetichus) and Ahmose Khnemibre (Amasis) that much of the narrative behind the Nitocris story as presented by Manetho took its final form. In addition to this there is clear evidence that Rhodopis, for whom the Third Pyramid was supposedly built, became simply another manifestation of Nitocris. We can tell this because both names can mean "rosy-cheeked,"[39] a term that closely matches what Eusebius's Epitome of Manetho says about Nitocris being, "the most beautiful of all the women, fair-skinned with red cheeks."[40] Thereafter it is stated that, "By her, it is said, the third pyramid was reared, with the aspect of a mountain,"[41] confirming the relationship not only between Nitocris and Rhodopis, but also between both of these women and the Third Pyramid at Giza.

Before ending this debate on the origins of Manetho's Nitocris and her relationship to Rhodopis, I have one further observation to make with respect to both these women's association with the Third Pyramid at Giza. According to legend it was "some of the nomarchs" who had become Rhodopis's lovers that built this monument as her final resting place.[42] (A *nomarch* in ancient Egypt was usually the governor of a *nome* or district). As we have seen, Rhodopis, before becoming queen of Egypt, was said to have been a *hetaira,* a courtesan, and *hetairai* generally only served elite members of society.

Rhodopis's profession in this respect could have a deeper meaning, particularly in terms of Egyptian religion, since it was the goddess Hathor who presided over music, dance, and sexuality, all actions that would have been closely associated with the concept of the hetaira. Hathor, as we saw in chapter 9, was strongly associated with Menkaure through his creation of the carved stone triads showing him in the company both of Hathor and of the local gods attached to those nomes that hosted estates belonging to the goddess. These triad slabs had stood in the king's valley temple located at the end of the causeway attached to Menkaure's pyramid. Close by, in what is today a Muslim cemetery, there is a small grove of sycamore trees that provide shade for an old holy well known as Bir el-Samman (Hammad el-Samman was a local Muslim saint), which might well have been associated with the cult of Hathor in dynastic times.[43] So did the goddess's divine presence in the nearby valley temple of Menkaure eventually become entangled with stories surrounding Rhodopis-Nitocris, arguably as late as the Twenty-sixth Dynasty?

Some evidence of this fact comes from knowledge that in Arabic medieval folklore the ghost of Nitocris was seen to haunt the area around the Third Pyramid, a tale recorded by French Egyptologist Gaston Maspero (1846–1916) in the following manner:

> It is said that the spirit of the Southern Pyramid [that is, the Third Pyramid or pyramid of Menkaure] never appears abroad, except in the form of a naked woman, who is very beautiful, but whose manner of acting is such, that when she desires to make people fall in love with her, and lose their wits, she smiles upon them, and immediately they draw near to her, and she attracts them towards her, and makes them infatuated with love; so that they at once lose their wits, and wander aimlessly about the country. Many have seen her moving round the pyramid about midday and towards sunset. It is Nitokris still haunting the monument of her shame and her magnificence.[44]

All this suggests something going on there that was more than simply the memory of a legendary sovereign named Nitocris or a celebrated courtesan named Rhodopis. In my opinion both of these personalities became attached to a preexisting female *genius loci* connected to the Third Pyramid, through lingering memories of Khentkhawes I, the daughter of Menkaure, and also through a strong belief in the presence locally of the goddess Hathor.

Even if all this is correct it says nothing about the picture of Nitocris offered by Herodotus in his work *The Histories,* which, we should recall, was written over 150 years *before* Manetho's *Aegyptiaca.* It is almost as if Herodotus's Nitocris is a completely different person. So who was this *other* Nitocris?

Having asserted that "Nitocris is doubtless the Neit-okre(t)" of the Sixth Dynasty in the notes accompanying his translation of Herodotus, W. D. Waddell adds that the "queen's reign ending the Dynasty is followed by a period of confusion, just as after Dyn. XII. when Queen Scemiophris

(Sebeknofrurè') closes the line."[45] Although this statement was simply a poignant observation on the part of Waddell a connection between the story of Nitocris as preserved by Herodotus and the events surrounding the end of Egypt's Twelfth Dynasty is, as we see next, a very real possibility indeed.

17

Sobekneferu as Nitocris

Herodotus's account in book II of *The Histories* of how Nitocris avenges "her brother, the king,"[1] by massacring those responsible for his murder, before taking her own life to evade further retribution, was conveyed to the Greek writer by the priests of Egypt, apparently those of the temple of Hephaestus (Ptah) at Memphis. So did this historical drama reflect real life events, or was it simply a fantasy with little if any basis in truth? If the former solution can be considered, is it remotely feasible that these events record the death of Amenemhat IV and the succession to the throne of his sister Sobekneferu?

Previously we envisaged a situation whereby Egyptian nationalists, concerned about Amenemhat IV's liberal policies regarding the growing influence of western Asiatic peoples settling in the north of the country, might have initiated a plot to remove him. We saw also how these individuals, perhaps involving members of a prominent priesthood, would almost certainly have sought the support of Sobekneferu, promising to back her claim to the throne if their wishes were met. If this imagined scenario during the reign of Amenemhat IV is in any way correct can Herodotus's account of Nitocris provide convincing evidence to support this hypothesis? To answer this question we will start with an analysis of what Herodotus says about Nitocris and her brother and examine how the reigns of these two monarchs relate to those of other Egyptian kings mentioned in book II of *The Histories*.

330 KINGS AND ONLY ONE WOMAN

As we have seen, after being informed about the reign of Min (or Menes), the legendary first king of Egypt, Herodotus is provided with the names of all 330 kings who had once ruled the country. "In all these many generations," the priests tell him, "there were eighteen Ethiopian kings, *and one queen,* native to the country; the rest were all Egyptian men."[2] (Current author's emphasis.)

The important statement here is that of all the 330 kings listed in the papyrus scroll, just one was a "queen," in other words a female sovereign. We can't say which female ruler the priests might have been referring to here. The fact, however, that they allude to just *one,* not two, three, or more women rulers, tells us that this particular monarch must have been particularly powerful for her to be remembered as Egypt's *sole* female ruler. Herodotus, of course, tells us her name was Nitocris.

No clue is given as to how this female monarch fits into the chronology of Egypt's 330 kings. In the knowledge, however, that Manetho's Nitocris— whom he records as the last ruler of the Sixth Dynasty—never existed tells us that Herodotus's Nitocris was somebody else altogether. Since Manetho only mentions one Nitocris, then is it possible he recorded Herodotus's Nitocris under a completely different name?

To answer this question, we need to look at what *other* female rulers Manetho lists in the Epitome. For instance, Hatshepsut, we find, is alluded to under the name of Amensis (also Amersis or Amesses), whom he says ruled for 22 years.[3] He also records the reign of Neferneferuaten (either Nefertiti or Meritaten), whom he refers to as Acheres (also Acherrhes or Akenchĕres),[4] allotting her a reign of 12 years. Although there is no indication of the gender of these kings in the Epitome they *are* recorded as female in the section of Manetho's *Aegyptiaca* included in a work by the first-century CE Jewish writer Flavius Josephus titled *Against Apion.*[5] The only other female ruler Manetho lists is Skemiophris/Sobekneferu, the last ruler of the Twelfth Dynasty.

So which, if any, of these monarchs would be the best candidate for the "one queen, native to the country" that Herodotus is told about by the priests of Egypt? Maybe we can whittle it down, since Herodotus's "queen," in other words Nitocris, is said to have been the *sister* of the previous king.

So how many of Manetho's female rulers were the sister of the previous male ruler?

THE BROTHER-SISTER CANDIDATES

In the Epitome of Manetho as recorded by Africanus and Eusebius the only time a brother-sister relationship between two successive rulers is mentioned is that between Ammenemes/Amenemhat IV and Skemiophris/Sobekneferu.[6] However, in Josephus's *Against Apion* he cites Amensis/Hatshepsut as being the "sister" of the previous king Amenophis, who is said to have reigned 20 years and 7 months.[7] Hatshepsut, of course, was the half-sister and royal wife of the previous king Thutmose II. In the Epitome of Manetho as recorded by Eusebius, Thutmose II would appear to be listed as a king named Chebron,[8] who is said to have ruled 13 years (even though Thutmose II's actual reign was perhaps as little as 3 or 4 years).

No other brother-sister relationships between rulers appear in the works of Manetho, our oldest Greco-Egyptian source of information on the chronicles of the kings of Egypt other than Herodotus's *The Histories*. So which of the two brother-sister relationships that the Egyptian writer lists corresponds with Herodotus's account of the relationship existing between Nitocris and her brother, the king? Is it Ammenemes–Skemiophris (Amenemhat IV–Sobekneferu) or is it Amenophis–Amensis (Thutmose II–Hatshepsut)? Even though it would be easy to say Amenemhat IV–Sobekneferu since they better fit what we know about the sociopolitical intrigues taking place during their reigns, more evidence is required to prove the case one way or another. This, as we see next, can be provided by looking more closely at the construction of Herodotus's narrative in book II of *The Histories*.

AMENEMHAT III AS KING MOERIS

After concluding his account of Nitocris and her brother, Herodotus straight away introduces the reader to another of those 330 kings mentioned by the priests of the temple. This is what he says:

> But of the other kings they related no achievement or deed of great note, save of Moeris, who was the last of them. This Moeris was remembered

as having built the northern forecourt of the temple of Hephaestus, and dug a lake, of as many furlongs in circuit as I shall later show; and built there pyramids also, the size of which I will mention when I speak of the lake. All this was Moeris' work, they said; of none of the rest had they anything to record.[9]

We know from references to "Moeris" elsewhere in Herodotus that he is here speaking of Amenemhat III who is thought to have made additions to the existing temple of Ptah (the Greek Hephaestus) at Memphis including the construction of its northern entranceway.[10] When Herodotus returns to the achievements of King Moeris later on in book II of *The Histories* he speaks about the building of the Labyrinth before turning his attention once more to the Fayum lake:

More marvellous [than the Labyrinth, which he has just told the reader "no words can tell its wonders"] is the lake Moeris, by which it stands. This lake has a circuit of three thousand six hundred furlongs, or sixty schoeni, which is as much as the whole seaboard of Egypt. Its length is from north to south; the deepest part has a depth of fifty fathoms. That it has been dug out and made by men's hands the lake shows for itself; for almost in the middle of it stand two pyramids, so built that fifty fathoms of each are below and fifty above the water; atop of each is a colossal stone figure seated on a throne. . . . The water of the lake is not natural (for the country here is exceeding waterless) but brought by a channel from the Nile; six months it flows into the lake, and six back into the river.[11]

According to Herodotus, it had been King Moeris who had undertaken this extraordinary hydrological venture in the Fayum. Other classical writers echo Herodotus's statements about this king. Diodorus Siculus, for instance, tells us that Moeris "excavated the lake" and cut a channel allowing the floodwaters of the Nile to fill its interior at the time of the inundation. This in turn allowed the reclamation and subsequent irrigation of the rich fertile lands existing beyond its shores. An engineering project on such a grand scale, Diodorus tells us, had required "myriads of men" laboring for many years,[12] whereby the king:

dug a canal, eighty stades long and three plethra wide, from the river to the lake, and by this canal, sometimes turning the river into the lake and sometimes shutting it off again, he furnished the farmers with an opportune supply of water, opening and closing the entrance by a skilful device and yet at considerable expense; for it cost no less than fifty talents if a man wanted to open or close this work. The lake has continued to serve well the needs of the Egyptians down to our time, and bears the name of its builder, being called to this day the Lake of Moeris. Now the king in excavating it left a spot in the centre, where he built a tomb and two pyramids, a stade in height, one for himself and the other for his wife, on the tops of which he placed stone statues seated upon thrones, thinking that by these monuments he would leave behind him an imperishable commemoration of his good deeds.[13]

The two "pyramids" mentioned both by Herodotus and by Diodorus refer to two colossi of Amenemhat III that were set atop rectilinear pedestals, each being in the range of 21 feet (6.4 meters) in height (see fig. 17.1). They survived through to the Middle Ages although by the eighteenth century all that remained of these gigantic statues were a few scattered fragments along with their somewhat dilapidated pedestals. These can still be

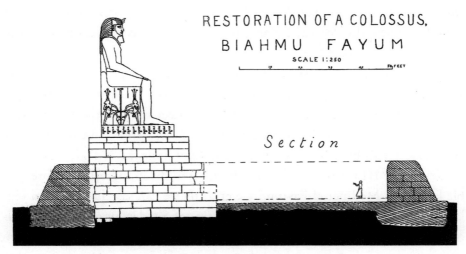

Fig. 17.1. Flinders Petrie's rendition of the twin colossi of Amenemhat III formerly located at Biahmu in the Fayum (from Petrie 1889, pl. XXVI). Only fragments of their pedestals remain today.

seen to this day at a site named Es-Sanan (meaning "the way" or "the road"), which lies amid cultivated fields just north of the village of Biahmu, some 3.7 miles (6 kilometers) north-northeast of the former site of Shedet.[14]

Before going any further it should be pointed out that the classical writers' bold assertions to the effect that Moeris/Amenemhat III dug out the Fayum lake are completely false. Known today as Birket Qarun, the lake is a natural body of slightly saline water with its surface currently around 141 feet (43 meters) below sea level. It covers an area of 125 square miles (202 square kilometers), is oriented west-southwest to east-northeast, and is approximately 25 miles (40 kilometers) in length and around 5.6 miles (9 kilometers) in width. The lake was formerly much larger and is thought to have been present when Neolithic peoples began settling in the region as much as 7,500 years ago,[15] with its connection to the crocodile god Sobek probably dating back to the beginning of dynastic history.[16]

The canal linking the Nile with the Fayum is called the Bahr Yusef ("Waterway of Joseph"). It is completely natural and enters the depression through the east-west oriented valley basin known as the Hawara Channel.[17] During the Twelfth Dynasty certain kings engaged in large-scale hydrological programs to clear sections of the channel to permit the floodwaters of the Nile to enter the Fayum depression.[18] Once the inundation had passed its peak, the excess floodwaters would flow back into the Nile. This is something that would have had the additional benefit of stopping Lower Egypt from becoming flooded each year, ensuring that it was an extremely fertile region in its own right.

As to which Twelfth Dynasty kings were responsible for these far-reaching hydrological projects, that remains unclear. Egyptologist Alan B. Lloyd writes that Senosret II, "cut a canal from the Bahr Yusef to Lake Qarun, added water catchment basins, and placed a dyke at el-Lahun,"[19] this being close to where the canal joins the Nile. In his words "Amenemhat III introduced further basins and dykes, obtaining more arable land near Medinet el-Fayum."[20] Certainly we can say that the land reclamation projects going on in the proximity of Shedet, immediately south of the lake, must have begun at the beginning of the dynasty since the word *shedet* simply means "the reclaimed place."[21] It was, of course, on this reclaimed land that the Twelfth Dynasty kings constructed the temple of Sobek of Shedet, adjoining which was a royal palace (see chapter 2).

There seems little doubt that the hydrological engineering programs that took place in the Fayum during the Twelfth Dynasty were the product of more than one monarch. By the age of Herodotus, however, it was only Amenemhat III under the name Moeris who was remembered as the principal engineer of these grand projects, which will have changed forever the face of the Fayum depression. Yet not only was Moeris/Amenemhat III celebrated as the builder the Bahr Yusef canal, he was also said to have created the Fayum's great lake. Very clearly this confusion came from the extent to which both him and his predecessors had dug out the Hawara Channel, their achievements becoming magnified across the centuries. One reason for this is probably because Amenemhat III was deified in death with a cult in his name surviving through until Roman times.[22]

The name Moeris comes from the phonetic spelling of the king's prenomen or throne name Ni-ma'at-Ra, meaning "He who belongs to the *ma'at* [divine truth and cosmic order] of Ra."[23] This would have been pronounced something like "Ne-ma-ray," corrupted eventually into Moeris, as well as other variations such as Lamares and Marres.

CHRONOLOGICAL RELATIONSHIP

The main point of importance to be gained from Herodotus's account of King Moeris is that the Greek writer introduces him *immediately* after recounting the story of Nitocris and her brother the king. This could simply be coincidence. On the other hand, it could indicate that in the minds of the priests of Egypt some kind of chronological relationship existed between these three separate rulers.

The idea of a chronological relationship existing between Nitocris, "her brother, the king,"[24] and the pharaoh named Moeris is strengthened in the knowledge that the next two kings Herodotus introduces are *also* from Egypt's Twelfth Dynasty. The first of these is Sesostris, who is said to have followed Moeris and "set out with a fleet of long ships from the Arabian Gulf and subdued all the dwellers by the Red Sea, till as he sailed on he came to a sea which was too shallow for his vessels. After returning thence back to Egypt, he gathered a great army (according to the story of the priests) and marched over the mainland, subduing every nation."[25]

Herodotus goes on to cite many more exploits and deeds of Sesostris,[26] although for the purposes of this book these need not be explored. All we need to know is that Sesostris can be identified as Senusret III, the predecessor and assumed father of Amenemhat III, the monarch's conquests of other nations based loosely on his recorded military campaigns against the Libyans, Nubians, and the Retjenu of Syria-Palestine.[27]

The next king that Herodotus focuses on is said to have been the son of Sesostris, his name being given as Pheros.[28] Almost certainly this was not his real name, since *pheros* is simply a corruption of the Egyptian *per 'aa* (from *pr-ʿȝ*), meaning "great house."[29] Originally this was a term that referred solely to the royal palace of the king, although in the New Kingdom it came to refer also to the ruling monarch and, as such, is the root behind the word *pharaoh.*

Despite his associations with the Egyptian term *per 'aa,* meaning "great house," the Pheros of Herodotus is considered to be based on the life and exploits, whether imaginary or otherwise, of Amenemhat II, the third king of the Twelfth Dynasty.[30] He ruled prior to Senusret II who in turn was followed on to the throne of Egypt by Senusret III. So Pheros was certainly not Sesostris's son as is stated by Herodotus.

Despite this minor confusion on the part of Herodotus, if we examine the order of kings he introduces to his narrative from Nitocris and "her brother, the king"[31] onward then a clear pattern emerges. For if we assume that Nitocris is Sobekneferu and her brother is Amenemhat IV, then we would have, in order of their appearance, entries relating to the eighth, seventh, sixth, fifth and, finally, the third ruler of the Twelfth Dynasty (see fig. 17.2).

So based on the contents of the "papyrus roll" shown to Herodotus by the priests of Egypt it would appear possible that the Greek writer was informed about five notable rulers starting with Nitocris and her brother, arguably Sobekneferu and Amenemhat IV, and then gradually stepping backward in time through the reigns of Amenemhat III, Senuset III, and, finally, Amenemhat II. Very clearly Herodotus, being unfamiliar with the order in which these kings reigned, or what their true familial relationship might have been, does his best to try and recount everything the priests have told him about the lives and deeds of these monarchs. He does make some mistakes, although whether these were down to him or they came from the priests who provided this information is unclear.

Herod. Ref.*	Herod. Ruler name	Egyptian Name	12th Dyn. Position
2.100	Nitocris	Sobekneferu?	Eighth
2.100	"brother . . . king of Egypt"	Amenemhat IV?	Seventh
2.101	Moeris	Amenemhat III	Sixth
2.102–2.111	Sesostris	Senusret III	Fifth
2.111–2.112	Pheros	Amenemhat II	Third

*Herodotus Book II, followed by the chapters in which the monarch features.

Fig. 17.2. List of Twelfth Dynasty kings featured in book II of Herodotus's *The Histories.* Note how they appear in the same sequence as they feature in the text, but in reverse order starting with Nitocris and "her brother, the king," suggesting that they are to be identified with Sobekneferu and her brother Amenemhat IV.

Thereafter in his narrative Herodotus goes on to say that "a man of Memphis" succeeded Pheros, and that his name was Proteus. He is said to have thrived during the age of Helen of Troy and the Trojan War.[32] Since these events occurred as much as 600 years after Egypt's Twelfth Dynasty, Herodotus has clearly now shifted his attention to a much later epoch corresponding most probably to Egypt's Nineteenth Dynasty.

After Proteus, who has no real equivalent in the Egyptian king lists, Herodotus informs us that the next king to rule the country was Rhampsinitus, whose life and deeds appear to be loosely based on those of the Twentieth Dynasty king Rameses III (1183/82–1152/51 BCE).[33] It is after this that Herodotus introduces his reader to the celebrated kings of the Fourth Dynasty beginning with Cheops (or Khufu), the builder of the Great Pyramid, and then moving on to his successors Chephren (Khafre) and Mycerinus (Menkaure), the builders of the Second and Third pyramids respectively.[34] Herodotus is clearly now heading into areas of ancient Egyptian history far removed from those of the kings of the Twelfth Dynasty.

In summary there seems to be sufficient grounds to suspect that Herodotus's story of Nitocris and the death of her brother is more likely based on events surrounding the reigns of Amenemhat IV and his sister Sobekneferu. What we know of the reigns of Thutmose II and Hatshepsut simply does not fit the profiles of Nitocris and "her brother, the king," especially since no convincing case has ever been made for Thutmose II being murdered, despite the fact that his reign only lasted for a period of 3 or 4 years.

So in the knowledge that Herodotus appears to bracket the reigns of Nitocris and her brother with those of three Twelfth Dynasty kings supports the hypothesis that these two legendary monarchs can be identified as Sobekneferu and her brother Amenemhat IV. If so, then it might now be possible to better break down what Herodotus says about Nitocris and the way she was able to gain her revenge on those deemed responsible for the death of her brother, and how, finally, she herself committed suicide to avoid further retribution from those seeking vengeance for her actions. Before, however, we can do this there are other more pressing matters that need to be addressed. For instance, if Sobekneferu really is Herodotus's Nitocris, then how did she come to bear a name that very clearly honors the goddess Neith, when she herself was a devotee of the crocodile god Sobek? It is this conundrum we tackle next.

18

Mother of Crocodiles

Following her death Sobekneferu would appear to have been deified by the kings of the incoming Thirteenth Dynasty.[1] They saw her as some kind of inspiration both in connection with their own nationalistic interests and also because of her patronage of the cult of Sobek. The actions of these monarchs ensured that an ancestral cult in Sobekneferu's name continued through the Second Intermediate Period and survived, seemingly, into the New Kingdom.

Having said this there are clear indications that Sobekneferu's individual memory as Egypt's first female ruler of Upper and Lower Egypt had started to fragment by the start of the New Kingdom, a situation emphasized by the fact that by this time even the whereabouts of her tomb had seemingly been lost. One apparent example of this situation surrounds the legendary builder of the Labyrinth.

As we shall see in part 6 of this book, there is ample evidence that Sobekneferu not only completed the construction of the Labyrinth but also established it as one of the most important religious centers in the whole of Egypt. Despite this, classical writers generally credit the monument's construction—or certainly its use as a royal tomb—to the king named Moeris, who can be identified as Amenemhat III (see chapter 17 as well as chapter 28). This is understandable since it was Sobekneferu herself who would appear to have deified her father following his death, thus ensuring that a cult in his name flourished through to Roman times.[2] One tradition, however, preserved by the Roman writer, naturalist, and natural philosopher Pliny the Elder (23/24–79 CE) speaks of the Labyrinth as the creation of "King Petesuchis or Tithöes."[3] So who exactly were Petesuchos and Tithöes?

GIFT OF THE CROCODILE GOD

The identity of Tithöes is outlined below, but it is Petesuchis that is of more immediate interest. Petesuchis, more usually written Petesuchos, means the "gift of Suchos," with Suchos being the Greco-Roman rendering of Sobek. The "King Petesuchis" Pliny identifies as the builder of the Labyrinth is, of course, Amenemhat III.[4] This seems inescapable, especially as the king is addressed in the temple of Renenutet at Medinet Madi as "son of Sobek."[5] His daughter Sobekneferu was, however, equally associated with the cult of Sobek, particularly at the Labyrinth. Not only was she arguably the god's patron during her reign but she also uniquely used the crocodile sign as part of her personal name and throne name.

So there is every reason to assume that by the Ptolemaic age (323–30 BCE) certain of Sobekneferu's deeds had become absorbed into myths surrounding not only her father, but also the deity she venerated, in other words Sobek. Should this be correct, then there is every chance that aspects of her life and memories of her reign were absorbed into the cult of other deities worshipped in the Fayum, particularly if they were associated with crocodiles.

THE CULT OF NEITH

One deity that fits the bill perfectly is Neith, the bisexual, self-created goddess of war and hunting, who was seen as either the mother of or the source behind so many other gods and goddesses.[6] Neith was one of the oldest deities in Egypt with several very ancient temples in the western Delta, which was her foremost region of veneration from very earliest times. Despite her powerful nature Neith did not gain widespread popularity until the Twenty-sixth Dynasty (664–525 BCE). It was then, as we have seen, that the kings of Sais revitalized Neith's worship in the city.

In addition to the multitude of aspects already mentioned, Neith was considered the mother of those snakes and crocodiles "who are in the abyss."[7] She bore the title "the nurse of crocodiles" and in religious iconography was shown being suckled by twin crocodiles (see fig. 18.1).[8] They signify the two children to whom she gave birth, one being the sun and the other the moon.[9] Most significant, however, is that Neith was considered the mother of Sobek, the principal deity both of the Fayum and of Sobekneferu.[10]

Fig. 18.1. The goddess Neith suckling two crocodiles. Statue in faience dating from the sixth to fourth century BCE housed today in the Staatliches Museum Ägyptischer Kunst, Munich, Germany. Photo by Vassil.

One of the goddess Neith's principal links with the Fayum was in her role as Mehet-Weret, which means the "Great Primeval Ocean" or the "Great Flood."[11] This was a deity usually depicted like Hathor as the Celestial Cow with the sun disk supported between her long horns (the two goddesses would have a close interconnection throughout dynastic history).[12] Neith in her form as Mehet-Weret (Greek: Methyer) presided over the primeval waters of creation signified in the night sky by the stream of stars making up the Milky Way and on the ground by the floodwaters of the Nile at the time of the inundation.[13] In the Fayum these floodwaters would surge along the Bahr Yusef canal into the Fayum lake, allowing it to be seen as a personification of the primeval waters as well as the abode of Mehet-Weret, who gives birth each day to the new sun.[14]

In the Greco-Roman papyrus known as the Book of the Fayum, Mehet-Weret appears several times. One representation shows her with her hands and forearms raised and twin streams of water pouring downward from her elbows (see fig. 18.2 on the next page). Horst Beinlich, an expert on the Book of the Fayum, suspects that this symbolism relates to the manner the Bahr Yusef canal splits apart just before it enters Medinet el-Fayum causing the surging waters to flow away in separate directions,[15] although it could

Fig. 18.2. The goddess Neith in her form as Mehet-Weret as shown in the Book of the Fayum.

have a celestial meaning and relate to the manner the Milky Way bifur-
cates into two separate streams of stars in the vicinity of the constellation of
Cygnus, the celestial bird, which is also known as the Northern Cross.

Mehet-Weret's association with the Fayum is probably very ancient
indeed and is arguably behind the hieroglyph used for the toponym Shedet.
This shows a horned bucranium atop a tower-like serekh and is used to
denote the town within inscriptions.[16] Indeed, sometimes this bucranium
appears alongside Sobekneferu's personal name (it is present, for instance,
on the British Museum cylinder seal—see fig. 2.1 on page 16). This was to
emphasize that the form of Sobek venerated by the monarch was specifically
that of Shedet in the Fayum.

Neith in the Fayum

In the Book of the Fayum, Neith is shown in association with her symbol
the forked acacia tree (see fig. 18.3), which might also reflect the manner

Fig. 18.3. Reconstruction of the shrine of Neith named the
"Acacia of Neith" as depicted in the Book of the Fayum.

in which the Milky Way splits into two separate branches in the vicinity of the Cygnus constellation. The presence of the goddess's forked tree in the papyrus text referred to a presumably very ancient cult shrine somewhere in the Fayum.[17] Named the "Acacia of Neith," it was one of three important sanctuaries in the vicinity of the lake.[18] The other sanctuaries listed are the "House of Life of Rasehet" and Shedet itself, which, of course, was Sobek's principal center of veneration in the Fayum.[19]

The existence of the "Acacia of Neith" shrine in the Fayum makes it clear that the goddess Neith must have been extremely important across the region, especially since she was the mother of Sobek. There are, however, other links between Neith and Sobekneferu in her role as builder of the Labyrinth.

Earlier we saw how Pliny the Elder recorded that the builder of the Labyrinth was "King Petesuchis or Tithöes." Petesuchos can be identified as Amenemhat III and perhaps even as Sobekneferu, while Tithöes is the Greek name of a Greco-Egyptian protective deity named Tutu, known as "the one who keeps enemies at a distance." Shown as a combination of winged sphinx and griffin, this fearsome creature had the body and legs of a lion, the wings of a falcon, the head of a human, and a tail in the form of a cobra.[20] Clearly, this was a composite creature that had absorbed aspects of other deities, although what's important is that Tutu or Tithöes was seen as the son of the goddess Neith.[21] It was for this reason that he was occasionally shown with a tripartite head, one of a man, one of a lion, and the third that of a crocodile identified with Sobek.[22] Tutu had power over the demons sent out by his mother, the first of which would always be in the form of a crocodile.[23]

Egyptologist Olaf E. Kaper of Leiden University, who has made a detailed study of the cult of Tutu, explains that the god was connected very strongly with the cult of the crocodile.[24] He adds that Tutu could also be seen as a divine king and may even have been a historical figure, as seems implied by Pliny's assertion that Tutu/Tithöes was responsible for the construction of the Labyrinth.[25] So whether its builder was seen as Sobek/Petesuchos or as Tutu/Tithöes, the mother in both cases was the goddess Neith, a key deity in the magico-religious traditions of the Fayum.

The Deep Bosomed One

In addition to this, there is another important connection between Sobekneferu, her father Amenemhat III, and the goddess Neith. A lime-

From Labyrinth.

Fig. 18.4. Inscription from the Labyrinth showing the only known reference to the goddess Dehdehet (from Petrie 1890, pl. XI, 1). Her name appears upright in the rectangular frame between Amenemhat III's throne name (*left*) and a variant of Sobekneferu's personal name (*right*). Outside the box on the right Amenemhat III's name appears for a second time.

stone block found in the vicinity of the Labyrinth bears an inscription linking both rulers with an obscure female deity named Dehdehet [*dh.dh.t*] (see fig. 18.4).[26] This is the only known inscription mentioning her name suggesting perhaps that Dehdehet was an epithet of a more familiar goddess venerated in the region.

Egyptian language scholar and classicist Terence du Quesne (1942–2014) felt that Dehdehet could be translated as the "Deep Bosomed One,"[27] bringing to mind pictorial representations of the bipedal hippopotamus shown in ancient Egyptian art with long drooping breasts (see fig. 18.5 on the next page). Usually this goddess is identified as Taweret, Opet, or Reret, all names applied to the She-hippopotamus. In the Book of the Fayum, however, a bipedal hippopotamus is shown with a crocodile on its back,[28] alongside which is the inscription, "Neith, the Great, Protector of her son, the First of her forms [Akhemu] in the middle of the Lake."[29]

It therefore seems likely that Neith, being a deity of extreme antiquity, was perhaps an original name of the hippopotamus goddess. (I shall have more to say about the greater antiquity of the cult of Neith in chapter 35.) If correct, then Dehdehet was probably an epithet of Neith, especially in the knowledge that in Fayumic tradition she was seen both as Mehet-Weret, the Great Flood, personified as the waters of the Great Lake, and as the mother

Fig. 18.5. Figurine of the
hippopotamus goddess
Taweret in the form
of a bottle held by the
Louvre Museum, Paris.
It dates from between
900 and 700 BCE.
Photo by Rama.

of Sobek in his role as the sun god. It was thus in her capacity as patron of
the cult of Sobek, as well as one of the two principal monarchs behind the
construction of the Labyrinth, that Sobekneferu's memory was most likely
preserved along with that of her father as Sobek/Petesuchos or as Tutu/
Tithöes, the offspring of Neith, Mother of Crocodiles.[30]

PORROMANRES, POIMANDRES,
AND AMENEMHAT III

Another potential link between Sobekneferu, her father, and the goddess
Neith is the "strange monument," found in 1953 at Kiman Faras on the site
of the former "Great Hall" of Shedet. Described by Labib Habachi in 1955[31]
and dating from the Ptolemaic age, it is made of hard limestone and shows
four figures on steplike pedestals that are so positioned as to allow for all
the heads to be at the same level (see fig. 18.6). Despite the carvings being
quite severely damaged, we can see that from right to left is a crocodile on a
divine perch (the god Suchos), a seated baboon (the sacred animal of Thoth-
Hermes), a recumbent hippopotamus (identified by Habachi as Taweret, but
more likely to be Neith), and, finally, a kneeling Egyptian male figure, his
hands resting on his thighs with his palms facing upward in a gesture of

prayer. He wears a kilt, as well as a *nemes*-headdress, and a false beard, which was a symbol of kingship.[32]

The monument's discovery on the site of Shedet's Great Hall has allowed the human figure to be identified as Amenemhat III in his capacity as a deified individual. It is in this guise that he appears in an early first century BCE hymn to Isis—found inscribed on a doorpost at the nearby temple of Medinet Madi and written by one "Isidorus"—where he is identified as "Porromanres, the Great, Deathless."[33]

Porromanres as a name is simply a corruption of Amenemhat III's throne name Nimaatre $(n(y)\text{-}m3\hat{t}\text{-}R^{\varsigma})$ prefixed with the Egyptian word for king, which is *per'aa,* the root of the word *pharaoh.* Porromanres is today considered to be the literary inspiration behind the Hermetic wisdom bringer Poimandres who, in a tract forming part of the *Corpus Hermeticum* titled *The Divine Pymander,* conveys the knowledge of Hermetica to Hermes Trismegistus, the Thrice Great Hermes.[34]

The Amenemhat III shown on the strange monument found at Kiman Faras would appear to have performed the role of intermediary between

Fig. 18.6. The strange monument (*left*) found in 1953 at Kiman Faras in Medinet el-Fayum and described Labib Habachi. On the right is a reconstruction that shows from right to left the crocodile god Sobek, the god Hermes-Thoth in the form of his sacred animal the baboon, a hippopotamus representing the goddess Neith as the mother of Sobek, and, left, Amenemhat III as the Greco-Roman deity named Porromanres, the apparent inspiration for the Poimandres of Hermetic tradition (from Habachi 1955, pl. XXI).

humanity and the gods shown by his side. As such he can be seen as Porromanres, an avatar of the god Thoth-Hermes, as well as the offspring of the crocodile god Suchos-Sobek, who is himself the offspring of Neith, seen in figure 18.6 in the form of a reclining hippopotamus.

THE CRATER OF POIMANDRES

Aside from featuring in the tract known as *The Divine Pymander,* Poimandres, whose name is usually interpreted as meaning "Shepherd of Men," also became a highly important figure in Greco-Egyptian alchemical tradition.[35] For instance, Zosmios of Panopolis, an alchemist from Panopolis (modern Akhmin in Upper Egypt) who flourished circa late third to early fourth century CE, writes to his "sister" Theosebeia asking her to turn away from the "false prophets," through whom the "daimones energise," and once she has purified herself hasten to Poimandres and baptize herself in the krater (a mixing bowl or cup).[36]

German philologist Richard Reitzenstein (1861–1931) saw compelling evidence in Zosimos's actions toward Theosebeia of the presence at Panopolis of what he called the Poimandres-Gemeinde, or Poimandres Community, which existed to preserve the wisdom of Poimandres. Its members included Zosimos and, seemingly, Theosebeia, who was seen as having turned away from the true gnosis to traffick with "daimones."[37]

In an influential book written in 1904 on the origins of Hermetic literature Reitzensten proposed that this Gnostic sect, perhaps connected to the Sethites, had been responsible for the construction of the purely Egyptian elements of the *Corpus Hermetica,* which he suspected dated back as far as the age of Amenhotep III (1388–1351/50 BCE), the father of Akhenaten.[38] Reitzenstein knew nothing of the modern theory that Poimandres was in fact Porromanres, the deified form of Amenemhat III. So it is this king, and not Amenhotep III, who now becomes the more likely candidate for the initial impetus behind the gradual evolution of the *Corpus Hermetica,* something begun when Sobekneferu made the decision to deify her father following his death.

Should all this be true then it helps support the idea that Dehdehet—the goddess mentioned in connection with Amenemhat III and Sobekneferu at the Labyrinth—is simply a form of Neith in her role as the mother of Sobek.

Plate I. Four views of the cylinder seal held by the British Museum displaying four out of five of the royal names of Sobekneferu. In order these show: A. The hieroglyphs for "beloved of Sobek of Shedet." B. The monarch's personal name, Sobekneferu, contained in a cartouche above which are the sage and bee signs. C. Sobekneferu's Nebty name, Sat-sekhem-tawy, and her Golden Horus name, Djedet-khau. D. The seal as seen from above.

Plate 2. The headless bust of Sobekneferu today housed at the Louvre Museum, Paris.

Plate 3. The Berlin bust of Sobekneferu, sadly now lost, with its nose restored (after Fechheimer [1914] 1920, pl. 58).

Plate 4. A small figurine of a royal woman held by the Metropolitan Museum of Art, New York, and thought to show Sobekneferu wearing the Heb Sed cloak. Courtesy of the Rogers Fund, 1965.

Plate 5. Sarcophagus of Neferuptah, Sobekneferu's sister, in the Egyptian Museum. Plates 5–8 used with permission of Meretseger Books.

Plate 6. The girdle and beaded skirt from the tomb of Neferuptah.

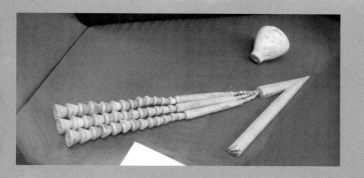

Plate 7 and 8. Flail and silver vase from the tomb of Neferuptah.

Plate 9. Wall panel from the temple of the snake goddess Renenutet at Medient Madi showing the original positions of, left, Amenemhat III; center, Neferuptah holding a sistrum; and, right, Renenutet. Photo by Ani Williams.

Plate 10. Amenemhat III or Amenemhat IV making offerings to the snake goddess Renenutet as seen at the Medinet Madi temple in the southern Fayum. The throne name of both kings appears above the figure's head. That, however, of Amenemhat IV has been chiseled out, something noted also at other locations in the temple. Photo by Ani Williams.

Plate 11. Artist Ahmad Sidky's impression of Neferuptah, Sobekneferu's sister, based on the wall panel showing her from the temple of Renenutet at Medinet Madi. (From Iskander and Farag, 1971.)

Plate 12. The so-called Black Pyramid of Amenemhat III at Dahshur.
Photo by Tekisch.

Plate 13. The pyramid of Amenemhat III at Hawara.

Plate 14. Section from the Abydos Canon or Abydos Table seen in the temple of Seti I at Abydos. From left to right we see the throne names of Twelfth Dynasty kings Senusret III, Amenemhat III, Amenemhat IV, and then that of Ahmose, the first king of the Eighteenth Dynasty. Sobekneferu's name, along with those of every ruler from the commencement of the Thirteenth Dynasty through the end of the Seventeenth Dynasty, is missing.

Plate 15. Red granite architrave at the site of the Labyrinth.

Plate 16. Site of the Labyrinth showing column drums from the Twelfth Dynasty complex at Hawara.

Plate 17. Statue of the crocodile god Sobek in the Ashmolean Museum, Oxford. Photo by Graeme Churchard.

Plate 18. Dimeh al Siba, the site of the former city of Soknopaiou Nesos, in the northern Fayum. Photo by Ani Williams.

Plate 19. The Qasr el-Sagha temple in the northern Fayum, with the Qasr el-Sagha rock fortress in the background. Photo by Ani Williams.

Plate 20. Polygonal blocks in one of the walls of the Qasr el-Sagha temple, resembling those seen in the Valley Temple of Khafre at Giza. Photo by Ani Williams.

Plate 21. Interior of the Qasr el-Sagha temple with its seven small shrines on the left-hand side. Photo by Ani Williams.

Plate 22. Carved doorframe of one of the seven shrines inside the Qasr el-Sagha temple. Photo by Ani Williams.

Plate 23. Carved doorframe of one of the chapels seen inside the temple of Renenutet at Medinet Madi. Its close similarity to those at the Qasr el-Sagha temple indicates that both buildings were probably built around the same time. Photo by Ani Williams.

Plate 24. Fossilized remains of an Eocene age whale at Widan el-Hitan in the northern Fayum. For the ancient Egyptians the presence of such remains might have reflected religious beliefs concerning both the process of death and the soul's journey through the underworld. Photo by Ahmed Mosaad.

Plate 25. Fragment of an ancient Egyptian mummy case acquired by Kenneth Grant in 1948 and later used by his Nu-Isis Lodge to make contact with the spirit of Sobekneferu. It was these magical workings that helped trigger the modern revival of interest in the female monarch. Used with permission of Starfire Publishing.

It explains also why Sobekneferu might have been interested in her since both she and her father would have been considered to embody the spirit of Sobek both in life and also in death.

Such ideas would have taken full form during the late Twelfth Dynasty and subsequently revived by the Saitic kings of the Twenty-sixth Dynasty, whom Herodotus implies in book II of *The Histories* were the builders of the Labyrinth.[39] Although what Herodotus says in connection with the Saitic kings can be shown to be incorrect (see chapter 27), what does seem clear is that they almost certainly revitalized the Fayum's cult of Sobek. These same ideas would be taken up in earnest during Greco-Roman times, when Amenemhat III would become a god in every sense of the word, and Sobekneferu's own achievements in connection with the cult of Sobek and her involvement in the construction of the Labyrinth had been absorbed into those of her father.

That the celebrated daughter of one of those Twenty-sixth Dynasty kings, Psamtik I, was herself named Nitocris, almost certainly helped popularize existing stories of a mythical queen of the same name who had thrived during some former age of Egyptian history.[40] That "queen," of course, was the original Nitocris, the one and only female ruler whom Herodotus is told had ruled Egypt. She, I am sure, can now be positively identified as Sobekneferu, and not as Hatshepsut or any other female ruler of Egypt.

SOBEKNEFERU AND THE KING LISTS

So how exactly did Sobekneferu's memory become so fragmented? She is included, for instance, in the Turin Canon, where she is recorded under the name Neferusobek.[41] She is present also in the Karnak Canon, created during the reign of the Eighteenth Dynasty king Thutmose III (1458/57–1429 BCE) and formerly located in the Akh-Menu Hall of the Temple of Amun-Re at Karnak (it can be seen today in the Louvre Museum, Paris). On this the monarch is included under her personal name of Sobekneferu.[42] She appears also within the Saqqara Canon (also known as the Saqqara Tablet) found at Saqqara in 1860 inside the tomb of a lector priest of Rameses II (1279–1213 BCE). Here the monarch is recorded under her throne name of Sobekkara.[43]

In contrast, Sobekneferu is ignored in the Abydos Canon or Abydos Table seen to this day in the mortuary temple of Seti I (1290–1279/78 BCE) at Abydos in southern Egypt.[44] Having listed all the kings up to and including Amenemhat IV the Abydos Table then skips forward to Ahmose I, the founder of the Eighteenth Dynasty who was responsible for the expulsion from Egypt of the Hyksos warlords around 1550 BCE (see plate 14). It could be argued that Sobekneferu and the kings of the Second Intermediate Period were ignored because they did not form part of Seti I's family lineage (the king himself is shown introducing the royal canon to his son, the future Rameses II). This is possible, although another way of interpreting Sobekneferu's absence from this king list is to consider the possibility that the Egyptian royal family during the reign of Seti I was trying to deliberately disassociate itself from any memory of those whom they saw as responsible for the tumultuous events surrounding the Second Intermediate Period. On this black list was any king seen as connected with the inception of the Hyksos invasion starting, it would seem, with Sobekneferu.

Complicating the matter, for future generations at least, was the fact that the priestly scribe or scribes responsible either for the Turin Canon or for one of its primary sources wrongly copied the name of a Sixth Dynasty king, changing it from Netjerkare, honoring the god Ra, to Neitiqerty, honoring the goddess Neith. This in turn led to Manetho identifying this king's reign with the rather nebulous figure of Nitocris, whose entries in the Epitome as recorded by Africanus and Eusebius are based more on the legendary figure of Rhodopis and her supposed association with the Third Pyramid at Giza than they are Herodotus's Nitocris.

The consequences of this simple scribal error in the Turin Canon, realized only recently by Kim Ryholt, caused Nitocris to be wrongly identified as the final ruler of the Sixth Dynasty, when really she was the last monarch of the Twelfth Dynasty. In summary then, there never was an Egyptian ruler named Nitocris who reigned in the Sixth Dynasty. The real Nitocris of legend was, I would argue, an abstract memory of the life and deeds of Sobekneferu, and with this thought we can now go on to examine more closely what Herodotus has to say about the vengeance of Nitocris following the death of her brother the king.

19

The Vengeance of Nitocris

Herodotus's account of the vengeance Nitocris exacted on those seen as responsible for the death of her brother, the king, may well have been based on some distant memory of what happened following the death of Amenemhat IV and the accession to the throne of his sister, Sobekneferu. If this is correct, then the Greek writer's narrative could contain kernels of information regarding what happened at the end of this close brother-sister relationship.

Let us go back to Herodotus's original narrative. Here he tells us that, "She, to avenge her brother (he was king of Egypt and was slain by his subjects, who then gave Nitocris the sovereignty) put many of the Egyptians to death by guile."[1] This is what he says took place following the king's death. If, however, Sobekneferu really was involved in some nationalistic plot to oust her brother—one that led to his untimely death—then why would she have wanted to punish those she saw as responsible for his murder? It just doesn't make sense.

What does make sense, however, is if she wanted to use the death of her brother as an excuse to crack down on any persons seen as a potential threat to her own reign. In other words, those people put to death were not necessarily the plot conspirators but political opponents whom she could accuse of being behind the murder. Doing this would also defer the blame away from her while at the same time allowing the true perpetuators of her brother's death to walk away unscathed. They, most likely, were those at the core of the forthcoming Thirteenth Dynasty, which, as we have seen, was nationalistic in nature and supported no doubt by the priesthood of Sobek.

In this knowledge Herodotus's words begin to make more sense, with Sobekneferu blaming her brother's death on his own closest allies, some of whom would surely have suspected that she was involved in the king's death. However, although this might have acted as a necessary fix in the short term, by taking this course of action Sobekneferu will have stirred up even further problems. It is a conclusion supported by the Greek writer's account of how after Nitocris had murdered those considered responsible for the death of her brother she "cast herself into a chamber full of hot ashes, thereby to escape vengeance."[2]

If Sobekneferu had simply put to death those genuinely responsible for her brother's murder, then why would she have afterward needed to "escape vengeance" herself? What this suggests is that her actions against her brother and his supporters triggered a revenge campaign initiated by those behind the gradually emerging Fourteenth Dynasty. This, as we know, was backed by the Canaanite elite in the north of the country and had been supported by Amenemhat IV before his death.

THE SPACIOUS UNDERGROUND CHAMBER

Returning to Herodotus's narrative, we find some intriguing statements regarding the manner that Nitocris is able to eliminate those seen as responsible for her brother's death, and these, as we shall see, will show us even more clearly that we are dealing with events that occurred toward the end of the Twelfth Dynasty. For instance, Nitocris is said to have, "built a spacious underground chamber; then, with the pretence of handselling it, but with far other intent in her mind, she gave a great feast, inviting to it those Egyptians whom she knew to have been most concerned in her brother's murder; and while they feasted she let the river in upon them by a great and secret channel."[3]

The idea of constructing "a spacious underground chamber" to exact her vengeance can be shown to refer to the Labyrinth at Hawara, at least half of which consisted of underground chambers. This is what Herodotus, elsewhere in book II of *The Histories,* has to say about this monumental structure:

Moreover they resolved to preserve the memory of their names by some joint enterprise; and having so resolved they made a labyrinth, a little way beyond the lake Moeris and near the place called the City of Crocodiles. I have myself seen it, and indeed no words can tell its wonders. . . . Though the pyramids were greater than words can tell, and each one of them a match for many great monuments built by Greeks, this maze surpasses even the pyramids. It has twelve roofed courts, with doors over against each other: six face the north and six the south, in two continuous lines, all within one outer wall. There are also double sets of chambers, three thousand altogether, fifteen hundred above *and the same number underground.* We ourselves viewed those that are above ground, and speak of what we have seen; *of the underground chambers we were only told;* the Egyptian wardens would by no means show them, these being, they said, the burial vaults of the kings who first built this labyrinth, and of the sacred crocodiles.[4] (Current author's emphasis.)

The Labyrinth, as we have seen, was commissioned by Amenemhat III and afterward completed by Sobekneferu. It therefore seems highly likely that the "spacious underground chamber" said to have been built by Nitocris is in fact an abstract memory of the Labyrinth's own "underground chambers." Moreover, the fact that the "spacious underground chamber" in the Nitocris story would have become the final resting place of those supposedly drowned when the waters overcame them seems to echo Herodotus's words about the Labyrinth's own "underground chambers" acting as "the burial vaults of the kings who first built this labyrinth."

THE GREAT AND SECRET CHANNEL

Even further confirmation of a connection between Herodotus's account of Nitocris and the Labyinth is determined by the fact that it was during the aformentioned "great feast" that the female sovereign let "the river upon them [that is, the murderers of 'her brother, the king'[5]] by a great and secret channel."[6] Is Nitocris's "secret channel" in fact an echo of claims made by various classical writers including Herodotus to the effect that King Moeris, that is Amenemhat III, dug the Bahr Yusef canal linking the Nile with the Fayum? This canal is, of course, natural, although it was almost certainly cleared during the reigns of one or more of the Twelfth Dynasty kings, reflecting Herodotus's statement about Nitocris enabling the River Nile to enter the "spacious underground chamber," presumably the Labyrinth, via "a great and secret channel."

The Hawara Channel, through which the Bahr Yusef canal flows, lies immediately to the south of the pyramid complex of Amenemhat III, which, of course, included the Labyrinth. The two were linked via a causeway, as much as 1.1 miles (1.75 kilometers) in length, which began in the vicinity of a valley temple that stood close to the canal's northern side, where today the village of Hawarat el-Maqta now stands. It then entered into the pyramid city via an opening in the southeastern corner of its terminus wall (see fig. 19.1).*

Clearly, Herodotus does not connect the "spacious underground chamber" and "great and secret channel" of the Nitocris story with his account elsewhere in book II of *The Histories* of, respectively, the glory of the Labyrinth and the digging of Lake Moeris with its connection to the Nile. In the knowledge, however, that the Greek writer starts to introduce the reader to the achievements of King Moeris/Amenemhat III directly after he tells the story of Nitocris supports the idea that the geographical setting in both cases is the Fayum.

In conclusion there seems every reason to suspect that the priests of Egypt conveyed to Herodotus a somewhat distorted and rather abstract account of the death of Amenemhat IV and the succession of Sobekneferu. It is a story that contains as a backdrop the memory of socioreligious activities that would take place at the Labyrinth as well as the hydrological engineering programs undertaken in the Fayum by the kings of the Twelfth Dynasty.

Having said this, I do not believe that Herodotus's account of Nitocris should be interpreted literally. Sobekneferu did not trick her adversaries into partaking in some great feast and then caused them to be drowned when water from a secret channel channeled from the nearby River Nile was allowed to fill the banquet hall (see fig. 19.2 on page 176)! What I *do* consider possible is that this narrative is a garbled account of very real events surrounding the death of Amenemhat IV and the subsequent tur-

---

*Having said this, since the causeway has not properly been explored, its full extent and relationship to the pyramid complex's valley temple must remain a matter of conjecture at this time.

Fig. 19.1. Map of Hawara showing the position of the Labyrinth and pyramid of Amenemhat III along with the suspected course of the complex's causeway to the Bahr Yusef canal in the south. Solid lines represent the known or suspected route of the causeway with broken lines signifying its hypothetical course.

moil following Sobekneferu's succession to the throne. Whether or not she would have been directly involved in her brother's death or whether this was left up to others will probably never be known. What does seem certain, however, is that his death is unlikely to have occurred so easily *without* her direct involvement.

Fig. 19.2. "The Vengeance of Nitocris" by Italian artist
Fortunino Matania (1881–1963). It was done to accompany the publication of a
story of the same name by American playwright and screenwriter
Tennessee Williams (1911–1983) based on Herodotus's account of Nitocris.
It was published in the August 1933 issue of the magazine
Britannia and Eve (pages 41–43).

REGICIDE OR FRATRICIDE?

To accuse Egypt's first female ruler of being complicit in regicide, that is the killing of a dynastic rival, and even of fratricide, the killing of one's brother, might seem like the stuff of historical novels. This is understandable. It should be pointed out, however, that Egyptologists have long attempted to fit the events described by Herodotus concerning the vengeance of Nitocris into some kind of historical context. This, for instance, is what Ancient Egypt Online has to say about the subject:

> Nitocris was the beautiful and virtuous wife and sister of King Metesouphis II (Merenre II), an Old Kingdom monarch who had ascended to the throne at the end of the Sixth Dynasty but who had been savagely murdered by his subjects soon afterwards. Nitocris then became

the sole ruler of Ancient Egypt and determined to avenge the death of her beloved husband-brother.[7]

So seeing Herodotus's account of Nitocris as reflecting real historical events should not be dismissed as ridiculous even if they might relate, not to the end of the Sixth Dynasty as has always been assumed, but to another time frame altogether. From the evidence presented within these pages that time frame would appear to have been the close of the Twelfth Dynasty.

It should also be pointed out that examples of regicide and attempted regicide are recorded in connection with at least two kings of the Twelfth Dynasty. For instance, Manetho in the Epitome of Africanus tells us that the second king of the Twelfth Dynasty, named as "Ammanemes," ruled for 38 years and was then "murdered by his own eunuchs."[8]

Which king this refers to, whether it be Amenemhat I, the founder of the dynasty, or Amenemhat II, who was its third ruler, is unclear, and whether or not this murderous act really took place goes unrecorded in contemporary accounts. What this story does imply, however, is that kings of the Middle Kingdom could become the subject of plots to kill them, in this case through the intervention of eunuchs.

Traditionally eunuchs would have been among the only nonroyal individuals allowed direct access to a ruling monarch giving them the perfect opportunity to commit murder if they chose to do so. That eunuchs formed an important function in the royal courts of ancient Egypt is not in doubt,[9] although what their influence might have been during the Middle Kingdom is unclear.

In addition to the murder of Ammanemes, we have an apparent example of attempted fratricide during Egypt's Twelfth Dynasty. The story in question comes from book II of The Histories by Herodotus and relates to the king named Sesostris, that is Senusret III, who is said to have conquered many foreign nations. The Greek writer informs his reader that on Sesostris's return to Egypt after many successful military campaigns he reached "Daphnae of Pelusium," this being a fortress town situated in the northeastern part of the country. While there, we are told, "his brother, to whom he had given Egypt in charge, invited him and his sons to a banquet and then piled wood round the house and set it on fire. When Sesostris was aware of this, he took counsel at once with his wife, whom (it was said) he was bringing with him; and she counselled him to lay two of his six sons on the fire and to make a bridge over the burning whereby they might pass over the bodies of the two and escape. This Sesostris did; two of his sons were thus burnt, but the rest were saved alive with their father."[10]

Again we cannot say whether this incident really occurred, although the fact that Senusret III was probably Amenemhat III's father, and therefore the grandfather of Sobekneferu, brings the concept of regicide, and indeed fratricide, dangerously close to the reigns both of Amenemhat IV and his sister. Thus from these accounts alone we can see that there is every reason to suspect murder and intrigue being involved with the monarchs of the Twelfth Dynasty, just as it was among the Ptolemaic kings of Egypt some 1,500 years later.[11]

The final part of Herodotus's narrative regarding the vengeance of Nitocris is highly enigmatic and far-reaching in its implications, for he tells us, "This was all that the priests told of her, save that also when she had done this she cast herself into a chamber full of hot ashes, thereby to escape vengeance."[12] If this in any way alludes to the final fate of Sobekneferu then what can we make of Herodotus's words? Did she really commit suicide at the end of her nearly four-year reign? It is this shocking prospect that we address next.

20

The Death of Sobekneferu

Sobekneferu's drastic measures to avoid the fragmentation of Egyptian society into two separate factions—one surrounding the nationalistic views of the embryonic Thirteenth Dynasty and the other supporting the more liberal policies of her brother Amenemhat IV—very likely led to her downfall and eventual death. As we have seen, Sobekneferu's intended political and economic reforms probably involved a clampdown on the growing influence of the western Asiatic population in the north of the country—something that is unlikely to have gone down well in certain quarters of Egyptian society.

Under such circumstances it therefore seems plausible that Sobekneferu was given an ultimatum by her adversaries—either stop what you are doing or face death. Unwilling to bend to their demands and be seen as weak in the minds of her subjects, perhaps it was death that she finally chose, although not death at the hands of her opponents but death by her own chosen means. This is certainly what Herodotus implies when he tells us that after Nitocris had disposed of her brother's murderers "she cast herself into a chamber full of hot ashes, thereby to escape vengeance."[1] If Sobekeneferu really was the historical Nitocris then this clearly implies that Egypt's first female ruler ended her own life.

CLEOPATRA'S DEATH BY SNAKE

Is it possible then that Sobekneferu took the same course as Cleopatra VII, Egypt's last female ruler who—unwilling to be submitted to disgrace and humiliation at the hands of Octavian (the future Augustus Caesar) following the death of her lover, the Roman politician and general Mark Antony—committed suicide? This was how the first century CE Greek biographer Plutarch described the scene surrounding Cleopatra's tragic death in 30 BCE:

> Cleopatra sent to Caesar [that is, Octavian] a letter which she had written and sealed; and, putting everybody out of the monument but her two women, she shut the doors. Caesar, opening her letter, and finding pathetic prayers and entreaties that she might be buried in the same tomb with Antony, soon guessed what was doing. At first he was going himself in all haste, but, changing his mind, he sent others to see. The thing had been quickly done. The messengers came at full speed, and found the guards apprehensive of nothing; but on opening the doors, they saw her stone-dead, lying upon a bed of gold, set out in all her royal ornaments. Iras, one of her women, lay dying at her feet, and Charmion, just ready to fall, scarce able to hold up her head, was adjusting her mistress's diadem. And when one that came in said angrily, "Was this well done of your lady, Charmion?" "Extremely well," she answered, "and as became the descendant of so many kings"; and as she said this, she fell down dead by the bedside.[2]

According to the classical writers Cleopatra either allowed a snake, an asp in the accounts, to administer the venom that killed her, or she was able to poison herself in some other manner. Plutarch records that two slight pricks on her arm were afterward noted and that maybe the poison had been hidden in a hollow comb.[3] If a snake *had* been involved in Cleopatra's death then it was presumably smuggled into her chamber concealed in a basket of flowers or figs, or perhaps in a water jar (see fig. 20.1).[4] However, no snake was ever found, so her means of committing suicide remains unclear. It has been suggested that the introduction of a venomous snake into the story of Cleopatra's death was deliberate, for since a snake carries sexual connotations it further emphasized the Roman opinion that the queen was little more than a "foreign seductress."[5] Whether or not this was the case is not important. There is, however, good reason to suspect that accounts of her death contain some highly symbolic elements.

Fig. 20.1. Steel engraving by John Sartain (1808–1897) of Caesar Augustus's now lost encaustic painting of Cleopatra VII showing her self-induced death through being bitten by an asp (Sartain 1885, frontispiece). The queen wears around her neck the knot of Isis showing her devotion to the goddess. The painting was found in 1818 within the ruins of Hadrian's Villa at Sorrento near Naples, Italy.

The fact that Cleopatra saw herself as an incarnation of Isis,[6] the Egyptian goddess of magic and medicine, could imply that the snake blamed for causing her death was a metaphor for her self-administration of the poison that killed her. This seems confirmed in the knowledge that in one ancient Egyptian legend Isis manufactures a snake out of dust, which is held together by spittle taken from the sun god Ra. She then makes the serpent bite the god, but because the creature has been made from his spittle he is unable to purge the poison from his body.

Realizing he is about to die, Ra asks Isis to use her magical powers to heal him. In return she says she will only do so if he reveals his secret name, something that Ra reluctantly does, saving his life.[7] This powerful story exemplifies Isis's magical powers as well as her ability to be able to administer poisons through the use of a snake. Snakes are, of course, primary symbols both of poison and of medicine, an association that probably began in places like Egypt many thousands of years ago and continues to this day with the snake being a universal symbol of the medical profession.

SECRETS OF THE GODS

So if Cleopatra was able to escape a terrible fate at the hands of Octavian by administering a poison into her body, then could Sobekneferu have departed this world in a similar fashion? Could this be what Herodotus is trying to tell us when he says that Nitocris "cast herself into a chamber full of hot ashes, thereby to escape vengeance"? If so, then how can a female ruler of Egypt commit suicide by casting herself into "a chamber full of hot ashes," or "embers" as it is written in some translations of the original Greek text?[8] Clearly, there must be either symbolic or highly abstract elements preserved in this account.

One possible interpretation of what Herodotus relates is that the "chamber" in question was a ritual room where smoke produced through the burning of incense on fire embers was able to create an intoxicating environment—one designed to induce altered states of consciousness. Chambers of this sort would have been used for the purposes of entering otherworldly realms to commune with spirit intelligences considered to inhabit such places.

In Greek Hellenistic tradition ritual chambers of this kind were known as *aduta* or *adyta,* the plural of *adyton* (Greek: Ἄδυτον and Latin *adytum*), a term generally interpreted as meaning "crypts" or a place "not to be entered."[9] They were usually "the hidden and secret parts of the temple,"[10] or its "innermost chambers."[11] Greek biographer Diogenes Laertius (fl. third century CE) records that the Greek philosopher Pythagoras descended "into aduta ['crypts'] while in Egypt," where he "learned the secrets of the gods."[12] Of course, aduta need not be underground—they can simply be a room or chamber set aside for communication either with the gods or with great ancestors. Such places are likely to have existed not only in Egyptian temples, but also in royal palaces.

INTOXICATING INCENSES

In the opinion of the author a ritual chamber of this kind is probably being alluded to in Herodotus's statement about the manner in which Nitocris is able to commit suicide, with the "hot ashes" or "embers" responsible for the female sovereign's death being a reference to intoxicating incenses. Incenses of this kind could well have featured in the rituals that took place in Egyptian aduta. Arguably the most famous adyton in classical tradition was the one located within the temple of Apollo at Delphi in Greece. For several centuries or more prophetesses who bore the title Oracle or Pythia made pronunciations while sitting on a tripod seat positioned above a natural vent that allowed the chamber to become filled with gases rising up from the Earth. These gases or fumes are thought to have created an intoxicating effect that enabled the prophetess to communicate with Apollo in his role as god of prophecy.

POISONS IN EGYPT

What incenses or substances might have served a similar function in the aduta of ancient Egypt is unclear. Possibly they included psychotropic—that is, psychoactive or hallucination-inducing—plants such as the opium poppy (*Papaver somniferum*), henbane (*Hyoscyamus muticus*), and hellebore (*Hellebori nigri rhizoma*), all of which were available in Egypt during dynastic times.[13] Moreover, opium, henbane, hellebore, along with another highly toxic plant named hemlock (*Conium maculatum*), are all listed as medicines in a Greco-Egyptian papyrus of the first century CE (Oxyrhynchus Papyri, No. 1088), confirming their use in ancient Egypt.[14]

One other psychotropic plant that would appear to have been known to the dynastic Egyptians was datura (*Datura stramonium*), or to give it its more common name, thorn apple. Datura grows wild in Egypt, and according to British Egyptologist Alfred Lucas (1867–1945) in his article "Poisons in Ancient Egypt" (1938) it was present in the country "from very early times."[15] Medieval Arab sources speak about the presence of the datura plant in Egypt and the Levant, with an account from 1248 written by the Andalusian botanist and pharmacologist Ibn al-Baytār (1197–1248 CE) affirming that datura was being cultivated in the fields near the port of Damietta on Egypt's Mediterranean coast.[16]

More pertinent to this current debate, however, is the fact that in Nubia, modern Sudan in northeastern Africa, smoke from datura leaves was used to relieve asthma and pulmonary problems.[17] This shows how toxins from the datura plant can be very easily absorbed into the lungs simply through exposure to its smoke (it can also, of course, be absorbed into the body through the use of smoking paraphernalia). Since, however, the ingestion of large quantities of datura can be lethal,[18] there is every reason to assume that intense amounts of smoke from toxic substances of this kind can very easily induce not only deathlike states, but also death itself.

Since all these plants can be highly dangerous in nature their use would have been closely monitored to make sure the right dosage was administered to create the desired effects safely and without any adverse effects. If, however, these safety measures were ignored, whether accidentally or on purpose, then death could very easily have followed.

RITUAL DEATH

Support for the idea that psychotropic plants of the type outlined above were available for use in ancient Egypt comes from new findings regarding the means by which Cleopatra was able to exit this world. In 2010 it was announced that Christoph Schaefer, a professor of ancient history at Trier University, Germany, was challenging the common, centuries-old belief that Cleopatra had committed suicide by allowing an asp to administer its fatal poison. Schaefer, working alongside German toxicologist Dietrich Mebs, was able to determine through an examination of surviving accounts of the queen's death that she had killed herself through the ingestion of hemlock mixed with wolfsbane and opium.[19] All of these plants can be classed as psychoactive in nature.[20] Each would have been able to bring about an altered state of consciousness whereby entry into a perceived spirit world would have become relatively easy, especially for the initiate.

Is this what Cleopatra had been trying to achieve—entry into the hereafter through some form of ritual death brought about by the ingestion of psychotropic plants? Was this done under the guidance and protection of Isis, the goddess of magic and medicine, who was thought to have the ability both to administer poisons and, where necessary, to provide their antidotes?

MORS VOLUNTARIA AND THE CULT OF ISIS

It is interesting to note that voluntary death was an important aspect of the cult of Isis, with initiates willingly forgoing their mortal lives during a ritual in which the goddess herself was seen to be in attendance. Such ritual deaths in the name of Isis were apparently acted out in a third-century CE religious shrine at Antioch, modern Antakya, in Turkey, known as the House of the Mysteries of Isis.[21] A surviving mosaic from the site, uncovered by a team from Princeton University,[22] shows a male initiate undergoing *Mors voluntaria,* a Latin term meaning "voluntary death." He is shown being led by the god Hermes to his "death," whether actual or symbolic, as the goddess Isis gestures him forward.

The Roman historian Florus (second century CE), in his work *Epitome of Roman History,* provides an account of Cleopatra's demise following the death of Antony. He tells us that she repaired to a mausoleum and, "There, having put on the elaborate raiment by the side of her beloved Antonius in a coffin filled with rich perfumes, and applying serpents to her veins thus passed into death as into a sleep."[23] Although these words were written as much as a century after Cleopatra's death there is a sense in them of the queen effecting her entry into the afterlife through a very specific process involving a drug induced sleep. Is there any reason why we should not consider the possibility that Sobekneferu, Egypt's first female ruler, did not exit this world in a similar manner? Did she also enter into a voluntary ritual death through the ingestion and/or inhalation of psychoactive and highly toxic substances? If so, then where and how might this have happened?

A CHAMBER FULL OF HOT ASHES

Herodotus tells us that Nitocris's final act was to throw herself in "a chamber full of hot ashes." If this does refer to an adyton or ritual room reserved for use exclusively by Sobekneferu then the chances are it was located in the royal palace adjoining the temple of Sobek at Shedet in the Fayum. Not only was this just a short distance away both from the Labyrinth and from the pyramid complex of her father at Hawara, but the entire palace presumably also functioned as a spiritual retreat connected with activities associated with the cult of Sobek. Sobekneferu would presumably have spent her time at this palace when not on official duties at the capital Itj-tawy, located some 28 miles (45 kilometers) to the northeast.

So was this how Sobekneferu ended her life, not by simply committing suicide, but by purposely entering into a kind of voluntary ritual death in the same manner that Cleopatra would herself choose to exit this world some 1,800 years later? Is this how the reign of Egypt's first female ruler

Fig. 20.2. Artist Russell M. Hossain's impression of Sobekneferu's ritual death, which, if correct, probably occurred at the royal palace attached to the temple of Sobek at Shedet in the Fayum.

ended—with a self-induced death caused by the ingestion of a cocktail of psychoactive substances, such as opium and datura? (See fig. 20.2 for artist Russell M. Hossain's impression of Sobekneferu's suspected death in a manner similar to that of Cleopatra.)

BEYOND SOBEKNEFERU'S REIGN

We can never be sure that this is exactly what did happen to the monarch, although there seems every indication that her reign ended abruptly. Indeed, Stefania Pignattari speaks of Sobekneferu's "sudden death" following a tangible crisis during her reign.[24] She goes on to add that without anyone to succeed her from her own dynasty the north was able to rise up and seize power.[25]

Here Pignattari is referring to the Canaanite-inspired Fourteenth Dynasty, which is thought to have run parallel with the nationalistically driven Thirteenth Dynasty ruling from Itj-Tawy. This rivaling dynastic power struggle went hand in hand with the steady rise in influence of the Delta's western Asiatic population, which Pignattari says was now requiring most of the country's resources simply to deal with the problem. As she also makes clear, both during Sobekneferu's reign and during the incoming Thirteenth Dynasty there were no mining operations in the Sinai and no private stelae being erected.[26]

All this coincided with a growing anxiety that was slowly increasing throughout the country. Some of this anxiety was due to a decrease in the Nile floods, something recorded by graffiti present on rocks located above the present level of the river below the fortress of Kumma (Semna East), close to Egypt's border with Nubia.[27] The implications of this disconcerting situation would have been disastrous for cultivation in the Nile Valley since the floodwaters would not have been sufficient to fully irrigate the fields. It has also been suggested that there was a famine at the end of Twelfth Dynasty, which accelerated still further Canaanite settlement in northern Egypt, preparing the grounds for the arrival en masse of the Hyksos sometime around 1700 BCE.[28] Clearly, there were major problems in Egypt during the age of Sobekneferu, and these must have impacted on the manner and timing of her death.

Egyptologist Nicolas Grimal, as already noted, suspected that the monarch's reign ended in violence,[29] while Alan Gardiner wrote that her period of rule was "so abnormal" it was a situation that by its nature contained the "seed of disaster."[30] However, there are no hints from any source that Sobekneferu's reign ended in bloodshed. No classical writer, for instance, talks in terms of a female ruler fitting the monarch's description being assassinated. All we have is Herodotus's account of Nitocris's suicide, which if now transferable to Sobekneferu tells us she took her own life when it became obvious that there was no longer any route forward for her personally. Somebody was coming for her, as Herodotus says of Nitocris, and just like Cleopatra, Sobekneferu took the option of deciding her own fate. Not only was this to avoid humiliation as well as potential incarceration and death, but it was also no doubt to ensure the future destiny of the country, while at the same time ensuring her own safe passage into the afterlife.

None of this implies that Sobekneferu's brief but somewhat tumultuous reign was a disaster. If she saw ruling the kingdom as her divine birthright then she would have had no other option than to eliminate any perceived opponents to achieve her goals. As the first woman to wear the double crown of Upper and Lower Egypt, restoring ma'at, "truth," "justice," and "cosmic order," to the Two Lands would have been her primary concern. Everything else would have come second.

    What fate befell Sobekneferu's body and where it might have been buried is unclear. These are questions that will have some answers before the end of this book. More important right now is to better understand who Sobekneferu's opponents were and how they might have been able to force her into committing an act of ritual death.

21

Enemies of Sobekneferu

Despite the country's western Asiatic population being at the center of Egypt's political struggles during the reign of Sobekneferu it is unlikely to have contributed directly to her death. Sobekneferu's policies might well have affected its future influence in the country, and the death of her brother and the elimination of his allies might not have been favorably received by its leaders, but they were not the monarch's enemies as we shall see.

So if the country's western Asiatic population was *not* Sobekneferu's enemy, then who was? The obvious answer is high-ranking court officials who had previously been loyal both to her father Amenemhat III and, after his death, to his successor, Amenemhat IV. The chances are they will have attempted to persuade her to change her policies back to those in place during the reign of her brother, something she would not have been willing to do believing that the future destiny of the country was in her hands, and in her hands alone. These same court officials would also, most assuredly, have been responsible for conveying messages between the monarch and any outside factions that had previously been loyal to her brother.

So who exactly were these outside factions if they did not belong to the country's western Asiatic population? Almost certainly they were connected to one or more of the country's powerful priesthoods. Clearly, this would not have been the priesthood of Sobek of Shedet, which remained loyal not only to Sobekneferu but also to the kings of the incoming Thirteenth Dynasty. Plus, of course, Sobekneferu, as the country's ruler, was their living patron, so they are extremely unlikely to have plotted against her.

One possible candidate worth considering is the priesthood of Amun at Thebes in the southern part of the country. During Sobekneferu's reign they had lost a certain amount of power and influence to the priesthood of Sobek, which during the reign of Sobekneferu had risen to become the country's state religion (see chapter 28). Having said this, the involvement of the priests of Amun in this affair is basically a nonstarter. The Thirteenth Dynasty, which as we know was loyal to the memory of Sobekneferu, reestablished a close bond with the cult of Amun and even proclaimed Thebes as its principal seat of power after Itj-tawy. It thus seems unlikely that its priests were involved in the downfall of Sobekneferu.

The same might be said of the priests of Osiris at Abydos, where some Twelfth Dynasty kings built cenotaphs to complement their pyramids in the north of the country. The fact that Sobek's principal animistic form, the crocodile, was a vehicle also of Seth, the god of chaos and disorder who murdered his brother Osiris, is something that would not have endured the Osiris priesthood to that of Sobek. This is true, and it is a matter we return to in chapter 36; however, this alone would not have been enough for the priests of Abydos to have wanted Sobekneferu dead.

THE PRIESTS OF HELIOPOLIS

There is only one other major priesthood that might have played a crucial role in the fall of Sobekneferu and this was the one at Heliopolis, home of the sun god Ra and also of the creator god Atum. As we saw in chapter 14 Atum had seemingly become Amenemhat IV's personal deity,[1] as is evidenced, for instance, from the inscription in the name of the god seen on the sphinx found in Beirut, Lebanon.

This strong interest in the cult of Atum would have ensured that the priests of Heliopolis were loyal to Amenemhat IV and his chief supporters, even after the king's death. They would have supported his social and economic policies, which, as we have seen, included both the establishment of a new kingdom in the Sinai region and, we must assume, the rise of Egypt's Canaanite-inspired Fourteenth Dynasty.

If so, then there would have been every reason for the Heliopolitan priesthood to have rejected the nationalistic policies of Sobekneferu and even to have actively plotted her downfall. This would have been especially so if they had come to realize that she was almost certainly behind the death of her brother and the elimination of his allies, who might well have included court officials directly in league with the priests of Heliopolis.

To better understand what might have been going on at Heliopolis toward the end of the Twelfth Dynasty, and how it fits into the gradually emerging story behind the fall of Sobekneferu, it will be necessary to explore age-old traditions that might have lingered in the Fayum until medieval times. I speak here of the rich body of source material that emerged in Egypt following the Arab invasion of the mid-seventh century CE, which has as its root stories from the Pentateuch, the first five books of the Hebrew Bible, as well as from the Holy Koran. These refer to the presence in Egypt of Joseph, the son of Jacob and great-grandson of Abraham, the great ancestor of the Israelite people.

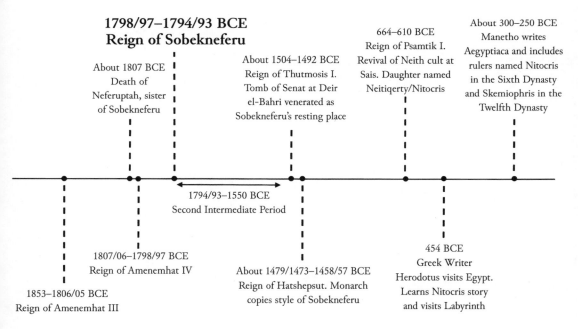

Fig. 21.1. Timeline of events associated with the life and subsequent cult of Sobekneferu from the Twelfth Dynasty through to the Ptolemaic period.

PART 5

FAITH

22

Joseph in Egypt

Before attempting any foray into Old Testament tradition it should be made clear that it is not the purpose of this book to attempt to confirm the historical validity of characters contained in the Hebrew Bible, or indeed those of the Holy Koran, which carries similar stories. Our interests lie principally in what medieval Arab-Islamic historians say regarding Joseph's alleged hydrological activities in Egypt's Fayum region and how they might relate to major engineering projects known to have taken place there during Egypt's Twelfth Dynasty. These, as we have already established, are accredited in classical sources to an Egyptian king named Moeris, who can be identified as Sobekneferu's father Amenemhat III (although the clearing of the Hawara Channel and other land reclamation projects had probably begun as early as the reign of Amenemhat I, the founder of the Twelfth Dynasty).[1]

If therefore it can be shown that Arab-Islamic accounts relating to Joseph's presence in Egypt are indeed a reflection of the activities surrounding the country's western Asiatic population during the age of Amenemhat III and his contemporaries, then they could offer tantalizing clues regarding the political, religious, and socioeconomic situation prevalent in Egypt at this time.

JOSEPH IN THE FAYUM

One of the most important medieval Arab works featuring Joseph's alleged activities in the Fayum is the *Kitāb al-ʿAdjāʾib al-kabīr* ("The Great Book of Marvels").[2] It is attributed to the noted littérateur Ibrāhīm Ibn Wasīf Shāh, known also as al-Wasīfī, who thrived no later than 1200 CE.[3] The book's text, apparently derived from earlier source material, talks about Joseph's time in Egypt, this being after he has successfully interpreted prophetic dreams experienced by the ruling monarch concerning an imminent seven-year drought that would otherwise have plunged the country into a severe famine. For his role in allowing Egypt to avoid this economic and humanitarian disaster, Pharaoh (the name given to the ruling king in the Hebrew Bible) elevates Joseph to a position of great power in the royal court, this being the story as told in chapter 41 of the book of Genesis.[4]

The account as given in the *Kitāb al-ʿAdjāʾib al-kabīr* picks up the biblical narrative after the pharaoh in question, named as Nahrāush, has "reigned 120 years," at which time, we are told, "Joseph created the Fayum."[5] The author speaks of how the Egyptians saw the king as growing too old to rule and so with his intelligence fading he is put "to the test," something that Joseph is asked to do on his behalf.[6] The aging monarch then speaks to the prophet saying, "I have given this land to my daughter; it is only an overflow for the waters; put it in order for her."[7] This is a reference to Egypt's Fayum depression prior to it being transformed into a fertile oasis and place of residence for the royal family (the "daughter" alluded to in the account will be discussed in chapter 24).

Thereafter, the narrative relates, Joseph embarked on various engineering projects, whereby he "managed to remove the waters, had the mud removed, dug the Menha and built Allahūn." It is said also that he "divided the waters and separated them; and all this in four months. Everyone was astonished at his skill. He was, it is said, the first in Egypt who practiced the art of engineering."[8]

Menha, or al-Manhi, is the name given to one of the principal canals in the Fayum region. The name itself is very possibly a corruption of the ancient Egyptian Mr-wr (*mi-wer*), which refers both to a town of this name in the vicinity of Lake Moeris and the Bahr Yusef, or Waterway of Joseph, a tributary of the Nile connecting the river with the Fayum. Most likely the town of this name was located at Kom Medinet Ghurab or Gurob opposite El-Lahun.[9] The lake itself (Egyptian *hone*) was called the "lake of Mi-wer,"[10] showing its relationship to the canal, while the Fayum as a whole was referred to by the ancient Egyptians as Ta-She, meaning "land of the lake."[11]

El-Lahun, as we saw in chapter 5, marks the site of a Twelfth

Dynasty town and necropolis that included the pyramid complex of Senurset II. Known as Re-hone it was located on the western edge of the Nile Valley,[12] close to where the Bahr Yusef enters the Fayum depression via the Hawara Channel.

That this Arab-Islamic account preserves some memory of the hydrological projects undertaken by one or more of the kings of the Twelfth Dynasty seems inescapable.

If all this is correct then who exactly is the king named in the *Kitāb al-ʿAdjāʾib al-kabīr* as Nahrāūsh, who ruled Egypt at the time of Joseph? No obvious clues are given, although he is probably the same as the pharaoh named al-Walid, or indeed his son Raiyan ibn al-Walid, who in Islamic tradition is said to have ruled Egypt during the age of Joseph.[13] He can be pretty firmly identified as Amenemhat III.[14] (The term *raiyan* or *raijan* is the term used in Arab-Islamic literature for the ruling king or pharaoh.)

CHRISTIAN COPTIC ROOTS

British archaeologist Claire J. Malleson has made a detailed study of the various Arab-Islamic accounts that feature the story of Joseph's presence in the Fayum. She writes that the earliest known source of this stratum of material comes from the writings of the Arab Egyptian historian Ibn 'Abd al-Hakam, who lived in the ninth century CE.[15] More significant, she says, is that some of it clearly derives from earlier Coptic Christian sources. Indeed, she points out that in a tenth century CE Arab work titled *Akhbar al-zaman* ("Chronicles of Time"), the author of which is disputed, it states that the Coptic name of the king that ruled during the life of Joseph was Nehrâous,[16] clearly a variation of the name Nahrāūsh. If so, then the likely source of this information was probably one of the monasteries existing in the Fayum prior to the Arab Conquest of Egypt in the mid-seventh century CE.[17]

Another important source providing useful information regarding Joseph's presence in the Fayum is a work by Murtadā ibn al-'Afīf, an Arab writer born 1154/1155 CE, perhaps in Jerusalem. He is known to have studied at Alexandria, Damascus, and Cairo, where he eventually died in 1237.[18] His book, *The Prodigies of Egypt* or *The Egyptian History,* was published in English in 1672.[19] It contains a plethora of archaic folktales regarding matters such as the antediluvian origin of the Great Pyramid and the conditions prevalent in Egypt at the time of the Great Flood. Also included are several brief accounts regarding Joseph's engineering activities in the Fayum.

These stories introduce the prophet by stating that when the Egyptian people saw that Joseph was becoming too old to make good decisions they asked the ruling monarch to step in and challenge him in some manner ("[Oh] Great King, Ioseph is now grown very ancient, his knowledge is diminished, his beauty is decay'd, his Judgment is impaired, and his Wisdom is departed from him"[20]). This is in contrast to the *Kitāb al-ʿAdjāʾib al-kabīr* where it is the king's diminishing condition that is being questioned and not that of Joseph as is the case with *The Prodigies of Egypt*.

Initially, the king objects to the remonstrations of his subjects and there, for a while, the matter rests. After two years, however, of being constantly subjected to the protests of his people the king finally decides to put Joseph to the test. His challenge will involve a place known as Alphiom,[21] a close approximation of the Coptic name for the Fayum, which is Phiom or Phiōm. This in turn derives most probably from the Ancient Egyptian *p3-ym* (Pa-yum in Coptic)[22] meaning "the Sea," a reference no doubt to Lake Moeris. Indeed, the Egyptian *ym* meaning "sea" in this instance probably derives from the Hebrew ים (*yam*), which also means "sea" as in ים סוף (*yam suph*), "the Bitter Sea," the Hebrew name given in the Bible for the Red Sea.[23]

According to *The Prodigies of Egypt* Alphiom at this time was called Geouna, adding that it was little more than "a Common Sewer to the Upper Egypt, and a passage for the water."[24] Joseph's designated task is to, "turn the water of Geouna, and force it thence, that you may have a new Province, and a new revenue."[25]

So the king, named only as "the Raijan," commands Joseph, "to cause three Chanels to be made; one Chanel coming out of High Egypt, from such a place to such a place; an Eastern Chanel, from such a place to such a place; and a Western Chanel."[26] We are thereafter told:

Ioseph got men together to carry on this work, and caused the Chanel of Manhi [this is the al-Menha or al-Manhi canal mentioned in the *Kitāb al-ʿAdjāʾib al-kabīr,* which can be identified with the Bahr Yusef] to be digg'd, from the Upper part of Asmounine to Lahon, which he caused also to be digged afterwards. Then he caused the Chanel of Alphiom to be digged. . . . That done, he got Labourers to cut down all the Reeds and

Tamarisk that was in it, and carry it away, and then the Nile began to flow into it, and Geouna became pure and clean ground.[27]

Once again this account seems to describe the hydrological works undertaken in the Fayum by one or more Twelfth Dynasty pharaohs. This includes the clearing of the Bahr Yusef waterway from its entrance at El-Lahun through the entire length of the Hawara Channel until it reached Lake Moeris (see fig. 22.1). What is more, these Arab accounts adequately match the alleged achievements of King Moeris as offered by the classical writers such as Herodotus,[28] Pliny,* as well as the first-century BCE Greek historian Diodorus Siculus.[29]

Even though the Bahr Yusef waterway is simply a natural extension of the Nile River there seems little doubt that King Moeris's achievements are those undertaken for the most part by Amenemhat III, who would seem to have been the true mastermind responsible for various land reclamation and irrigation projects in the region, including perhaps the clearing of the Hawara Channel. As Bonnie M. Sampsell in *A Traveler's Guide to the Geology of Egypt* explains, "He [Amenemhat III] had the . . . [Hawara Channel] widened and deepened and fitted with sluice gates. Water amounting to up to 10 percent of the flood discharge was admitted to the depression during peak flood and returned to the Nile (less that which had evaporated) after the crest of the flood had passed."[30]

These same feats of engineering came to be accredited to Joseph, a Hebrew slave who in the Hebrew Bible is said to have become "ruler over all the land of Egypt."[31] That Semitic-speaking peoples were present in the Fayum at this time, engaged in monumental engineering programs under the command of the reigning king, is not in question. As John van Seters writes: "It was undoubtedly from the Eastern Delta that Amenemhat III drew large bands of workmen for his projects in the Fayum."[32] Van Seters is referring to the Nile Delta's western Asiatic population, who, as we have seen, achieved positions of authority during the reign of Amenemhat III. Did this include the supervision of Semitic-speaking work gangs employed

---

*Pliny 1855, bk. XXXVI, 16. Although Pliny mentions the lake of "Mœris" being an "excavated . . . immense artificial piece of water," he doesn't name the king responsible for this engineering feat. That said, he is clearly quoting secondhand from an earlier source who does name Moeris as the lake's creator. Most obviously this was Herodotus.

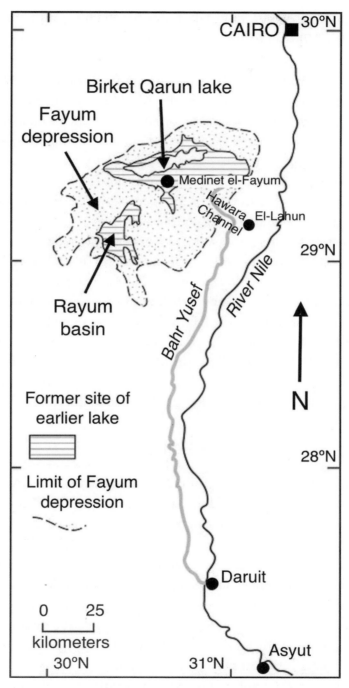

Fig. 22.1. Map showing the course of the Bahr Yusef Canal
that splits away from the River Nile in the vicinity of
Dairut and Asyut.

both in the construction of canals and in the clearing of the Bahr Yusef waterway from El-Lahun all the way to the royal palace and temple of Sobek at Shedet?

Of course, Amenemhat III would not himself have supervised enormous engineering projects of the sort described here. Their execution would have been placed in the hands of governors proficient in organizing large workforces that could be rallied to undertake such mammoth tasks. Major projects of this sort would have been overseen by the vizier, who was the highest-ranking official in Egypt other than the king himself. Curiously, it was this same rank of office that Joseph is considered to have achieved when Pharaoh made him "ruler over all the land of Egypt."[33]

Whether or not Joseph was indeed a historical character is, as stated at the start of this chapter, not of any major concern to this narrative. He is here simply a literary vehicle for a stratum of historical material that might easily reflect the activities in the Fayum of the country's western Asiatic population during the reign of Amenemhat III. In this spirit we should further examine the story of Joseph as presented in the Pentateuch, the first five books of the Hebrew Bible. In its current form this dates from the time of the building of the Second Temple following the return from captivity in Babylon of the Jewish nation during the second half of the sixth century BCE.

THE LIFE OF JOSEPH

According to the Hebrew Bible, Joseph (Arabic-Islamic Yusef) was the son of Jacob, who was the son of Isaac and grandson of Abraham, the great patriarch of the Israelites.[34] Having been despised, abused, and almost left for dead by his brothers, Joseph is sold to some Ishmaelites, the ancestors of the Arabs, who in turn sell him on to Midianite merchants.[35] These were the Semitic-speaking, nomadic inhabitants of the land of Midian, located in what is today the Jordanian Highlands east of the Jordan Valley. Both the Ishmaelites and Midianites are likely to have operated the caravans that ran between Egypt, Canaan, and the Sinai Peninsula, and were probably linked to the much later Nabateans of Petra in Jordan.

According to the book of Genesis, the Midianites take Joseph down into Egypt where he is sold to Potiphar, the captain of the pharaoh's guard.[36] Joseph serves Potiphar as his chief slave servant until he is falsely

Gen. XLI. *Joseph explique à Pharaon ses songes.* S. I. 15.
15–37. Jozef verklaart Farao zyne droomen.

Fig. 22.2. Engraving by Halma Scheits showing Joseph interpreting Pharaoh's
dreams (from Scheits 1710, pl. VT15).

accused by Potiphar's wife of attempting to force himself upon her.[37] Joseph is brought before a court where he is tried and found guilty of this crime, leading to his imprisonment.[38] It is only after he successfully interprets Pharaoh's dreams about the seven years of prosperity that will be followed by seven years of severe drought that he is finally released from prison (see fig. 22.2 on the previous page).[39] It is Joseph's advice on how Egypt should prepare for this drought, and what is to be done when the inhabitants of Egypt and neighboring Canaan come to Pharaoh asking for grain, that results in him becoming "ruler over all the land of Egypt."[40]

CONTROLLING THE NILE FLOODS

There is no mention in the Hebrew Bible of Joseph being responsible for major engineering projects in the Fayum. All he does is stock the granaries full of grain during the seven years of plenty and then hand it out to Egyptians and Canaanites alike during the seven years of drought.[41] Having said this, there could well be a link between the biblical story of Joseph's

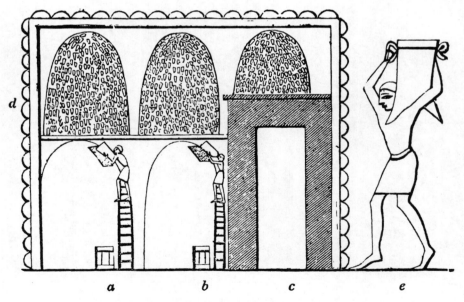

Fig. 22.3. Ancient Egyptian granaries in Thebes (from Wilkinson 1837, II, fig. 122). Similar granaries might have been used in the famous Bible story of Joseph and his interpretation of Pharaoh's dream of seven years of prosperity followed by seven years of drought.

granaries (see fig. 22.3) and the hydrological works that took place in the Fayum during the reign of Amenemhat III. I say this, for the clearing of the Hawara Channel and the digging of the canals and irrigation ditches would not only have enabled the Fayum depression to become greatly fertile, it would also have relieved Lower Egypt of excessively high floods.[42]

These high floods would appear to have been a major problem during the reign of Amenemhat III. Harvard Egyptologist Barbara Bell has made a detailed study of the high water levels of the Nile as was recorded on the cliffs above the Middle Kingdom fortress of Semna, close to the Second Cataract on the border with Lower Nubia.[43] Such excessively high floods, which occurred throughout most of Amenemhat III's reign,[44] would have drowned the cultivated lands of Lower Egypt, making it impossible for seeds to be successfully planted during the next growing season.

By diverting some of the floodwaters into the Fayum depression it alleviated the threat of flooding in Lower Egypt. This is something that would appear to have been one of the principal motivations behind the clearance of the Hawara Channel, which not only lowered the levels of the inundation in Lower Egypt but also allowed the Nile floodwaters to flow into Lake Moeris while at the same time irrigating the Fayum's cultivated lands.

That "Joseph," as a literary figurehead of the Nile Delta's western Asiatic population, is singled out in Coptic-Arabic tradition as having been involved in these engineering projects does then start to tie in with the biblical narrative. This, of course, sees him as responsible for successfully navigating Egypt through the country's seven years of drought, the reason why Pharaoh made him "ruler over all the land of Egypt."[45]

Does this story refer to the involvement of Joseph and Egypt's western Asiatic population in ensuring the success of this mammoth engineering project, which enabled Lower Egypt to avoid a potential famine? This was the conclusion drawn by Egyptologist David Rohl in his own study of Joseph's presence in Egypt during the reign of Amenemhat III.[46] What Rohl makes clear, however, is that Joseph was not only vizier to *this* king, but that he also retained the same position during the reigns of Amenemhat IV and Sobekneferu, and might even have gone on to be vizier to the first two kings of the Thirteenth Dynasty.[47]

That Amenemhat III was pharaoh at the time of Joseph has long been recognized. As far back as 1925 British archaeologist

Arthur Weigall (1880–1934) wrote that during Joseph's time the ruling king, whom he names as Amenemhat III, "took such trouble to study the Nile-levels at the Second Cataract and carried out such great irrigation works that we may well suppose a series of low Niles and consequent famines to have caused his engineers to bestir themselves."[48] The king thereafter caused "a new canal to be made, and this canal to this day is called 'Joseph's Canal;' (*Bahr Yusuf*) by the Egyptians,"[49] this all being part of the great irrigation works undertaken by this pharaoh.[50]

Weigall sums up the situation in the following manner:

> Assuming that the Biblical Yusuf or Joseph is referred to [in the naming of the canal], it may be pointed out that traditions relating to events in ancient Israelite history generally came to be adopted by the Egyptians in early Christian times and in the early years of the Mohammedan age, when the Hebrew scriptures were recognized, and that, previous to this, the Jews in Egypt were in sufficient numbers to have kept alive the memory of their ancient connections with that country. Thus in the case of this canal, the Jews of the early centuries A.D. may well have been able to point to it and to relate how their fathers had handed down a reliable record that it was made by their national hero, Joseph.[51]

Although we know today that the Bahr Yusef canal is not of artificial construction, Weigall's observations a century ago were pretty spot on with regards Amenemhat III's relationship with the biblical character of Joseph. Since then others have come to similar conclusions, the findings of David Rohl being an obvious example. Other modern scholars such as Stefania Pignattari have also concluded that the Raijan of Arab-Islamic literature who ruled Egypt at the time of Joseph was Amenemhat III.[52]

So what more can we glean from the role Joseph, as the figurehead of Egypt's western Asiatic population, played during the reigns of Amenemhat III, Amenemhat IV, and Sobekneferu? One major clue, as we see next, comes from the priestly background of Joseph's so-called slave master when first he enters Egypt.

23

The Heliopolitan Connection

One very significant clue gleaned from the book of Genesis regarding the life of Joseph concerns his so-called slave master when first he arrives in Egypt. This was Potiphar, who is said to have been "an officer of Pharaoh, [and a] captain of the guard."[1] His name is thought to be a corrupted form of a Late Egyptian title meaning "He whom Ra has given."[2]

The connection with the sun god Ra is revealing since Potiphar, recalled later in the biblical narrative under the slightly altered name of Potipherah (or Potiphera),[3] is said to have been a priest of On, the Hebrew name for Heliopolis.[4] This conclusion comes from a verse in Genesis chapter 41, which reads, "And Pharaoh called Joseph's name Zaphnath-Paaneah; and he gave him to wife Asenath the daughter of Potipherah priest of On."[5] The Hebrew word On is derived from the city's original Egyptian name, which was I'wnw, meaning "the pillars."

AMENEMHAT IV AND THE ROLE OF HELIOPOLIS

With Amenemhat IV's patronage of Heliopolis and his active promotion of its creator god Atum, perhaps the priests of Ra had begun to feel that their importance was on the ascendancy once more. If correct, then we can understand why the king's death, almost certainly at the hands of Sobekneferu, would not have been greeted too kindly by them. This seems especially so in the knowledge that she had once more elevated the god Sobek to the role of state god in Egypt, a matter explored in chapter 28.

If the priests of Heliopolis really were responsible for the downfall and perhaps even the voluntary death of Sobekneferu, then how might the figure of Joseph have figured into this scenario as the apparent vizier of Egypt during the reigns not only of Amenemhat III, but also potentially those of Amenemhat IV and Sobekneferu?[6]

As the supposed husband of Asenath, the daughter of the "priest of On," was Joseph in any way complicit in the political intrigues surrounding Amenemhat IV's association with the Heliopolitan priesthood and, following the king's death, the eventual fate of Sobekneferu? More importantly, did she know Joseph personally? If she did then what was the nature of their relationship, and would they even have gotten along? It is these matters we address next.

24

When Sobekneferu Met Joseph

The realization that Sobekneferu might have known "Joseph"—whether he be an important Hebrew who rose to become vizier of Egypt or just a composite character expressing the greater achievements of Egypt's western Asiatic population—is a tantalizing possibility and one that needs to be explored. As far-fetched as this scenario might seem there are clear indications that some memory of the female monarch's presence in the Fayum has been preserved in Arab-Islamic stories celebrating Joseph's engineering achievements in the region.

PHARAOH'S DAUGHTER

The accounts in question refer to a royal woman, the daughter of the ruling Pharaoh, whom we shall call Pharaoh's Daughter. This is because her actual name has, sadly, been lost to history, a fact confirmed by Claire Malleson following her own detailed examination of the Arab-Islamic stories regarding Joseph's presence in the Fayum.[1]

Our first clear mention of Pharaoh's Daughter comes from the *Kitāb al-ʿAdjāʾib al-kabīr* attributed to the noted twelfth century CE littérateur Ibrāhīm Ibn Wasīf Shāh. When Joseph is charged with undertaking engineering projects in the Fayum, the king tells him: "I have given this land to my daughter; it is only an overflow for the waters; put it in order for her."[2] Then in *The Prodigies of Egypt,* written in the twelfth century CE by the

Arab writer Murtadā ibn al-'Afīf, as the Raijan or pharaoh is explaining to Joseph the task he must perform in Alphiom/Geouna he is told:

> You know how dear such a Daughter of mine is to me, and you see it is time I should assign her some place where she may be Mistress, and whereof the Revenues may be sufficient to maintain her: and I do not find any Lands besides my own which I can give her, unless it be Geouna: For that Land is neither too near, nor at too great a distance, and there is no coming into it of any side, unless it be through desart and dangerous places: the case will be the same with her, none can come near her on any side, but through desart and dangerous places.[3]

Both these accounts, which almost certainly derive from earlier source material, make clear the importance of Pharaoh's Daughter in what Joseph is to perform in the region. Since we know these hydrological projects climaxed during the reign of Amenemhat III, it is possible that the Pharaoh's Daughter alluded to in these accounts is in fact Sobekneferu. So do these stories preserve a Semitic account of Sobekneferu's role both as the daughter of Amenemhat III and as Egypt's first female pharaoh?

If correct, then knowledge that the *Kitāb al-'Adjā'ib al-kabīr* tells us that the king had "given this land [that is, the Fayum] to my daughter" is surely a reference to the royal palace and temple complex at Shedet in the Fayum, which dates mainly from the reign of Amenemhat III and would appear to have become a principal residence of Sobekneferu during her reign (see chapter 2).

Turning now to *The Prodigies of Egypt* the reference to the Raijan wishing to "assign her [his daughter] some place where she may be Mistress, and whereof the Revenues may be sufficient to maintain her" also seems to confirm that the account is talking about Shedet and its royal palace. The allusion, however, to the fact that "Revenues may be sufficient to maintain her" is, I believe, a reference to the true function of the Labyrinth monument at Hawara, a matter explored in chapter 28. So is there any further evidence that the Pharaoh's Daughter of the Arab accounts is in fact Sobekneferu?

Following the account in the *Kitāb al-'Adjā'ib al-kabīr* regarding Joseph's engineering projects in the Fayum we read that after the death of Nahrāūsh, the king at this time, he is succeeded by his son Darmagūsh, known also as Dārim ibn Al Rīan (Darim, son of the Raijan).[4] We are told that this "prince followed a line of conduct quite different from that which his father had followed. Joseph was his lieutenant, but if, in certain cases, he adopted his opinions, in others he ignored them."[5]

AMENEMHAT IV IN THE ARAB ACCOUNTS

So if the king named in the *Kitāb al-ʿAdjāʾib al-kabīr* as Nahrāūsh can be identified with Amenemhat III then was Darmagūsh, his successor, based on a memory of his son and heir Amenemhat IV? This seems likely in the knowledge that Amenemhat IV was succeeded to the throne in preference to his sister Sobekneferu, the reason perhaps why she is described only as Pharaoh's Daughter and never as a reigning monarch.

In other Arab-Islamic accounts of Joseph such as that preserved in the multivolume work titled *The Meadows of Gold and Mines of Gems,* written in 947 CE and attributed to Al-Masʿūdī (died circa 956 CE), known as the "Herodotus of the Arabs," it tells us that Darem ibn er-Reyan, that is Darmagūsh the son of Raijan, was the last of his line,[6] a statement that fits well with what we know from the king list or royal canon of Abydos (see chapter 18). This ignores Sobekneferu along with the entire list of kings that reigned during the Second Intermediate Period and only resumes with Ahmose, the first king of the Eighteenth Dynasty and founder of Egypt's New Kingdom.

KAMOSE, AHMOSE, AND THE EXPULSION OF THE HYKSOS

According to Masʿūdī the king that succeeded Darem ibn er-Reyan was Kames ben Madan. He was followed onto the throne of Egypt by al-Walid ibn Moçab, whom we are told was the pharaoh who reigned at the time of Moses.[7] As noted by cultural anthropologist Anastasia Banschikova, Kames ibn Madan is surely Kamose, the last king of the Seventeenth Dynasty.[8] He and his brother and successor, Ahmose, were responsible for the eventual defeat of the Hyksos and their final expulsion from Egypt. So in keeping with the Abydos king list seen to this day in the temple of Seti I, the medieval Arab sources completely ignore the reigns of

Sobekneferu and the kings of the Second Intermediate Period and resume, in their case, with Kames ibn Madan, in other words Kamose. He, and not his brother Ahmose, is seen as the first of a new line of kings following the Second Intermediate Period, one of Egypt's darkest and most confusing periods of history.*

Whether or not Ahmose can be identified with Kames ibn Madan's successor al-Walid ibn Moçab, the pharaoh who ruled during the age of Moses, and "knew not Joseph,"[9] is hard to say. That said, there is every reason to assume that the crucial role played both by Kamose and by Ahmose in expelling the Hyksos from Egypt might easily have contributed to the story of the Israelites, in other words the Nile Delta's western Asiatic population, leaving Egypt under the command of Moses, the story as told in the book of Exodus.[10]

With all this in mind, the statement in the *Kitāb al-ʿAdjāʾib al-kabīr* about Darmagūsh following, "a line of conduct quite different from that which his father had followed" makes complete sense of the more liberal policies adopted by Amenemhat IV upon his accession to the throne. If we are to take this as a reference to the political situation in Egypt at this time, then his conduct could very easily be described as "quite different" from those adopted by his father Amenemhat III.

Whereas Amenemhat III had allowed western Asiatic peoples not only to settle in the north of the country but also to assume positions of power at many levels of society Amenemhat IV went one step further. He encouraged an open borders policy, decided to create a new Egyptian kingdom in the Sinai, and increased still further the influence of the country's Asiatic population. This political engineering helped catalyze the rise in the Nile Delta of the Canaanite-led Fourteenth Dynasty, which came to rival the more nationalistic Thirteenth Dynasty that rose to prominence around the same time.

In addition to this Amenemhat IV rejected the cult of Sobek, so favored by his father, and instead adopted the Heliopolitan creator god Atum as his personal deity. Thus to find that a king in the medieval Arab accounts who

---

*Masʿūdī writes that Kames ibn Madan was an Amalekite, that is a member of the western Asiatic tribal peoples who feature heavily both in the Hebrew Bible and in the Holy Koran.

can be identified as Amenemhat IV and crops up as the brother of Pharaoh's Daughter is therefore intriguing indeed, especially since these accounts allude to engineering projects carried out in the Fayum during the reign of Amenemhat III. So there seems every reason to conclude that the references to Pharaoh's Daughter do indeed preserve some memory of Sobekneferu's presence at the royal palace and temple complex of Shedet located as it was then on the shores of the Fayum's great lake, close to the termination of the Bahr Yusef waterway.

SOBEKNEFERU OR NEFERUPTAH?

It could be argued, of course, that the stories relating to Pharaoh's Daughter refer not to Sobekneferu, but to Amenemhat III's elder daughter Neferuptah. She certainly stood to inherit the Fayum if she had lived long enough to sit alongside her half brother Amenemhat IV as co-ruler of the Two Lands. Could she have been the Pharaoh's Daughter mentioned in the medieval Arab accounts and not Sobekneferu? It is a theory that is certainly worth consideration; however, since the stories of Joseph's activities in the Fayum would presumably have been passed down orally across many generations, until they were finally set down in writing, the chances are that those featuring Pharaoh's Daughter relate to Amenemhat III's *most memorable* daughter, who, of course, was Sobekneferu. Not only did she succeed to the throne of Egypt, but she also became the country's first female ruler of the Two Lands, an incredible feat that should hopefully have ensured the preservation of her memory across the millennia, no matter how abstract it might have become.

WHEN JOSEPH MET SOBEKNEFERU

There seems little escaping the fact that Sobekneferu would have known Joseph. This seems especially so if, as David Rohl has proposed,[11] the Hebrew who became "ruler over all the land of Egypt"[12] was vizier of Egypt into the reigns of the first two kings of the Thirteenth Dynasty. That Joseph would appear also to have spent some time in the Fayum also tells us that he must have frequented the royal palace at Shedet, one of the likely residences of Sobekneferu.

If the Hebrew Bible is correct in its statement that Potiphar, Joseph's slave master when he first enters Egypt, was a priest of Heliopolis under the slightly altered name of Potipherah,[13] then certain facts might be gleaned about Sobekneferu's apparent relationship with Joseph. According to the book of Genesis it was Potipherah's daughter Aseneth that Joseph took as wife.[14] If this is true, then it confirms Joseph's close alliance with the Heliopolitan priesthood. Is it possible therefore that in his capacity as vizier Joseph acted as intermediary between the priests of Heliopolis and the female monarch, bringing to her their demands or requests, while at the same time offering advice on how best to proceed on certain key issues, the role perhaps of a spin doctor in today's politics?

As we have seen Sobekneferu would appear to have supported the nationalistic factions of Egypt, which wanted to clamp down on her brother's more liberal policies regarding immigration and the expansion of influence of the country's western Asiatic population. Since this is something that would have greatly increased the power and influence of the Heliopolitan priesthood there would have been every reason for them to have put pressure on the female monarch to desist in her own stricter policies and resume those implemented by her brother.

THE ROAD TO DESTRUCTION

To gain support for their demands the priests of Heliopolis would perhaps have attempted to convince important and influential members of the royal court, as well as the country's native and foreign populations, that the female monarch was taking the nation down a road of destruction. They would surely have highlighted the fact that everything had been fruitful during the reigns of her father and brother, particularly because of the celebrated engineering projects undertaken in the Fayum, which would have brought a long-lasting fruitfulness and prosperity to Lower Egypt in particular.

Yet now, following the succession to the throne of Sobekneferu, the Nile floodwaters were so low that the cultivated lands both in the Nile Valley and also in the Fayum were no longer capable of producing successful harvests, a situation that if allowed to continue would only bring about famine and disaster. As we saw in chapter 3, this comes from knowledge that in

Fig. 24.1. The inscription recording the height of the floodwaters in Year 3 of Sobekneferu's reign as preserved on rocks above the River Nile close to the Kumma fortress marking the border between Egypt and ancient Nubia (modern Sudan). The floodwaters rose to just 6 feet (1.83 meters) above the current average water level today, which would appear to have been very low indeed (from Habachi 1954, XIII, C).

Year 3 of Sobekneferu's reign the floodwaters at the time of the inundation at Kumma on the border with Nubia only reached 6 feet (1.83 meters) above the modern-day average (see fig. 24.1).[15] This was extraordinarily low and as a consequence would have left the entire Nile Valley basin and Fayum depression bereft of the rich muddy deposits necessary for the sowing of seeds at the beginning of the next growing season.

This unfortunate situation would have been made worse by the fact that some of the excess floodwaters that had previously drowned parts of Lower Egypt were now being successfully diverted into the Fayum's great lake via the newly cleared Bahr Yusef canal. This would have meant even less water for irrigation in the Nile Valley and Delta region when the floodwaters were particularly low, as was the case certainly during Year 3 of Sobekneferu's reign.* The failure of the floodwaters to successfully irrigate the Nile Valley basin would undoubtedly have been put down to divine intervention, or the lack of it to be more precise, something that a religious priesthood like that at Heliopolis would have seized upon and used to their advantage.

---

*We do not have any records from Kumma relating to her other years of rule, so there are no clear indications whether the annual floodwaters were high or low at this time.

THE RULER AS THE TRUE HORUS AND "RAINMAKER"

The king in his or her capacity as the incarnate god Horus and so-called divine rainmaker was considered directly responsible for the fruitfulness of the Nile floodwaters.[16] So their absence at the time of the inundation would unquestionably be blamed on the ruler in question. Making matters worse was the fact that, as a water god, Sobekneferu's own patron deity Sobek was seen as presiding over the fruitfulness of the land brought about by the success of the annual inundation.[17]

Undoubtedly the Heliopolitan priests would have seized upon the connection between Sobek's influence and the poor state of the inundation to question the female monarch's choice of divine patron. They would also have pointed out that nothing like this had happened during the reign of her brother, proof that he had expressed a harmonious relationship with the concept of ma'at, cosmic order, something that she was failing to do during her own reign.

In addition to this, the Heliopolitan priests would have rightly spread rumors that Sobekneferu was responsible for the death of her brother, the king, which, along with the gods denying Egypt a fruitful harvest, provided proof that she was an interloper, a false Horus king. As a consequence of these accusations, their ultimatum to Sobekneferu would have been simple—either step down as monarch or the gods would intervene and she would be removed forcibly.

THE FATE OF SOBEKNEFERU

It should be pointed out that Barbara Bell in her detailed study of the effects of climate on Egypt during the Middle Kingdom and Second Intermediate Period wrote that, "in a time troubled both by poor floods and unusual uncertainty about the identity of the true Horus King, a king would be secretly murdered or expected to commit suicide when his coronation was not followed in due season with floods adequate to avert scarcity."[18]

If correct, then this, I suspect, is exactly what played out during the reign of Sobekneferu. Low water levels at the time of the inundation provided the priests of Heliopolis with the perfect opportunity to put pressure on the monarch to either take her life or be murdered. Sobekneferu was forced therefore to abandon her reign and, as a consequence, entered into a ritual death. This then becomes the most likely final fate of Sobekneferu, her act of suicide done selflessly to ensure the future cosmic balance of the Two Lands.

Before, however, all this took place there seems every likelihood that Joseph, as vizier of Egypt, would have relayed to Sobekneferu the accusations being leveled against her by the Heliopolitan priesthood. He would surely have advised her that if she did not either revert to the more liberal policies of her brother, and in doing so return the country back to prosperity, the priests of Heliopolis would take matters into their own hands. What this would have meant is doing whatever it took to get influential members of the royal court to forcibly remove her from the throne and, as a consequence, suffer the same fate as her brother, in other words death (the scenario as recorded by the Greek writer Herodotus in his valuable account of what happened to Nitocris following the death of her brother, the king—see chapters 19 and 20).

Such then was the suspected relationship between Joseph and Sobekneferu—he the Hebrew who became "ruler over all the land of Egypt"[19] advising her on how the country was turning against her and that if she did not do something about it then she would be murdered. One suspects that this would have been among the final conversations that the two of them would have had before she made the decision to end her life. Based on this fact I would say that these two important individuals were not so much friends, but valued acquaintances that shared common interests, especially toward the end. He advised Sobekneferu of her impending fate, and she accepted his word.

Despite any antagonism that may have existed between Sobekneferu, the Heliopolitan priesthood, and Egypt's western Asiatic population, symbolized in Hebrew and Arab-Islamic tradition by the stories of Joseph, there does appear to have existed, as we see next, certain links between the female monarch and the Semitic-speaking peoples of the Nile Delta during her formative years.

25

Sobekneferu—
The Asiatic Connection

So far we have learned about the tumultuous reign and eventual fall of the first woman in Egyptian history to wear the double crown of Upper and Lower Egypt. Now it is time to explore further back in time in an attempt to piece together what might have occurred during Sobekneferu's formative years. This appears to be a fruitful exercise for there exist tantalizing clues suggesting that she could well have mixed with northern Egypt's Asiatic community when just a child. If correct then it means she might easily have been influenced by its Semitic-based beliefs and practices.

To understand how this might have come about we must return to Tell el-Dab'a in the eastern Nile Delta, where in 1941, as described in chapter 5, Egyptologist Labib Habachi investigated three life-size statues of Sobekneferu as well as a religious shrine found nearby.[1] This potential evidence of the presence there of a Sobek temple active during the female monarch's reign prompted Habachi to speculate that Sobekneferu might have had some special relationship with the area. For him the fact that, "the queen left so many statues in the district leads us to think that she might have resided there or at least have chosen the place as a summer resort."[2] He goes on to write, "it is quite likely that she was related with the district, perhaps being born or brought up there."[3]

THE LAND OF GOSHEN

These are powerful thoughts offering the possibility that during her youth Sobekneferu might have resided at Tell el-Dab'a, and could even have been born there. If correct then there is every reason to assume that she would have come into contact with high-ranking members of the area's western Asiatic population, most obviously officials or governors associated with the royal court of her father, Amenemhat III. Did this include Joseph who, having successfully navigated Egypt through seven years of drought due to his stockpiling of grain,[4] was able to convince the king to allow his brothers, his father Jacob, and their extended family (see fig. 25.1 on the next page) to settle in the "land of Goshen"?[5] This was the name by which the Hebrews knew the eastern Nile Delta. More specifically, we are told, Joseph's family made their home in the city of Raamses,[6] or Pi-Rameses as it was called by the Egyptians. This was the name given to Tell el-Dab'a and its environs after a new city was built there during the reign of Rameses II (1279–1213 BCE).[7]

Thus there seems every chance that if Sobekneferu had spent her childhood in Tell el-Dab'a then she might well have come into contact not only with Joseph, but also with his extended family who had come to settle in Tell el-Dab'a.[8] It would, of course, be Joseph's family that would go on to become the foundation of the Israelite peoples who, according to the book of Exodus, were forced into slave labor in order to build the "treasure cities" of Raamses and Pithom during the reign of the so-called Pharaoh of the Oppression, who "knew not Joseph."[9]

DEVOTION TO THE GODDESS

Was it through this presumed contact with the Nile Delta's western Asiatic population that Sobekneferu first began to take a personal interest in magico-religious beliefs and practices? As we saw in chapter 8, this would appear to have included some form of devotion to the goddess Hathor, who presided over dancing, music, sexuality, love, and poetic inspiration, among many other things.

So at Tell el-Dab'a did Sobekneferu come into contact with certain religious practices relating not only to Hathor, but also to her Semitic

Fig. 25.1. Engraving by the French artist and illustrator Gustave Doré (1832–1883) of the biblical figure of Joseph revealing his identity to his brothers following their arrival in Egypt (from Doré 1866, pl. 28).

Fig. 25.2. Small red sandstone Sphinx found at Serabit el-Khadim on which were carved inscriptions both in Egyptian and in the so-called Sinaitic script (from Petrie 1906, pl. 141). The Egyptian inscription reads "Hathor, Lady of Turquoise," with the Sinaitic inscription honoring "Ba'alat," which means "The Lady" (Gardiner 1916, 15).

counterpart Ba'alat, whose name means, simply, "the lady"? As Ba'alat Gebal, "Ba'alat of Byblos," this Canaanite goddess was venerated at Byblos in what is today Lebanon, while another form of her was venerated at Serabit el-Khadim in the Sinai Peninsula as is shown from various Semitic-based inscriptions found at the site (see fig. 25.2).[10]

That a Canaanite form of Hathor was venerated at Tell el-Dab'a during the Thirteenth Dynasty (and arguably before) is not in doubt. Scarabs found there show highly abstract forms of Hathor with clear Canaanite overtones, suggesting that the goddess in question was an amalgamation of Hathor and her Semitic counterpart.[11] The discovery of huge oak tree pits in the eastern part of the city has suggested to Manfred Bietak and his colleagues that a temple dedicated to the Semitic goddess Ashera once existed there.[12] Whether or not Ba'alat and Ashera were one and the same goddess is unclear, although at Tell el-Dab'a both would appear to have been syncretized with Hathor.

As we have seen, there is good reason to suspect that before fully coming to realize it was her divine birthright and future destiny to become Egypt's first female pharaoh Sobekneferu probably trained as a priestess, something that scholars such as Kara Cooney and Kelly-Anne Diamond have indicated themselves.[13] If Sobekneferu, as a young princess, did initially dedicate her life to a particular deity it was almost certainly Hathor/Ba'alat.

There is also, as discussed in chapter 7, grounds to suggest that when still a princess Sobekneferu might have acted as a foreign envoy on behalf of her father. This is supported by the discovery of the highly important statue fragment of Sobekneferu found at the Canaanite cult center of Tel Gezer in modern-day Israel. If Sobekneferu had indeed mixed with members of the Nile Delta's western Asiatic population during her early life, then the chances are she would have been familiar with their spoken language, something that would have greatly impressed Canaanite rulers and dignitaries.

THE RIGHT TO RULE

At some point Sobekneferu made the decision to do whatever was necessary for her to succeed to the throne of Egypt. Should the small figurine of a female ruler in dark green schist housed today in New York's Metropolitan Museum of Art truly show Sobekneferu, then the fact that the individual is shown wearing the Heb Sed cloak probably does indicate that the monarch underwent some kind of ritual trial, the outcome of which helped convince her she was the legitimate heir to the Two Lands.

This, of course, was something we explored in chapter 6, and should this theory prove correct then almost certainly the deity involved with this process was Hathor, whose role included the legitimization of a king's right to rule following the successful completion of the Heb Sed ritual.

Such a spiritual awakening on the part of Sobekneferu might easily have had something to do with her suspected childhood upbringing at Tell el-Dab'a. It is also possible that members of the city's western Asiatic community saw her as someone unique and special whose future destiny, if steered in the right direction, might well benefit their own long-term plans for further settlement in the country. The fact that the medieval Arab accounts say that the engineering projects Joseph undertook in the Fayum were to create a permanent residence for Pharaoh's Daughter on behalf of the Raijan (Amenemhat III) does imply some kind of special relationship between Joseph and Sobekneferu during her formative years.

Should all this be true, then where exactly might Sobekneferu have undergone her proposed personal initiation to "legitimize" her right to rule? Did it occur at Tell el-Dab'a, where Hathor/Ba'alat might have played some role in her early life? It is indeed possible. Alternately, it could have taken place in the Sinai, at Serabit el-Khadim, a cult center both of Hathor and of Ba'alat. Even though Sobekneferu's name has not been found at the site I see no reason why she would not have gone there during the reign either of her father or of her brother. We must also not forget that during his reign, when Sobekneferu probably acted as his royal wife or even as an unofficial co-ruler, it was Amenemhat IV's intention to create a new kingdom in the Sinai. Should this plan have been realized then there seems little question that Serabit el-Khadim would have acted as its spiritual seat of power.

THE MONARCH'S BETRAYAL

Whether or not Sobekneferu really was brought up in Tell el-Dab'a might never be known. Despite this, there seems every reason to suspect that during her youth as a princess growing up in northern Egypt she would have been on familiar terms with influential leaders of the country's western Asiatic population. Its priests and officials might even have seen Sobekneferu as their future hope should anything happen to her brother the king.

How then might these people have felt when on succeeding to the throne the monarch changed the immigration policies originally introduced by her father and extended by her brother—policies that had been particularly favorable to the growth and expansion of their communities throughout Egypt? I suspect that to them it would have seemed like a complete betrayal. This was not only because she might well have grown up alongside their own children in the Eastern Delta, but also because they had probably supported her cause during her early years and had continued to do so even after she had taken up residence in the royal palace at Shedet.

Whether or not members of Egypt's western Asiatic population supported the proposed actions of the priests of Heliopolis against Sobekneferu is unclear. They might not have actively done so, but replacing her with a ruler more sympathetic to their own long-term interests in Egypt would surely have been more favorable than leaving her on the throne.

PREMONITIONS OF IMPENDING DOOM

As history tells us, Sobekneferu and the nationalistic supporters of the incoming Thirteenth Dynasty were right to have been concerned about the long-term future of Egypt, for the rise of the Canaanite-led Fourteenth Dynasty unquestionably opened the door for the eventual take over of the country by the Hyksos warlords just a few generations later. They had begun to settle in the Nile Delta by around 1700 BCE and by 1650 BCE they had control both of Memphis and the capital, Itj-tawy.[14] It was this loss of sovereignty that had led to one of Egypt's darkest periods, something that Sobekneferu and the fledgling kings of the Thirteenth Dynasty had surely sensed was coming.[15] Indeed, French Egyptologist Pierre Montet (1885–1966) even proposed that Amemenhet III and his family had experienced premonitions concerning the impending collapse both of the royal dynasty and of Egypt as a whole.[16]

So, despite what some might see as the nationalistic actions of Sobekneferu and the incoming Thirteenth Dynasty, we can understand why they would have done what they did to prevent the inevitable fragmentation and break-up of the country. Although they eventually failed in their efforts, the Thirteenth Dynasty survived long enough to pass on the baton of Egyptian sovereignty to the first kings of the Seventeenth Dynasty, some of whom, like their predecessors, bore names honoring the crocodile god Sobek. They would rise up against the Hyksos and establish Egypt's New Kingdom, once more bringing stability, wealth, and prosperity to the Two Lands.

Such then were the circumstances surrounding the fairly short reign of Sobekneferu. This much we can surmise about her life, but what more can we glean from the fragmentary legacy she left behind in the wake of her sudden exit from this world? What, for instance, became of her body? Did it receive the funerary rites so important to the soul's passage into the afterlife? Clearly, it did not end up in what might have been her intended final resting place—the now demolished northern pyramid at Mazghuna, located around 1.6 miles (2.6 kilometers) south of the Dahshur pyramid field.

To answer the question as to what became of Sobekneferu following her death we must begin to explore key monuments attributed to her reign. This will help us to better understand why she and her contemporaries saw the Fayum as so important not only to the royal dynasty, but also to the destiny of Egypt.

PART 6

TWO LANDS

26

Sobekneferu the Builder

It is generally thought that during the reign of Sobekneferu very few building projects were undertaken, and those that did were confined to the Fayum region.[1] To some degree this is true, with the female monarch seemingly ignoring southern Egypt completely. In Middle Egypt the situation, however, seems to have been slightly different. There is evidence that the monarch was responsible for the construction of at least one major structure at Heracleopolis Magna (Egyptian *Hemen-nesw*), a very ancient city located around 9 miles (14 kilometers) south-southwest of the entrance to the Fayum depression.[2]

Excavations at a mound site there named Kom el-Aqarib, close to the modern town of Ehnasya el-Medina, revealed a small temple from the reign of Rameses II.[3] Among its ruins archaeologists came across an architrave in secondary use bearing an inscription in the name of Sobekneferu. Its presence at the site led Egyptologist Indo Matzker to propose that the female monarch had been responsible for the construction there of a major monument.[4] Whether or not this structure was administrative or religious in nature remains unclear. It is also worth recalling that Kom el-Aqarib was the alleged findspot of a damaged cylinder seal bearing Sobekneferu's throne name examined in a Cairo "dealer's shop" by British Egyptologist Percy E. Newberry (see chapter 2 and fig. 2.4 on page 25). Was this even further evidence of the female monarch's presence in Heracleopolis Magna?

Outside the Fayum the only other building project thought to have occurred during Sobekneferu's reign was at Tell el-Dab'a in the Nile Delta where in 1941 Labib Habachi investigated the three life-sized statues of Sobekneferu found more or less in situ (see chapters 5 and 25). Habachi speculated that a temple of Sobek had existed on the site during the reign of the monarch, and that it had remained in use during the Thirteenth Dynasty.[5]

Then there is the unfinished pyramid at Mazghuna North, immediately south of the Dahshur pyramid field, which might well have been built as the sovereign's final resting place during the reign of her brother Amenemhat IV, its southern counterpart, at Mazghuna South, having been built for the king himself. The fact, however, that when investigated by British archaeologist Ernest Mackey in 1910 no evidence of a royal burial was found in the Mazghuna North pyramid means that any connections between this funerary complex and Sobekneferu must remain circumstantial at best.[6] That said, tentative evidence does exist to show her connection with the site as we shall see in chapter 34.

BUILDING PROJECTS IN THE FAYUM

Beyond these building activities Sobekneferu, during her reign, would indeed appear to have concentrated her efforts within the Fayum depression, which is surrounded on all sides by the Libyan Desert.[7] Why this should have been the case is probably down to highly crucial geographical factors that dominated the religious and political activities of the Twelfth Dynasty. These would have concerned the region's role not only as the main cult center for Sobek, but also the fact that the line of division between Upper and Lower Egypt corresponded with the approximate geographical latitude, not only of the capital Itj-tawy (modern Lisht) in the Nile Valley, but also the Fayum region north of the great lake.[8]

Sobekneferu would inevitably have spent a considerable amount of her time at the royal palace attached to the temple of Sobek at Shedet (modern-day Kiman Faras on the northwestern outskirts of Medinet el-Fayum).* This was the site of the Greek city of Crocodilopolis, close to the shores of Lake

---

*During the reign of Ptolemy II (who ruled Egypt 283 to 246 BCE) a new city would be built nearby that was named Arsinoe in honor of his sister and co-regent Arsinoe II. (Ptolemy II crowned her ruler of Upper and Lower Egypt and deified her following her death around 268 BCE. Arsinoe II would thereafter become the Fayum's patron goddess through till the end of the Roman period).

Moeris. It is even possible that, after the dynastic capital of Itj-tawy, Shedet was Sobekneferu's primary residence. This seems confirmed in the knowledge that an inscription on a bead dating from the monarch's reign addresses her as "beloved of Sobek of Shedet—Horus who resides in Shedet, lord of the land of the lake, who resides in the palace."[9] Although the palace mentioned would seem to be that of the god Sobek, the fact that Sobekneferu is cited as the living Horus who resides in Shedet would tend to suggest that this relates to the same place, in other words the city's temple of Sobek with its adjoining royal palace.

We also have to assume that Sobekneferu would have officiated at ceremonies taking place in the temple of the snake-headed goddess Renenutet at Medinet Madi to the southwest of Shedet. This is despite the fact that her name is not found anywhere in the temple. Only those of her father Amenemhat III and her brother Amenemhat IV are found there, and when they are they are often placed side by side.

Why the female monarch's name does not appear at the Medinet Madi temple is curious, especially considering her relationship with the god Sobek, who was the complex's other divine patron. The simple solution for her omission from reliefs and inscriptions is that the temple was completed in its entirety while her father was still alive, almost certainly during his co-regency with Amenemhat IV (see chapter 3).

It might also be important to recall that one of the wall scenes in the Medinet Madi temple shows Sobekneferu's sister Neferuptah in the company of their father. She uses a sistrum rattle, sacred to the goddess Hathor, to pacify the snake-headed Renenutet (see fig. 8.4 on page 81 and plate 9). The presence of this relief, which survived through to modern times, would have been a constant reminder to Sobekneferu that it was her sister and not her who had been chosen by her father to rule the country alongside Amenemhat IV. This, together with the fact that the temple was partially the handiwork of her brother and contained several reliefs showing him alongside her father, was reason enough perhaps for Sobekneferu to concentrate her efforts on building projects elsewhere in the Fayum depression.

It should also be pointed out that where the throne names of Amenemhat III and Amenemhat IV are seen together at Medinet Madi, in some places those of the latter king have been chiseled out. Clearly, this was not the act of a later dynasty opposed wholesale to the kings of the

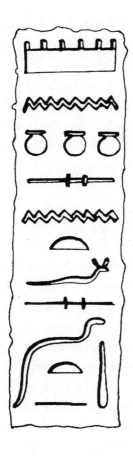

Fig. 26.1. Inscription from a granite block found at the Labyrinth that reads "[she made it as] her monument to her father, living forever" (from Habachi 1954, pl. XIII, B).

Twelfth Dynasty otherwise both names would have been erased, and not just one. One wonders whether this occurred during Sobekneferu's reign, an act perhaps carried out by the female monarch's followers reflecting her wish to disassociate herself from her brother's own reign. If so, then it is yet further evidence that their relationship did not end well.

As we have seen, Sobekneferu's greatest architectural achievement during her reign would appear to have been the completion of her father's pyramid complex at Hawara,[10] the site having been chosen after the king abandoned work on his other pyramid complex at Dahshur on the edge of the Nile Valley.

At Hawara, Sobekneferu zeroed in on her father's overly large mortuary temple situated immediately south of the Hawara pyramid.[11] Her name has been found among its ruins on lintels, on columns, on architraves, and in relief inscriptions, at times alongside that of her father Amenemhat III.[12] One inscription on a granite block found at the site even reads "[she made it as] her monument for her father, living forever"[13] (see fig. 26.1 on the previous page), confirming her involvement in this grand building project.

It was, of course, this dual relationship between the two monarchs that has occasionally led to suspicions that Sobekneferu entered into a co-regency with her father shortly before his death.[14] This, however, was not the case; she likely used his name to bolster her own legitimacy as the true heir to the throne of Egypt.[15]

HEB SED COURT THEORY

Why Amenemhat III's mortuary temple should have been so large probably had something to do with its similarity in design to the pyramid complex of Djoser, the first king of the Third Dynasty (about 2686–2600 BCE). This is located at Saqqara on the west bank of the Nile opposite the Old Kingdom capital of Memphis. On the south side of the king's famous step pyramid, in the same position as Amenemhat III's own mortuary temple, Djoser built a massive funerary complex that included a Heb Sed court. This took the form of a large rectangular arena where the Heb Sed festival would take place.[16] It is therefore possible that Amenemhat III's mortuary complex at Hawara was likewise designed with Heb Sed festivals in mind.[17]

We have already seen just how important Sobekneferu saw the Heb Sed festival to the legitimization of her reign. Thus there seems every reason to suspect that one of the reasons why she took a particular interest in her father's mortuary complex was because of its perceived importance both to her deified father and to the goddess Hathor. As previously made clear, the goddess was seen to preside over the continued legitimization of a king's reign following the successful completion of the Heb Sed ritual. Fragments of statues of Hathor were found at the site of Amenemhat III's funerary complex indicating the presence there of a shrine or chapel to the goddess.[18] Indeed, other than the crocodile god Sobek, it would appear that Hathor was one of the main deities venerated at the complex.[19]

What seems most significant about Sobekneferu's involvement in the construction of her father's funerary complex is that she didn't just put the finishing touches on preexisting structures begun when her father was still alive. She would appear to have transformed the complex from a mortuary temple, complete with its Heb Sed court, into a major religious center that classical writers would come to refer to as the Egyptian Labyrinth. It is this remarkable monument of the past that we explore next.

27

The Magnificent Labyrinth

According to the classical writers, the Labyrinth at Hawara in Egypt's Fayum region was one of the most magnificent architectural achievements of the ancient world. It was said to have consisted of a series of interconnected buildings containing halls, rooms, chambers, and chapels, all arranged around a central open court beneath which was a vast subterranean network of corridors and chambers.[1]

Herodotus in book II of *The Histories* tells us, "I have myself seen it, and indeed no words can tell its wonders. . . . Though the pyramids were greater than words can tell, and each one of them a match for many great monuments built by Greeks, this maze surpasses even the pyramids."[2] He further writes that it had: "twelve roofed courts, with doors over against each other: six face the north and six the south, in two continuous lines, all within one outer wall. There are also double sets of chambers, three thousand altogether, fifteen hundred above and the same number underground."[3] (See figure 27.1.)

When British archaeologist and Egyptologist W. M. Flinders Petrie first surveyed the site of the Labyrinth in 1888 he found it covered an enormous area, approximately 800 x 1,000 feet (244 x 305 meters) in size and 18.38 acres (7.44 hectares) in extent;[4] this being enough space to contain not just all the main temples of Karnak and Luxor, but the Ramesseum on the Theban West Bank as well.[5] "In short," Petrie wrote, "all of the temples on the east of Thebes, and one of the largest on the west bank, might be placed together in the one area of the ruins at Hawara. Here we certainly have a site worthy of the renown which the labyrinth acquired."[6] More modern estimates, based on the limits of the complex's temenos wall, suggest it could have been even larger, perhaps as much as 1,263 feet (385 meters) by 518 feet (158 meters),[7] even though today all that remains of the Labyrinth are vast fields of excavation ditches and mounds, interspersed with the occasional cut and dressed red granite fragment or hard white limestone column segment seen sticking up out of the ground (see plates 15 and 16).

Fig. 27.1. Imaginative interpretation by German Jesuit scholar and polymath Athanasius Kircher (1602–1680) of the Egyptian Labyrinth published in his book *Turris Babel* (from Kircher 1679, 78). Surrounding a central maze we see the 12 roofed courts alluded to by Herodotus in *The Histories* (1920, bk. II, 148), each of which is allotted to a different nome. Beyond these are 48 statues in shrines presumably signifying the local gods of the different nomes. Arched entrances are seen at the four corners of the structure.

Even before Petrie got to Hawara, the site had been investigated across a period of two months during the late spring of 1843 (see fig. 27.2) by pioneering German Egyptologist Karl Richard Lepsius (1810–1884). In a report of the ruins of the Labyrinth written by him that year he describes the setting in the following manner:

> An immense cluster of chambers still remains, and in the centre lies the great square, where the courts once stood, covered with the remains of large monolithic granite columns, and of others of white hard limestone, shining almost like marble. . . . The whole is so arranged, that three immense masses of buildings, 300 feet broad, enclose a square place, which is 600 feet long and 500 feet wide. The fourth side, one of the narrow ones, is bounded by the Pyramid, which lies behind it; it is 300 feet square. . . . A canal of rather modern date, passing obliquely through the ruins . . . cuts off exactly the best preserved portion of the labyrinthian chambers, together with part of the great central square, which at one time was divided into courts.[8]

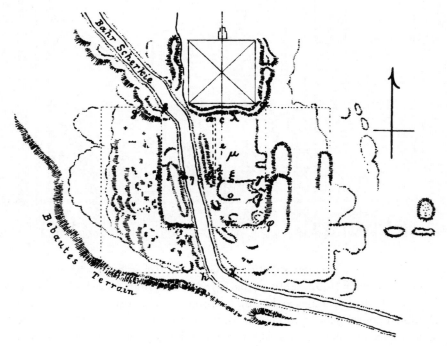

Fig. 27.2. Plan of the pyramid of Amenemhat III at Hawara, along with the ruins of the Labyrinth, made by Karl Lepsius in 1843 (from Lepsius [1904] 1970, 11).

WHO BUILT THE LABYRINTH?

Herodotus seems to imply that the builders of the Labyrinth were twelve rulers of Egypt's Late Period,[9] the most renowned of whom was Psamtik I, known to the Greeks as Psammetichus. These kings thrived just two centuries before Herodotus's own age, so their choice as builders does seem a little odd. This, however, is what the "Egyptian wardens" who maintained the Labyrinth must have told the Greek writer.[10]

Despite the fact that Pliny the Younger, writing in the first century CE, repeats Herodotus's suggestion that the Dodecarchs were responsible for the construction of the Labyrinth,[11] this assertion is clearly in error. We can say this with some certainty in the knowledge that there has existed ample evidence, ever since Lepsius first explored the site in 1843, that the monument's principal architect was Amenemhat III. The German archaeologist makes this clear, informing his reader that, "The fragments of the mighty columns and architraves which we have dug up from the great square of the halls, exhibit the name-shields [that is, the cartouches] of the sixth king of this same 12th Dynasty, Amenemha[t] III. Thus the important question of its place in history is answered."[12]

That said, from Lepsius's notes of his field explorations at the site it is clear also that he found various fragments with inscriptions bearing the "shield" or royal name of "Skemiophris," in other words Sobekneferu, showing that she too was responsible for construction work at the Labyrinth (see fig. 27.3).[13]

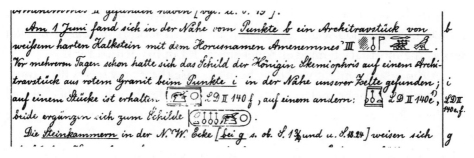

Fig. 27.3. Karl Lepsius's handwritten record from June 1, 1843, speaking about his discovery at the site of the Labyrinth of architraves and fragments bearing the names both of Amenemhat III and of "Skemiophris," in other words Sobekneferu (from Lepsius [1904] 1970, 15).

These discoveries by Lepsius constitute the first contemporary evidence of the female monarch's existence outside of Manetho's entry for Skemiophris in the *Aegyptiaca* and her presence in king lists, such as those of Turin[14] and Karnak,[15] which had begun emerging on to the Egyptological scene during the early to mid 1820s. Petrie himself found compelling evidence that the principal builder of the Labyrinth was Amenemhat III, with Sobekneferu's name also being present on various architraves and columns found at the site.[16]

Manetho himself credits Amenemhat III as the builder of the Labyrinth. In the Epitome of his *Aegyptiaca* as recorded by Africanus, for instance, the fourth king of the Twelfth Dynasty is given as, "Lachares (Lamares), [who ruled] for 8 years." He, it is said, "built the Labyrinth in the Arsinoite nome as his own tomb."[17] The Arsinoite nome constituted the district around Arsinoe, the capital of the Fayum during the Ptolemaic period.

Lachares is simply a corrupted form of Amemenhat III's throne name Nimaatre. The fact that Manetho only allots him a reign of 8 years when Amenemhat III ruled at least 45 years suggests some confusion with the reign of his successor Amenemhat IV, who ruled for a minimum of 9 years.

Strabo in the *Geography,* writing at the end of the first century BCE, does not record who built the Labyrinth, although he does tell us that, "Imandes is the name of the man buried there."[18] Diodorus Siculus, writing in the same century, attributes the Labyrinth to a "native king" called Mendes, "whom some call Mares." This he built as his tomb.[19] Imandes, Mendes, and Mares are all no doubt further corruptions of Amenemhat III's throne name Nimaatre. The fact, however, that Manetho, Strabo, and Diodorus Siculus collectively state that the Labyrinth was constructed as the sepulcher of the monarch in question seems to affirm that the structure's primary function was as the mortuary temple of Amenemhat III in his deified form.

Although this might well have been the case there now seems little question that it was Sobekneferu who, following the death of her father, picked up the mantle and transformed his mortuary complex into something quite extraordinary. Remember too that Pliny wrote that the "king" responsible for the construction of the Labyrinth was "Petesuchis or Tithois,"[20] names we have already linked with Sobek, Neith, and through them both Amenemhat III and Sobekneferu (see chapter 18). Why the female monarch's involvement in the Labyrinth complex was ignored by classical writers probably can be put down to two basic reasons. Firstly, in the past no one really understood the importance of Sobekneferu and the impact of her reign, and, secondly, the far more celebrated achievements of her father meant that he alone must have been the sole builder of the Labyrinth.

What also is important to remember is that Sobekneferu's brother, Amenemhat IV, would appear to have had nothing to do with the Labyrinth; his name is not found there at all.[21] Why not? Why did he not honor his father's memory? The fact that Amenemhat IV would seem to have avoided the Labyrinth might be put down to the fact that, unlike his sister during her reign, he did not need to justify his legitimacy to the throne by continually associating himself with the monuments of his father.[22] His rule was assured in the knowledge that his father had chosen Sobekneferu's sister Neferuptah to become his royal wife and co-ruler, and not Sobeknerferu.

Amenemhat IV's choice to ignore the Labyrinth also fits well with what we know about his growing disinterest in the cult of Sobek and the Fayum in general, along with his desire instead to patronize the cult of Atum at Heliopolis. Working on the Labyrinth would perhaps have placed too much strain on his reign, especially since his intentions were seemingly to abandon the Fayum and found a new kingdom in the Sinai, with Serabit el-Khadim perhaps as its main seat of power (see chapter 14).

So, following the death of Neferuptah, Amenemhat IV left any remaining construction work at the site of the Labyrinth to his sister Sobekneferu. She would probably have begun work there immediately upon the death of her father and probably continued to add to the complex up until the end of her reign. The question then becomes—what exactly was she doing there? What was she attempting to achieve?

The fact that the classical writers came to see the Labyrinth as perhaps the greatest monument in the whole of Egypt, grander even than the pyramids at Giza, suggests she really did achieve something quite extraordinary. What exactly will require us to better understand how this mammoth project was executed and how the female monarch was able to establish the Labyrinth as, quite literally, the center of the known world.

28

At the Center of It All

Why exactly Sobekneferu focused her attention so heavily on the Labyrinth has never been properly explored. Naturally, her primary concern would have been the completion of her father's funerary complex to honor his memory and to establish him as a deified king, quite literally as a deity to be worshipped by the inhabitants of Egypt. It is clear, however, that much more was going on there, not only during the reign of Amenemhat III, but also afterward during that of Sobekneferu herself.

The first thing to note is the building's name, the Labyrinth, which remains an enigma to this day. Pliny the Elder tells us that the Egyptian Labyrinth, built "according to tradition 3,600 years ago,"[1] was the first of four, the other structures of this name being on Lemnos, in Etruria (modern Italy), and on the Island of Crete in the Aegean Sea.[2] This final example, arguably the most famous of them all, was designed by Daedalus on behalf of King Minos of Knossos, with its purpose being to contain the half-bull, half-human creature known as the Minotaur to whom tributes were paid every 9 years in the form of 7 maidens and 7 youths. Pliny goes on to state that,

> Whatever the truth may be, there is no doubt that Daedalus adopted it [that is, the Egyptian Labyrinth] as the model for the labyrinth built by him in Crete, but that he reproduced only a hundredth part of it containing passages that wind, advance and retreat in a bewilderingly intricate manner.[3]

All that might be gleaned from this description of the Cretan Labyrinth is that its Egyptian counterpart must likewise have been thought to contain a similar subterranean network of winding passages. As to the name itself, this is almost certainly pre-Greek in origin and derives probably from the Lydian word *labyrs*,[4] meaning "double handed axe." If correct, then how this name came to be associated with the Labyrinth in Egypt is unclear; all we know is that the term was first used to describe Amenemhat III's funerary complex by Herodotus in the mid-fifth century BCE.

THE SACRED CROCODILES

As to the true purpose of the Egyptian Labyrinth, this assumedly had something to do with the original function of its subterranean chambers, for as Herodotus informs us "the Egyptian wardens" there would not permit him to see the monument's "lower chambers." The reason they gave for this was that these were "the burial vaults of the kings who first built this labyrinth, *and of the sacred crocodiles.*"[5] (Current author's emphasis.)

The "burial vaults of the kings" Herodotus refers to were assumedly those of the Dodecarchs, whom he was told built the Labyrinth. The reference, however, to "the sacred crocodiles" was, presumably, an indication of the presence there of an active cult of Sobek, something confirmed seemingly by Flinders Petrie in 1888. Close to the site of the Labyrinth he uncovered a cemetery filled with mummified crocodiles ranging in size from tiny babies to fully grown adults 15 feet (4.6 meters) long.[6]

In the same cemetery Petrie found a number of crocodile dummies made from bundles of reed and grass with an egg or single bone placed inside.[7] Most if not all these crocodile burials dated to the Greco-Roman period, although it is clear the cult of Sobek must have played an important role at the Labyrinth from the very beginning. This seems certain in the knowledge that various broken statues and reliefs of the crocodile god, all clearly dating to the late Twelfth Dynasty, were found there by Petrie.[8] Most of these were simply stone fragments (see fig. 28.1 on the next page). Others were better preserved showing the god in anthropomorphic form with the head of a crocodile. Only the torsos and heads were preserved, and in almost every case the arms and snout had been broken off, seemingly as acts of iconoclasm. A few were in better condition showing the god wearing a striated and tripartite

Fig. 28.1. Damaged statues from the site of the Labyrinth showing (top left) the head of the goddess Hathor and (top right and bottom left and right) the crocodile god Sobek of Shedet (from Petrie 1912, pl. XXVI).

Fig. 28.2. Crocodiles carved on the stone "altar" found by Petrie close to the site of the Labyrinth (from Petrie 1912, pl. XXVII, 4).

wig that terminated in horizontal bands below the neckline (see plate 17). One surviving statue fragment showed Sobek's right arm holding the *was*-staff.[9]

In addition to the discovery of statues of Sobek Petrie also found, close to the southeastern corner of the Hawara pyramid, a limestone block on which were carvings of two crocodiles with traces also of a third (see fig. 28.2).[10] Being so close to the Labyrinth strongly suggested it had come from there.

Then on the north side of the pyramid, at the site of a Roman tile kiln, Petrie came across a stone slab bearing the names of three different forms of the god Sobek, each associated with a different location.[11] The spacing between the names matched exactly that of the crocodiles on the stone block, leading him to suspect that this slab had once been placed on top of the possible altar showing the three crocodiles found on the other side of the pyramid.[12] These facts, along with the various relief inscriptions from the Labyrinth mentioning Sobek of Shedet in connection with both Amenemhat III and Sobekneferu,[13] make it clear the crocodile god was the principal deity venerated there.[14]

BOOK OF THE FAYUM

Some idea of what might have been going on at the Labyrinth after its completion can be gleaned from the Greco-Roman papyrus text known as the Book of the Fayum, introduced in chapter 18. Written almost certainly in the Fayum, it describes the geomythical landscape and cultus places in the vicinity of the depression's great lake and Bahr Yusef canal; it also provides an account of how the lake itself came into being.[15] Prominence, of course, is given to Sobek of Shedet and his cult center at Shedet (Crocodilopolis or Arsinoe).

Ra, in the form of the crocodile god Sobek, is said to have been the first god to emerge out of the primeval waters of the great lake, which was seen as a personification of Mehet-Weret (the "Great Flood"), in other words Neith in her role both as the heavenly cow and as the She-hippopotamus who gives birth to Sobek. Indeed, it was in his form as the crocodile god that the sun, under the name Sobek-Ra, was seen to swim through the waters of the great lake each night before being born anew on the eastern horizon at dawn the following morning.[16]

Litany of the Crocodiles

What seems of primary importance with respect to the function of the Labyrinth is a section of the Book of the Fayum known to modern scholars as the Litany of the Crocodiles.[17] It takes the form of a series of vignettes containing a crocodile, a form of the god Sobek, that symbolizes the soul or active spirit of the local god associated with each of the 42 nomes of Egypt—22 in Upper Egypt and 20 in Lower Egypt—along with a list of the offerings to be made to them by priestly representatives of the different nomes.[18] For instance, in the case of the first of the Upper Egyptian nomes, which was home to the ram god Khnum, guardian of the twin sources of the Nile, we read that, "This is Sobek, Lord of the Two Caves that are the source of the Nile. He is given 10,620 *hetep*-offerings and 365 *djefau*-offerings. He lives from the fish next to Sobek in his Lake."[19] Another example is: "Sobek: lord of the fish *nome* (12th Upper Egyptian administrative district); he is Ra; 10,700 offerings are given to him in the Lake."[20]

STORIES OF CREATION

Although the details of these offerings to the different forms of Sobek were only set down in Greco-Roman times, they seem to reflect religious observances that almost certainly had their origins as far back as the Twelfth Dynasty. This can be seen from the creation myths associated with Sobek contained in the Book of the Fayum. One story, or instance, relates how eight primeval gods, known as the Ogdoad, are said to have dug out the lake, which was then filled with the primeval waters of Nun to become Mehet-Weret, the Great Flood, to create the first temple of Sobek; that is, Lake Moeris itself.[21] A similar story about the lake being "dug out" is found in book II of Herodotus's *The Histories*. This tells how this mammoth project was undertaken by "men's hands" and not those of primeval gods.[22] These legends are likely to have been extremely ancient and probably derived from the same primary source material.

So the geomythical world described in the Book of the Fayum is not simply Greco-Roman in origin, but probably dates back to a very early age indeed. This is something that Egyptologist John Tait has concluded himself, observing that, "The possible points of contact with the Book of the Fayum in Herodotus' fifth century account include the various series of cult-places in the papyrus . . . the series of mummified crocodiles, the 'images of animals' in the central registers, and also the dimensions of the Fayum."[23]

It therefore appears possible that Sobekneferu set up the Labyrinth not only as a place of veneration for her deified father, but also as a place of worship for Sobek in his role as a creator god associated with the death and rebirth of the sun each day and as the true source of the local gods serving all 42 nomes of Egypt. The idea of different forms of Sobek providing the spiritual nourishment for each of the different nomes of Egypt is something hinted at in the crocodile carvings seen on the limestone block found at the site of the Labyrinth by Petrie. They match the positions of regional forms of Sobek named on the stone slab found nearby. In his opinion, the two blocks, when placed together, formed part of "a row of sacred crocodiles of various localities, placed side by side on an altar or high table of stone."[24]

If this scenario can be accepted in connection with the suspected function of the Labyrinth, then can we envisage priestly representatives from all the 42 nomes making their way to the Labyrinth on, say, a yearly basis to supplicate Sobek in his role as the active spirit of their own particular god? Such activities would almost certainly have begun during the reign of Sobekneferu and then continued in some manner through to the Ptolemaic period when the Fayum region's geomythic reality was finally recorded in the Book of the Fayum.

THE LABYRINTH AS THE CENTER OF EGYPT

If all this is correct then it seems possible that Sobekneferu was able to establish the Labyrinth not only as the showcase religious center of the Fayum, but also as the geopolitical center of Egypt. This view is supported by yet another piece of evidence from the Book of the Fayum, which describes the Fayum as the "center of Egypt,"[25] and that here the "gods receive nourishment in their crocodile form."[26]

There, a distance of 61⅔ Iteru (approximately 400 miles or 644 kilometers based on an iteru length of 6.5 miles or 10.5 kilometers) is provided as the distance between Aswan in the extreme south of the country and the Fayum (it is in actuality closer to 382 miles or 615 kilometers).[27] This led Egyptologist Horst Beinlich to comment, "Such statistics—especially the use of fractions—implies that the land was measured exactly."[28] As well as this very specific distance, the north-south and east-west limits of the country are also described,[29] all this no doubt being inspired by the belief that both the capital Itj-tawy on the edge of the Nile Valley and the Fayum depression to its west marked the place of division between Upper and Lower Egypt.

ASSEMBLY OF THE NOMES

There are clues also from the classical writers that the Labyrinth represented a kind of microcosm of the whole of Egypt with chapels set aside for each of the country's 42 nomes. Strabo, for instance, writing in the *Geography,* tells us:

In addition to the things mentioned [in the vicinity of Lake Moeris], this Nome has the Labyrinth. Near the first entrance to the canal, and on proceeding thence about thirty or forty stadia, one comes to a flat, trapezium-shaped place, which has a village, and also a great palace composed of many palaces—as many in number as there were Nomes in earlier times; for this is the number of courts, surrounded by colonnades, continuous with one another, all in a single row and along one wall, the structure being as it were a long wall with the courts in front of it.[30]

Elsewhere in *The Geography* we read that, "the total number of nomes was equal to the number of the courts in the Labyrinth; these are fewer than 30."[31] (The 30 nomes refers to a division of the country into 11 Theban nomes, 4 others around Pelusium in the Nile Delta, and then 30 more for the rest of the country. It is these, seemingly, that are alluded to by Pliny the Elder.[32])

Strabo, who like Herodotus visited the Labyrinth, provides evidence enough to suggest that the "courts" found inside the Labyrinth each served one of the nomes of Egypt, something he confirms himself with the following words:

It is said that this number of courts was built because it was the custom for all the Nomes to assemble there in accordance with their rank, together with their own priests and priestesses, for the sake of sacrifice and of offering gifts to the gods and of administering justice in matters of the greatest importance. And each of the Nomes was conducted to the court appointed to it.[33]

Here Strabo almost spells out what might have been going on in the Labyrinth even at the time of his own visit there in the first century BCE. Having said this, his statement that its "great palace" was "composed of many palaces—as many in number as there were Nomes in earlier times" tends to suggest that this assembly of all the nomes was something that happened there in the past, his account of the ceremonies taking place having been given to him perhaps by the Labyrinth's resident priests or wardens.

Pliny also, from the sources he used to create his account of the

Labyrinth, talks about the connection between its design and layout and the different Egyptian nomes. In his words:

> It would be impossible to describe in detail the layout of that building and its individual parts, since it is divided into regions and administrative districts which are called nomes, each of the 21 nomes giving its names to one of the houses. A further reason is the fact that it also contains temples of all the gods of Egypt.[34]

On this topic John Tait observes, "The common notion that the sub-sections of the labyrinth in some sense represented all the nomes of Egypt can be related to the listings in the Book of the Fayum,"[35] with those listed being the 42 forms of Sobek to which offerings were made to honor the fact that the crocodile god was the true spiritual source behind the gods of all the different nomes.* As accurate as this observation might seem, it is certainly not new.

As early as 1886 Dutch Egyptologist and museum director Willem Pleyte (1836–1903), in a detailed study of available versions of the Book of the Fayum, concluded that the text preserved a memory of the existence within the Labyrinth of an adyton of Sobek containing 42 chapels, one each for the 42 nomes of Egypt (see fig. 28.3).[36] He also points out that although Amenemhat III has adequately been shown to be the builder of the Labyrinth, both through archaeological exploration and classical references, the fact that the name of Sobekneferu, the Greek Skemiophris, has also been found there attests to the part she played in this building project.[37]

THE FUNCTION OF ITJ-TAWY

All this tells us that the Labyrinth was a plan originally conceived of by Amenemhat III, then ignored by Amenemhat IV, but afterward fully realized by Sobekneferu. Why this mammoth building project took place at

---

*Alan B. Lloyd in his study of the Labyrinth rejected the idea that it was divided up into courts serving the different nomes of Egypt, the claim made by Strabo 1932, bk. XVII, ch. I, section 37. Lloyd's argument centered on the fact that during the reign of Senusret III the importance of the nomes had been minimized in favor of a new political unit, and that it was unlikely therefore that his successor, Amenemhat III, would go on to "gratify a political entity which his father had done his best to destroy." See Lloyd 1970, 94 n. 1.

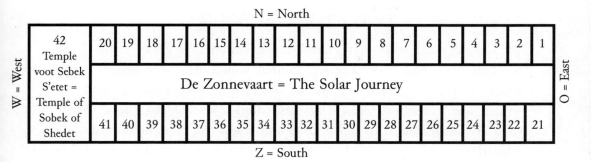

Fig. 28.3. Willem Pleyte's impression of the Labyrinth's 42 shrines, each one
dedicated to the one of the local gods of the 42 different nomes of Egypt.

Hawara in the Fayum, as opposed to Itj-tawy (modern Lisht), which also
straddled the line of demarcation between Upper and Lower Egypt, might
well have had something to do with Amenemhat III and Sobekneferu's attitude toward Egypt's chosen capital at this time.

Itj-tawy was perhaps seen more as an administrative seat of power than
as a place of ancient sanctity. Even though Lisht was the location of a Middle
Kingdom necropolis set aside for royal and elite burials—which included
the pyramid complexes of Amenemhat I and his son Senusret I, the first two
kings of the Twelfth Dynasty—it never became a long-lasting cult center
and place of pilgrimage.

After the Thirteenth Dynasty Itj-tawy was abandoned, its necropolis
plundered by tomb robbers, and its location lost. That was until American
archaeologist and Egyptologist Sarah Parcak, the world's leading expert on
space satellite remote sensing technologies, used LIDAR (Light Detection
and Ranging) in an attempt to find its location. This revealed the presence
in the vicinity of Lisht of an enormous urban center, which will almost certainly turn out to be Itj-tawy itself.[38]

The same fate did not befall the Labyrinth, and the Fayum as a whole,
which retained its role as an important spiritual and administrative center
up until the Coptic Christian era. So if Sobekneferu did indeed establish the
Labyrinth as a place of assembly of the representatives of the different nomes
then this was a deliberate attempt on her part to consolidate all the spiritual
and religious power of Egypt at a single location—one that might well have
been deemed the true point of unification of the Two Lands.

TWELVEFOLD SYMBOLISM

We should recall also that Herodotus recorded that even in his time the Labyrinth had "twelve roofed courts, with doors over against each other: six face the north and six the south, in two continuous lines, all within one outer wall. There are also double sets of chambers, three thousand altogether, fifteen hundred above and the same number under ground."[39]

Although the "twelve roofed courts" Herodotus alludes to are perhaps meant to represent the twelve kings he was told were responsible for the construction of the Labyrinth, there is a huge amount of symbolism in what he says. Twelve is an important cosmological number symbolizing not only the division of the heavens into twelve equal parts, but also the universal concept of a twelvefold division of countries, nations, tribes, cities, pieces of land, or assemblies of people, all focused around a centrally positioned seat of power.[40] This is reflected even in the twelvefold nature of the Dodecarchs said by Herodotus to have built the Labyrinth.

These ideas are further indicated in the fact that Herodotus records that six of the Labyrinth's royal courts "face the north and six the south, in two continuous lines." This tells us two things. First, that the central area between these two sets of six courts, which would appear to have faced each other mirror fashion, symbolized two counterbalanced halves of a whole. Second, it tells us that this dual relationship with respect to the Labyrinth's royal courts was emblematic of the consolidation of Egypt's spiritual and religious power, signifying—again, symbolically at least—the coming together of all the nomes of Upper and Lower Egypt. In some ways the dualistic relationship existing between the building complex's twelve courts, six on one side and six on the other, might be compared with the symbiotic function of the yin and yang symbol in Daoist tradition. This same type of harmonic relationship is implied by the symbolism of the Labyrinth.

RED TEMPLE—WHITE TEMPLE

Even further evidence of this harmonic combination of the spiritual powers of both Upper and Lower Egypt in the design and layout of the Labyrinth is found in the observations of Karl Lepsius following his exploration of its ruins in 1843. He felt he had identified a "red temple" made of red granite occupying the northern half of the Labyrinth, and a "white temple" made of hard white limestone occupying its southern half.[41]

Accepting that Lepsius's interpretation of what he recorded at the site of the Labyrinth is accurate,* then what he was implying is that there were two different colors and types of stone relating to the two separate halves of the monument. This is extraordinarily significant since the red granite of Aswan was emblematic of Upper Egypt, while the hard white limestone, from the Tura hills south of Cairo, was emblematic of Lower Egypt. Bringing the two together in architectural harmony was a sign of the unification of Upper and Lower Egypt. This was similar to the manner that the lotus flower and papyrus plant were themselves used in Egyptian architecture to symbolize, respectively, Upper and Lower Egypt.

The lotus flower and papyrus plant, of course, played the same function in the visual device known as the sema-tawy seen on the sides of royal thrones. Remember, it is present on the side of the stone seat and legs of a statue housed today in New York's Metropolitan Museum of Art that is now known to form the lower half of the famous Berlin bust showing Sobekneferu (see chapter 4). Thus Lepsius's observation that a "red temple" dominated the north side of the Labyrinth while a "white temple" dominated its southern area is yet further evidence that both Upper and Lower Egypt were represented in symbolic form there.

Additionally significant is the fact that the red temple, symbolizing Upper Egypt, was located in the Labyrinth's northern half, representative of Lower Egypt, while the white temple, symbolizing Lower Egypt, was in its southern half, representative of Upper Egypt. If Lepsius's observations were indeed correct then it implies that the deliberate placement of these temples was meant to counterbalance each of the Two Lands they represented on a microcosmic scale. This is something that the twelve courts, six on one side and six on the other, described by Herodotus, was also quite clearly meant to

---

*Eric P. Uphill, in his own study of the classical and modern sources of information on the Labyrinth, confirms that Lepsius's interpretation of the division of the site is clearly based on the distribution of the red and white stone columns and lintels, but adds a cautionary warning to the effect that "the answer was not quite as simple, in that the granite building had limestone walls, while the limestone columns could have been associated with granite elements such as doorways or altars." See Uphill (2000) 2010, 3.

signify—the harmony and unification of Upper and Lower Egypt at a single location seen as the center of Egypt.

There seems little question that Sobekneferu was the creative genius behind the realization of this mammoth architectural project that was intended to bring together all the country's spiritual power in one single place, arguably within the structure's central open court, which was described by Herodotus in the fifth century BCE and identified, seemingly, by Lepsius in 1843.

THE ABGIG MONOLITH

What type of monument the monarch might have erected at the center of the Labyrinth to symbolize this harmonization process can only be guessed at today, although conceivably it was a pinnacle of some kind, similar in style to the gigantic red granite monolith erected during the reign of the Twelfth Dynasty king Senusret I (1956–1911/10 BCE) at Abgig, a small village around 1.9 miles (3 kilometers) southwest of Medinet el-Fayum (see fig. 2.2 on page 17 for a map of the Fayum showing the position of Abgig).[42] This remarkable monument was originally 42 feet (12.9 meters) in height with sides 7.9 feet (2.4 meters) in width at the base tapering to around 4.6 feet (1.4 meters) at the top. It stood on a stone plinth 11.8 feet (3.6 meters) wide made up of four huge slabs of hard white limestone (see fig. 28.4). The Abgig pillar remained in situ up until the nineteenth century, when, finally, it toppled over and broke into two pieces. It remained in this state until it was eventually re-erected in the middle of a roundabout in Medinet el-Fayum, where it can be seen to this day.

The pillar has relief carvings and inscriptions on all four sides. These relate to the manner that the king receives into his presence the gods and goddesses of both Upper and Lower Egypt. They include Atum and Ra-harakte of Heliopolis, Thoth of Hermopolis, and Montu and Amun of Thebes. There is also a crocodile god represented who is almost certainly Sobek (the inscription is damaged). No evidence of any building has been found in the vicinity of the monolith's original location, suggesting it must have stood at the center of some kind of open court, like that which existed at the Labyrinth.

Italian Egyptologist Marco Zecchi proposes that the Abgig pillar is

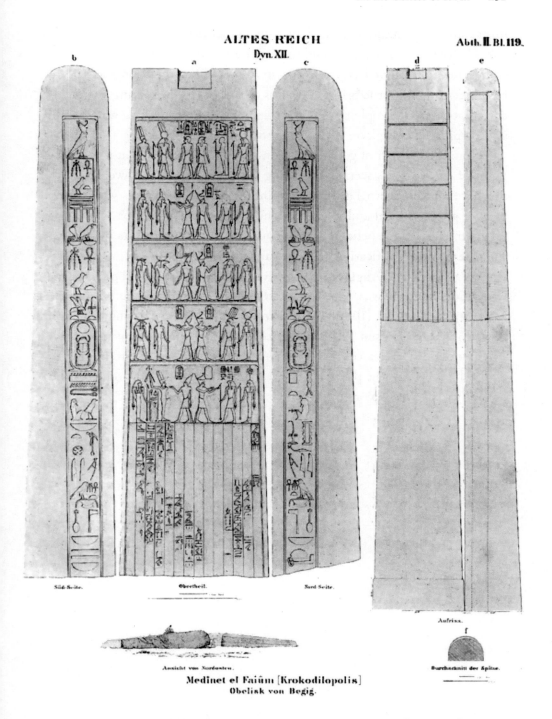

Fig. 28.4. The monolith of Senusret I formerly at Abgig in the Fayum and today standing in the city of Medinet el-Fayum (from Lepsius 1904, II, 119).

unlike any other monument in Egypt, being neither a stela nor a true obe-lisk. He feels it is solar-related and was inspired by the concept of the *benben*-stone, the stone of first creation that in Heliopolitan tradition was said to have emerged out of the primeval waters of Nun at the beginning of time. If correct, this would imply that by the reign of Senusret I, Abgig was, Zecchi says, "a pillared cult place, with strong solar connections."[43]

From the number of gods present on the pillar it is clear that its original point of erection was seen as a meeting place of the divine powers of both southern and northern Egypt, something that Zecchi suspects would have been of great political and religious significance.[44] In many ways, the Abgig pillar emphasized the belief that the Fayum, in similar with Itj-tawy, marked the true point of unification of Upper and Lower Egypt.

Very clearly the Abgig monolith would have dominated the landscape when Sobekneferu was involved in the construction of the Labyrinth, located just 6.2 miles (10 kilometers) to the east. Was she trying to realize everything that Senusret I had attempted to achieve with the erection of the Abgig monolith over a century beforehand? Was she herself attempting to establish Hawara as the place of first creation in the physical world? It is this possibility that we explore next.

29

Navel of the World

In ancient Greek cosmological tradition, places of first creation were known as *omphali* (singular *omphalos*), the word for "navel." They acted not only as centers of countries or kingdoms, but also as, quite literally, centers of the physical world. Everything in the known universe was seen to come into being from a single centralized location that was invariably marked by a navel stone or obelisk of some kind.[1] Omphali are found everywhere from Easter Island (Rapanui) in the Pacific Ocean to Cusco in Peru and Delphi in Greece. All are seen as terrestrial navels signifying the place of emergence of all creation, both in the past and in the present day.

Various temples in Egypt were promoted by their priesthoods as points of first creation, a belief perpetuated by so-called foundation texts inscribed on their walls. Among the cult centers that claimed this status included Karnak (cult center of the god Amun) in southern Egypt, Hermopolis (the cult center of the god Thoth) in Middle Egypt, and Heliopolis, the cult center of the creator god Atum in northern Egypt.[2]

At this last location a building known as the Temple of the Phoenix marked the place of first creation, where Atum or Ra was said to have shone forth after emerging from the waters of Nun as a primordial hill, island, or mound at the beginning of time.[3] Almost certainly the temple contained a pillar similar to the stone monolith formerly at Abgig in the Fayum.[4] This pillar, as we saw in the previous chapter, is thought by Marco Zecchi to have acted as a kind of *benben*-stone[5]—one meant to signify the region as the center of creation.

SOBEK AS CREATOR GOD

In her creation of the Labyrinth, Sobekneferu may well have been attempting to complete an extraordinary plan—one originally conceived by her father Amenemhat III, but ignored by Amenemhat IV—to fully establish Hawara as the center of the Two Lands. Why Sobekneferu and her father might have believed this even possible comes down to their presumed conviction that the Fayum constituted a place of primordial creation associated with the concept of *zep tepi*—the "first time" or "first occasion." In other words, they had come to believe that it was from the Fayum's great lake that not only the physical world, but also the entire cosmos had come into being.

Some idea of what Amenemhat III and his daughter might have believed in this respect can be found in the Book of the Fayum. As we saw in chapter 28, it contains a legend to the effect that the Fayum's great lake was dug out by eight primeval gods known as the Ogdoad,[6] and that afterward it was filled from beneath with the primeval waters of Nun to create Mehet-Weret, the Great Flood, which in turn became the first "temple" of Sobek.[7]

One of the book's illustrations shows the crocodile god at the center of the Fayum's great lake (see fig. 29.1). He wears the red crown of Lower Egypt sticking up from which are double plumes, ram's horns (a symbol of the god Amun-Ra), and the solar disk. In the accompanying legend the crocodile is described as the one "who was created from himself, who emerged from the Wadj-wer [the Great Green]" at the moment of first creation. He is described also as the oldest son of Mehet-Weret, the "Great Flood," in her role as the

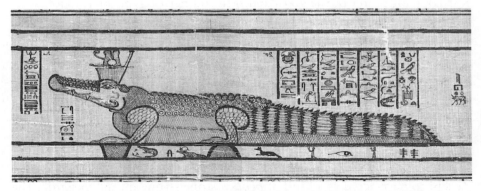

Fig. 29.1. A form of the crocodile god Sobek-Ra in the Fayum's great lake from the Book of the Fayum. It wears the red crown of Lower Egypt with twin plumes, ram's horns (a symbol of Amun-Ra), and the solar disk.

genius loci of the Fayum's great lake.[8] Mehet-Weret, as previously noted, is none other than the goddess Neith, the mother of Sobek.

The "primeval crocodile" seen on the waters of the Great Flood is identified in the text as "Sobek of Shedet," who is himself a form of the falcon-headed-god Ra-harakte, this being Ra in his form as Horus of the Two Horizons.[9] It is a reference to the manner that Ra in the form of the crocodile god swims through the waters of the Fayum lake from sunset on the western horizon through to his rebirth on the eastern horizon at dawn the following morning.[10]

Although it is difficult to prove that the Fayum's inherent cosmogony truly predates the construction of the Book of the Fayum, there are good reasons to suspect that many of its mythological themes long preexisted the age of Herodotus and most likely had their inception during Egypt's Middle Kingdom. If correct, then their existence might well have influenced decisions being made by Amenemhat III and Sobekneferu regarding the design, layout, and ultimate purpose of the Labyrinth.

It is even possible that the Labyrinth, once completed and fully operational, took over some of the religious functions that had previously taken place in the temple of Sobek at Shedet located on the shores of the great lake. Its cult of the crocodile went back at least to the Old Kingdom and may even have existed as early as the First Dynasty.[11] In this knowledge, it is conceivable that the Book of the Fayum is very possibly the last remnant of beliefs and practices associated with the cults of Sobek and Neith going back across a period of 3,000 years to the very beginnings of dynastic Egypt.

MIRROR OF THE COSMOS

In summary then, it would appear feasible that Sobekneferu deliberately established the Labyrinth as both a mirror of the cosmos and as a microcosm of Egypt. In doing so she perpetuated preexisting beliefs concerning the region's role as the true place of first creation, something that according to the Book of the Fayum was said to have occurred during *zep tepi,* the "first time" or "first occasion."[12] Did she additionally believe that these creative forces continued to affect the outside world through the power of the god Sobek in his role as the active spirit of the local gods of the 42 nomes of Egypt, something that their priests and administrators would have to honor each year with offerings to the form of the crocodile god attached to their own particular district?

The fact that Amenemhat III's mortuary complex might also have functioned as a Heb Sed court would only have added to the Labyrinth's assumed cosmological function. Sobekneferu would no doubt have seen the Labyrinth's placement close to what the kings of the Twelfth Dynasty saw in terms of the line of demarcation between Upper and Lower Egypt as emblematic of her own divine right to rule the Two Lands. The fact also that both her personal name (Sobekneferu) and throne name (Sobekkara) both included the theophoric form of the name Sobek must only have strengthened her conviction that she was justified in establishing the Labyrinth to channel and focus the influence of the crocodile god in his role as the great primeval one who was created at the beginning of time and was thus the living spirit of *all* gods of Egypt. In asserting this belief and insisting that representatives of the various different nomes come to the Labyrinth to make offerings to Sobek as the animating essence of their own local gods, Sobekneferu may in fact have been attempting to initiate a form of monotheistic religion, one that predated Akhenaten's Aten faith by as many as 450 years.

Sobekneferu did not, of course, proclaim Sobek to be the *only* god of Egypt, although it is possible that having been brought forth by his mother Neith, the She-hippopotamus, in her form as Mehet-Weret, the "Great Flood," Sobek was considered the first born of all the gods. That Sobek was given such a high status in the Egyptian pantheon of gods during Sobekneferu's reign unquestionably elevated him to the position of primary state god in Egypt. It was a status he would retain into the Thirteenth Dynasty, where as many as seven of its rulers were named Sobekhotep, meaning "Sobek is satisfied" or "Sobek is contented."

What Sobekneferu managed to achieve with respect to the Labyrinth was, I believe, quite remarkable. For the duration of her brief, but clearly eventful, reign this would have afforded her immense power and prestige, although as we have seen there was too much against her and her regime for this process to continue without it being hindered by outside influences such as rival priesthoods. After just 3 years, 10 months, and 24 days on the throne she would appear to have been deposed and forced to take her own life. As outlined in chapter 21, the monarch's most obvious opponents were the priests of Heliopolis, and in the knowledge that they must have seen their cult center as the true site of first creation, what Sobekneferu was doing in the Fayum—at the Labyrinth in particular—simply could not be allowed to continue. Her promotion of the Fayum both as the center of the country and as Egypt's true place of first creation, something that gave Sobek a virtual monotheistic status, simply had to be stopped. The chances are her opponents would have done whatever was necessary to put a stop to this situation, the consequences of which have already been outlined in this book.

THE VENGEANCE OF NITOCRIS REVISITED

Some knowledge not only of Sobekneferu's downfall but also of her apparent involvement in the establishment of the Labyrinth as the place of assembly of the different nomes would appear to have been preserved in Herodotus's account of the vengeance of Nitocris. It will be recalled that following the death of "her brother, the king,"[13] the queen "built a spacious underground chamber; then, with the pretence of handselling it, but with far other intent in her mind, she gave a great feast, inviting to it those Egyptians whom she knew to have been most concerned in her brother's murder." As we are informed, "while they feasted she let the river in upon them by a great and secret channel," thus drowning them all.[14]

As argued in part 4 of this book, Herodotus's Nitocris was almost certainly Sobekneferu, while "her brother, the king" can be identified as Amenemhat IV. The "spacious underground chamber" mentioned in the story is, I feel certain, a reference to the Labyrinth's own "underground chambers" mentioned elsewhere in book II of Herodotus's *The Histories*.[15] The fact also that the Bahr Yusef waterway through which the waters of the Nile reached Lake Moeris lay immediately south of the Labyrinth is surely an allusion to "the river" let into the "spacious underground chamber" via "a great and secret channel" that drowned the invited guests attending the "great feast."

The "great feast" in turn is perhaps a distorted memory of the arrival in the Fayum each year of priestly representatives of the different nomes. All this, along with Herodotus's further statement that once Nitocris had done away with those whom she saw as responsible for the death of her brother "she cast herself into a chamber full of hot ashes, thereby to escape vengeance,"[16] recalls other events that took place during Sobekneferu's reign. They include the murder of Amenemhat IV and afterward her own death, seemingly by suicide.

Sobekneferu's demise ended the Twelfth Dynasty, although from its ashes arose the Thirteenth Dynasty, whose kings continued what she had started. They recognized Itj-tawy as Egypt's capital, although are likely to have settled any differences with the priests of Heliopolis since they would have needed their participation in rites of kingship including the authentication of the royal titulary, the titles adopted by every ruler of Upper and Lower Egypt on ascending the throne.

The Thirteenth Dynasty rulers strove to uphold Egypt's independence despite the growing fear of Lower Egypt being overrun by the Hyksos, something that would begin around 1700 BCE. Lastly, the kings of the Thirteenth Dynasty would appear to have deified Sobekneferu, in the same manner that she had deified her own father.[17]

The Labyrinth, along with the royal palace and temple of Sobek at Shedet, was probably ransacked and at least partially destroyed when the Hyksos finally overran first Memphis and afterward the capital Itj-tawy. It would have been around this time that the kings of the Thirteenth Dynasty abandoned the Fayum as their seat of power and established themselves fully at Thebes in the south of the country.

What became of the Labyrinth after this time is unclear, although from what Herodotus tells us there is every reason to believe it was restored to its full glory by the kings of the Late Period, seemingly those of the Saite or Twenty-sixth Dynasty. They, as we saw in chapter 16, Psamtik I in particular, were responsible for the popularization of the cult of Neith at her great religious center of Sais, the dynasty's chosen capital in the Nile Delta. It was probably at this time that Sobekneferu's memory became confused with the name Nitocris, arguably because of Neith's role as mother of Sobek.

So why did Sobekneferu and her immediate predecessors, including her father Amenemhat III, come to believe so strongly in the power of Sobek of Shedet as the creator god of Egypt? What was it about this region that so convinced them to see it as the center of the country and as the place of unification of the Two Lands? Answering these questions, as we see next, will eventually provide us with some real clues regarding the final fate of Sobekneferu's body.

PART 7

ANCESTORS

30

The Mystery of Mazghuna North

It was in 1910 that the British archaeologist Ernest Mackay began investigating a series of ancient cemeteries located in the desert immediately south of the Dahshur pyramid field and a little way to the west of the Mazghuna railway station situated in the nearby Nile Valley. Most of the graves he opened had previously been ransacked, but enough archaeological materials remained to show that some of the cemeteries belonged to the Fifth and Sixth Dynasties of Egypt's Old Kingdom. Others, however, only dated to Roman times.[1]

While in the area Mackay decided to take a look at the substructures of two former pyramids that lay nearby (see fig. 30.1 for a map of the location).[2] Carved directly out of the bedrock, they included corridors, chambers, and long entrance shafts inside which were huge blocks of quartzite, making up architectural features such as roof slabs, lintels, plug blocks, and monolithic sarcophagi.

From the similarity in style of the plug blocks seen in both pyramids, it was clear to Mackay that they had been built at the same time.[3] This, along with certain other features noted also in Amenemhat III's pyramid at Hawara, such as the presence of enormous quartzite burial chambers, led Mackay to conclude that the two pyramids—Mazghuna North and Mazghuna South as they became known—were probably built for his immediate successors.[4] The south pyramid was perhaps destined for Amenemhat IV, especially since there was some evidence of it having per-

Fig. 30.1. Map showing the positions of the Mazghuna North and Mazghuna South pyramids in relation to the Dahshur Pyramid field and surrounding area.

haps contained a burial, with the unused Mazghuna North pyramid having been intended for his sister Sobekneferu.*

---

*Mackay himself suggested the north pyramid was perhaps intended for Amenemhat IV with its southern counterpart being built for Sobekneferu. This was based on the fact that the southern pyramid was larger (see Mackay 1912, 37). As logical as this solution might seem, the fact that only the southern example possessed a seemingly functional (mortuary?) chapel and showed some evidence of having received an interment (see Mackay 1912, 45-46), suggests that this was always intended as the first of the two to be built and used. The fact also that the southern pyramid was said by Mackay to be "merely a copy" of Amenemhat III's pyramid at Hawara tends to back up the idea that this, and not its northern counterpart, was the first of the two pyramids to be built (see Mackay 1912, 49). Since Amenemhat IV preceded Sobekneferu, this therefore implies that the southern pyramid was intended as the former monarch's intended tomb.

When Mackay first approached the site of the Mazghuna North pyramid—having been informed of its existence by local workmen—the only thing he could see was a large area covered with limestone chips. This was all that remained of the pyramid's superstructure, which had been entirely made from stone.[5] Not a single block remained in situ above ground level, indicating that the pyramid must have been destroyed in antiquity. Its substructure, on the other hand, remained almost entirely intact.

Mackay decided to explore the site, although there was an immediate problem. A small Coptic cemetery occupied the central area of the large scattering of limestone chips.[6] Since it still appeared to be in use its disturbance was not going to be greeted too kindly by the local Coptic community. So Mackay decided that he would have to work around its edges, perhaps finding a way to go beneath it without disturbing the graves. Why exactly the Copts decided to place their cemetery on this spot, as opposed to anywhere else in the area, is a mystery, suggesting perhaps that the site had long been seen as holy ground.*

After surveying the area as best as possible, Mackay managed to gain entrance into a long shaft, oriented due east with a series of 31 steps cut into its bedrock floor.[7] It descended downward at an angle of 13.5 degrees into a small chamber where an enormous quartzite plug, rectangular in shape, waited in a readymade wall slot to be moved into place.[8]

BENEATH THE PYRAMID

From there onward a series of winding corridors and chambers, one containing a second quartzite plug, led eventually into the pyramid's burial chamber. Inside this stone-cut sepulcher was a monolithic piece of quartzite. Cut into this was the rectangular shape of a sarcophagus along with a smaller square compartment to contain the canopic jars that would have held the deceased's internal organs. A huge quartzite lid weighing as much as 10 tons (9 metric tonnes), with a rounded upper surface and squared off ends, lay ready to be slid into position.[9]

The fact that the huge stone plugs and lid of the sarcophagus had never

---

*Curiously, this cemetery has since become the stuff of mystery and imagination, and was featured in the 1985 thriller *The Mummy Case* by Elizabeth Peters.

been used made it clear to Mackay that the pyramid's substructure could never have contained a royal burial. What is more, he found no evidence of a mortuary chapel that would have been necessary for the preparation of the body prior to final interment. Despite these observations, plunderers had still entered the substructure in an attempt to find treasure as was evidenced by the fact that a wall between a corridor and a blocked up chamber had been broken down, while the floor of the corridor had all but been destroyed.[10] It should also be pointed out that Mackay was told that French archeologist and engineer Jean-Jacques de Morgan, who famously excavated the pyramid of Amenemhat III at Dahshur (see chapter 12), had tentatively explored the substructure of the Mazghuna North pyramid some twenty years earlier.[11] What he might have found is not recorded.

ENTERING THE AFTERLIFE—PYRAMID ORIENTATION

Mackay noted two somewhat peculiar features about the Mazghuna North pyramid, which might well have been constructed as Sobekneferu's final resting place. The first of these was its descending shaft. This came down from a small stone chamber at its eastern end, which was in turn accessed by

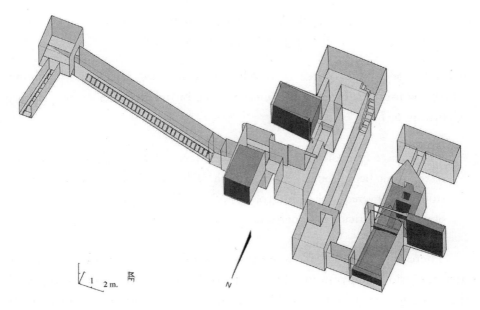

Fig. 30.2. Substructure of the Mazghuna North pyramid by Franck Monnier.

a staircase entered from the north (see fig. 30.2). The long descending shaft or passageway of a pyramid would normally be oriented north-south—the north being the direction of the afterlife.[12]

The fact that the Mazghuna North pyramid's descending shaft (or more correctly, its *ascending* shaft, since this was in fact meant for the soul to ascend toward the stars) was uniquely directed due east, something Mackay deemed to be "quite unknown."[13] Very clearly, there must have been different motivations behind the monument's design and layout, even from those behind the construction of its southern counterpart just a third of a mile (half a kilometer) away. This has a north-south orientated descending shaft entered from the south and leading to a burial chamber at the northern end of the substructure.[14]

The easterly placement of the Mazghuna North pyramid's descending shaft could simply have been to thwart tomb robbers searching for its entrance. This is possible, although unlikely, since the orientation of shafts and passages was usually determined through cosmological considerations. So orienting a pyramid's descending shaft east-west, as opposed to north-south, suggests the presence of conflicting ideas on what happened to the soul upon its exit from the pyramid.

THE RED PLASTERING
ON QUARTZITE SURFACES

A further peculiarity noted by Mackay in connection with the Mazghuna North pyramid's substructure concerned the burial chamber's sarcophagus. According to him:

> The exposed faces of the sarcophagus were very well finished, the surface of the stone being rubbed down smooth. When this had been done the stone was covered with a thin coating of red-coloured plaster, the reason of which is difficult to understand, as there were no flaws to conceal.[15]

There was, however, far more to the simple use of red plaster to cover surfaces inside the pyramid. Mackay determined that *all* exposed surfaces of the white quartzite blocks used in the tomb were painted in a similar manner, while on various of them were drawn "several series of vertical strokes in black upon the red surface," each series of strokes being between "fine horizontal lines."[16] Puzzled by this discovery, which was not present in the Mazghuna South pyramid, Mackay observed:

> It is difficult to explain why only the quartzite blocks should have been selected for this purpose, the marking not being found on any limestone masonry. It could hardly have been for the purpose of ornamentation, because it occurs on the ends of the plug blocks which would be concealed in their recesses when the chamber was closed. Similarly the northern outside face of the sarcophagus was also marked, and I could not have seen this if the limestone bed, upon which the lid rested, had not been destroyed.[17]

Red in ancient Egypt could denote male gender, with this being seen in the fact that the skin of statues or reliefs showing men were often painted red. Red was also a symbol of sekhem, great strength and divine power through its association with the redness of flames, the might of the sun, and the color of blood, particularly that of your enemies. All these attributes were embodied in the lioness-headed goddess Sekhmet, the personification of sekhem as a female deity.

In the papyrus text known as the Book of the Heavenly Cow, found in the tomb of Eighteenth Dynasty king Tutankhamun,[18] Hathor as Sekhmet reigns down fire on the world after men turn against the sun god. The goddess would have wiped out humanity had she not been stopped by the intervention of the other gods, who caused her to stop her reign of terror.

The association between the color red and the leonine form is something seen, for instance, in connection with the Great Sphinx at Giza.[19] We know from ancient reports that the monument was once painted red, probably symbolic of the creature's strength, although whether it ever represented the goddess Sekhmet is unclear.

All of this information only becomes relevant to this current study if the Mazghuna North pyramid really was to become the final resting place of Sobekneferu as some scholars suggest.[20] Was she responsible for the design and layout of the pyramid, including the red plastering of all its white quartzite blocks?

SEKHEM-SOBEKNEFERU

In chapter 5 we saw how a Thirteenth Dynasty papyrus found at Harageh speaks of a site named Sekhem-Sobekneferu, a reference seemingly to Sobekneferu's funerary complex.[21] If this was the intended name of the Mazghuna North pyramid, then the use of the term *sekhem* could be reflected in some manner within its design. Just possibly the quartzite features of the tomb were painted red to uphold the principles of sekhem, even in death, while at the same time serving as a warning to those who might dare to disturb the deified monarch's eternal slumber. We should also not forget that Sobekneferu set up a large stone sphinx at Khatana, on the site of the Hyksos city of Avaris in the eastern Delta. Was this meant to convey the idea of the monarch's absolute power (sekhem) through her adoption of the sphinx form, symbolic of the goddess Sekhmet?

All this might well help explain why the interior of the Mazghuna North pyramid was painted red, and even perhaps why Sobekneferu's funerary complex was called Sekhem-Sobekneferu. The problem, of course, is that we have no hard evidence that the pyramid was intended for her, so any theories regarding its design and layout must remain tentative at the very least.

If, however, the Mazghuna North pyramid *had* been intended as Sobekneferu's final resting place then it can only be imagined that in the wake of her sudden and unexpected death alternative plans were put in place for her final interment. As Stefania Pignattari points out, the successors of Sobekneferu might not have allowed the monarch to be interred in a finished tomb due to the prevailing political situation at the time of her death.[22] If, like Cleopatra during a much later age of Egyptian history, Sobekneferu took her life unexpectedly and without due announcement, then perhaps she was buried in secret to ensure her remains were not disturbed by those opposed to her strict regime.

Wolfram Grajetzki has proposed that her burial place should be looked for either at Hawara or at Dahshur.[23] Pignattari suggests she could have been interred in one of two minor pyramids at Dahshur.[24] That her father Amenemhat III commissioned the construction of the Black Pyramid at Dahshur, which was used to inter at least two of his royal wives along with various of his daughters, does make this idea appealing. Having said this, the fact that the Black Pyramid lies just 1.5 miles (2.5 kilometers) distance from the Mazghuna North pyramid might equally be used to explain the female monarch's decision to site her pyramid at Mazghuna, particularly if the location had been chosen *before* her father switched his attention to Hawara.

In the end, however, Sobekneferu was never interred at Mazghuna, meaning that her tomb has to be located elsewhere, and in the current author's opinion one place to start looking for it is the Fayum depression, which, as we have seen, would appear to have held a deep spiritual meaning to Sobekneferu on a number of levels. This, along with the fact that the Fayum's great lake was seen as a personification of Mehet-Weret, a form of the goddess Neith, the mother of Sobek,[25] makes it clear that both Sobekneferu and her closest supporters might have chosen a burial site somewhere in the region. In this way her rebirth would have been assured through her role as an avatar of the crocodile god.[26]

So what *did* happen to her? Where might she have allowed herself to be buried to reflect her true personal beliefs? To answer these questions we will need to examine a highly enigmatic building in the Fayum depression that would appear to have been of special interest to Sobekneferu. I speak here of the curious megalithic temple located at the foot of the Qasr el-Sagha rock formation on the north side of the great lake. This strange structure, as we see next, can help explain why the female monarch believed the region to be so important to her greater destiny.

31

Temple of the Crocodile

In 1888, prior to beginning his exploration of the site of Labyrinth at Hawara, British archaeologist and Egyptologist Flinders Petrie took time out to examine the historical sites that lay beyond the northern shores of the Birket el-Qarun lake. Accompanying him on this expedition was the inspector of public works for the Fayum province, Mr. Marshall Hewat.[1]

On arrival in the area the two men visited the enigmatic ruins of Dimeh al-Siba, which means "Dimeh of the Lions." This was an important Greco-Roman settlement that might well have been situated on an island in the great lake. Today, however, it is little more than a series of isolated ruins jutting out of the Libyan Desert like some nameless city of the sands from a H. P. Lovecraft story (see plate 18).

In Ptolemaic times Dimeh al-Siba was named Soknopaiou Nesos (meaning "Island of Soknopaiou," from the Egyptian "Sobek-en-Pai"),[2] an important center for the worship of the crocodile god Sobek under his Greek name of Soknopaios. Although only founded during the reign of Ptolemy II in the third century BCE, there is evidence all around the ruins of human activity going back beyond the earliest Egyptian dynasties to the Neolithic age.[3]

Petrie and Hewat then continued their journey, traveling around 4.3 miles (7 kilometers) farther north to the uppermost limits of the Fayum depression. In this very striking—but eerily silent—desert landscape, devoid of any modern human habitation, they climbed slowly upward until, without forewarning, they came upon what they had gone there to see. It was an unusual stone building standing on the southernmost edge of an escarpment known to geologists as the Qasr el-Sagha formation.

It was the structure's proximity to this geological feature that led to it becoming known as the Qasr el-Sagha temple, and it is somewhere that Sobekneferu and her contemporaries would unquestionably have seen as very important indeed. To start with, the temple is at almost exactly the same latitude as the Twelfth Dynasty capital of Itj-tawy,* some 30 miles (50 kilometers) to the east. So like Itj-tawy, the Qasr el-Sagha temple would have been seen to mark the line of division between Upper and Lower Egypt. This is a point to remember as we begin to explore this strange structure, which, like Dimeh al-Siba, today sits quite isolated in the Libyan Desert.

THREE-DIMENSIONAL JIGSAW PUZZLE

The Qasr el-Sagha temple possesses several highly unusual features, making it almost unique to the dynastic architecture of ancient Egypt. To start with its exterior walls are made up of three basic levels of construction— the lowest composed of rough "tafl rock" extracted from the platform on which the structure sits. The middle section is of white sandstone, with the uppermost layer being of hard limestone.[4] Much of the rectangular building's external masonry is polygonal in nature, enabling its stone blocks to slot together without the need for mortar. This creates what can only be described as a three-dimensional jigsaw puzzle (see fig. 31.1 and plate 19).

Fig. 31.1. The Qasr el-Sagha temple as drawn by Flinders Petrie for his book *Ten Years Digging in Egypt 1881–1891* (from Petrie 1912, fig. 78).

---

*The pyramid of Amenemhat I at Lisht is at latitude 29°34.492'N with the Qasr el-Sagha temple at 29°35.706'N. This provides a variance of around 1.214'. These figures were determined using Google Earth.

Normally, stone temples in ancient Egypt were built using regular blocks, their exposed surfaces cut and dressed to create a perfect finish. This, however, was not the case with the Qasr el-Sagha temple (see plate 20). Its exterior walls bear an uncanny resemblance to those of pre-Incan and Incan buildings in Peru, which also employ the use of polygonal masonry in their construction.

Sitting on a flat, rocky platform, the temple is approximately 70 feet by 28 feet (21.5 by 8.5 meters) in size, meaning that it displays an almost perfect 5:2 ratio in its design (see fig. 31.2).[5] Such exact proportions were often incorporated into ancient Egyptian architecture in honor of the first sacred enclosure and temple built during the primordial age when the gods still inhabited the earth.[6] What *is* curious, however, is that in ancient Hebrew cubits of 21 inches (53.34 centimeters) the temple's exterior walls would have been precisely 40 cubits by 16 cubits in size, something that seems unlikely to be coincidence. There are no indications that western Asiatic peoples were involved in the construction of this building, although the use of a cubit of 21 inches is intriguing to say the least.

The building's long axis is oriented 20.3 degrees south of west or, alternately, 20.3 degrees north of east allowing its only doorway, located midway along its southern wall, to face out toward the lake below. Today the Birket el-Qaran is around 5.6 miles (9 kilometers) away from the edge of the Qasr el-Sagha formation, but in the distant past its waters would have come up as far as the raised platform on which the temple stands.

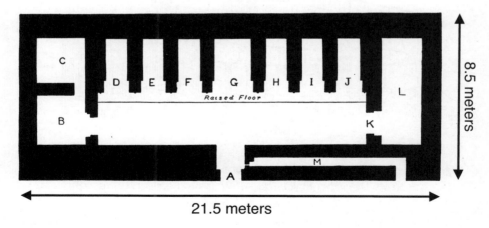

Fig. 31.2. Plan of the Qasr el-Sagha temple
(from Caton-Thompson and Gardner 1934, pl. LXXIV, 3).

INTERNAL FEATURES

On entering inside the temple Petrie found himself in a long, narrow corridor that ran the entire length of the building and allowed access to small rooms located at either end. On the north side of the corridor were a series of seven cells or shrines divided from one another by stonewalls and carved doorframes that had once supported double doors (see plate 21). The floors of the shrines were elevated, meaning that a step had to be navigated to enter inside them. The long corridor was designed to enable access to these small shrines, meaning that it had probably functioned as an offering hall during ceremonies performed at the structure. The central shrine was slightly larger than the rest, suggesting it served a more prominent role than the others. All seven cells would probably have contained the statue of a god.[7]

One further compartment, completely hidden with no entrance door at all, lay beyond the westernmost of the seven shrines. The only means of entering it was via a small crawl hole situated at ground level in the small room on its southern side. The purpose of this blind room is unclear. Since the crawl space allowing access to this enclosed compartment would not have been visible when the door of the room was open, some Egyptologists have concluded it must have functioned as a place of storage, perhaps for temple paraphernalia.[8] Equally, it could have had a ritual usage, maybe as a compartment set aside for the veneration of a god whose myth cycle called for its image to be hidden from general view.

Above the seven small shrines is a roof that runs the entire length of the building, the cornices on its southern extent forming a parapet wall. There is no roof at all above the offering hall. Indeed, from the unfinished exterior walls to the missing roof it could be argued that the temple was never completed, with what we see today being the condition it has stood since the age of Sobekneferu and her contemporaries.

Just about a third of a mile (500 meters) northwest of the temple, rising out of a line of hills known as the Gebel Qatrani formation,[9] is a monumental rock feature that goes by the name Qasr el-Sagha. The name is Egyptian Arabic and means "Fortress of Gold," a reference seemingly to the structure's uncanny likeness to an unimaginable stone citadel left over from some forgotten age of humankind. It is from this formidable structure that the rocky platform on which the temple sits gains its name.

DATING THE TEMPLE

It was almost certainly the proximity of this towering rock fortress that prompted eager treasure hunters to tear up the temple's floor looking for hidden chambers and secret hiding places. They will have carried away anything of value it might have contained, making it difficult to determine the building's age, especially since it contains no carvings, no reliefs, and no inscriptions. Petrie himself was unable to come to any conclusions regarding its age,[10] advocating only that, "Some more excavation might disclose a clue to its meaning."[11]

Schweinfurth's Temple

Petrie was not, however, the first European to sets eyes on the Qasr el-Sagha temple. Four years earlier, in 1884, the German botanist, ethnologist, and explorer George August Schweinfurth (1836–1925) had come across the structure during his own explorations of the northern Fayum.[12] (This we know since he carved his initials and the date "1884" on one of the blocks there.)[13] Indeed, prior to Petrie publishing details of the site the building had already become known as Schweinfurth's temple.[14]

Exploring the platform on which the temple sits, Schweinfurth noted on its southern side "mounds of ancient pottery" of the "most weather worn appearance."[15] This had led him to propose, "that the old temple, as well as the original settlement or formation [to its west], is one of the monuments belonging to the oldest times."[16]

Many other visitors to Qasr el-Sagha since the age of Petrie and Schweinfurth have searched for clues as to the temple's true age and purpose. Most Egyptologists are today happy to accept the findings of the German husband and wife team Dieter and Dorothea Arnold. They investigated the site in the 1970s and concluded to their satisfaction that it was built either during the reign of Senusret II or during that of his successor Senusret III; they, of course, being Sobekneferu's great-grandfather and grandfather respectively. It was a deduction made following the discovery beneath some construction rubble found near the temple of several examples of mid-Twelfth Dynasty ceramics, which when tested using a dating technique known as thermoluminescence provided dates during the reigns of these two pharaohs.[17] Similar pottery was found in association with the Twelfth Dynasty settlement just to the west of the temple.[18]

Others, however, have had different opinions on the age of the Qasr el-Sagha temple as the Arnolds themselves acknowledge.[19] In fact, several early visitors to the site came away convinced it belonged to the Old Kingdom. These opinions were based on the building's exterior walls, which bear close similarities to funerary temples built at Giza for the kings of the Fourth Dynasty. For instance, the mortuary temple and valley temple of Khafre (builder of the Second Pyramid), as well as the Sphinx Temple located on the eastern side of the Sphinx monument, were all constructed using huge megalithic blocks, some as much as 50 to 100 tons (45 to 90 metric tonnes) apiece.

Polygonal masonry, however, is seen today only in two Egyptian temples—Khafre's valley temple at Giza and, to a lesser degree, the Osireion, the cenotaph of the Nineteenth Dynasty pharaoh Seti I (1290–1279/8 BC), situated at the rear of the king's funerary temple at Abydos in southern Egypt.

THE BASALT QUARRIES OF WIDAN EL-FARAS

The discovery by the English archaeologist and Egyptologist Gertrude Caton-Thompson (1888–1985) in the vicinity of the Qasr el-Sagha temple of abundant stone tools in the form of "crescent-grinders and hand-picks, typical of the early dynasties,"[20] led her to suspect that the site had been "an Old Kingdom centre."[21] This seems confirmed in the knowledge that immediately to the west of the temple is the start of an ancient paved road, lined mostly with slabs of sandstone and basalt, that runs north-northwestward for roughly 6 miles (10 kilometers) and terminates in the vicinity of four basalt quarries situated on the hill ridge forming the highest part of the Gebel Qatrani formation.[22] The location itself is known as Widan el-Faras, meaning the "ears of the horse," a reference to two prominent sandstone peaks that form a gigantic gateway into the area of the quarries.[23]

Black Basalt Floors
The Widan el-Faras quarries were unquestionably exploited during the Old Kingdom, their highly distinctive black basalt being used to construct the floors of various funerary structures within the Memphite necropolis. They

include the mortuary temple of Khufu situated on the east side of the Great Pyramid at Giza,[24] as well as various Fifth Dynasty temples at Saqqara and Abusir.* Mining operations, however, ceased at the quarries toward the end of the Old Kingdom, arguably due to transportation problems after the Bahr Yusef canal began to silt up, making it impossible for vessels to pass from the Fayum's great lake into the River Nile.[25]

The problem was fixed, of course, during the Twelfth Dynasty with the clearing of the Hawara Channel.

The road itself begins in the vicinity of a former port or quayside about a third of a mile (half a kilometer) southwest of the Qasr el-Sagha temple. It then continues as a poorly preserved, winding track until it reaches the escarpment near to where the building stands. It then assumes a linear course of better-preserved stone slabs that come to an end in a rocky gulley known as Wadi Ghorab, the "Valley (of the) Crow."[26] What seems significant about this ancient paved road is that for much of its way it is aligned directly toward the temple site, something that seems absolutely purposeful (see fig. 31.3 for a map of the northern Fayum region).

SOBEKNEFERU LINKS?

So although there's nothing to prove that the Qasr el-Sagha temple was built during the Old Kingdom, there are grounds to suspect that the site itself was important at this time. The question then becomes what possible relationship might there have been between this strange temple and the world of Sobekneferu?

The fact that either her great-grandfather Senusret II or her grandfather Senusret III were likely responsible for the building's construction brings its sheer existence into Sobekneferu's sphere of influence. More importantly, Egyptologist Ian Shaw of Liverpool University has proposed that striking similarities exist between the structure's interior architecture and that of the late Twelfth Dynasty temple of Renenutet at Medinet Madi (see plates 22 and 23). This could indicate that both were built around the same time,

---

*Basalt is used for floors in the mortuary temples of Userkaf and Pepi I at Saqqara, the mortuary temples of Sahure, Neferirkare, and Nuiserre at Abusir, and also in the valley temple of Sahure at Saqqara. See Hoffmeier 1993, 118–19; Bloxam and Storemyr 2002, 28.

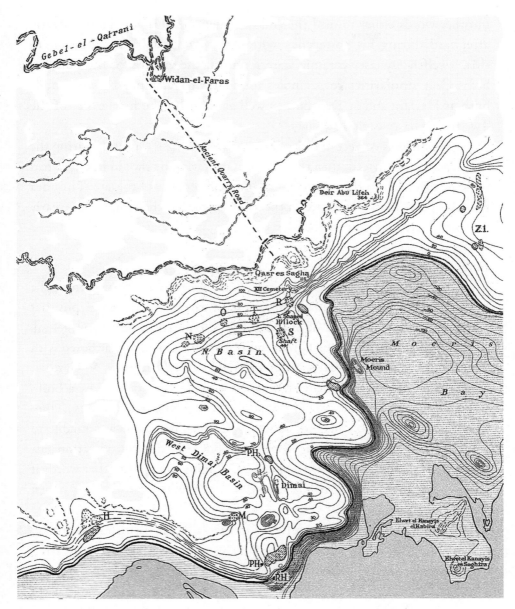

Fig. 31.3. Section of a map of the northern Fayum above the Birket Qarun lake (from Caton-Thompson and Gardner 1934, pl. CXIV). The Wadi el-Faras quarries and Gebel Qatrani hills are seen at the top left. From there the ancient quarry road leads southwest toward the Qasr el-Sagha temple. Note also Dimeh al-Siba (ancient Soknopaiou Nesos) located due south of Qasr el-Sagha; site Z.1, where Gertrude Caton-Thompson found a Neolithic stone circle, and also the position of the Deir Abu Lifa monastery northeast of Qasr el-Sagha. Please note that some spellings on the map differ from those used in this present book.

in other words either toward the end of Amenemhat III's reign or directly afterward during his co-regency with Amenemhat IV.[27] In addition to this, Twelfth Dynasty ceramic ware found in the vicinity of the building bears clear similarities to examples found at Amenemhat III's pyramids both at Hawara and at Dahshur, as well as at Lisht, the former site of the Twelfth Dynasty capital Itj-tawy.[28]

If Ian Shaw is correct and the Qasr el-Sagha temple was built during the lifetime of Sobekneferu, then there is no reason why she should not have had some involvement in the construction and maintenance of the site. This idea becomes particularly attractive in the knowledge that the temple was clearly associated with the cult of Sobek.

Beloved of Shedet

The Qasr el-Sagha temple's association with Sobek is confirmed from the discovery there by Caton-Thompson of a relief carving with hieroglyphs that read *Shedti mery,* "beloved of Shedet."[29] As she noted in her monumental, two-volume work *The Desert Fayum,* published in 1934 and coauthored with her colleague, the geological lecturer and field surveyor Elinsor W. Gardner (1892–1980), "The sign Shedet represents a shrine surmounted by a bull's skull and horns on a pole. . . . The word means 'He of Shedet,' and is a common title of the crocodile-god, Sebek."[30] Caton-Thompson was unable to determine the exact date of the inscription, but after due consideration suspected that the relief was "later than the Old Kingdom."[31] In other words it almost certainly belonged to the second half of the Twelfth Dynasty, when the cult of Sobek was at its height in the Fayum.

It should be recalled that on the cylinder seal in the British Museum on which are recorded the royal titles of Sobekneferu, the monarch is referred to as "Beloved [*meryt*] of Sobek Shedety," which uses the same hieroglyph of a bull's skull on a pole to denote the term "of Shedet." It could be argued, of course, that this inscription is feminized, while the relief inscription found by Caton-Thompson showed the word "beloved" [*mery*] in its male form, and so cannot be referring to Sobekneferu. However, the damaged cylinder seal from the monarch's reign noticed by Percy E. Newberry in a "dealer's shop" in Cairo and said to have been found at Kom el-Aqarib, near the site of the ancient city of Heracleopolis Magna (see chapter 2), included the line, "Sobekkara, beloved of Shedet."[32] The word "beloved" was written in its masculine form [*mery*], meaning there is no reason why the relief inscription found by Caton-Thompson at Qasr el-Sagha could not have been alluding to Sobekneferu as "beloved of Shedet." In addition to this, there exist other tentative clues that point persuasively to the fact that Sobekneferu had a strong interest in this site. These we explore in chapter 33.

The View from Qasr el Sagha

That the Qasr el-Sagha temple was being used to venerate Sobek of Shedet does make good sense. Being located on high ground overlooking the lake means that the crocodile god's role as the form taken by the sun god Ra to swim through its waters from sunset to sunrise each night could have been celebrated there to full effect. The Fayum's great lake is also one of the few places in Egypt where, from a certain vantage point, the sun can be seen to both rise from and set down into a large expanse of water.[33]

One of the best places to witness this spectacle during the Middle Kingdom would have been the Qasr el-Sagha temple. Its position on the lake's northern shores would have made it ideal for this purpose. In addition to this, Sobek of Shedet's role as the vehicle used by the sun god Ra to navigate the waters of the lake is, as we see next, dimly recalled in a legend concerning the foundation of the Qasr el-Sagha temple.

According to the story a young pharaoh was fleeing from wild dogs that were pursuing him. He ran as fast as he could until, eventually, he found himself on the shores of the great lake. At that moment a friendly crocodile appeared that allowed the pharaoh to climb onto its back. The animal carried him into deeper waters until finally they came upon an island. Here the young pharaoh was able to keep safe until the dogs gave up their chase. To honor the kindness offered to him by the crocodile, the king built the Temple of the Crocodile, the name given to the Qasr el-Sagha structure.[34]

It is a legend that seems to echo, in a somewhat abstract manner, the manner in which the sun god Ra was daily carried through the waters of the great lake in the form of a crocodile or perhaps even on the back of a crocodile.[35] It also brings the cult of Sobek right to the door of the Qasr el-Sagha temple. However, the story of the foundation of the Temple of the Crocodile is not simply some fanciful tale created by the inhabitants of the Fayum to explain how the structure came to be there. Diodorus Siculus in the first century BCE recorded almost exactly the same story, albeit with some added twists.

THE DEIFICATION OF THE CROCODILES

In Book I of his *The Library of History*, Diodorus includes a section concerning "the deification of crocodiles."[36] It begins with an explanation of why people in Egypt's Nile Valley eat crocodiles and how hunters are able to catch them. Thereafter he cites an account he had been "given of these beasts," writing:

> For some say that once one of the early kings [of Egypt] whose name was Menas, being pursued by his own dogs, came in his flight to the Lake of Moeris, as it is called, where, strange as it may seem, a crocodile took him on his back and carried him to the other side. Wishing to show his gratitude to the beast for saving him, he founded a city near the place and named it City of the Crocodiles; and he commanded the natives of the region to worship these animals as gods and dedicated the lake to them for their sustenance; and in that place he also constructed his own tomb, erecting a pyramid with four sides, and built the Labyrinth which is admired by many.[37]

There can be little doubt that in this legend "Menas," presumably Menes, the legendary first king of Upper and Lower Egypt, is synonymous with the "young pharaoh" featured in the legend regarding the foundation of the Qasr el-Sagha temple. This, of course, is located on the north side of Lake Moeris, while the former site of Crocodilopolis, ancient Shedet, is to be found on its southern shores at what is today Kiman Faras at the northwestern limits of Medinet el-Fayum.

THE FOUNDATION OF CROCODILOPOLIS

According to Diodorus, Menas, after being saved by the crocodile, went on to found, not the Qasr el-Sagha temple, but Crocodilopolis, which, along with the lake, thereafter became the principal place of worship of the crocodile god. As we have seen, there is every reason to suspect that Sobek was venerated in the Fayum as early as the Old Kingdom, and arguably as early as the First Dynasty.[38] More significant, however, is that Diodorus's section on the "deification of the crocodiles" doesn't just refer to the age of Menes, it clearly recounts the foundation of Shedet as the principal cult center of Sobek during the reigns of Amenemhat III and Sobekneferu.

The fact that Diodorus's "Menas" is said to have "commanded the natives of the region to worship these animals as gods and dedicated the lake to them for their sustenance," and then constructed there, "his own tomb, erecting a pyramid with four sides, and built the Labyrinth which is admired by many," appears to confirm this fact.

Quite obviously Diodorus is here referring to the construction of the Hawara pyramid complex and Labyrinth monument, initially by Amenemhat III, and then afterward by Sobekneferu. She, as we saw in chapter 28, would appear to have set up the Labyrinth both as a microcosm of Upper and Lower Egypt and as the socio-religious center of the country.

Why exactly the female monarch might have come to believe the Fayum oasis deserved this divine status could well have had something to do with how she and her contemporaries perceived the importance not just of the Qasr el-Sagha temple, but also of the site itself. Not only did it mark the approximate line of demarcation between Upper and Lower Egypt, something determined when Amenemhat I established Itj-tawy as Egypt's capital at the beginning of the Twelfth Dynasty, but there is also every reason to suspect that the entire northern Fayum was seen as a place of the ancestors, *and* of the gods they worshipped. It is this fascinating topic that we explore next.

32

Place of the Ancestors

All around the Qasr el-Sagha temple is considerable evidence of prehistoric activity going back *millions* of years. In its vicinity, among the expanses of desert sand, are huge petrified tree stumps from a former great forest. There are also the fossilized remains of extinct species of whales and giant sea snakes that thrived when the region still formed part of a vast sea some 37 million years ago.[1] Seeing the winding backbones and rib cages of these enormous creatures, which remain in situ today at a site named Wadi el-Hitan (see plate 24), the "Valley of the Whales," conjures thoughts of huge underworld monsters of the sort the deceased in ancient Egyptian tradition would have had to encounter and successfully navigate in order to reach the hereafter.* From all this it becomes easy to understand why the northern Fayum might have come to be seen as a realm of the ancestors.

Adding to this conclusion would have been the large scattering of Neolithic stone tools and sites found throughout the area. This was something made clear by the extensive field studies carried out in the northern Fayum by Gertrude Caton-Thompson and her colleague Elinsor Wight

---

*Snakelike creatures are shown accompanying the text of the Book of Two Ways (also known as the "Guide to the Ways of Rostau"), which features for the first time in Middle Kingdom coffins and forms part of the much greater body of literature known as the Coffin Texts (see Faulkner 1973 and Faulkner 1977). These pictorial representations of netherworld creatures constitute the first appearance of similar imagery found in association with New Kingdom books of the dead such as the Amduat and the Book of Gates. For more on this subject see Hill 2018.

Gardner between 1928 and 1934.[2] Not only did they investigate the presence there of a number of prehistoric settlements, but Caton-Thompson records the survival of a prehistoric stone circle, perhaps 7,000 years old, located some 3.75 miles (6 kilometers) east-northeast of the Qasr el-Sagha temple.

SITE Z.I

Known as Site Z.1, this ringlike structure was made up of six large blocks of limestone and sandstone, one of which remained standing. Some of the stones displayed so-called cup marks—small circular hollows of a type well known from prehistoric standing stones in Europe and Anatolia. Neolithic flint implements as well as a knife of Old Kingdom date were found inside the circle.[3] Caton-Thompson was of the opinion that this monument was one of the oldest in the entire depression.[4] So its close proximity to the Qasr el-Sagha site should be noted, especially since it would presumably have been in much better condition during the age of Sobekneferu and her contemporaries.

ANCESTRAL GODS

Then, of course, there is the black basalt quarries of Widan el-Faras situated in the hills at the end of the 6.2-mile-long (10 kilometer), ancient paved road that commences in the vicinity of the Qasr el-Sagha temple. The pharaohs of the Twelfth Dynasty would undoubtedly have been aware of these quarrying operations undertaken by their great ancestors of the Fourth and Fifth dynasties. Strengthening the connection between the kings of the Twelfth Dynasty and those of the Old Kingdom is the fact that looking north from the Widan el-Faras quarries the observer during the age of Sobekneferu would have seen in the distance the pyramid fields of Dahshur, Saqqara, and Giza.[5]

All this singles out the Qasr el-Sagha temple as an important place of veneration not just of the crocodile god Sobek, but also with any spirit or deity considered to have inhabited the northern Fayum. What then can we find out about these local gods and goddesses and how might they have been of interest to the female monarch?

THE BLACK LAND

The first clue as to the northern Fayum's most ancient sanctity comes from the fact that the black basalt marking the summits of the highest hills in the Gebel Qatrani range might well have served a nonutilitarian function. Its dark appearance connected it with the nutrient-rich black silt left behind by the floodwaters of the annual inundation. Its presence in the Nile Valley each year gave Egypt its ancient name, which was Kemet (*kmt*) or Khem (*km*), meaning the "black land." The minerals present in this highly fertile sediment enabled the successful growth of planted seeds. Its failure to appear due to low floods would have spelt disaster to the peoples of Egypt. So, inevitably, the black sludge became sacred in its own right.

The Earth God

In 1993 archaeologist and Egyptologist James K. Hoffmeier proposed that the black basalt floors used in Old Kingdom funerary temples reflected the regenerative powers of this fertile black sediment, which was itself seen as sacred to the earth god Geb.[6] In support of this hypothesis Hoffmeier cited the fact that the earth god played an important mortuary role in the Pyramid Texts, stating that, "In many spells Geb is directly involved in the burial and the ascension of the king to the sky."[7]

This last fact seems important as in addition to the floors of Old Kingdom funerary temples, the black basalt of Widan el-Faras was used in the manufacture of royal sarcophagi inside which the regeneration and ultimate resurrection of the deceased was expected to take place.[8] (Note: Pyramid Texts were inscribed on the interior walls of pyramids from around 2350 BCE to the end of the Old Kingdom, circa 2181 BCE. They were a corpus of spells and sayings meant to help the internee navigate his or her way to the hereafter.)

Hoffmeier's ideas regarding the connection between the earth god Geb and the black basalt used in the construction of Old Kingdom funerary temples and royal sarcophagi were afterward embraced by James A. Harrell and Thomas M. Bown, two leading experts on the geology of the Fayum's Gebel Qatrani formation.[9] So did Geb really become the divine protector of the area's black basalt quarries?

Although no inscriptions to this effect are known to have been found, Geb was certainly venerated in the Fayum. In Ptolemaic and later Roman times, Sobek and Geb were combined together under the name of Soknebtunis-Geb, their cult center being Tebtunis (modern Tell Umm el-Baragat), an ancient town located on the south side of Lake Moeris.[10]

SNAKE DEITIES

One of Geb's primary animistic forms was that of the snake; indeed, from as early as the Pyramid Age he was seen as the father of all snakes. It was an attribution born out of the fact that the snake was a primary symbol of creation and regeneration, particularly in association with the fertility both of the Nile Valley and of the Fayum depression following the annual inundation.[11] This is something we have already explored in connection with Renenutet, the snake-headed goddess venerated by the ancient Egyptians as the bringer of a successful harvest. Not only was she divine patron of the Twelfth Dynasty temple at Medinet Madi, but she was also a wife of the earth god Geb.

That Geb and Renenutet are both associated with the Fayum and each have serpentine forms should alert us to the fairly obvious fact that the region would appear to have been associated in the past with a primeval *genius loci* ("spirit of the place") in the form of a snake. One of its identities was no doubt as the goddess Renenutet, with another being Geb, who could well have functioned as divine protector of the Widan el-Faras quarries and thus the Gebel Qatrani hills as a whole. What then might have been the identity of this snake deity during the age of Sobekneferu?

The Snake Goddess

Papyrus documents dating from the Greco-Roman period found at Dimeh al-Siba (ancient Soknopaiou Nesos) in the northern Fayum speak of a snake deity named Nephershati (*n3-nfr-ir-ṣdy*),[12] who was called Neforsatis (Νεφορσατης) by the Greeks.[13] Since the last part of the name, *ṣdy*, shows as its determinative the snake glyph, British Egyptologist Francis Llewellyn Griffith (1862–1934)—who was responsible for a detailed study of the demotic papyrus texts from Dimeh al-Siba housed in the Rylands Library, Manchester, England—suspected that Nephershati was a snake goddess.[14]

A cult in the name of Nephershati is certainly thought to have existed in the northern Fayum by the Late Period (664–525 BC),[15] if not earlier, although during Greco-Roman times this snake deity would appear to have merged with the goddess Isis to become Isis-Nepheres, who was also worshipped in the Fayum.[16] As we saw in chapter 20 in connection with the fate of Cleopatra, Isis was divine patron of magic and medicine, her principal symbol being the snake.

Nephershati's cult center was clearly Soknopaiou Nesos, modern Dimeh al-Siba, where she was seen as the genius loci of a sacred pool known as the Great Green (*Wt-wryt*), the site of which is lost today.[17] The term Great Green could be used to refer to the Mediterranean Sea as well as the Fayum's great lake,[18] since both were considered visible manifestations of the primeval waters of Nun.[19] So it seems likely that the sacred pool at Soknopaiou Nesos was representative of these primeval waters, which in the Book of the Fayum were said to have welled up to create the great lake.[20]

Soknopaiou Nesos, as we saw in chapter 31, was a major cult center of

Fig. 32.1. The snake goddess Renenutet from the Medinet Madi temple. Photo by Ani Williams.

Fig. 32.2. Carving on an altar from the temple of Renenutet at Medinet Madi of the Greco-Roman snake goddess Thermouthis, who combined aspects of Renenutet and Isis-Nepheres. Photo by Ani Williams.

the god Soknopaios, a Greek form of Sobek. During Ptolemaic times Isis would herself become the consort and even the mother of Soknopaios under the name Thermouthis, a snake goddess who combined aspects both of Renenutet and of Isis-Nepheres (see figs. 32.1 and 32.2).[21] So it's clear that the entire region was seen as the domain of a deified snake that had many identities.

The ruins of Soknopaiou Nesos, we should recall, are just 5 miles (8 kilometers) distance from the Qasr el-Sagha temple and just 5.6 miles (9 kilometers) away from the Widan el-Faras quarries. Gertrude Caton-Thompson recorded that since there existed at Dimeh al-Siba traces of human activity going back to the Neolithic age, worship of Sobek must have begun there at a very early date indeed.[22] More crucially, she concluded that there must have been a connection between Soknopaiou Nesos and Qasr el-Sagha.[23]

In this knowledge, it seems possible that the Qasr el-Sagha temple was a place of veneration not only of the crocodile god Sobek, but also of a primeval deity in the form of a snake. If so, then what was its name? Was it Geb? Was it Renenutet, or could it have been Nephershati? More crucially, what could any of this have meant to Sobekneferu and her own personal association with the northern Fayum? It is these questions we address next.

33

The Seven Snake Gods

The first clue as to the original identity of the Fayum's primeval serpent comes from knowledge that the earth god Geb and the snake goddess Renenutet had a son. His name was Nehebkau, which means "Assigner of Kas."[1] A *ka* (plural *kau*) was a form of the human soul that helped animate the physical body and remained close to the tomb once its occupant had been laid to rest.

In ancient Egyptian art Nehebkau was shown as a snake with human arms and legs, or as a serpent with two or more heads, or as a snake-headed human figure (see fig. 33.1).[2] Egyptian priests would invoke Nehebkau to

Fig. 33.1. The snake god Nehebkau from the Papyrus of Ani, ch. LXXXVII (from Budge 1913, pl. 27).

cast magical spells either to protect a person from snakebites or to cure them of a snakebite if they'd already been bitten.[3]

THE BIRTH OF RA

Nehebkau also played a crucial role in the Heliopolitan creation myth. As a god form he is said to have been the first thing to stir within the primeval waters of Nun prior to the coming into being of the physical universe. This he did by becoming the moving coils of a great snake that formed the outer limits of material existence, from which emerged the god Atum, the "Complete One," who rose out of the waters of Nun as a primeval mound, hill, or island and shone forth his light on the first day.[4]

For Atum, or Ra as the deity was also known, to completely break free of the waters of nothingness he had to kill Nehebkau, an act often signified by the sun god adopting the form of a feline and using a triangular knife to slice off the serpent's head.[5]

Sometimes this feline is identified as the Great Cat named Mau, but there are indications that this act could also have involved other, more familiar feline deities such as Bastet and Sekhmet.[6] Both deities were linked with the veneration of Nehebkau, in that they were able to control or negate his serpentine influence.[7]

Nehebkau's role in the Heliopolitan creation myth is recalled in Spell 449 of the Pyramid Texts, which reads: "[The deceased king in his role as Ra] is the flood's outflow, emerging from it when water came into being. He is Kas-Assigner [Nehebkau], who(se body) has many folds."[8] The floodwaters here are those of the Nun, which was thought to have brought forth all the world's water including, of course, that which filled the Fayum's great lake.[9]

CULT OF THE SNAKE GOD

Nehebkau's cult center is unclear, although he would appear to have been venerated at Heracleopolis Magna, which lies immediately south of the entrance to the Fayum.[10] The city certainly served the cults both of Bastet and of Sekhmet, the last of whom was wife of Ptah, the city's divine patron. Heracleopolis Magna, as we saw in chapter 26, was one of the few places beyond the limits of the Fayum where Sobekneferu would appear to have commissioned the construction of a major building. The fact that she would seem to have possessed a special interest in the concept of sekhem, divine power or strength, personified as the goddess Sekhmet, might well explain why she wanted to leave her mark on this city. In the Book of the Heavenly Cow, it was at Heracleopolis Magna that Sekhmet is said to have begun her terrifying rampage, "wading about in the blood of men" for three nights, after its inhabitants turned away from worshipping the sun god Ra.[11]

Had Sobekneferu been familiar not only with Nehebkau's connection with Heracleopolis Magna, but also with the city's association with Bastet and Sekhmet? If so, then perhaps Heracleopolis came to be seen as the spiritual center of the monarch's own personal interest in the concept of sekhem.

THE SEVEN COBRAS

According to the Coffin Texts—a corpus of spells that began appearing on coffins during the Middle Kingdom to help the deceased enter the afterlife—Nehebkau is associated with the magical force known as *heka* (plural *hekau*). This was personified as a god of the same name and as a serpent-headed goddess named Urt-hekau (or Weret-hekau), which means "Great one of magic." Spell 85, for instance, states that Nehebkau, "swallowed seven cobras to consume their *heka* and gain magical power."[12] Elsewhere, in Spell 374, these seven *uraei*-snakes are said to have afterward become seven of the god's vertebrae.[13] From various references to the swallowing of the seven *uraei*-snakes to gain *heka*-magic found in the Pyramid Texts we know that the vertebrae in question were those that support the neck.[14]

Nehebkau was not the only deity associated with the *heka*-magic gained by consuming the seven cobras. Spell 612 of the Coffin Texts associates these same seven cobras with the goddess Hathor. This tells us:

TO BECOME HATHOR. How happy are those who see the festival in this place of mine! I am seated on the throne of Khopri [or Khepri, the scarab beetle and proto-form of Ra], I give judgement in company with the seven cobras. . . . I have swallowed the seven uraei, because I am Hathor, Mistress of rams, the serpent who laughs with Edjo [or Wadjet, the cobra god of the north], the great wild cow of the Mansion.[15]

Fig. 33.2. Hathor's "fetish object" occasionally shown worn as a headdress by the goddess in ancient Egyptian art (from Budge [1934] 1988). Within its doorway we see a raised cobra while on its outside we see either the cow horns of the goddess or twin cobras ready to strike. It seems likely this structure was some kind of ritual shrine containing a deity in the form of a snake.

Not only do these statements link Hathor with the magic power of the seven cobras, but it seems that the goddess herself could assume the form of a snake, making her into some kind of mistress of snakes. Indeed, one of the symbols of Hathor was a snake housed in a conical shaped structure protected either by cow horns or twin cobras (see fig. 33.2).[16]

All this is important because the seven cobras that bestow the power of heka on those who swallow them might well have been synonymous with what are known as the "seven Hathors." These were seven spirits under the command of the goddess. They feature in certain ancient Egyptian stories where they appear to people in order to foretell the future, an act of *heka-magic* in its own right.[17] As we have seen, Hathor would seem to have had her own shrine in the Labyrinth and was perhaps favored by Sobekneferu because of Hathor's role in the legitimization of a pharaoh's right to rule following the successful completion of the Heb Sed festival (see chapter 9).

What then might all this mean to our understanding of the Qasr el-Sagha temple, and how does it relate to the world of Sobekneferu? The answer comes in what else we know about the snake goddess Nephershati venerated at Dimeh al-Siba, ancient Soknopaiou Nesos, for the full break down of her Egyptian name reveals something very significant indeed.

THE DISCOVERIES OF EVE REYMOND

The first element of Nephershati's name, *N3-nfr*, means, simply, "beauty," in the same manner that Sobekneferu, or Neferusobek, means "beauties (*neferu*) of Sobek." The second element of Nephershati's name, *ir-ṣdy*, is, however, more problematic. According to Egyptologist Eve Reymond (1923–1986), who made a comprehensive study of the papyri found at the site of the former city of Soknopaiou Nesos in the 1930s, the word *ṣdy* conceals, "a wide range of meanings and we may suggest for its interpretation 'secret,' holy,' or take it with the meaning 'ground,' 'plot of land,' 'region,' 'waters,' or 'supernatural powers.'"[18] On the other hand the verb *ir,* she wrote, implies "to make" or "to create,"[19] leading her to comment:

> There is, therefore, a distinct possibility that the Dime [that is, Soknopaiou Nesos] deity [Nephershati] had a pronounced creative capacity. The expression *ir-ṣdy* by itself, disregarding the variety of meanings suggested, brings to mind, in connection with the creation, another Egyptian deity who was conceived to be a snake with creative powers. This is the *'Ir-tꜣ*, the 'Earth-Maker'. . . . It may be surmised that in the doctrine of the Sobek priests the original plot of land that emerged from the Nun at the commencement of the world was habitually described by the word *ṣdy*, and consequently the original Creator of waters and earth was called *'Ir-ṣdy*.[20]

Thus to Reymond, Nephershati was the memory of a primeval snake, whose gender was seemingly neutral, that stirred in the primeval waters of Nun before the emergence of the sun god on the first day of creation. This, of course, was the same role the god Nehebkau played in Heliopolitan tradition.

As Reymond wanted to make clear, "We should be inclined to admit that the Dime deity represented as a snake may have been for Dime, and perhaps for other Fayyumic places, what the Earth-Maker was in other temples."[21] In other words, her proposed primeval serpent was probably venerated at more than one site in the Fayum from very earliest times, with one of those sites being Soknopaiou Nesos, just five miles (eight kilometers) distance from the Qasr el-Sagha temple. If Caton-Thompson was right in suspecting a relationship between these two sites, then I believe there is every reason to conclude that the Fayum's primeval serpent, who would later emerge as the snake goddess Nephershati, would indeed have been venerated at Qasr el-Sagha during rites that in Reymond's opinion would have involved "creation and ancestry."[22]

Nephershati, under the name Nepherses, features in the Book of the

Fayum as a form of Isis,[23] while Isis herself is described in the text as "The Divine Wife Shedet,"[24] making her a manifestation of the Fayum itself. One illustration shows Isis greeting a standing snake,[25] which might be the same serpent mentioned elsewhere in the text under the name Aha-nefer,[26] arguably another name for the Fayum's genius loci in the form of a serpent.

THE FAYUM AS A PLACE OF CREATION

In the knowledge that both Nehebkau and Hathor gained their *heka*-magic through swallowing the seven cobras, could it be possible that the Qasr el-Sagha temple's seven shrines were dedicated to seven local gods who could take the form of snakes? Textual evidence from the Book of the Fayum seems to suggest this might well have been the case. Let me explain.

The principal hieroglyphic form of the Book of the Fayum is referred to as the B/H/A manuscript, with the initials standing for the museum collections that originally housed its three main fragments.[27] One of the fragments contains a highly abstract map of the Fayum's great lake. On its shores are seen deities in the form of snakes, crocodiles, a baboon, along with two mummiform figures that have scarab beetles for heads.[28] All are positioned either on the map's left side—symbolizing both the east and south, the directions associated with the source of the Nile, Upper Egypt, and the rising of the sun—or on its right side, representing the north and west, the directions of darkness, death, the outflow of the Nile, the entrance to the underworld, and, of course, Lower Egypt.[29] This makes sense of the suspicion that as early as the Middle Kingdom the northern Fayum was seen as a place of the ancestors.

Much of the text accompanying the map has been lost.[30] One version of the papyrus, however, written in hieratic script and found at Tebtunis, the Greco-Roman center of the cult of Geb-Sobek in the southern Fayum,[31] preserves around 90 percent of this missing text, although it has no corresponding map. What it says is very revealing indeed. Horst Beinlich, who has attempted to tie together this new information with the Book of the Fayum's B/H/A manuscript, observes:

One facet of the text that must be restored here is particularly interesting. It says that, upon the birth of the sun god from Mehet-Weret [that is, the

Fayum's great lake], other gods were also born. *These are characterized as snakes,* which were the most ancient form of all gods. Presumably *there were a total of seven of these gods,* but not all their names are preserved.[32] (Current author's emphasis.)

What this shows is that there was a firm belief in Fayumic tradition that when Neith in her guise as Mehet-Weret, the Great Lake, gave birth to the sun god Ra in his guise as the crocodile god, seven *other* gods came into being at the same time. *These gods took the form of snakes.* This alone tells us how the Fayum, in the eyes of the Twelfth Dynasty monarchs, came to be seen as Egypt's primary place of first creation ahead of the claims of other cult centers such as Heliopolis or Thebes. Was this one of the reasons why Sobekneferu and, we must assume, her father Amenemhat III came to believe that the Fayum had to be established as the center of Egypt—because it was considered the true and original place of creation in the physical world?

Seven Powerful Spells

Taking the matter one step further is a text from the temple of Esna in southern Egypt. It describes how Neith was able to create the world by uttering "seven powerful spells"[33] or "seven magical words."[34] Neith, we know, was also considered "the mother of the snakes and crocodiles,"[35] and was said to have brought into being the serpent named Apep, an equivalent to the god Nehebkau, by spitting upon the primeval waters.[36] Thus there can be little doubt that Neith was seen as the progenitor of the seven snake gods that emerged from the waters of the great lake in Fayumic tradition. If this is indeed the case, then these snake gods are perhaps synonymous with the seven cobras that when swallowed gave a person the power of *heka*-magic. In this manner the seven cobras can be seen as emblematic of the "seven powerful spells" used by Neith in her creation of the world.

Cosmological ideas of this nature, attached to the cult both of Neith and of Sobek, thus become relevant to the architectural design of the Qasr el-Sagha temple, in particular its seven shrines, which may well have contained statues of seven local gods. Could these seven gods have assumed the form of snakes? It should be recalled that in the Book of the Fayum it records the presence somewhere on the lake's shores of a cult shrine of Neith called the "Acacia of Neith," known also as the "Temple of the Acacia."[37]

A partially preserved illustration accompanying the text shows the goddess and her young son, who although named as Horus, that is, the rightful heir to the throne of Egypt, is very clearly an incarnation of Sobek-Ra.[38] This is affirmed in the fact that what little can be seen of the remaining figure shows the snout of a crocodile. The rest of the child, who stands in front of Neith, is completely missing (see fig. 18.3 on page 163 for a reconstruction of this illustration).[39]

Unfortunately, the location of this lost shrine of Neith is unclear, although there is no reason why it could not have been on the north side of the great lake. It is, of course, tempting to link it with the Qasr el-Sagha temple, although this would be little more than wild speculation at this time.

In the opinion of the present author there is enough evidence to suggest that the unique nature of the Qasr el-Sagha temple marks it out as very special indeed. Although a structure probably existed on the site before the age of Sobekneferu, it seems likely she had a hand in its reconstruction and maintenance. Arguably it was restored and renovated during the reign of her brother, Amenemhat IV, perhaps at her instigation, with the same architects responsible for the internal design of the temple of Renenutet at Medinet Madi being brought in for this purpose.

If all this is correct then there is good reason to suspect that the building was used at this time to conduct ceremonies involving seven gods who could take the form of seven *uraei*-snakes.

Is it possible that at the Qasr el-Sagha temple Sobekneferu celebrated the coming forth from the Fayum's great lake of the sun god Ra in his form as the crocodile god Sobek, as well as the emergence from its waters of a primeval snake later recalled as the snake goddess Nephershati? I think this is very likely indeed.

THE SOBEKNEFERU SCARAB

There is, I have to add, one object relating to Sobekneferu that might well provide compelling evidence that the monarch had a personal interest in *heka*-magic. It is a glazed steatite scarab, pierced longitudinally, of late Twelfth Dynasty origin that was acquired by the British Museum in 1960 (acquisition number EA66159). In size, it is 0.788 inches (2 centimeters) in length, 0.52 inches (1.32 centimeters) in width, and 0.34 inches (0.86 centimeters)

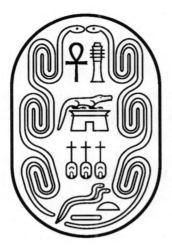

Fig. 33.3. Scarab bearing the name of Sobekneferu found in Egypt and purchased by the British Museum in 1960 (Acquisition number EA66159). Illustration by Nick Burton.

in depth. Unfortunately its provenance is unclear, with the only information offered on the museum's website being that it was found in Egypt.[40]* Apparently, it was purchased through the auction house Spink & Son, having formerly been in the collection of the Reverend George Denis Nash (1866–1943). He was an avid collector of ancient Egyptian antiquities, and during the 1920s and 1930s spent winters in Egypt. He died in 1943 and following the death of his widow Spink & Son handled the sale of his Egyptological collection across a period of two years between 1959 and 1960.[41]

With an upper surface in the familiar shape of the scarab beetle, the object's underside displays hieroglyphs (cut in high relief) for Sobek and *neferu,* the former above the latter (see fig. 33.3). The name is not contained in a cartouche, meaning that the piece dates to before the monarch ascended the throne. That the Sobekneferu in question is the ruler of this name is asserted on the British Museum's website.[42]

Over the name Sobekneferu is an ankh next to a *djed*-pillar, symbolizing, respectively, life and stability. A border around the hieroglyphs is composed of a continuous line incorporated into which is a series of six spiraling scrolls. This was a familiar style of decorative design for scarabs in the late Twelfth Dynasty, although in this case the border, instead of being continuous, is severed both at the top and at the bottom. Each side of the border

*I wish to thank Melissa Thiringer for bringing the Sobekneferu scarab to my attention during the writing of this book.

ends in a snake's head at the top and a snake's tail at the bottom, making it clear the spiraling scrolls are to be viewed as serpentine coils.

In addition to this, the snake tail on the left-hand side extends beneath the name Sobekneferu to introduce a hieroglyph showing two cobras, one above the other. This represents the combined letters "dd," which means "stable, enduring, pillar;" as in the *djed*-pillar itself. There is also another hieroglyph next to the twin cobras, which appears to be an upturned hemisphere. If correct, then this signifies the letter "t," used to feminize a word. Thus the "dd" hieroglyph is being feminized to form the word *ddt,* usually expanded to *djedet,* which appears also on the British Museum cylinder seal as part of Sobekneferu's Golden Horus name. This was Djedet khau (*ddt-h'w*), which, as we saw in chapter 2, means something like "Stable is she [*djedet*] in rites of kingship [*khau*]." Thus the entire statement implied by the hieroglyphs on the scarab is: "With life [*ankh*] and stability [*djed*] Sobekneferu [she] endures [*djedet*]."* (See fig. 33.4.)

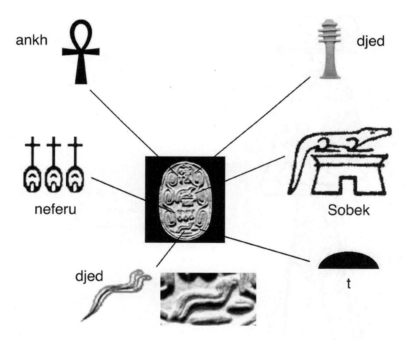

ankh

djed

neferu

Sobek

djed

t

Fig. 33.4. Hieroglyphic components of the Sobekneferu scarab, which spell out "With life [*ankh*] and stability [*djed*] Sobekneferu [she] endures [*djedet*]."

---

*A horizontal line appears below the twin cobras, which I have been unable to properly identity.

HEKA MAGIC

Twin cobras were representative of the goddesses Isis and Nephthys, and in particular the manner they used *heka*-magic to bring Osiris back to life after being murdered by his twin brother Seth. With the *djed*-pillar being an abstract representation of Osiris's backbone, his raising became synonymous with the erection of the *djed*-pillar, something achieved using the combined magical powers of the two goddesses—hence the use of the twin cobras to symbolize the *djed*-pillar.

So the implication of the hieroglyphic inscription seen on the scarab was to provide life and stability to Sobekneferu through the intervention of *heka*-magic, its influence confirmed not just by the twin cobras making up the djed hieroglyph but also by the scrolled border formed out of twin snakes facing each other. (As a god-form Heka was shown clutching twin snakes—see fig. 33.5.)

Fig. 33.5. The god Heka shown holding twin snakes symbolizing the *heka*-magic he controls. Illustration by Heshbi.

Glazed steatite scarabs of this type would have formed part of a finger ring where the scarab is attached via a thick metal wire to the horns of a crescent shaped ring, made usually out of gold or silver. This then acted as a magical seal in the form of a revolving bezel, its owner denoted by the inscription on the scarab's base. In time the wire would inevitably deteriorate causing the two parts of the ring to part, leaving the scarab as the only identifiable indication of ownership. In this case the name is Sobekneferu, strongly suggesting that the original scarab ring belonged to her. Such items would have been talismanic in nature indicating that its inscription might well reflect Sobekneferu's own personal belief in *heka*-magic.

The clear relationship between the *heka*-related inscription on the scarab and the spells from the Coffin Texts about Hathor and Nehebkau swallowing the seven cobras to gain the *heka*-magic is intriguing to say the least. Add to this the possible connection between the seven snake gods of the Book of the Fayum and the seven shrines in the Qasr el-Sagha temple, which Sobekneferu arguably helped reconstruct, and it tells us there is every chance the monarch might well have used the site for *heka*-related rituals, perhaps even to ensure her own future destiny.

GREAT ONE OF POWER

One final piece of evidence potentially linking Sobekneferu with the Qasr el-Sagha temple is a small sandstone fragment found at the site and described by Dieter and Dorothea Arnold in their book *Der Tempel Qasr el-Sagha* (1979).[43] Made from sandstone, it preserves part of an inscription. Visible are the hieroglyphs for *neb* (*nb*), meaning "gold" or "lord," and *tawy* (*t'wi*), meaning "the Two Lands." This alone, as the Arnolds write, must refer to a king of Upper and Lower Egypt, and arguably one associated with the temple. Which king, however, the Arnolds do not say, although since they are sure the temple is of Twelfth Dynasty date very probably the ruler in question belonged to this dynasty.

Next to the hieroglyphs for *neb* and *tawy* is another partial sign, the rest of it now lost. Looking like the side and top of a rectangle, the Arnolds suggest it is part of the hieroglyph known as F36;[44] this being an ideogram meaning *semy* (*sma*), "balance,"[45] as in *sema-tawy*, "balance of the Two Lands." It is the present author's opinion, however, that a much better match

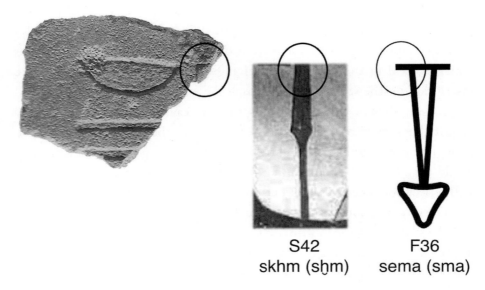

S42   F36
skhm (sḫm)   sema (sma)

Fig. 33.6. The sandstone fragment found at Qasr el-Sagha next to the hieroglyphs S42 *skhm* (*sḫm*) and F36 *sema* (*sma*). (By Dieter and Dorthea Arnold, 1979.)

for what can be seen of this partial sign is the hieroglyph S42,[46] which means *skhm* (*sḫm*), the root behind the word *sekhem,* meaning "power" or "might" (see fig. 33.6).*

If correct this would be a very significant realization since the three signs together *sekhem, neb,* and *tawy* form the main part of the Nebty or Two Ladies name of Sobekneferu, which, in full, is Sat-sekhem-nebet-tawy, meaning, as we saw in chapter 2, "Daughter of power [*sat sekhem*], mistress of the Two Lands [*nebet tawy*]." Interestingly, the inscription found at Qasr el-Sagha it without a cartouche, which would be correct since a monarch's Nebty name was not usually framed inside a cartouche or serekh. The only argument against the connection with Sobekneferu's Nebty name might be that the *neb* sign does not have alongside it the additional sign for the letter "t," the upturned hemisphere, feminizing the word to *nebet.* Yet as we have seen Sobekneferu's royal names and titles were written either in male form or in female form, so any such argument is meaningless.

---

*I floated this interpretation of the partial sign to two Egyptologists, Kara Cooney and Jan Summers Duffy, neither of whom saw it as impossible.

If this assessment of the carved fragment proves to be correct then not only would it link Sobekneferu directly with Qasr el-Sagha, but it would also be only the second occasion the female monarch's Nebty name has been recorded; it being present on the British Museum cylinder seal and nowhere else. What is more, finding the monarch's Nebty name at Qasr el-Sagha could imply that she was invoking there the force of sekhem, divine power or might personified as Sekhmet, the more terrifying aspect of the goddess Hathor. As we saw earlier in this chapter, Sekhmet along with another feline goddess, Bastet, were invoked to combat or control the influence of the primeval snake named Nehebkau.[47] Both deities were venerated at Heracleopolis Magna where Sobekneferu would appear to have left behind a major monument of some kind.

One pressing question still remains, however, and this is what happened to Sobekneferu after her death and where *was* she buried? If she was not interred in the Mazghuna North pyramid, then perhaps she was buried somewhere in the Fayum region, and arguably even in the vicinity of the Qasr el-Sagha temple. As we see next, this symbolic location might well have provided her with a suitable resting place where her loyal followers could continue to pay their respects to her, even in death.

34

Sobekneferu's Final Resting Place

The only real clue as to Sobekneferu's potential final resting place is the Mazghuna North pyramid and, as already explored in earlier chapters, there is good reason to believe that this was indeed her *intended* tomb. That, however, was before the monarch's reign ended with, I believe, her ritual death.

Since Sobekneferu would appear to have died suddenly and seemingly by her own instigation it was perhaps realized by her closest followers that her body risked being abused and even destroyed by her enemies. For this reason her burial was probably carried out in secret at a location known only to a few select individuals. Most obviously they would have included priests from the temple of Sobek at Shedet, next to which in the adjoining palace the monarch may well have met her fate in an adyton through the inhalation and ingestion of psychotropic substances that allowed her to enter into an eternal sleep.

So where might she have been buried? As we saw in chapter 5 the monarch's final resting place would appear to have borne the name Sekhem-Sobekneferu, meaning the "power," "might" or "strength" of Sobekneferu. The name almost certainly alludes to her interest in the concept of sekhem and its personification as the goddess Hathor in her guise as Sekhmet, Lady of Terror.

If, through ritual processes, the monarch came to believe that Hathor had somehow been responsible for legitimizing her rightful vocation as Egypt's true Horus king then there are grounds to suspect that the monarch would have chosen a place of burial that reflected her devotion to this goddess. This would presumably have included Hathor's role as the swallower of the seven uraei or cobras to gain the power of the *heka*-magic. This, alongside Sobekneferu's devotion to the cult of Sobek, could well suggest that the Qasr el-Sagha temple was seen as important to her intended journey into the afterlife. What is more, these suspicions are supported by a very curious fact indeed.

THE QASR EL-SAGHA ALIGNMENT

The Qasr el-Sagha temple is aligned approximately 20.3 degrees north of east (or, equally, 20.3 degrees south of west). If this axis line is projected east-northeastward for a distance of 35 miles (56 kilometers) it targets the Mazghuna North pyramid, Sobekneferu's *intended* place of interment. The line does not target the Mazghuna South pyramid, only its northern counterpart.

The idea of long-distance alignments playing some role in the location of Twelfth Dynasty pyramids might not appeal to everyone. However, the Mazghuna North pyramid's apparent relationship with monuments in

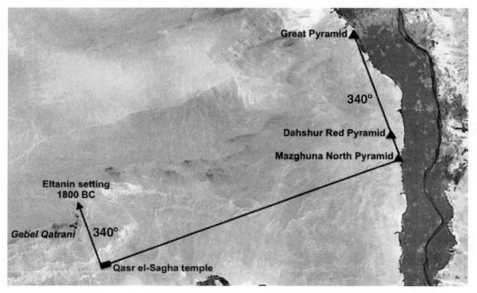

Fig. 34.1. Map showing the axial alignment of the Qasr el-Sagha temple with the Mazghuna North pyramid and the perpendicular alignment at 340 degrees northwestward toward the Red Pyramid of Sneferu and the Great Pyramid of Khufu at Giza.

the surrounding landscape does not end there. If the alignment from the Qasr el-Sagha temple to the Mazghuna North pyramid is then extended at right angles north-northwestward it targets the peaks of two major pyramids. The first is the Red Pyramid at Dahshur, attributed to the Fourth Dynasty pharaoh Sneferu, with the second being the Great Pyramid at Giza, built by Sneferu's son Khufu. All three pyramids—Mazghuna North, the Red Pyramid, and Great Pyramid—are on the same alignment, which is perpendicular to the line connecting the Qasr el-Sagha temple with the Mazghuna North pyramid as defined by the temple's long axis (see fig. 34.1).

ALIGNING WITH THE ANCESTORS

Could such long-distance alignments have been part of a plan by the kings of the Twelfth Dynasty to connect with the Fourth Dynasty pyramid builders who might have been seen as great ancestors? This possibility is given credence in the fact that Amenemhat I, the founder of the Twelfth Dynasty, used red granite blocks specifically taken from Khafre's funerary monuments at Giza to construct his pyramid complex at Lisht, the site of the Twelfth Dynasty capital of Itj-tawy. According to American Egyptologist Mark Lehner this was done because the blocks were deemed to have a "spiritual efficacy,"[1] something that Amenemhat I perhaps wished to harness in order to establish a special connection not just with Khafre but also with the Fourth Dynasty kings as a whole.

We know also that Sneferu, the founder of the Fourth Dynasty and grandfather of Khafre, was venerated as a god during the age of Amenemhat III and Amenemhat IV. This can be seen from the existence of various inscriptions found at the cult shrine of Hathor at Serabit el-Khadim in Sinai honoring Sneferu as a "great god" and divine protector of the mining expeditions undertaken by the kings in question.[2]

SNEFERU AND ARCHAISM

In addition to these facts, Italian astrophysicist and archaeoastronomer Giulio Magli has determined several examples of harmonization between the pyramids built at Dahshur by Twelfth Dynasty kings and those in the same proximity built by Sneferu. They include the orientation and placement of structures, similarities between the angles of ascent of pyramids, and parallel alignments toward solstices.[3] All this, he proposes, was part of a deliberate act of what he calls "archaism," with Amenemhat III's role in this grand scheme summed up as follows: "When the architects of Amenemhet III started the project of the king's pyramid [at Dahshur], they apparently took into account the existing monuments [from the reign of Sneferu] in order to harmonize the new element in the human-made landscape and, one would be tempted to say, to keep *Maat,* the Cosmic Order, in the already old royal Necropolis."[4]

So aligning the Mazghuna North pyramid with the Red Pyramid at Dahshur and the Great Pyramid of Khufu at Giza does make good sense as this would connect its intended internee with the world of Sneferu and Khufu respectively. It should be recalled also that the Qasr el-Sagha temple, itself locked into this Fourth Dynasty inspired geometry, was built using polygonal masonry of a style seen also in the design of the Valley Temple of Khafre. This hints at the possibility that the Qasr el-Sagha temple was built to resonate with funerary architecture belonging to the Fourth Dynasty.

Then, of course, we have the importance of the black basalt from the Widan el-Faras quarries used in the construction of various Fourth and Fifth Dynasty funerary complexes. This includes the paved floor of Khufu's mortuary temple located on the east side of the Great Pyramid.* Positioning the Qasr el-Sagha temple at the end of an ancient paved road built to access these Old Kingdom basalt quarries adds further weight to the idea that the placement both of this structure and of the Mazghuna North pyramid were deliberately chosen to lock them into a landscape geometry reflecting a deep interest in the rulers of the Fourth Dynasty.

All this helps us focus on the fact that a clear spatial relationship would appear to have existed between the Qasr el-Sagha temple in the northern Fayum and the Mazghuna North pyramid on the edge of the Nile Valley. With Sobekneferu as the probable intended internee of the Mazghuna North pyramid can we credit her with some involvement in the creation,

---

*A large fragment of a black basalt statue of Khafre was found in his valley temple at Giza, although whether or not the basalt came from Widan el-Faras is unclear. See "Fragment of Basalt Standing Statue of Khafre" 2020.

or at least the perpetuation, of this landscape geometry? If so, then it tells us that she might well have seen the Qasr el-Sagha temple as important to the fate and destiny of her eternal soul. What is more, the placement of the Mazghuna North pyramid at the end of an alignment featuring both the Red Pyramid and the Great Pyramid, respectively built by Sneferu and his son Khufu, would tend to indicate that she saw herself as related to these important Fourth Dynasty pharaohs.

Taking all this into consideration, and assuming that the female monarch was not interred in one of the unclaimed minor pyramids at Dahshur or Saqqara, then her most likely burial site would be somewhere in the northern Fayum region, and arguably in the vicinity of the Qasr el-Sagha temple. Should this prove correct, it is even possible that the temple might actually have featured in mortuary rituals conducted in the name of the monarch following her death.

PLUNDERED SHAFT TOMBS

Where exactly a royal female of Sobekneferu's status might have been interred is impossible to say, although what can be said is that in a cliff face immediately southwest of the Qasr el-Sagha temple, Gertrude Caton-Thompson uncovered a cemetery in which were the entrances to several shaft tombs of dynastic origin. One explored on January 26/27, 1925, seemed of special interest.

For two whole days, as high winds and fierce sandstorms raged outside, Caton-Thompson and her excavation team gradually cleared the tomb's descending shaft of many tons of built-up sand. She described the shaft as a square-cut tunnel some five feet (1.5 meters) in width and in height that descended at an angle of 31 degrees on an azimuth bearing of 205 degrees for a distance of 59 feet (18 meters).[5]

Two spherical amethyst beads, a green glaze scarab, as well as a wooden oar from a model funerary boat were found before they finally came upon a carved oblong pit that formed the tomb's burial chamber. Its level floor was around 5 feet (1.5 meters) lower than the ending of the descending passageway (see fig. 34.2). In size it was 9 feet, 11 inches (3 meters) in length and 4 feet 11 inches (1.5 meters) in width, with its domed roof rising to a height of approximately 15 feet (4.6 meters).[6]

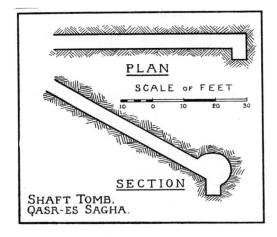

Fig. 34.2. Plan of the shaft tomb explored by Gertrude Caton-Thompson in the Twelfth Dynasty cemetery southwest of the Qasr el-Sagha temple (from Caton-Thompson and Gardner 1934, pl. LXXXV, 20).

Unfortunately, however, the tomb had been completely robbed of all grave goods with the only thing remaining being a few scraps of painted plaster. Caton-Thompson concluded that the tomb, which was of exceptional size, belonged to the Middle Kingdom.[7] Indeed, on maps included in her and Elinsor Gardner's two-volume work *The Desert Fayum,* the cemetery containing the shaft tomb is said to date from the Twelfth Dynasty,[8] making it contemporary with the construction of the nearby Qasr el-Sagha temple. (See fig. 31.3 on page 275 for a map showing the area of the cemetery.)

Despite the immense sophistication and great size of this shaft tomb located so close to the Qasr el-Sagha temple I am not suggesting it was the final resting place of Sobekneferu. It is possible, however, that following the monarch's death a shaft tomb of this type was sequestered for use by her devotees. If so, then her tomb might well be located either in this particular Twelfth Dynasty cemetery, or in one close by, in the cliffs perhaps to the north, which form the southernmost extension of the Gebel Qatrani formation.

There we see a whole series of hewn out caves with evidence of rectilinear burial pits. Some of these were used for the interment of monks from the nearby Deir Abu Lifa monastery, founded during the mid-seventh century CE by a saint named Panoukhius (known also as Abu Lifa).[9] Other pits, however, might well have contained burials from a much earlier age.

Just maybe the monks of the monastery held some knowledge concerning the whereabouts of Sobekneferu's tomb. If so, was this knowledge passed on to the earliest Arab-Islamic explorers to reach the northern Fayum in the early medieval period?

What certainly seems feasible is that the monasteries of the Fayum were perhaps responsible for preserving stories regarding Sobekneferu's role as "Pharaoh's Daughter." As we saw in chapter 24, in Arabic-Islamic literature she was granted the Fayum as her royal residence by the Raijan that ruled during the age of Joseph. These stories were almost certainly echoes both of the massive hydraulic works undertaken in the Fayum during the reign of Amenemhat III and of the completion of the Labyrinth during the reign of his daughter, Sobekneferu.

Certain aspects of these Coptic-Arab stories now make better sense with our greater understanding of what Sobekneferu was attempting to achieve at the Labyrinth. In *The Prodigies of Egypt,* for instance, written by Murtadā ibn al-'Afīf, the Raijan explains to Joseph the task he must perform in the Fayum. He says, "You know how dear such a Daughter of mine is to me, and you see it is time I should assign her some place where she may be Mistress, and whereof the Revenues may be sufficient to maintain her."[10]

Are the "Revenues" mentioned in the account a distorted memory of the manner that representatives of the different nomes would converge on the Labyrinth to make offerings to the form of Sobek deemed the active spirit of their own local god? I suspect the answer could be yes.

All this, of course, is simply speculation, although I would certainly encourage future Egyptologists, who might wish to embark on a search for the lost tomb of Egypt's first female monarch, to begin their investigations in the northern Fayum, and in particular in the vicinity of the Qasr el-Sagha temple. I firmly believe this will ultimately pay dividends and reveal more information about the monarch's final resting place, and what might have become of her in death.

Did, for example, the funerary rituals carried out in her name permit her to live forever? Did she go on to reach an afterlife among the stars, or does her soul remain in a limbo state, never quite having achieved the same type of immortality as that of other more famous pharaohs such as Rameses II, Tutankhamun, and Akhenaten, or indeed female monarchs such as Hatshepsut, Nefertiti, and Cleopatra? These are, of course, metaphysical questions that have no real answers, although something else has, over the past 120 years, caused Sobekneferu to return to popular consciousness, albeit in a somewhat unorthodox manner. At the turn of the nineteenth century a certain gothic horror writer—already the author of a book titled *Dracula*—began work on a new novel in which an ancient Egyptian queen is raised from the dead in Victorian England. That writer, of course, was Bram Stoker.

As we see next, there exists convincing evidence that Stoker chose Sobekneferu as the inspiration for his resurrected Egyptian queen. In doing so he catalyzed the female monarch's emergence as a modern pop icon. How exactly this came about and what its implications are to the story of Sobekneferu is revealed in this book for the first time.

PART 8

RESURRECTION

35

Goddess of the Seven Stars

In 2017 cinema audiences were treated to the latest reboot of the classic horror movie franchise featuring the resurrection of an ancient Egyptian mummy. Titled, inevitably, *The Mummy,* and starring Tom Cruise, it was an action-packed thriller that sees the return to life of a princess named Ahmanet. She wreaks havoc across modern-day London before finally being defeated.* It is a compelling concept—an ancient Egyptian royal female becoming flesh and blood again in a different age. Ahmanet, however, is just the latest incarnation of a fictional character that appears for the first time in a novel written by celebrated Irish gothic novelist Bram Stoker (1847–1912) and published by William Heinemann in 1903. Stoker (fig. 35.1), of

Fig. 35.1. Photograph of Bram Stoker, author of *Dracula* (1897) and *The Jewel of Seven Stars* (1903) among many other books, thought to have been taken in 1906.

*For more information, see the appendix, "Sobekneferu on Film and Television."

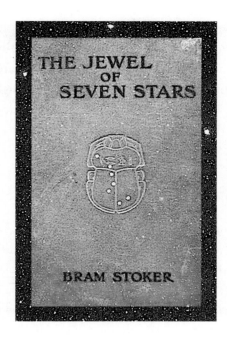

Fig. 35.2. The cover of the first edition of *The Jewel of Seven Stars* by Bram Stoker (1847–1912) published by publishers William Heinemann in 1903.

course, was the author of *Dracula,* which had been published six years earlier in 1897.[1]

With the somewhat enigmatic title of *The Jewel of Seven Stars* (fig. 35.2),[2] Stoker's Egyptian novel tells the story of how an ancient queen and sorceress named Tera is able to return to this world by first overshadowing and then finally replacing the 18-year-old daughter of Abel Trelawny, an English collector of antiquities. So shocking was the book's ending deemed by its post-Victorian audience that Stoker was persuaded to replace it in future editions.

Who exactly Stoker's Queen Tera might have been, historically speaking, has intrigued Egyptological students, as well as commentators of the Irish author's works, for over a century. Even though Hatshepsut is generally assumed to have been the role model for the character of Tera there is today growing evidence that Stoker's true inspiration was in fact Sobekneferu. How this came about is a fascinating story, and one that simply has to be told since it has had a dramatic impact on the female monarch's role in modern pop culture today.

In *The Jewel of Seven Stars* Stoker informs his reader that Queen Tera lived "forty or fifty centuries"[3] ago and that she was the only daughter of

King Antef,[4] one of the rulers of Egypt's Eleventh Dynasty. Now, there *was* indeed a king named Antef who ruled at this time. In fact, there were four kings all named Antef who reigned during this dynasty, which is today dated to circa 2046–1976 BCE. Yet none of them had a notable queen or daughter fitting Queen Tera's description. Not that this is a problem, of course, as Stoker's book is simply a work of fiction. However, he must have got his inspiration from somewhere.

THE CASE FOR HATSHEPSUT

With regards to Queen Tera's historical background Stoker informs his reader that, "Prominence was given to the fact that she, though a Queen, claimed all the privileges of kingship and masculinity. In one place she was pictured in man's dress, and wearing the White and Red Crowns. In the following picture she was in female dress, but still wearing the Crowns of Upper and Lower Egypt."[5] These statements ably describe Hatshepsut who did indeed wear the double crown of Upper and Lower Egypt, and is depicted in statuary and reliefs both in male and in female attire.

In addition to this, Hatshepsut's tomb was discovered in 1902, the same year Stoker wrote his Egyptian novel. Such a monumental event would surely have influenced his decision to base the character of Queen Tera on Hatshepsut, especially since she was one of Egypt's most famous female rulers.

All this is pretty convincing evidence in favor of Hatshepsut being the role model for Stoker's Queen Tera, as is the fact that, in death, the female monarch's name was erased from inscriptions in a similar manner to how the Irish writer tells us Tera's name was also struck from monuments following her death.[6]

There are, however, problems with this solution regarding the true identity of Queen Tera. Firstly, Hatshepsut lived a minimum of 500 years *after* the intimated "forty to fifty centuries" ago that Stoker tells us Queen Tera ruled Egypt. Moreover, even though Hatshepsut's tomb was first entered in 1902—by British archaeologist Howard Carter, then Chief Inspector of Antiquities for Upper Egypt, and his American colleague Theodore M. Davis (1838–1915)—it was of minor interest since it was found to be empty.[7] More important, exploration of the tomb did not begin until March 1903,[8] well after Stoker had written *The Jewel of Seven Stars*. Indeed, Doubleday,

Page & Company had deposited a copyright patent for the book's *republication* as early as 1902,[9] even though it would be Harper and Brothers of New York who would finally publish the novel's first U.S. edition in 1904. In addition to this, it would not be until 1906 that the first academic book containing a full description of Hatshepsut's tomb would finally appear.[10] Thus it seems unlikely that Carter's exploration of the tomb convinced Stoker to base his character of Queen Tera on Hatshepsut. What is more, those who assume this was the case completely ignore Sobekneferu, who was the first woman to wear the double crown of Upper and Lower Egypt.

THE CASE FOR SOBEKNEFERU

As we know, Sobekneferu was herself depicted in statuary in both male and female attire. What is more, a tentative link exists between Sobekneferu and a king named Antef, Queen Tera's fictional father. The king list known as the Royal Tablet of Karnak, the details of which would have been freely available to Stoker when he wrote *The Jewel of Seven Stars,* shows a king named Antef succeeding Sobekneferu. This has sometimes led to speculation that she was married to him.[11] Could it have been *this* King Antef that was the real inspiration behind Queen Tera's father? Maybe, although one might question just how much Stoker actually knew about any of this when he came to write his book.

Bringing us closer to the true inspiration behind the character of Queen Tera is what Stoker has to say about her connection with the goddess Hathor, who he informs us governed "beauty, and pleasure, and resurrection."[12] A relief of the goddess seen in the fictional tomb of Queen Tera shows Hathor within the "Boat of the Moon." She is depicted, we are told, "cow-headed and bearing the disk and plumes," and alongside her is, "the dog-headed Hapi, the God of the North. It [the boat] was steered by Harpocrates [a form of Horus] towards the north, represented by the Pole Star surrounded by Draco and Ursa Major."[13] Here Stoker is implying that Hathor presided over the stars of the northern night sky, in particular those of the constellations of Draco and Ursa Major, which turn about the celestial pole each night.

Stoker further informs his reader that the seven stars of the Plough, the name given to the Big Dipper in Britain, signify the goddess's "seven forms,"[14] a reference to the Seven Hathors:

She [Tera] was born, we learn in the Stele of her tomb, in the seventh
month of the year—the month beginning with the Inundation of the Nile.
Of which month the presiding Goddess was Hathor, the Goddess of her
[Tera's] own house, of the Antefs of the Theban line. . . . Again, in this seventh month—which, by later Egyptian astronomy began on October 28th,
and ran to the 27th of our November—on the seventh day the Pointer of
the Plough just rises above the horizon of the sky at Thebes.[15]

We learn also that it is the influence of these seven stars, "the symbols
of the constellation which we call the Plough," that not only governed Tera's
birth, but also her destiny,[16] which was to live again in this world. In addition to this Stoker notes that, "Seven was to her [Tera] a magic number; and
no wonder" since she had "seven fingers on one hand, and seven toes on one
foot."[17] Moreover, we read that:

In a marvellously strange way, therefore, are grouped into this woman's
life these various things. The number seven; the Pole Star, with the constellation of seven stars; the God of the month, Hathor . . . whose seven
forms ruled love and the delights of life and resurrection.[18]

To ensure her future destiny Queen Tera constructs a tomb in which
is placed a number of objects that must be used to ensure her resurrection,
which is to happen "after a long time and in a more northern land, under
the constellation whose seven stars had ruled her birth."[19] They include
seven lamps, each symbolizing one of the seven forms of Hathor,[20] a seven-
sided box or coffer, a table of "bloodstone" on which the coffer is to slot into
place,[21] and the eponymous Jewel of Seven Stars, carved into the likeness of a
scarab beetle and mounted on a ring.[22] Of this we are told: "With a talisman
of a rare ruby with seven stars in the same position as in that constellation
which ruled her birth, each star of the seven having seven points—in itself a
geological wonder—it would have been odd if she had not been attracted by
it."[23] All these items will be required to engage in the "Great Experiment"[24]
to bring the queen back to life.[25]

The purpose of this detailed exposition of the Egyptological background to
The Jewel of Seven Stars will become clear in due course. The bigger question

for the moment is why in his novel did Stoker decide to so heavily feature the importance of the cyclic motion of the stars and constellations around the celestial pole? Also, how did any of this relate to Hathor, the goddess ruling Tera's destiny, whose seven forms are said by Stoker to have symbolized the seven stars of Ursa Major?

EGYPTOLOGICAL SOURCE MATERIAL

Stoker was very well read on ancient Egypt. His private library contained many books on Egyptology. According to Stoker's biographer William Hughes a sale of its contents at Sotheby's on July 7, 1913, included, "Budge's *Egyptian Ideas of the Future Life* (1900); *Egyptian Magic* (1899); *Easy Lessons in Egyptian Hieroglyphics* (1899–1902); *The Mummy* (1893); *The Book of the Dead: The Papyrus of Ani in the British Museum* (1895); *A History of Egypt* . . . (9 vols. 1902) as well as Flinders Petrie's 1895 *Egyptian Tales Translated from the Papyri.*"[26]

The list contains those books on Egyptology that made it to Sotheby's for the sale of Stoker's personal possessions following his death on April 20, 1912. His library, however, would almost certainly have contained many more volumes of value, plus we know that Stoker would have had the opportunity to consult additional source material for his Egyptian novel in the Reading Room of the British Museum. Indeed, we read on the museum's website that those granted tickets to its prestigious Reading Room during its formative years included, "Karl Marx, Lenin (who signed in under the name Jacob Richter) and novelists such as Bram Stoker and Sir Arthur Conan Doyle."[27]

Hughes was able to trace several statements made by Stoker in *The Jewel of Seven Stars* to similar statements made by Budge in *The Mummy*,[28] while it is clear from the novelist's own words that during his writing of the book he had access to works "by [Samuel] Birch and [Karl Richard] Lepsius and [Ippolito] Rosellini and [Francesco] Salvolini, by [the Frenchman] Mariette Bey and by Wallis Budge and Flinders Petrie and the other scholars of their times."[29] All are distinguished names from the field of Egyptology.

Stoker could very easily have composed the Egyptological elements of his novel from material lifted from one or more of these important primary sources. Of this we can be fairly sure. None, however, are likely to have persuaded him to feature sevenfold stellar-based symbolism as the spiritual and magical motivation behind the actions of Queen Tera, whom he portrays as an earthly incarnation of the goddess Hathor in her role as goddess of the seven stars. This type of material was simply not available in any standard reference work on Egyptology at the time he wrote his novel. So where exactly did this material come from, and what inspired him to use it in the first place?

The Works of Gerald Massey

Only one writer from the Victorian age provides precisely the source material featured in Stoker's *The Jewel of Seven Stars* and this was Gerald Massey (1828–1907), a quite brilliant poet and writer on matters relating to the mythology and sky lore of ancient Egypt (see fig. 35.3). In two separate works, 1881's *A Book of the Beginnings* and 1883's *The Natural Genesis,** he features Sobekneferu extensively, connecting her with a strong belief among the Egyptian peoples in the existence of a primeval deity, a keeper of cosmic time, who was thought to control the movement of the stars around the northern celestial pole, and through this action the destiny of humankind.

Massey states that in ancient Egypt this primordial deity—which he terms the "Mother-Goddess of Time"[30]—was seen as a sky figure marked out by the stars of the constellation of Draco, identified with the ancient Greek dragon-monster Typhon, as well as by the seven stars of Ursa Major, the Great Bear. Indeed, Massey proposed that it was the constant turning of these seven stars about the Pole Star—like some giant cosmic crank handle—that caused this age-old deity to become universally identified with sevenfold symbolism.[31]

GODDESS OF THE SEVEN STARS

One of the most recognizable forms of this creatrix of human destiny, Massey explains, was the goddess Hathor. In *A Book of the Beginnings*, for instance, he writes:

---

*Massey continued this same theme in a third book in the series titled *Ancient Egypt the Light of the World,* published in 1907, four years after the publication of Stoker's *The Jewel of Seven Stars.*

Fig. 35.3. Photograph of historian and mythologist Gerald Massey (1828–1907) dated to around 1856.

Hathor, the cow-headed genitrix, is septiform in the seven Hathors or cows; the Great Serpent or Dragon [of the constellation Draco] is seven-headed, and so in various ways the one constellation [Ursa Major, the Great Bear] is also the sevenfold in accordance with the phenomena, and in no other form of phenomena do we meet with the seven in one satisfying all the requirements of the various illustrations.[32]

Massey refers to this "Typhonian genitrix,"[33] as he calls her, from whom all time is created, as "Goddess of the Seven Stars,"[34] "Goddess of the Seven Stars of the north,"[35] and as "Goddess of the Seven Stars of Ursa Major."[36]

In Egypt, according to Massey, this Typhonian creatrix was identified not only with the seven forms of Hathor, but also with a sky figure in the form of a bipedal hippopotamus.[37] "In the celestial north," he says in *A Book of the Beginnings*, "was the mythical birthplace where the Great Mother Taurt [or Taweret], the Goddess of the Great Bear and Seven Stars, was represented as the bringer-forth from the [primeval] waters [of Nun] in the shape of a hippopotamus."[38]

From the New Kingdom onward this particular sky figure, shown usually as the She-hippopotamus with a crocodile on its back, is frequently seen in star ceilings of tombs or temples, as well as on coffins and in connection with what are known as the Ramesside star clocks.[39] To the ancient Egyptians this She-hippopotamus was identified under the name Reret [*rrt*], a word simply meaning "sow," a term applied equally to a pig or a hippopotamus. It related to the She-hippopotamus's role as cosmic mother who in the Book of the Fayum is identified as Neith, the mother of Sobek. She can be identified also as Taweret or Isis-Djamet,[40] both being names that would come to be attached to a much older deity in the form of a hippopotamus identified as Neith, who was known as "the oldest goddess, the Mother of the Gods."[41]

As a sky figure the She-hippopotamus with the crocodile on its back would appear to have been identified with the stars of Draco.[42] On the long, crocodile tail-like "hair" hanging down the hippo's back we see seven dots with a further dot on the top of her arm, which reaches out to hold upright Meskhet, the Bull's Leg or Ox Thigh, a sky figure usually identified with the seven main stars of Ursa Major.[43]

In the opinion of the present author, the seven dots on the hippo's arm signify the seven stars of Ursa Major, the movement of which the She-hippopotamus controls through her strength. If so, then the single dot on her arm is probably meant to represent the Pole Star in its role as the pivot or turning point of the heavens, making her the controller of cyclic time.*

---

*At the beginning of the Pyramid Age the closest star to the celestial pole was Thuban (Alpha Draconis or α Dra), in the constellation of Draco. This therefore acted as Pole Star. Even by the commencement of the Middle Kingdom, however, the slow wobble of the Earth's axis across its cycle of around 26,000 years had caused the celestial pole to move away from Draco into the constellation of Ursa Minor, although no bright star was now close enough to the celestial pole for it to be deemed Pole Star. It was a situation that prevailed through until Polaris (α Ursae Minoris) came close enough to the celestial pole for it to take up the role of Pole Star some 2,000 years ago. Thus the appearance on the arm of the She-hippopotamus of a dot apparently representing the Pole Star was probably just a symbolic gesture recalling a time when Thuban signified the turning point of the heavens.

STARS AND SKY FIGURES

Confirmation of this surmise comes from the fact that if the principal stars of Draco and Ursa Minor are overlain on an image of the She-hippopotamus with the crocodile on its back shown as part of the stunning astronomical ceiling in the tomb of King Seti I (KV17) on the Theban West Bank, the match is almost perfect. As can plainly be seen, the bright orange star Eltanin (Gamma Draconis or γ Dra) corresponds with the eye of the crocodile (see fig. 35.4). At the same time, the stars of Ursa Major correspond

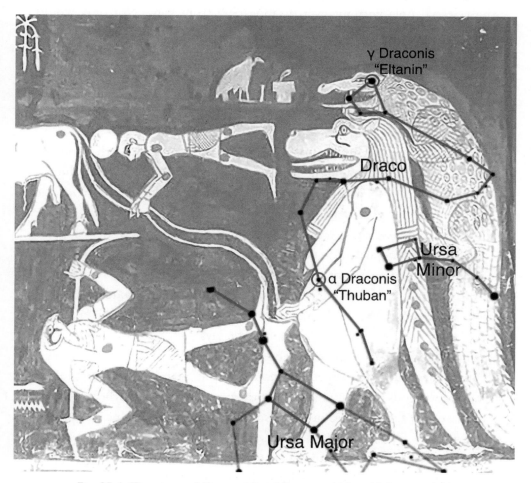

Fig. 35.4. The stars of Draco, Ursa Minor, and Ursa Major overlaid
on the hippopotamus and crocodile sky figure as seen on the astronomical ceiling
found inside the tomb of Seti I (KV17) in the Valley of the Kings on the
Theban West Bank.

very well with the position of Meskhetyu, the Ox Thigh, held upright by the She-hippopotamus.

This realization seems to confirm the relationship between this complex sky figure—combining both the hippopotamus and the crocodile and representing Neith and her son Sobek—with the stars of Draco, Ursa Minor, and Ursa Major. Linking them all is the fact that during the dynastic age all three constellations were circumpolar, in that they never set below the horizon. All of their stars (with one exception, the bright star Eltanin in Draco, which we look at in chapter 37) simply revolved around the celestial pole without ever disappearing from view. Not only would this have made them of extreme importance to the ancient Egyptians, but each of these asterisms could have been interpreted as in some manner responsible for controlling the turning of the heavens and the destiny of humankind.

Mother of the Crocodile

For Massey, the She-hippopotamus could be identified as the goddess Hathor, with the crocodile she carries on her back being Sobek. Although he was the son of Neith, Hathor came to be associated with some of the aspects of this much older deity including her role as a celestial cow under the name Mehet-Weret.[44] In this respect, Massey informs his reader, "Hathor is called the hippopotamus-goddess . . . the feminine Sebek . . . and is thus doubly identified as a form of the goddess of the seven stars."[45] He goes on: "The crocodile is the secondary form of the hippopotamus-goddess . . . both are bringers on of the Typhonian genitrix."[46] In this manner the crocodile becomes her son who is both Sobek and, he says, Sut, Sutekh, or Seth,[47] the Egyptian god of chaos, disorder, and the desert. He, in turn, was simply a form of the monstrous serpentine giant Typhon, who in Greek mythology attacked the gods of Olympus, causing them to flee to Egypt where they hid out in animal forms[48] (and in doing so became the zoomorphic gods of the Egyptians?).

As "Lord of Avaris" Seth was the chief god among the Hyksos kings whose capital city was Avaris. Although Seth and Sobek were separate deities, one of the forms of Seth was as the crocodile, while in some texts Seth was the father of Sobek.[49]

The true mother of Sobek was, of course, Neith, who was herself shown as the She-hippopotamus with the crocodile on her back in the Book of the Fayum. Confirming her identity in this form is the inscription accompanying the illustration in question, which reads, "Neith, the Great, Protector of her son [Sobek-Ra], the First of her forms (Akhemu) in the middle of the Lake."[50] The manner these two figures, the bipedal hippopotamus and crocodile, are shown in the Book of the Fayum matches almost exactly the way the She-hippopotamus with the crocodile on its back appears in astronomical sky ceilings, such as that seen in the tomb of Seti I (KV17). (See fig. 35.5 for a side-by-side comparison.) This suggests there was originally some kind of relationship between the manner Neith and Sobek are portrayed in the Book of the Fayum and the function and identity of their astronomical counterparts, which, as we have seen, appear to correspond with the constellations of Draco, Ursa Minor, and, in the case of the Ox Thigh, Ursa Major.

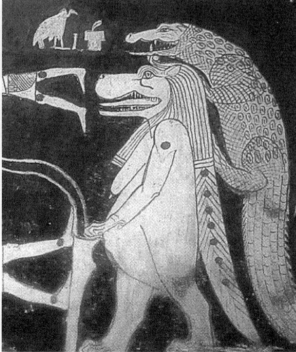

Fig. 35.5. Side-by-side comparison of (left) Neith as a bipedal hippopotamus with the crocodile god Sobek on her back from the Book of the Fayum and (right) the hippopotamus and crocodile sky figure shown on the astronomical ceiling in the tomb of Seti I (KV17) in the Valley of the Kings.

PREDYNASTIC ORIGINS

The relationship of Neith and Sobek with the northern night sky is arguably extremely ancient. In the Pyramids Texts, for instance, Spell 317 speaks of the deceased king as Sobek, who has come from "the leg and the tail of the Great One, she who resides in the brilliant light." Sobek is said to enter the waterways of Mehet-Weret (that is, the Great Flood), where he "brings the green brilliance to the Great Eye (or: Eye of the Great One) which resides among the pastures," after which he "arises as Sobek, son of Neith."[51]

The term "Great One," *taweret,* is usually seen as a formal name of the She-hippopotamus, although in the Pyramid Text's Spell 317, it is very clearly being used as a title of Neith, a fact confirmed in the knowledge that the deceased king is addressed as "Sobek, son of Neith."

Pyramid Texts scholar J. D. Degreef suspects that Spell 317 has celestial connotations and could be a reference to the hippopotamus and crocodile sky figure found in the circumpolar region of the northern night sky. If so, then it had to have existed in the sky lore of the ancient Egyptians when the Pyramid Texts first started appearing on the interior walls of pyramids in around 2350 BCE. More speculatively, Degreef proposes that the identification of the She-hippopotamus and her son Sobek with this archaic sky figure could be much older still, dating back perhaps to Predynastic times.[52] This would be a remarkable discovery in the knowledge that the crocodile god's main cultus place was Shedet in the Fayum, where his cult is thought to have existed as far back as the First Dynasty, circa 3100 BCE. If Degreef is correct in his assessment of Spell 317, then would this sky lore have been knowledge revealed to Sobekneferu as a living embodiment of the crocodile god during her lifetime? Almost certainly the answer is yes.

The idea of a primordial deity, a keeper of cosmic time, identified not only as the She-hippopotamus with a crocodile on her back, but also with Hathor in her role as Goddess of the Seven Stars, was something unique to the works of Gerald Massey during the Victorian age. So to find similar themes cropping up in Bram Stoker's *The Jewel of Seven Stars* is difficult to ignore. It suggests very strongly that he had read one or more of Massey's books and had decided to incorporate some of these ideas in his Egyptian novel.

THE BURTON CORRESPONDENCE

Stoker's interest in Massey's work might well have come from his friend-
ships with members of London's occult scene. What we can say is that the
two men had a mutual friend in British explorer, writer, scholar, and sol-
dier Richard Francis Burton (1821–1890). In surviving correspondence, it is
clear that Burton was very taken by the theories put forward by Massey in *A
Book of the Beginnings*. In a letter dated April 7, 1881, Burton tells Massey
that he is in receipt of his book, which has been kindly sent to him.[53] On
April 22 Burton writes again to Massey informing him that he has now had
a chance to read both volumes of the book and is very impressed with its
ideas.[54] Then, in a letter written to Massey on April 28, 1881, Burton says
to his friend: "Returning to the Beginnings, I have mentioned it to many
friends and shall continue to do so."[55] In the knowledge that Burton was
a close friend of Stoker,[56] there would have been every opportunity for the
former to have alerted the latter of the book's merits.

Supporting the view that Stoker had knowledge of *A Book of the
Beginnings* when he came to write his Egyptian novel is the rather curious fact that Massey informs his reader that the ancient Egyptian word for
"time" is *tera* or *terah*.[57] (Actually, it is *neheh*, which means "cyclic time,"
although Massey might not have known this when he wrote his book.)

Since Massey calls his Typhonian genitrix the "Mother-Goddess of
Time," Stoker's choice of the name Tera for his own embodiment of this
same cosmic deity should be noted. That said, Stoker's most obvious reason for calling the novel's female antagonist Tera was surely to evoke in the
reader an almost subliminal sense of *terror* every time the queen's name is
mentioned!

None of this would be of any direct relevance to the matters under discus-
sion in this present book were it not for the fact that Massey, as we see next,
singles out Sobekneferu as the ancient Egyptian ruler responsible not only
for reviving the age-old cult of his Typhonian genitrix, but also for initiating
a religious revolution in her promotion of the crocodile god Sobek.

36

Servants of Sobek

It was through Sobekneferu's explicit actions, Gerald Massey writes in *A Book of the Beginnings*, that the kings of the Thirteenth Dynasty—no less than seven of whom bore the name Sobekhotep—had adopted the worship of Sobek-Ra, the son of the Typhonian genitrix. To them Sobek-Ra was a "star god" who presided over all "reckoning by solar time."[1] As this was happening at the capital Itj-tway the incoming Hyksos rulers of Avaris were likewise adopting the worship of this same primeval deity under the name of Sut, Sutekh, or Seth, who could also be represented as a crocodile.[2]

A RELIGIOUS REVOLUTION

Through the actions of the "Sebekhepts," or "Servants of Sobek,"[3] as Massey calls the Sobek kings of the Thirteenth Dynasty, and the Hyksos kings of Avaris, Sobekneferu came to be seen as an earthly incarnation of the Goddess of the Seven Stars, identified both with the septiform Hathor and, as we have seen, with the She-hippopotamus Neith, the mother of Sobek. (Note: The Egyptian word *hotep* is usually translated as meaning "to be at peace," "satisfied," or "contented," making Sobekhotep "Sobek is satisfied" or "Sobek is contented.") The female monarch's important status in this scenario is made clear in the following paragraph from *A Book of the Beginnings*:

> My own reading of the facts is that at the beginning of the 13th dynasty
> only a religious revolution had occurred through Queen Sebek-nefer-Ra,
> who delighted to assume the character of the Divine Genitrix as mother

of the son, i.e. the Virgin Mother, who alone produced the son from herself without the initial fatherhood, a role that was tempting to a woman who reigned alone. She was the continuer of Sebek as Ra.[4]

Earlier, Massey had introduced the reader to Sobekneferu and the Sebekhepts, the Sobek rulers of the Thirteenth Dynasty, in the following manner:

The last monarch of the twelfth dynasty is Sebek-nefer-Ra. According to [Heinrich] Brugsh-Bey [a well-known German Egyptologist—see below] she was the sister of the last king of the dynasty, Amenemhat IV, and an heiress through whom the succession went by marriage to a new race, the Sebekhepts or servants of Sebek. Possibly the name of this Queen conveys the information that she was the continuer (Nefer) of Sebek as the ram-headed Sun-god Ra, whereas he had previously been the Crocodile-god of the Fayoom, or Country of the Lake. Whether she is out of place here and should be the first of the thirteenth dynasty matters little. She marks the end of the twelfth, and is the first known royal Sebek on all the monuments, and the next dynasty is full of them; it is, in short, the Sebek dynasty.[5]

AGE OF THE RAM

In referring to Sobek-Ra as a ram Massey is alluding to Amun-Ra, the name given to the sun god from the commencement of the New Kingdom. This combination of Amun and Ra could be shown as a ram-headed human figure or as a seated ram. In the Book of the Fayum Amun-Ra is pictured as a composite figure with a ram's head, a lion's body (making him a ram-headed sphinx), and the tail of a crocodile,[6] showing that he embodies aspects of Sobek-Ra, that is, the sun in its form as the crocodile god Sobek.

The purpose behind Massey emphasizing the fact that Sobek-Ra was depicted as a ram was to show how Sobekneferu's revival of the Typhonian genitrix and her promotion of the god Sobek marked the transition from the astrological Age of Taurus (the Bull), where the bull had been a principal symbol of old world religions, to the Age of Aries (the Ram), where the ram became the most dominant religious symbol of the ancient world.[7]

So through her religious revival of the cult of Sobek-Ra, Sobekneferu had thus become the initiator of a new age and in doing so had shaken up Egypt's religious system for centuries to come, a matter summed up by Massey in the following way:

> The introduction [by the female monarch] of Sebek as the ram-headed [Amun-]Ra implies a religious revolution. The capital of Shat [that is, Shedet], called by the Greeks Crocodilopolis in the district of the lake Mœris, identifies the Typhonian nature of the old Sebek, with whom the Osirians were in enmity. In the list of Nomes the province of Lake Mœris was struck out as being hostile to Osiris.[8]

This is correct, the province of Lake Moeris was apparently ignored in some later lists of the nomes of Egypt because of the part it played in Sobekneferu's religious revolution and the sheer fact that Seth, the god of chaos and disorder, could assume the form of a crocodile, associating him with the god Sobek.[9] Indeed, and as previously mentioned, in some traditions Seth was actually the father of Sobek, bringing him even closer to the crocodile god of the Fayum. Seth, of course, in the Osirian myth was the murderer of his brother Osiris, who was both god of the underworld and god of the dead.

It was Osiris's son Horus who would go on to defeat Seth, the scene often shown as Horus spearing a crocodile representing his father's murderer. It was an artistic theme that continued to appear through into Coptic Christian times (see fig. 36.1), with the crocodile now identified as the monster Typhon or as the devil himself.

Many of these ideas Massey derived from an influential work by German Egyptologist Heinrich Karl Brugsch (1827–1894) titled *Histoire d'Egypte* ("History of Egypt"). Originally published in Leipzig, Germany, in 1859,[10] an English translation of the book, titled *A History of Egypt Under the Pharaohs,* had appeared in 1879, just two years before the publication of *A Book of the Beginnings.*[11] It is clear that it was this edition that Massey drew from quite extensively, particularly with respect to what Brugsch, or Brugsch-Bey as he was known, has to say about the reign of Sobekneferu and the construction of the Labyrinth. To quote him:

Fig. 36.1. Coptic panel showing Horus as a knight on a horse using a lance to slay the god Seth, the murderer of his father Osiris. Seth is shown in the form of a crocodile.

Blocks of stone, covered with traces of the names Amenemhat III., and of the queen who followed him, Sebeknofru, are all that remain near the pyramid of Ellahoon [this should be Hawara, not "Ellahoon," as in El-Lahun] as the last farewell greeting to us of the once celebrated Egyptian Labyrinth. The province which anciently contained Lake Mœris has not had the good luck to be frequently mentioned in the texts engraved on the walls of the Egyptian sanctuaries. They hated it, and they hated its inhabitants, because of the worship with which they honoured the god Sebek, the tutelary divinity of this region, and the crocodile, his sacred animal. This last being for the adorers of Osiris, one of the forms of the god Set, the Satan of the Egyptian mythology, we can very well explain the singular circumstances that, in the list of *nomes,* the province of Lake Mœris is struck out as hostile to Osiris.[12]

Whether or not this actually was the case is unclear. More important is the fact that what Brugsch-Bey wrote on the subject was taken seriously by Massey. That Brugsch-Bey had additionally written that "we may suppose that Queen Sebek-nofru-ra, the heiress of the twelfth dynasty," had "transmitted the worship of the god Sebek" to her successors, the "Servants of Sobek" or "Sobek-hotep" kings of the Thirteenth Dynasty,[13] was seen by Massey as confirmation of the dynamic impact of Sobekneferu's religious revolution. This, as we have seen, included the creation of a near monotheistic religion with Sobek as the living spirit of the gods of all the nomes or districts of both Upper and Lower Egypt with the Labyrinth as the country's seat of spiritual power.

THE CULT OF OSIRIS

Osiris was an important god at Abydos in the south of the country, where some of the kings of the Twelfth Dynasty had created secondary tombs or cenotaphs. This was done in the belief that in death every king was transformed into Osiris, so having a symbolic or even a primary interment near the god's ancient cult center helped ensure this transformation process took place.

In addition to being important at Abydos, however, Osiris was revered also at Heliopolis, where he formed part of the *Ennead,* the nine principal gods of Egypt. The Ennead consisted of Atum—who was self-created and emerged out of the primeval waters of Nun—his offspring Shu (Air) and Tefnut (Moisture), their offspring Geb (Earth) and Nut (Sky), and their offspring, the two sets of twins, Seth and Nephthys, and Osiris and Isis, all of which would perhaps have had shrines at Heliopolis.

That Sobekneferu might have been seen to have triggered the onset of the Second Intermediate Period through her devotion to the crocodile as a symbol both of Sobek and of Seth could very easily have resulted in the priests of Osiris, not only at Abydos but also at Heliopolis, striking the Fayum from the list of nomes of Egypt, all just as Brugsch-Bey had implied.

Of possible relevance here is the fact that Sobekneferu would appear to have been ignored in some king lists, such as the one found in the temple of Seti I at Abydos in southern Egypt. It omits every ruler from Sobekneferu until the end of the Seventeenth Dynasty.[14] As mentioned in chapter 18, one reason for these omissions could be that Seti I only wanted to include in his canon of kings those monarchs whom he saw as direct ancestors of his own royal line. The fact, however, that those rulers missing from the list, beginning with Sobekneferu, might well have been seen as having contributed to one of Egypt's darkest hours cannot be ignored. Is it possible that she was expressly blamed for the onset of the calamities that had befallen Egypt at this time?

THE DARK ARTS

With all this in mind we can perhaps understand why Massey came to see Sobekneferu as a powerful female ruler—one who went against the grain of orthodoxy to revive a religious cult that might well have been perceived as particularly dark in nature. This is surely something that would have appealed to Bram Stoker when he came to create the character of Queen Tera for his Egyptian novel. According to him she was struck from the records following her entry into the tomb, this being because of the dark magics she had employed to avoid a conventional death and instead enter into a kind of eternal slumber until the time of her resurrection.[15]

There seems little question that the English language edition of Brugsch-Bey's *Histoire d'Egypte* was a major influence on what Massey wrote in *A Book of the Beginnings,* and that it was here that he first began to zero in on the impact Sobekneferu had not only on the Sebekhept rulers of the Thirteenth Dynasty, but also on the Hyksos warlords of Avaris and, afterward, the rulers of the Eighteenth Dynasty. Among them would have been enlightened individuals such as Seti I, who was named after the god Seth. He would appear to have been involved in building projects at the temple of Sobek in Kom Ombo, southern Egypt.[16] The temple would be entirely reconstructed during Greco-Roman times with excerpts from the Book of the Fayum carved on its walls.[17]

So does anything Massey say resonate with what we know about Sobekneferu's reign from archaeological exploration? The answer, remarkably, as we see next, is a resounding *yes.*

Path of the Headless One

In addition to the monarch's promotion of the cult of Sobek, and her sus-pected interest in the goddess Hathor, there is only one goddess she is con-nected with in inscriptions and this is Dehdehet [*dh.dh.t*]. Her name appears alongside that of Sobekneferu and her father Amenemhat III in a wall relief from the Labyrinth. As already made clear in chapter 18, Egyptian language scholar Terence du Quesne felt the name Dehdehet could be translated as the "Deep Bosomed One,"[1] conjuring to mind artistic representations of the She-hippopotamus Taweret or Neith who is generally shown with long, dropping breasts in her role as "the oldest goddess, the Mother of the Gods."[2]

Does this imply that Massey was right, and Sobekneferu did indeed venerate the She-hippopotamus, with Dehdehet simply being an epithet of Neith, the mother of Sobek? If so, then can we find any confirmation that Sobekneferu and her contemporaries identified both Neith and her son Sobek with the sky figure showing the bipedal hippopotamus with a croco-dile on its back, which can be identified with the constellations of Draco and Ursa Minor? The answer is yes, we can.

THE QASR EL-SAGHA TEMPLE REVISITED

As previously noted, the long axis of the Qasr el-Sagha temple in the north-ern Fayum is aligned 20.3 degrees south of west or, alternately, 20.3 degrees north of east. If tracked eastward this line hits, at a distance of 35 miles (56 kilometers), the Mazghuna North pyramid. From there, a line at right angles north-northwestward (at an azimuth bearing of approximately

340 degrees) hits the peaks both of the Red Pyramid at Dahshur and the Great Pyramid at Giza.

This much we have already established, with the presence of these long distance alignments meant perhaps to lock in the Qasr el-Sagha temple and the Mazghuna North pyramid with key monuments erected by important kings of the Fourth Dynasty, namely Sneferu and his son Khufu.

Returning to the long axis of the Qasr el-Sagha temple, if a line is projected at right angles north-northwestward to match the building's cross axis it targets at a date of 1800 BCE, the epoch of Sobekneferu, the setting of the star Eltanin (Gamma Draconis or γ Dra) as it sinks below the Gebel Qatrani hills (see fig. 37.1).

In addition to this the alignment featuring the Mazghuna North pyramid, the Red Pyramid of Dahshur and Great Pyramid of Giza would itself have targeted the setting of Eltanin during this same epoch. In other words, from an elevated position in the vicinity of the Mazghuna North pyramid the star would have been seen to set each night into the Red Pyramid, beyond which in the distance and on the same alignment would have been the Great Pyramid. It is a celestial spectacle that is unlikely to have gone

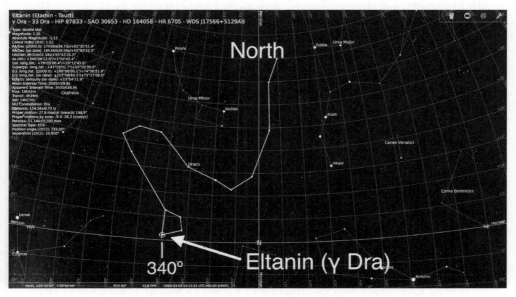

Fig. 37.1. The setting of the star Eltanin (Gamma Draconis or γ Dra)
for the epoch of 1800 BCE as viewed from the coordinates of the
Qasr el-Sagha temple using an extinction altitude of just over 1 degree.
This image was made using the Stellarium planetarium.

unnoticed by Sobekneferu and her contemporaries. This seems especially so in the knowledge that the Mazghuna North pyramid might well have been constructed as her final resting place, although, of course, it was never used for this purpose.

THE HEAD OF THE CROCODILE

As described in chapter 35, when the stars of Draco and Ursa Minor are superimposed over the sky figure made up of the She-hippopotamus with the crocodile on its back Eltanin corresponds with the eye of the crocodile god, making it the Eye of Sobek (see fig. 35.4 on page 319). Some might doubt the accuracy of this match, so perhaps it is best just to say that the star Eltanin would have corresponded with the head of the crocodile (although some sources report that the star signified the head of the hippopotamus).[3]

Being such a prominent star in the She-hippopotamus/crocodile sky figure, and the only one in any of the three main circumpolar constellations at this time to set below the horizon each night, could Eltanin have had some special function with regard to time-reckoning in ancient Egypt? Might the star's setting, followed just a few hours later by its rising on the north-northeastern horizon, have marked it out as important, its distinctly orange hue confirming its uniqueness? Did its cyclic movement come to be associated with the celestial mechanism seen as responsible for the turning of the stars about the celestial pole, the very attribute given to the combined She-hippopotamus and crocodile sky figure by Massey?

Since Eltanin signified the head of the celestial crocodile, might its nightly "beheading" as it sank beneath the horizon have influenced the development of extremely ancient myths in which the sun god Ra beheads the primeval Apep serpent? In addition to being a cosmic snake Apep (Greek: Apophis) could also either be depicted as a "monster crocodile"[4] or be aided in its duties by a crocodile named Seshsesh.[5] So an association between Apep and a primeval crocodile seems clear, which if correct links it with the gods Sobek and Seth, both of whom were themselves identified as crocodiles.

In the knowledge that in Greece and Persia, as well as among the ancient Semitic peoples of the Levant, the constellation of Draco was identified as a celestial serpent or dragon (see fig. 37.2),[6] the connection between Apep and the sky figure made up of the She-hippopotamus and crocodile in ancient

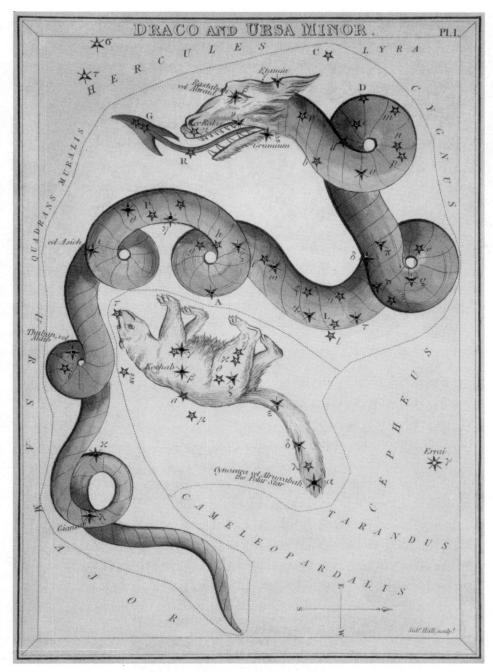

Fig. 37.2. Draco as the celestial snake by British engraver and cartographer Sidney Hall (1788–1831) showing the star Eltanin (here spelled "Etamin") in the creature's head (after Hall and Aspin 1824, pl. 1: "Draco and Ursa Minor"). Ursa Minor is located immediately beneath Draco.

Fig. 37.3. The cat of Ra severing the head of Apep (Apothis),
the primeval serpent as shown in the Papyrus of Hunefer, a funerary text or
Book of the Dead named after a scribe named Hunefer who lived in the
Nineteenth Dynasty (1194/93–1186/85 BCE).

Egyptian sky lore becomes a very real possibility, especially since the star Eltanin was said to mark its head.[7]

In chapter 33 we saw how in order to emerge from the primeval waters of Nun as the primeval hill and shine forth his light at dawn on the first day, the god Atum, a.k.a. Ra, had to kill Nehebkau, the primeval serpent. Symbolically, this act is told in the story of how the Great Cat named Mau uses a knife to sever the snake's head (see fig. 37.3).

Since this same myth is told in association with the cosmic serpent called Apep,[8] it seems clear that Apep and Nehebkau were originally one and the same, strongly suggesting that the idea of chopping off the head of a primordial crocodile, dragon, or serpent could indeed preserve the memory of how each night the star Eltanin would set beneath the horizon as viewed from the latitude of northern Egypt.

THE HEAD OF THE SERPENT

Interestingly, the name Eltanin is derived from the Arabic *Al-Tinnin*, meaning "The Serpent," or even *Al Ras el-Tinnin*, "The Head of the Serpent,"[9] while in modern (and seemingly ancient) Hebrew *tannin*, תַּנִּין, can mean both "great sea monster" and "crocodile."[10] *Al-Tinnin* was probably an original name for the constellation of Draco.[11]

Was this ancient cosmological sky lore reflected in the alignment of the Qasr el-Sagha temple toward the setting of the star Eltanin in circa 1800 BCE? Remember, this is the same direction of orientation as the building's seven small cells, which probably once contained statues of seven local gods.

As we saw in chapter 33, the northern Fayum would appear to have been the location of an age-old cult featuring a genius loci in the form of a primeval serpent whose existence was first identified by Egyptologist Eve Reymond. This primeval serpent was almost certainly linked with the seven snake gods said in the Book of the Fayum to have emerged from the great lake at the same time the sun god Ra arose from its waters in his form as the crocodile god Sobek or Sobek-Ra.[12] Remember, the lake was seen both as a manifestation of the goddess Neith in her guise as Mehet-Weret, the Great Flood, and also as the waters of Nun, out of which the sun arose after killing the primeval snake that in Fayumic tradition was, according to Reymond, the "original Creator of waters and earth" under the name 'Ir-ṣdy.[13]

We cannot say for certain whether Sobekneferu might have been aware of this alignment toward the star Eltanin along with its role as the head or eye of a celestial crocodile identified as Sobek, and seen in the sky attached to the back of his mother, the She-hippopotamus, Neith. If, however, Pyramid Texts scholar J. D. Degreef is correct in his proposal that the hippopotamus and crocodile sky figure found in the circumpolar region of the northern night sky does indeed go back to the beginning of dynastic history then this would surely have been knowledge passed on to the female monarch by the priests of Sobek at Shedet. If so, then the alignments toward the setting of the star Eltanin found both at the Qasr el-Sagha temple and at the Mazghuna North pyramid would unquestionably have reflected her own personal interest in the cosmic significance of Sobek and his mother, Neith, the Dehdehet, or Deep Bosomed One, mentioned in the inscription found at the site of the Labyrinth.

If Gerald Massey were alive today I am sure he would agree with these sentiments since it was his opinion that the female monarch, as an avatar of Sobek and his mother, the She-hippopotamus Neith, had single handedly managed to revivify the stellar beliefs of this age-old Typhonian cult and in doing so had ushered in a new aeon of cosmic awareness that was readily taken up by her successors, the Sebekhept kings of the Thirteenth Dynasty. Her actions, however, only resulted in the Fayum being struck off the list of Egyptian nomes by the followers of Osiris while she herself was blamed for triggering the Second Intermediate Period.

This then was the hypothesis explored by Victorian mythologist Gerald Massey in his various books—not just *A Book of the Beginnings,* published in 1881, and its sequel, *The Natural Genesis,* published two years later in 1883, but also in *Ancient Egypt the Light of the World,* published in 1907, three years after the release of Stoker's *The Jewel of Seven Stars.* There seems little question that the Irish novelist was familiar with Massey's books, and that their portrayal of Sobekneferu as an avatar of the Goddess of the Seven Stars helped inspire the character of Queen Tera in Stoker's Egyptian novel; her name being derived from what he saw as the Egyptian word for "time": *tera.*

In fact, it is true to say that prior to Hatshepsut's own remarkable story being pieced together in the early twentieth century, far more intrigue surrounded Sobekneferu than it did her. Of course, we cannot prove categorically that Sobekneferu was the sole inspiration behind Stoker's Queen Tera (and we can never dismiss the possibility that her character was not in some way influenced by what Stoker knew about Hatshepsut). What can be said, however, is that the evidence presented within these pages does make sense of Sobekneferu being the principal inspiration behind the book's enigmatic Egyptian female ruler, who, as we shall see in the book's appendix titled "Sobekneferu on Film and Television," would go on to feature in various horror movies based on the story as told in Bram Stoker's *The Jewel of Seven Stars.* In this new guise, the spirit of Sobekneferu lives on not only as an icon of gothic fiction, but also as the figurehand of influential occult traditions that have now brought her back to life in the modern world. It is these that we look at in the book's final chapter.

38

Typhonian Gnosis

Between 1972 and 2002, occultist, mystic, novelist, poet, and writer Kenneth Grant (1924–2011) produced three nonfiction trilogies expounding the magical rites of cults and religions worldwide that he saw as forming part of a universal, interconnected occult tradition many thousands of years old.[1] They included the voudon rites of Haiti and the United States, the kaula tantric cults of India, the religions of Seth and Sobek in ancient Egypt, and the Thelemic magic of occultist, poet, mountaineer, and writer Aleister Crowley (1875–1947). He was Grant's mentor shortly before his death in Hastings, West Sussex, in 1947; Grant being at this time Crowley's secretary.[2]

Fig. 38.1. Kenneth Grant and his wife Steffi at the time of their marriage in 1946. Used with permission of Starfire Publishing.

All of these different strands of religion, Grant came to understand, were driven by esoteric doctrines that contained psychosexual formulae and Ophidian (serpent-inspired) symbolism resonating as one to create what he saw as magic's left-hand path. This primeval current, which Grant proposed had developed originally among indigenous peoples in Africa and in Asia, he would come to refer to as the Draconian or Typhonian tradition. The Typhon in question was, of course, the Greek god-monster and primeval dragon of this name that in ancient Egypt would come to be equated with Seth and Sobek, as well as their shared animal form, the crocodile.[3]

It is, however, Grant's references to Sobekneferu and her perceived revitalization of what he saw as the Draconian cult that are of interest to our current understanding of the female monarch's reemergence into popular consciousness. In *Cults of the Shadow*, published in 1975, for instance, he writes: "It is not until the reign of Queen Sebek-nefer-Ra at the beginning of the thirteenth dynasty that the Draconians returned again in full force. This Queen was an initiate of the most profound Mysteries of the Cult, and her temperament was such that she revelled in assuming the role of the Great Mother. [The XIIIth dynasty] was known as the Sebek Dynasty because at this time . . . the sun began to rise in the Sign of the Ram."[4]

Grant continues the theme by saying, "the lamb or ram of Ra was a nominal terminal used by the Sebekhepts (devotees of Sebek) of the XIIIth Dynasty . . . [each of whom] was a devotee of Sebek, the son of the Goddess of the Seven Stars."[5]

Separately, he informs the reader that, "Sebek-nefer-Ra was the first royal Sebek on all the monuments, and the reign of the Sebekhepts continued until the end of the XVIIth Dynasty. It was during the reign of Queen Sebek-nefer-Ra that the Draconian Cult attained its maximum power."[6] Then, in a footnote accompanying his summary of Sobekneferu and her religious revolution, he adds: "She [Sebek-nefer-Ra] assumed the god-form of Typhon, the ancient goddess, who supposedly conceived without the intervention of the male."[7]

The ancient goddess alluded to here is the ancient Egyptian She-hippopotamus in her guise as the primeval dragon. This ancient deity, as we saw in chapter 35, was represented in the night sky by a sky-figure identified as a bipedal hippopotamus with a crocodile on its back. It was marked out by stars from the constellations of Draco and Ursa Minor and was connected also with the Ox Thigh sky-figure signified by the seven main stars of Ursa Major. As a form of Neith, the She-hippopotamus was the mother of Sobek as well as the controller of cosmic time in her role as Goddess of the Seven Stars.

THE TYPHONIAN CURRENT

Already we should be alerted to the fact that almost everything Grant says on these matters can be found also in the works of Gerald Massey[8] and Heinrich Brugsch-Bey,[9] two scholars that Grant acknowledges as primary sources of inspiration for his ideas on the Egyptian roots of the Draconian tradition. There is, however, in Grant's Typhonian Trilogies an even greater emphasis on the importance of Sobekneferu through her promotion of the cult of Sobek and the fact that she was responsible for the Sebekhept rulers of the Thirteenth Dynasty adopting the crocodile god in his form as Sobek-Ra. Through her influence they became devotees of the Goddess of the Seven Stars, with Sobekneferu being seen as her living embodiment on earth.

As Massey implies himself, the adoption of the ram (Amun-Ra) as a form of the sun god Sobek-Ra marked the point of transition between the age of Taurus (the Bull) and the astrological age of Aries (the Ram), which, as we saw in chapter 36, was thought to have triggered a new revolution in Egyptian religious thought.

The historical validity of such statements can, of course, be quite easily questioned, although there does seem every reason to believe that with the setting up of the Labyrinth as the central place of worship for the local gods of all the nomes of Upper and Lower Egypt, Sobekneferu can very well be said to have initiated her own religious revolution during her reign. What is more, the only deity she is associated with directly other than Sobek is Dehdehet, the "Deep Bosomed One." As we have seen, the term was almost certainly as epithet of Neith, the She-hippopotamus at the core of Sobekneferu's stellar-based religious cult.

DIVINE LINEAGES

Grant's own promotion of these ideas within his Typhonian Trilogies— which remain essential reading for occultists today—introduced

Sobekneferu to a whole new generational audience that would come to see the monarch as the primary incarnation of the Typhonian current in ancient Egypt. Grant saw her as the initiator of a powerful magical lineage that has produced its own avatars down through the ages. It is, however, what led him to this conclusion that is of the greatest interest to this present work, for it would appear to have come from ritualistic activities conducted by the magical group set up by Grant and his wife Steffi called the Nu-Isis Lodge.*

During one of the group's inaugural magical workings in the mid-1950s, a decorated ancient Egyptian mummy case fragment was introduced to the proceedings (see plate 25). Grant wanted to see if one of its members, a woman named Mira, could connect with its past. So with the lodge room used for the gathering draped with ancient Egyptian themed hangings, an assembled group of ten, including an officiating priestess, opened the circle to the sound of lutes and pipes.[10]

Mira quickly entered into an altered state of consciousness and, with the coffin fragment to hand, began gazing into a mirror raised at a slight angle.[11] Grant would afterward record that what Mira saw in the mirror was a "dazzlingly" beautiful ancient Egyptian royal woman. She was reclining on "cheetah pelts" that covered a mobile divan being carried by a group of black-robed figures moving at great speed through a seemingly endless tunnel.[12] According to Grant in his 1992 book *Hecate's Fountain*, the woman described by Mira, "was identifiably that of the 13th Dynasty, under the reign of Queen Sebek-nefer-Ra, one of the greatest exponents of the Draconian Tradition within historic times."[13] He goes on:

> To anticipate events: it had become apparent that the hierarch of the mummy-casing [used in the working] had also been an High Priestess in a Temple of Set endowed by Queen Sebek-nefer-Ra. The temple had survived ravages and depredations by the Osirians, who, for centuries had sought to obliterate all traces of the "abhorréd" Typhonian Cult.[14]

---

*I wish to thank Paul Weston for compiling all the material relating to Kenneth Grant's interest in Sobekneferu, including the magical workings of the Nu-Isis Lodge. This was published in Weston's book *Atargatis* (2018), the relevant sections of which were provided to me by the author. For more information, see Weston 2018.

This was a reference to the manner Massey, and before him the German Egyptologist Brugsch-Bey, had written that in the wake of Sobekneferu's promotion of the cult of Sobek and the subsequent events that had led to one of Egypt's darkest hours, the Fayum, as the chief center for the worship of the crocodile—a symbol of the god Set—had been struck from the list of nomes or districts making up the Two Lands (see chapter 36).

Although the ancient Egyptian woman glimpsed by Mira during the Nu-Isis Lodge's magical working is not specifically identified, the inference is that she was either a "High Priestess" in the service of Sobekneferu, or the monarch herself. In some ways it doesn't matter which, since it was the impact this session had on Grant that galvanized his interest, not just in Sobekneferu, but also in the influence of her magical current down through the ages.

THE FLORENCE FARR CONNECTION

In *Hecate's Fountain* Grant writes that the mummy case fragment introduced to the session had previously been used as a "psychic focus" by "one of the splinter groups of the Golden Dawn directed by soror S.S.D.D." and had come into his possession in 1948 "through the kindness of a collector."[15] The acronym S.S.D.D. is an allusion to the magical motto adopted by Florence Farr (1860–1917) a talented actor, composer, musician, director, writer, on entering an occult society known as the Hermetic Order of the Golden Dawn. It stands for "Sapientia Sapienti Dona Data," which is Latin and means, "Wisdom is given as a gift to the Wise."[16]

A plate illustration in Grant's book *Aleister Crowley and the Hidden God* (1973) shows the mummy case fragment with the following caption accompanying it: "Fragment of a sarcophagus used in the Golden Dawn for establishing magical contact with the khu [spirit] of an Egyptian princess."[17] Both statements imply that the artifact had formerly belonged to Farr and had been used by her and her own Sphere group, which formed part of the Golden Dawn, to make contact with a female spirit she called the "Egyptian Adept."

Contact with the spirit had begun following extensive visits by Farr to the British Museum's Reading Room while researching her book *Egyptian Magic*, published in 1896.[18] During these visits she would spend time meditating in front of a mummy contained inside a coffin labeled as a "lady of the college of the God Amen-Ra at Thebes."* The name given to this mummy was Mutemmenu, this coming from the inscription on the coffin, although it was much later realized that the mummy was in fact male and only dated back to Roman times.

Clearly, Grant knew about these spiritual communications otherwise he would not have mentioned the artifact's link both to Farr and to the Golden Dawn "splinter group." Farr, it should be pointed out, is not known to have ever identified the Egyptian Adept with Sobekneferu. The fact, however, that Farr's extensive communications with the Egyptian Adept might well have influenced the development of the character of Margaret Trelawny in Bram Stoker's *The Jewel of Seven Stars,* a matter dealt with elsewhere by the current author,[19] seems oddly coincidental, if nothing else.

As we have seen, the character of Queen Tera—who overshadowed Margaret for some while before finally replacing her completely—had almost certainly been created by Stoker after reading Massey's portrayal of Sobekneferu as a living embodiment of his Goddess of the Seven Stars. So if the character of Margaret was indeed inspired by Farr's magical communications with the Egyptian Adept then Grant's perception of Sobekneferu as a living spirit whose influence could still be felt today suddenly becomes of particular interest to this debate.

THE STELLAR LODE

This can probably be seen in the fact that even before the first magical workings of his Nu-Isis Lodge Grant had started gathering material for a series of fictional stories. One of special note is *The Stellar Lode,* which is thought to have been completed by Grant in 1956, this being around a year after the formation of the Nu-Isis Lodge in 1955.[20] An initial installment of the novella reached publication in 1991,[21] although it was not until 1995 that the complete story was made available for the first time.[22] The main focus of the plot is a "small sphere, like a skryer's crystal,"[23] purchased from a curio shop in Chelsea, West London, which had previously belonged to an artist

---

*The mummy's British Museum catalogue number is EA6704. It was purchased by the museum as far back as 1835. See Tully 2018, 135.

named Hilary Morgan.[24] It had come into his possession during the eleven years he'd spent in Egypt, most of it apparently in the Fayum.

According to the narrative, which is worth examining in detail, around midnight one evening, while in the "smoky room" of a club in the Fayum filled with "alcohol and drug-laden fumes," Morgan is said to have been drawn, almost hypnotically, to a "mysterious woman." Said to have been around 30 years of age, she was seated at another table dressed in attire of an "odd nature."[25]

Having joined her, the strange woman stands up and compels him to follow her out into the open air, after which they move through a starry landscape that to Morgan seems only vaguely familiar. Eventually they reach "a valley containing the almost-obliterated remains of an ancient temple."[26] From there they enter an "ancient gallery" before descending into a "shaft cut in the rock at an angle of approximately forty degrees."[27] Passing through underground chambers they eventually come upon a "regal tomb" hidden deep within an underground cavern situated "beneath the Lake,"[28] this presumably being a reference to the Fayum's Birket Qarun lake.

The "subterranean crypt" is found to contain the sarcophagus of a royal female, "probably a queen, and certainly a high princess," named Hat-Abaft-Sume. There and then, the woman guides him to find the shew-stone, described as a "magnificent jewel," within which is not only a shining star, but also the soul of the queen.[29] After that she is nowhere to be seen, having disappeared completely.

Realizing that the strange woman who had guided him to discover the shew-stone was in fact the living spirit of Hat-Abaft-Sume, Morgan is inspired to start painting abstract, almost surrealistic landscapes and settings featuring ancient Egypt. So remarkable are these paintings that they become highly prized in the art world.

Following the painter's death, the talisman is sold in the aforementioned curio shop. The rest of the book details what happens to those who come into contact with the shew-stone and how the ancient Egyptian queen it holds is able to affect their lives.

Hat-Abaft-Sume, we are told, had been, "one of the most evil and alluring queens of history,"[30] and yet she is also seen as the materialization of a "primal Star-Goddess."[31] As a monarch she had ruled at the commencement of the Eighteenth Dynasty, although, crucially, we learn that her reign "was a revival of the power she had previously wielded as Sebek-nefer-Ra-Nu in the XIIIth Dynasty."[32] So the real identity of the "mysterious woman" encountered by Morgan is finally revealed as Sobekneferu herself!

There seems little question that *The Stellar Lode* echoes important themes from Bram Stoker's *The Jewel of Seven Stars,* which I understand was one of Grant's favorite novels.[33] Here, however, the raising of Queen Tera has been replaced with the release of Hat-Abaft-Sume, while Stoker's eponymous Jewel of Seven Stars is transformed into a "magnificent jewel," a crystal sphere used as a shew-stone. More pertinently, the ritual undertaken toward the end of the story to free the hold that the "evil and alluring" queen Hat-Abaft-Sume/Sebek-nefer-Ra-Nu has on any owner of the shew-stone is referred to as the "Great Experiment."[34] This, of course, is a nod to the "Great Experiment" used to resurrect Queen Tera in *The Jewel of Seven Stars.*

Bringing us back to Florence Farr's influence on the magical activities of the Nu-Isis Lodge and Grant's own personal interest in Sobekneferu is the fact that in *The Stellar Lode* the person who buys the shew-stone from the curio shop in Chelsea is a woman named Flavia Keene. After getting it home she becomes self-absorbed in connecting with the ancient Egyptian realms accessed via the crystal's ability to affect the consciousness of its owner. She also finds herself glimpsing the entity contained inside the shew-stone, which, of course, turns out to be Hat-Abaft-Sume/Sebek-nefer-Ra-Nu.

It might be suggested that the character of Flavia Keene was influenced by Grant's knowledge of Florence Farr, this connection having come from the mummy case fragment given to him in 1948, the same year he apparently began work on *The Stellar Lode.*[35] This mummy case fragment, as we have seen, had formerly belonged, or so Grant came to believe, by Farr and had been used by her Sphere group to communicate with the spirit known as the Egyptian Adept.

So although the shew-stone from *The Stellar Lode* was most likely modeled on Stoker's Jewel of Seven Stars, if the character of Flavia Keene was indeed based on Florence Farr, then the role the mummy case fragment played in real life was probably the same as that played by the fictional jewel in Grant's novella. In both cases the artifact in question acted as a conduit to the living spirit of an ancient Egyptian female. If correct, this would be further confirmation of the impact that Farr's communications with the

Egyptian Adept had on the emergence of Sobekneferu both in Stoker's Egyptian novel and in modern pop culture in general.

THE NINTH ARCH

By the publication in 2002 of *The Ninth Arch,* Grant's final install-ment in his Typhonian Trilogies, Sobekneferu, or Sebek-nefer-Ra as he calls her, is directly identified with Stoker's Queen Tera. Statements such as "Tera was a herald of Queen Sebek-nefer-Ra of the XIIIth dynasty, she who revived the Typhonian Cult in ancient Khem"[36] and "The Oracle is ThERA, Queen of the Seven Stars who reigned in the Thirteenth Dyasty as Queen Sebek-nefer-Ra"[37] make it clear that Grant had by now come to realize that the fictional Queen Tera and the historical Sobekneferu were one and the same.* Both women, one fictional and the other real, had, in his words, "brought over from an indefinitely ancient past, prior even to Egypt, the original Typhonian Gnosis."[38]

The seemingly subversive and occasionally forceful manner that Sobekneferu has been able to push her way back into popular consciousness following 3,800 years of near obscurity has been quite remarkable, and quite unlike the journey taken by any other ancient Egyptian female ruler. What is more, her presence in pop culture today is on the rise. Look on the internet and you will find dozens of blogs, articles, stories, and videos that celebrate Sobekneferu's life in every way. They range from the sublime to the ridiculous.

Some Christian historians, for instance, have come to believe that Sobekneferu was the Pharaoh's daughter who pulled Moses out of the bul-rushes and raised him as her own through to adulthood.[39] Others believe that Sobekneferu was the founder of entire dynasties of so-called Dragon kings that have secretly guided the destiny of humankind down through the

---

*Without wishing to diminish the importance of Grant identifying Stoker's Queen Tera with Sobekneferu it should, however, be noted that *The Ninth Arch* makes reference to material from *The Seventh Sword* (1991), a work written by the present author (see Grant 2002, 80, 84, 126 n. 41). In the chapter titled "The Star of Egypt" (Collins 1991, 223–29), it not only notes Grant's interest in the Egyptian monarch (Collins 1991, 227–28), but also proposes that Bram Stoker "either consciously or unconsciously, based his Queen Tera on the historical figure of Sobek-nofru-re" (Collins 1991, 228). Whether or not these ideas inspired Grant to finally con-nect Queen Tera with the historical Sobekneferu we shall never know, but connect her he did.

ages. Historical writer Iona Miller wrote that these priest kings have always adhered to an occult lineage kept alive by a secret society known as the Dragon Court.[40] Through certain noble houses this bloodline of the Grail continues to thrive today. It is from one of its more recent descendants, the late Nicholas de Vere, that knowledge of the Dragon Court tradition has come down to us in the modern age.[41]

Then there are the dramatic personal experiences of those who claim to have had psychic encounters with Sobekneferu,[42] echoing Farr's contact with the Egyptian Adept and Grant's connections with the female monarch through the Nu-Isis Lodge workings. Sobekneferu, or Neferusobek as some Egyptologists prefer to call her, also now has her own feast day. It is listed as July 23,[43] one day after that of Mary Magdalene, which is July 22. I would

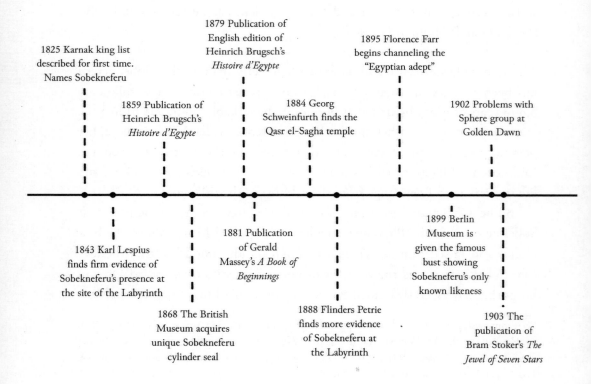

Fig. 38.2. Timeline of related events in Sobekneferu's reemergence into popular consciousness across the past 200 years.

like to think that people around the world do indeed celebrate the monarch's life and achievements on this special day.

This then is the story of Sobekneferu, mighty ruler, religious revolutionary, and—through the writings of intuitive authors such as Gerald Massey and Kenneth Grant—avatar of a primordial creatrix identified as Goddess of the Seven Stars. In a manner similar to how Bram Stoker imagined the eventual fate of Queen Tera in *The Jewel of Seven Stars,* it is almost as if Sobekneferu has herself existed across the ages in a state of eternal slumber, ever awaiting the time she might awaken out of the darkness of obscurity and live again in this world. Hopefully, in some small way, this book has done enough to make that happen.

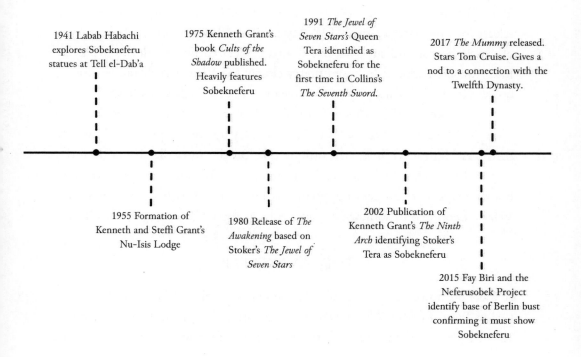

1941 Labab Habachi explores Sobekneferu statues at Tell el-Dab'a

1975 Kenneth Grant's book *Cults of the Shadow* published. Heavily features Sobekneferu

1991 *The Jewel of Seven Stars's* Queen Tera identified as Sobekneferu for the first time in Collins's *The Seventh Sword.*

2017 *The Mummy* released. Stars Tom Cruise. Gives a nod to a connection with the Twelfth Dynasty.

1955 Formation of Kenneth and Steffi Grant's Nu-Isis Lodge

1980 Release of *The Awakening* based on Stoker's *The Jewel of Seven Stars*

2002 Publication of Kenneth Grant's *The Ninth Arch* identifying Stoker's Tera as Sobekneferu

2015 Fay Biri and the Neferusobek Project identify base of Berlin bust confirming it must show Sobekneferu

Sobekneferu on Film and Television

Across the years there have been several attempts at cinematic adaptations of Bram Stoker's gothic novel *The Jewel of Seven Stars,* first published in 1903. They probably start with 1970's *Curse of the Mummy,* a made-for-TV film release forming part of British TV's Mysteries and Imagination anthology series of classic horror and supernatural dramas.[1] Created into a television play by John Russell Taylor, it followed pretty closely the Victorian theme of Stoker's book, with Isobel Black playing the role of Margaret Trelawny/Queen Tera.

Then came 1971's *Blood from the Mummy's Tomb,* directed by Seth Holt and Michael Carreras.[2] With a screenplay by Christopher Wicking, the film was Hammer Film's own unique take on the story. Set in modern-day England with flashbacks to Tera's entombment it is seen by many as the best horror adaption of Stoker's Egyptian novel in which British actress and model Valeria Leon plays a somewhat voluptuous Margaret Trelawny/Queen Tera.

THE AWAKENING

It was not, however, until 1980 and the release of the Mike Newell directed Orion Pictures film *The Awakening* that Stoker's Queen Tera came much closer to being identified with the historical Sobekneferu.* For the movie,

---

The Awakening (film cut with original ending included), (1980) 2007 DVD; *The Awakening* (with original ending removed) (1980) 2012 DVD. See also the tie-in novel written by Ronald

which starred Charlton Heston as Egyptologist Matthew Corbeck, Queen Tera is renamed Queen Kara. She is said to have ruled Upper and Lower Egypt in "1800 BC," the *exact* timeframe of Sobekneferu. This choice of date cannot be coincidence and tells us that the three writers behind the screenplay—Allan Scott, Chris Bryant, and Clive Exton—must have come to realize that the only female monarch that matched Stoker's Queen Tera was Sobekneferu, who, as we know, did indeed reign around 1800 BCE. However, since they had to stick to the narrative they could not use the name Sobekneferu, so instead opted for Kara, a shortening of the monarch's throne name—Sobekkara. Plus Kara was close enough to Tera, Stoker's original name for the queen.

In the film, it is Corbeck's daughter Margaret—played by American actress Stephanie Zimbalist—who is very gradually taken over by Kara's spirit. This was inevitable consequence of her birth in a Cairo hospital coinciding with her father opening Kara's coffin, still in situ within the sarcophagus, to expose her mummified remains for the first time in 3,800 years.

Margaret's transformation into Kara is very gradual at first, especially since she lives in New York with her mother, who'd left Corbeck after he'd decided to put the discovery of the tomb ahead of becoming a devoted father. Having felt compelled to go to London to see her father on her eighteenth birthday, Margaret's contact with the mummy of Queen Kara accelerates her connection with the dead monarch. She also comes to realize that her father had not only been Tera's father during her lifetime, but that as king he had forced her to marry him; her revenge being to murder her father as he was inspecting his own tomb and then kill anyone who had ever set eyes on him. "She must have killed thousands," Corbeck admits, as he tells the story to his daughter.

Margaret's full transition into the evil queen takes place as Corbeck conducts a major ritual to resurrect Kara inside the Egyptian room of the London Museum of Antiquities (which is clearly meant to be the British Museum). In Egyptian style shift dress Margaret, now almost entirely under Kara's control, joins her father in the museum, urging him to complete the

---

(*cont.*) Chetwynd-Hayes to accompany the film's release. Titled *The Awakening* (1980), it has a worldwide cult of Kara emerging even before the queen's eventual resurrection by Matthew Corbeck in the London Museum of Antiquities, a plot arc ignored by the film's scriptwriters.

ritual, which he does only to find there is nothing inside the mummy wrappings but withered flesh and bones. It is then that he realizes what is going on. Having now fully taken over Margaret's body, we next see Kara snarling at her father and wearing full Egyptian style eye makeup! In the chaos that ensues a large statue of Kara topples over killing Corbeck as the museum's Egyptian room goes up in flames.

The film's closing scene shows Kara now standing at the museum's colonnaded entrance, flames rising up behind her. With arms raised she gazes out over a darkened London skyline contemplating her next move in this unsuspecting world she has now found herself within. Interestingly, in some versions of the film this final scene has been cut.[3] Instead it ends with the resurrected Kara watching Corbeck's death as flames lick up around her—a strange echo of how the ending to Stoker's original novel was also censored.

THE MUMMY

If we skip over 1997's *Bram Stoker's Legend of the Mummy,* directed by Lou Gossett Jr., which was a pretty mediocre adaption of *The Jewel of Seven Stars* set in modern-day United States, we come, finally, to 2017's cinematic blockbuster *The Mummy.* Directed by Alex Kurtzman and released by Universal Studios, it starred Tom Cruise and Russell Crowe. Although Bram Stoker's novel was not credited as being the inspiration behind the film's backstory it surely was, something that has not gone unnoticed by movie critics and horror aficionados alike.[4]

The Bram Stoker connection with the film makes sense, especially as *The Mummy* was to have been the first of several movies forming part of Universal's "Dark Universe" series. This would have revolved around an extended universe featuring all the studio's classic movie monsters including Stoker's own Dracula, Mary Shelley's Frankenstein, Wolf Man, the Phantom of the Opera, as well as Dr. Jekyll and Mr. Hyde, who appears in *The Mummy* played by Russell Crowe. Due, however, to the extremely poor reception of *The Mummy,* Universal's Dark Universe was shelved indefinitely, with only 2020's *The Invisible Man* seen as belonging to the series.

There is, however, a slight nod to the world of Sobekneferu in 2017's *The Mummy.* The ancient Egyptian princess brought back to life following the discovery of her tomb—a role played quite brilliantly by Algerian actor, dancer, and model Sofia Boutella—bears the name Ahmanet. This is very obviously a shortening of Amenemhat, the name of Sobekneferu's father and brother, and the principal name used by the rulers of the Twelfth Dynasty.

There are other modern adaptions of Stoker's *The Jewel of Seven Stars,* but in all honesty they are so bad they are not worth devoting any time to here. I would recommend readers seek out 1970's *Curse of the Mummy* and 1971's *Blood from the Mummy's Tomb* and watch them instead. Both, however, are not even in the same league as 1980's *The Awakening,* which is the only one where many of the scenes were shot on location in Egypt. The character of Kara is also both compelling and chillingly alluring in her final manifestation. In addition to this, the original soundtrack by celebrated French composer Claude Bolling (1930–2020) is totally evocative of ancient Egypt and was played many times during the writing of this book. Both the soundtrack and the film are available for free on YouTube.

THE ADVENTURE OF THE ERSATZ SOBEKNEFERU

Turning briefly now to television, Sobekneferu crops up in an episode of the show *Elementary,* a modern take on Arthur Conan Doyle's fictional detective Sherlock Holmes set in current-day New York. A corpse of a woman is discovered that is being slowly transformed into a fake Egyptian mummy— and not just any mummy. If the forger had succeeded in their masterwork it would have been passed off as the lost mummy of Sobekneferu, hence the episode's title, "The Adventure of the Ersatz Sobekneferu" (first screened on July 2, 2018).

In the dialogue some background information is given about the female monarch. Holmes, played by British actor Jonny Lee Miller, tells his companion Dr. Jane Watson (Lucy Liu), that Sobekneferu had died under mysterious circumstances, "in her late twenties, over 3000 years ago." He goes on to say that she had "almost certainly" been killed "by her brother's son, Sobekhotep, and/or his allies. He succeeded her to the throne, and records written during his dynasty studiously avoid any mention of how she died. That's a sure sign that his regime was involved. Only fair, I suppose, since she likely murdered his father to seize power in the first place."[5]

These observations, whether historically accurate or otherwise, certainly make it clear that the episode's scriptwriters had done some serious background research on the intrigues surrounding Sobekneferu's reign. The suggestion that she murdered her brother, Amenemhet IV, the father of Sobekhotep I, the first king of the Thirteenth Dynasty, conforms precisely with the findings of this book (see chapter 15). That said, the idea that Sobekhotep I murdered Sobekneferu as revenge for her father's death is much less likely, for as we have seen the kings of this dynasty were not only strongly supportive of the cult of Sobek, and retained the existing capital of Itj-tawy, but would also seem to have deified Sobekneferu and continued a cult in her name (see chapters 5 and 15).

The greater question is why the show's writers chose to feature Sobekneferu in the episode. That the monarch's tomb, and thus her mummy, have never been found, does, of course, make her a suitable candidate for use in such a story. That said, the fact that Arthur Conan Doyle's character of Sherlock Holmes is firmly rooted in the Victorian era once more suggests a cursory nod back to the storyline of Bram Stoker's *The Jewel of Seven Stars*. An additional nod to Stoker's book, and in particular the Jewel of Seven Stars itself, is the fact that during the episode we learn that an "amulet" in the shape of a scarab beetle bearing Sobekneferu's royal name had been found alongside the corpse being transformed into a mummy. As we have seen, the Jewel of Seven Stars was itself fashioned into the shape of a scarab beetle. All this then brings Sobekneferu one step closer to being recognized as the true inspiration behind Stoker's choice of a resurrected female monarch in his highly influential Egyptian novel.

Notes

Abbreviations: n.d. = no date given; n.p.n. = no page number(s) given.

PART 1. DISCOVERING SOBEKNEFERU

CHAPTER 1.
FEMALE PHARAOHS

1. Reeves 2005.
2. See Gabolde 1998.
3. See Tyldesley 2006, 33–34.
4. Waddell (1940) 1964, 54 n. 2.
5. Hassan 1943, 1.
6. Hassan 1943, 3.
7. Vanderzwet 2005.
8. Vanderzwet 2005.
9. Vanderzwet 2005.
10. Manetho, fr. 20, Syncellus after Africanus; fr. 21, Syncellus p. 109, after Eusebius; fragment 21b of Armenian version of Eusebius. See Waddell (1940) 1964, 53–57.

CHAPTER 2.
RULER OF THE TWO LANDS

1. Cooney (2018) 2020, 87.
2. See Diamond 2020 for a full study of the subject of female masculinity during the reign of Sobekneferu.

3. Zecchi 2010, 46–47.

4. Callender 1998b, 48; Grajetzki 2006, 30.

5. Grajetzki 2006, 68; Pignattari 2018, 101.

6. Zecchi 2010, 47.

7. Zecchi 2010, 24.

8. Zecchi 2010, 42–43.

9. Beinlich 2013, 48.

10. Zecchi 2010, 42.

11. Callender 1998b, 47; Pignattari 2018, 13, 108; Zecchi 2010, 108.

12. Habachi 1954, 467.

13. Egyptian Museum item number JE 72663.

14. Diamond 2020, 9.

15. Diamond 2020, 9.

16. See, for instance, Forman and Quirke 1996, 116; Callender 1998a, 236; Callender 1998b, 52; Pignattari 2018, 12.

17. Stevenson 2019, 72.

18. Newberry 1943a, 74–75.

19. Habachi 1954, 463–64.

20. Habachi 1954, 463.

CHAPTER 3.
SOBEKNEFERU—THE STORY AS WE KNOW IT

1. Pignattari 2018, 85–86.

2. Pignattari 2018, 23–31 and the references therein; Grajetzki 2006, 61.

3. Lundström 2014a; Baker 2008, 30–32.

4. Pignattari, 2018, 23–31 and the references therein; Grajetzki 2006, 61.

5. Manetho, bk. II, fr. 34, Syncellus p. 110 after Africanus; fr. 35, Syncellus after Eusebius. See Waddell (1940) 1964, 66–73.

6. Manetho, bk. II, fr. 34 from Syncellus after Africanus. See Waddell (1940) 1964, 68–69.

7. Lundström 2014b; Baker 2008, 455–57.

8. Pignattari 2018, 13.

9. Newberry 1943a, 74–75; Gardiner (1961) 1976, 141; Tallet 2005, 253.

10. Callender 1995, 228. See also Pignattari 2018, 13 and 13 n. 104.

11. Tallet 2005, 178–79; Piganattari 2018, 12.

12. Hayes 1953, 194.

13. Gardiner (1961) 1976, 141; Callender 1998b, 47.

14. Callender 1998b, 47.

15. Grimal (1988) 1992, 185; Ryholt 1997, 197; Pignattari 2018, 99.

16. Grimal (1988) 1992, 179; Callender 1998b, 50.

17. Grajetzki 2001, 24 entry 3.8; Theis 2009, 318–19; Cooney (2018) 2020, 26.

18. Pignattari 2018, 101.

19. Pignattari 2018, 101.

20. Manetho fr. 41a, Syncellus after Africanus; fr 41b, Syncellus after Eusebius; fr. 41c, of Armenian version of Eusebius. See Waddell (1940) 1964, 74–75.

21. Pignattari 2018, 101.

22. Saretta 2016, 137–45.

23. Pignattari, 2018, 82, 84.

24. Pignattari 2018, 101–2.

25. Grimal (1988) 1992, 171.

26. Gardiner (1961) 1976, 141.

27. Graffito no. SNM34390. See Callender 1998b, 50; Pignattari 2018, 69, 99.

28. Callender 1998b, 50.

29. Zecchi 2010, 17, 101; Ragheb 2019.

30. Callender 1998b, 50.

31. Callender 1998b, 50.

CHAPTER 4.
THE WOMAN BEHIND THE PHARAOH

1. Louvre inventory number E27135. For a full description see Louvre Collections "statue. Sobekkarê Néferousobek (1789–1786 [BCE])."

2. Callender 1998b, 51.

3. Callender 1998b, 52; Diamond 2020, 7.

4. Cooney (2018) 2020, 85.

5. Cooney (2018) 2020, 85.

6. Diamond 2020, 8.

7. Callender 1998a, 235.

8. See, for example, Fechheimer (1914) 1920, pls. 57–58.

9. Fay et al 2015.

10. Berlin acquisition number 14475: greywacke, height 5.5 inches, width 3.5 inches, depth 2.4 inches (14 x 9 x 6.2 centimeters).

11. Haney 2020, appendix B, especially p. 599.

12. Cooney (2018) 2020, 83.

13. Cooney (2018) 2020, 86.

14. Dunham 1960, 33, pls. 40 a–c.
15. Reisner 1929; Žabkar 1975; Žabkar and Žabkar 1975.
16. Fay et al 2015.
17. For the work of the Neferusobek Project see Fay et al 2015.
18. Fay et al 2015, 89.
19. Callender 2018.
20. Herodotus 1920, bk. II, ch. 99. All quotations from Herodotus are from the Loeb Edition, translated by A.D. Godley unless otherwise stated.
21. Callender 1998b, 48; Grajetzki 2006, 30.
22. Callender 1998b, 48; Grajetzki 2006, 30.
23. Grajetzki 2006, 57.
24. Email communication with Kara Cooney, December 3, 2021.

CHAPTER 5.
THE CULT OF SOBEKNEFERU

1. Habachi 1954, 458–60, 467–70.
2. For more information on the history of excavations at the site see Bietak 2007.
3. Habachi 1954, 458.
4. Habachi 1954, 460–61.
5. Habachi 1954, 460–61.
6. Adapted from Habachi 1954, 459.
7. Adapted from Habachi 1954, 460.
8. Habachi 1954, 469.
9. Habachi 1954, 469.
10. Habachi 1954, 459.
11. Adapted from Habachi 1954, 459.
12. Habachi 1954, 459.
13. Diamond 2020, 6. See also Callender 1998b, 45.
14. Diamond 2020, 6. See also Baines 1995, 9–11.
15. Cooney (2018) 2020, 87.
16. Metropolitan Museum of Art accession no. 29.3.1, "Large Kneeling Statue of Hatshepsut ca. 1479–1458 B.C." and accession no. 30.3.1, "Large Kneeling Statue of Hatshepsut ca. 1479–1458 B.C."
17. Forman and Quirke 1996, 116; Callender 1998a, 236; Callender 1998b, 52 Pignattari 2018, 12.
18. Naville 1887, 21–22; Habachi 1954, 462; Porter and Moss (1934) 1968, 9.
19. Habachi 1954, 462.

20. Naville 1887, 21.

21. Naville 1887, 21.

22. Naville 1887, 21.

23. Naville 1887, 21.

24. Naville 1887, 22.

25. Naville 1887, 22.

26. Marseilles no. 223. See Maspero 1890, 114 (no. 23); Grajetzki 2001, 24 entry 3.8; Theis 2009, 318–19; Cooney (2018) 2020, 26.

27. Grajetzki 2001, 24 entry 3.8; Theis 2009, 318–19; Cooney (2018) 2020, 26.

28. Gillam 1995, 233.

29. "TT60—Antefoqer and Senet" 2011.

30. Tallet 2005, 258: Tallet 2013, 82.

31. Adapted from Gardiner 1920, 28, pl. XXXVa, no. 2

32. Adapted from Gardiner 1920, 28, pl. XXXVa, no. 3.

33. Davies, Gardiner, and Davies 1920.

34. Gardiner 1920, 27–29; Davies, Gardiner, and Davies 1920, pl. XXXVa, nos. 2 and 3.

35. Pignattari 2018, 15.

36. Engelbach and Gunn 1923.

37. Grajetzki 2004, 54–56; Grajetzki 2006, 63.

38. Canhão 2019/2020, 9.

39. Grajetzki 2006, 63.

CHAPTER 6.
SOBEKNEFERU AND THE HEB SED MYSTERY

1. Metropolitan Museum of Art accession number MMA 65.59.1. See "Statuette of a Late Middle Kingdom Queen" 2016.

2. "Statuette of a Late Middle Kingdom Queen" 2016.

3. Callender 1998b, 52.

4. Pignattari 2018, 14.

5. Cooney (2018) 2020, 85 n. 12 on 338–39.

6. Callender 1998b, 52; Pignattari 2018, 14.

7. Callender 1998a; Callender 1998b, 52, 54.

8. Callender 1998b, 54.

9. Brooklyn Museum accession number 56.85. See "Head from a Female Sphinx," 2008.

10. "Head from a Female Sphinx" 2008.

11. "Head from a Female Sphinx" 2008.

12. See, for instance, Alm 2018.

PART 2. ROAD TO DESTINY

CHAPTER 7. SOBEKNEFERU IN CANAAN

1. Weinstein 1974, 51.

2. Weinstein 1974, 51–52; Hayes 1953, 183, 194.

3. Hayes 1953, 183, 194; Arnold 1992, 58 item no. 23.

4. Ryholt 1997, 213; Bart 2016.

5. Ryholt 1997, 213; Tallet 2005, 178–79; Pignattari 2018, 12, 77.

6. Seters (1966) 2010, 74; Grajetzki 2006, 61; Pignattari 2018, 77.

7. Ortiz 2013, s.v. "Gezer," 468–74.

8. Ortiz 2013, s.v. "Gezer," 469.

9. Hasson 2016.

10. Grajetzki 2006, 62; Bietak 2007; Pignattari 2018, 14.

11. Habachi 1954, 468–69.

12. Zecchi 2010, 87.

13. Seters (1966) 2010, 76–77.

14. Baines 1987; Grajetzki 2013, 5; Pritchard 2016, 230.

15. Collins and Little 2022, chs. 26–27.

16. Seters (1966) 2010, 76; Grajetzki (2009) 2012, 35.

17. Grajetzki (2009) 2012, 112, 131.

18. Giveon 1978, 29; Seters (1966) 2010, 75–76.

19. Grajetzki (2009) 2012, 35.

20. Seters (1966) 2010, 76.

21. Allen 2008; Grajetzki 2013, 5.

22. Allen 2008, 38.

23. Allen 2008, 32–38.

24. Allen 2008, 36.

25. Tallet 2005, 181-182; Grajetzki 2013, 5.

26. Newberry 1893, pl. 31.

27. Newberry 1893, pl. 28.

28. Newberry 1893, pl. 30–31, 38.

29. Newberry 1893, pl. 26, cols. 157–58; Allen 2008, 29.

30. Allen 2008, 29.

31. Allen 2008, 31.

32. Ryholt 1997, 293–94; Seters (1966) 2010, 78; Pignattari 2018, 82–84.

33. Pignattari 2018, 83.

34. Seters (1966) 2010, 77–80, 87–88, 93.

35. Saretta 2016, 137–45.

36. Seters (1966) 2010, 90.

37. Seters (1966) 2010, 94.

CHAPTER 8. THE VENGEFUL GODDESS

1. Gillam 1995, 234; Diamond 2020, 5–7.

2. Petrie 1906, chs. 5–11, 13; Seters (1966) 2010, 87–88, 91, 93; Pignattari 2018, 28.

3. Giveon 1978, 61.

4. Petrie 1916, 66; Giveon 1978, 61; Maier III (1986) 2018, 89.

5. Petrie 1916, 97–98; Giveon 1978, 62, 65.

6. Petrie 1916, 97–99.

7. Petrie 1916, 148, figs. 150 no. 9, 152 nos. 6–11, 154 nos. 1–14. Other similar cat figurines representing the serval have been found at another mining site, this one near Timna in the Negev region of Israel. See Giveon 1969, 50.

8. Petrie 1916, 148.

9. Petrie 1916, 67–69, 103, figs. 83 and 84.

10. Giveon 1978, 62; Maier III (1986) 2018, 89; Pignattari 2018, 70–71.

11. Hackley, 2014, 81.

12. Giveon 1978, 62.

13. Darnell, Darnell, Freeman, and Hendrickx 2002, 130.

14. Giveon 1978, 62.

15. Zecchi 2010, 53; Pignattari 2018, 88–91.

16. Zecchi 2010, 53, 55; Pignattari 2018, 88–91.

17. Gillam 1995, 234.

18. Zecchi 2010, 55; Pignattari 2018, 12.

19. See Gutbub 1961, 46–50; Fukaya 2019, 58–60.

20. Giveon 1978, 71.

21. Gillam 1995, 233.

CHAPTER 9.
DIVINE RIGHT TO RULE

1. Callender 1998b, 54.

2. See Collins 2006, 176–78, for a full review of this topic.

3. Friedman 2011, 25.

4. Friedman 2011, 25.

5. Friedman 2011, 25.

6. Friedman 2011, 40.

7. Friedman 2011, 25–26.

8. Ryholt 1997, 296–97.

9. Ryholt 1997, 294.

10. Ryholt 1997, 294.

PART 3. SEEDS OF DESTRUCTION

CHAPTER 10.
THE SISTER OF SOBEKNEFERU

1. Farag and Iskander 1971, pl. IV.

2. Farag and Iskander 1971, 2.

3. Farag and Iskander 1971, ix, 5.

4. Farag and Iskander 1971, 105.

5. Farag and Iskander 1971, 24.

6. Farag and Iskander 1971, 106.

7. Farag and Iskander 1971, 106–7.

8. Farag and Iskander 1971, 106.

9. Farag and Iskander 1971, 106.

10. Farag and Iskander 1971, 60, pl. XXXIX a and b.

11. Farag and Iskander 1971, 40, 70–71.

12. Farag and Iskander 1971, 13–15, figs. 8, 9, 10.

13. Farag and Iskander 1971, 9–10, 106.

14. Farag and Iskander 1971, 58, 106.

15. Farag and Iskander 1971, 14–15, figs 8–10, 20.

16. Farag and Iskander 1971, 15 fig. 10.

17. Farag and Iskander 1971, 58, 106, figs. 30, 31, 32.

18. Grajetzki 2014, 63.

19. Grajetzki 2014, 63–64.

20. Grajetzki 2005.

21. Grajetzki 2014, 64.

22. Callender 1998b, 52.

23. Pignattari 2018, 6.

24. Zecchi 2010, 80–82.

25. Gillam 1995, 234.

26. Pignattari 2018, 7.

27. Pignattari 2018, 6, 8.

28. Dodson and Hilton 2004, s.v. "Neferuptah B", 98; Pignattari 2018, 7.

CHAPTER 11.
THE KING'S DAUGHTERS

1. Pignattari 2018, 7.

2. Waddell (1940) 1964, 66 n. 1.

3. Manetho, fr. 34, Syncellus, p. 110 after Africanus. See Waddell 1940 (1964), 66–69.

4. Waddell (1940) 1964, 66 n. 1.

5. Manetho, fr. 34, Syncellus p. 110 after Africanus. See Waddell (1940) 1964, 66–69.

6. Weinstein 1974, 51.

7. Hayes 1953, 194.

8. Callender 1998b, 47. See also Pignattari 2018, 30.

9. Habachi 1954, 463, 466, pl. XIII B.

10. For a co-regency between Amenemhat III and Amenemhat IV see Petrie 1894, vol. 1: 195; Habachi 1954, 465; Grajetzki 2006, 61; Pignattari 2018, 23–31 particularly 23, 25–28. For a short co-regency of around one year see Ryholt 1997, 212.

11. Petrie 1890, 8; Farag and Iskander 1971, 105; Pignattari 2018, 8.

12. Farag and Iskander 1971, 58.

13. Shanine 2008.

14. Dodson and Hilton 2004, s.v. "Nubhotepet," 98.

15. Dodson and Hilton 2004, s.v. "Sithathor," 98.

16. Dodson and Hilton 2004, s.v. "Hathorhetepet," 96.

17. Diamond 2020, 6. See also Callender 1998b, 45.

18. Cooney (2018) 2020, 87.

CHAPTER 12.
FATE OF THE DYNASTY

1. Dodson and Hilton 2004, s.v. "Aat," 96.

2. Verner (2001) 2002, 427.

3. Magli 2010.

4. Morgan, Legrain, and Jéquier 1903, 98–109.

5. Morgan, Legrain, and Jéquier 1903, 100, figs. 147 and 148.

6. Morgan, Legrain, and Jéquier 1903, 102.

7. Arnold 1987. For a comprehensive summary of all excavations and discoveries at the site of the Black Pyramid see Hamilton 2020.

8. Dodson and Hilton 2004, 96.

9. Grajetzki 2014, 193.

10. Dodson and Hilton 2004, 99.

11. Pignattari 2018, 5, 16.

12. Ryholt 1997, 210.

13. Ryholt 1997, 210.

14. Ryholt 1997, 210.

15. Ryholt 1997, 211.

16. Ryholt 1997, 211.

17. Ryholt 1997, 297.

18. Ryholt 1997, 208.

19. Ryholt 1997, 208 cf. Habachi 1954, 462, pls. xiv–xv.

20. Pignattari 2018, 10.

21. Pignattari 2018, 14.

22. Ryholt 1997, 213.

23. Pignattari 2018, 96; Canhão 2019/2020, 8.

24. Pignattari 2018, 107.

25. Pignattari 2018, 107.

26. Manetho, fr. 34, Syncellus, p. 110 after Africanus. See Waddell (1940) 1964, 66–69.

27. Ryholt 1997, 213.

28. Waddell (1940) 1964, xv–xvii.

29. Syncellus in Mosshammer 1984.

30. Bedrosian 2008.

31. Manetho, fr. 34, Syncellus p. 110 after Africanus. See Waddell (1940) 1964, 66–69.

32. Manetho, fr. 35, Syncellus, p. 112 after Eusebius (see Waddell [1940] 1964, 68–71), and Manetho fr. 36 of the Armenian version (see Waddell [1940] 1964, 71–73).

33. Waddell (1940) 1964, xvi–xvii.

34. Ryholt 1997, 213.

35. Pignattari 2011, 35–36.

36. Pignattari 2011, 35–36.

37. Canhão 2019/2020, 16.

38. British Museum acquisition number EA58892. See The British Museum website. Hall 1928, 88, states that the sphinx is made of augite-diorite.

39. Adapted from Hall 1928, 88.

40. Hall 1928, 87–88.

41. Metropolitan Museum of Art accession Number: 08.200.2. See "Head of a King, possibly Amememhat IV," Metropolitan Museum of Art.

42. "Head of a King, possibly Amememhat IV," Metropolitan Museum of Art.

43. "Bust of Amenemhat III (1843–1798 B.C.)."

44. See "Bust of Amenemhat III (1843–1798 B.C.)."

45. Petrie 1890, 17.

46. Petrie 1890, 8, 15, 17.

47. Petrie 1890, pl. v.

48. Petrie 1890, 8, 15, 17.

49. Petrie 1890, pl. v.

50. Petrie 1890, 8.

51. Petrie 1890, 8.

52. Iskander and Badawy, 1948 (1965), 64; Farag and Iskander 1971, 105.

53. For a summary of all Middle Kingdom double or dummy burials see Grajetzki 2017.

CHAPTER 13. SIBLING RIVALRY

1. Callender 1998b, 47.

2. Newberry 1943a, 74–75; Tallet 2005, 253.

3. Ryholt 1997, 294.

4. Ryholt 1997, 294.

5. Mackay 1912, 37.

6. Mackay 1912, 37–55.

7. Mackay 1912, 49.

8. Mackay 1912, 37, 54.

CHAPTER 14. FLAWED VISIONS

1. Ryholt 1997, 293–94; Pignattari 2018, 84.

2. Pignattari 2018, 82.

3. Ryholt 1997, 294.

4. Seters (1966) 2010, 87.

5. Pignattari 2018, 84.

6. Ryholt 1997, 294.

7. Pignattari 2018, 82.

8. Ryholt 1997, 294.

9. Petrie 1894, vol 1: 187; Grimal (1988) 1992, 179; Callender 1998b, 49–50; Grajetzki 2006, 61; Pignattari 2018, 12, 14.

10. Ryholt 1997, 107.

11. Pignattari 2018, 109.

12. Pignattari 2018, 85–86, 92.

13. Brönn 2006, 45, 55, 87.

14. Seters (1966) 2010, 172.

15. British Museum acquisition number EA58892. See The British Museum website.

16. Adapted from Hall 1928, 88.

17. Pignattari 2018, 109.

18. Eyma and Bennett 2003, 13–14; Pignattari 2018, 109.

19. Pignattari 2018, 109.

20. Seters (1966) 2010, 88–89.

21. Ryholt 1997, 294.

22. Seters (1966) 2010, 87–88.

23. Seters (1966) 2010, 87, 91.

CHAPTER 15. THE FALL OF EGYPT

1. Grajetzki 2001, 24 entry 3.8; Theis 2009, 318–19; Cooney (2018) 2020, 26.

2. Ryholt 1997, 294.

3. Ryholt 1997, 294.

4. Bietak 2007; Pignattari 2018, 101.

5. Manetho fr. 41a, Syncellus after Africanus; fr. 41b, Syncellus after Eusebius; fr. 41c, of the Armenian version of Eusebius. See Waddell (1940) 1964, 74–75.

6. Ryholt 1997, 295–96.

7. Pignattari 2018, 101.

8. Ryholt 1997, 294.

9. Ryholt 1997, 296–97.

PART 4. REGICIDE

CHAPTER 16.
THE MYSTERY OF QUEEN NITOCRIS

1. Cicero bk. I, 5.

2. Herodotus 1920, bk. II, ch. 99.

3. Herodotus 1920, bk. II, ch. 100.

4. Herodotus bk. II, ch. 100. In Heidel (1935) 2019.

5. Manetho, fr. 20, Syncellus after Africanus. See Waddell (1940) 1964, 54–55.

6. Manetho, fr. 21a, Syncellus after Africanus. See Waddell (1940) 1964, 54–55.

7. Eratosthenes, listing no. XXII (after Syncellus). In Bunsen 1848, vol. I, 671–72. See also Bunsen's comparison listing in the same volume between Eratosthenes and Manetho, 123–30.

8. Eratosthenes, listing no. XXII (after Syncellus). In Bunsen 1848, vol. I, 671–72.

9. Bury, Cook, Baynes 1954, 307.

10. Dio Cassius 1925, bk. LXII, 6. For a comprehensive review of all classical references to Nitocris see Zivie-Coche 1972.

11. Waddell (1940) 1964, 54 n. 2.

12. See Ryholt 2014 for a full description of the Turin Canon.

13. Ryholt 2014.

14. Ryholt 2000.

15. See, for instance, Málek 1982, 96.

16. Ryholt 2000, 93.

17. Ryholt 2000, 93.

18. Ryholt 2000, 93.

19. Ryholt 2000, 92.

20. Ryholt 2000, 93.

21. Stern 1883, 23 n. 2. See also Hall 1925, 296, and Ryholt 2000, 93.

22. Ryholt 2000, 100.

23. Newberry 1943b, 51 n. 8.

24. See Caminos 1964.

25. Newberry 1943b, 51 n. 7.

26. Manetho, fr. 20, Syncellus after Africanus. See Waddell (1940) 1964, 54–55.

27. Manetho fr. 21a, Syncellus after Africanus. See Waddell (1940) 1964, 54–55.

28. Herodotus 1920, bk. II, chs. 124–29.

29. Waddell (1940) 1964, 54 n. 2.

30. Vanderzwet 2005.

31. Hassan 1943, 13.

32. Petrie 1894, vol. 1: 105.

33. Herodotus 1920, bk. II, ch. 134.

34. Strabo (1917) 1932, bk. XVII, ch. 808.

35. Diodorus Siculus 1933, bk I, ch. 64.

36. Herodotus 1920, bk. II, ch. 134.

37. Ælian (1665) 1670, bk. XIII, ch. xxxiii.

38. Herodotus 1920, bk. II, ch. 134.

39. See Hall 1904.

40. Manetho, fr. 21a, Syncellus after Africanus. See Waddell (1940) 1964, 54–55.

41. Manetho, fr. 21a, Syncellus after Africanus. See Waddell (1940) 1964, 54–55.

42. Diodorus 1933, bk. I, ch. 64.

43. Eady 1968; Lesko 1999, 84.

44. Maspero 1903, 286, 289. cf. Murtadā 1666, 65.

45. Waddell (1940) 1966, 54 n. 2.

CHAPTER 17.
SOBEKNEFERU AS NITOCRIS

1. Herodotus, bk. II, ch. 100. In Heidel (1935) 2019.

2. Herodotus 1920, bk. II, ch. 100.

3. Manetho, fr. 52, Syncellus after Africanus. See Waddell (1940) 1964, 110–12.

4. Lundström 2016.

5. Josephus 1926, bk. I, ch. 15.

6. Manetho, fr. 34, Syncellus after Africanus. See Waddell (1940) 1964, 67–69.

7. Josephus 1926, bk. I, ch. 15.

8. Manetho, fr. 53, Syncellus after Eusebius. See Waddell (1940) 1964, 114–15, as well as Manetho fr. 51, Theophilus, Ad Autolyc. bk. 3. ch. 19, in Waddell (1940) 1964, 106–9.

9. Herodotus 1920, bk. II, ch. 101.

10. Petrie 1909, 2 cf. Diodorus bk. I, ch. 51.

11. Herodotus 1920, bk. II, chs. 148–49.

12. Diodorus 1933, bk. I, ch. 51.

13. Diodorus 1933, bk. I, ch. 52.

14. See "The Pedestals of Biahmu" 2013.

15. Caton-Thompson 1927; Caton-Thompson and Gardner 1934.

16. Zecchi 2010, 5–7.

17. Evans 1987, 67.

18. Caton-Thompson and Gardner 1929, 31.

19. Lloyd 2010, 343.

20. Lloyd 2010, 343.

21. Evans 1987, 69.

22. Riad 1958.

23. Adapted from Evans 1987, 68.

24. Herodotus (1935) 2019, bk. II, ch. 100, trans. Heidel.

25. Herodotus 1920, bk. II, ch. 102.

26. Herodotus 1920, bk. II, chs. 102–111.

27. Liotsakis 2014, 503, 507, 513.

28. Herodotus 1920, bk II, chs. 111–12.

29. Gardiner 1927/1957, 75, 565.

30. Lloyd 2002, 422.

31. Herodotus (1935) 2019, bk. II, ch. 100, trans. Heidel.

32. Herodotus 1920, bk. II, chs. 112–20.

33. Herodotus 1920, bk. II, chs. 121–22, 124.

34. Herodotus 1920, bk. II, chs. 126–36.

CHAPTER 18.
MOTHER OF CROCODILES

1. Grajetzki 2001, 24 entry 3.8; Theis 2009, 318–19; Cooney (2018) 2020, 26.

2. Riad 1958.

3. Pliny 1855, bk. XXXVI, ch. 19.

4. Wilcken 1884.

5. Zecchi 2010, 77 n. 314.

6. For a good summary of all monuments and attributes of Neith, particularly in the Western Delta and Fayum, see El-Weshahy and Mosleh 2004.

7. Pinch 2002, s.v. "Neith," 169–70.

8. Pinch 2002, s.v. "Neith," 169–70.

9. Kaper 2003, 75.

10. Pinch 2002, s.v. "Neith," 169–70; Zecchi 2010, 17.

11. Pinch 2002, s.v. "Neith," 169–70; Beinlich 2013, 42.

12. Graves-Brown 2010, 163–64.

13. Zecchi 2010, 17; Mohamed 2017.

14. Pinch 2002, s.v. "Neith," 169–70; Zecchi 2010, 17.

15. Beinlich 2013, 42–43, fig. 17.

16. Zecchi 2010, 5–8.

17. Beinlich 2013, 34, 70.

18. Beinlich 2013, 34.

19. Beinlich 2013, 34.

20. Kaper 2003, 41; Pinch 2004, s.v. "Sphinx," 206.

21. Kaper 2003, 26, 30, 106–8.

22. Kaper 2003, 62, 98, 160–64, 195, 321, 323.

23. Kaper 2003, 28, 60–61.

24. Kaper 2003, 125.

25. Kaper 2003, 60.

26. Petrie Museum no. UC 14337: Petrie 1890, pl. XI.1; Habachi 1954, pl. XII.B.

27. Personal communication with the author.

28. Beinlich 2013, 56, fig. 32.

29. Beinlich 2013, 56.

30. El-Weshahy and Mosleh 2004; Ritner 2018, 284.

31. Habachi 1955.

32. Habachi 1955.

33. Venderlip 1972. For the text of the "Divine Pymander" featuring Poimandres see Hermes Mercurius Trismegistus 1650/1884.

34. Jackson 1999; and see Bull 2018, 121–31.

35. Jackson 1999, 95, 99; Bull 2018, 122.

36. Mead (1906) 1992, 179, 185–86.

37. Reitzenstein 1904, 8–9, 132–34, 183–84, 186, 266–67 n. 2. See also Fowden (1986) 1993, xxii–xxiii, for a summary of Reitzenstein's ideas on the existence and influence of the Poimandres-Gemeinde.

38. Reitzenstein 1904, 124, 309.

39. Herodotus 1920, bk. II, ch. 148 in relation to bk. II ch. 151 and the "twelve kings" mentioned there. See also Lloyd 1988 for a full explanation of this topic.

40. Newberry 1943b, 51 n. 7.

41. Lundström 2021c.

42. Lundström 2021a.

43. Lundström 2021b.

44. Lundström 2011.

CHAPTER 19.
THE VENGEANCE OF NITOCRIS

1. Herodotus 1920, bk. II, ch. 100.

2. Herodotus 1920, bk. II, ch. 100.

3. Herodotus 1920, bk. II, ch. 100.

4. Herodotus 1920, bk. II, ch. 148.

5. Herodotus (1935) 2019, bk. II, ch. 100, trans. Heidel.

6. Herodotus 1920, bk. II, ch. 100.

7. Hill 2019.

8. Manetho, fr. 34, Syncellus after Africanus. See Waddell (1940) 1964, 66–68. The statement is found also in the Epitome of Eusebius. See Manetho fr. 35, Syncellus from Eusebus. See Waddell (1940) 1964, 68–70.

9. See Jonckheere 1954.

10. Herodotus 1920, bk. II, ch. 107.

11. For the excesses of Egypt's Ptolemaic dynasty of kings, see Ager 2006.

12. Herodotus 1920, bk. II, ch. 100.

CHAPTER 20.
THE DEATH OF SOBEKNEFERU

1. Herodotus 1920, bk. II, ch. 100.

2. Plutarch 1906, "Life of Antony," ch. lxxxv.

3. Plutarch 1906, "Life of Antony," ch. lxxxvi.

4. For theories surrounding the means of Cleopatra's death based on classical accounts see Gurval 2011.

5. Grout 2017.

6. Wright 2019.

7. Hill 2010a.

8. Herodotus (1935) 2019, bk. II, ch. 100, trans. Heidel.

9. Jenkyns 2013, 249.

10. Jenkyns 2013, 249.

11. Larson 2007, 70–71.

12. Diogenes Laertius 1964, bk. 8 ch.3.

13. Lucas 1938, 199.

14. Oxyrhynchus Papyri, No. 1088, early first century: Medical Receipts. See Hunt 1911, 110–15 (hellebore, 113–14; hemlock, 113; henbane, 113; opium, 113).

15. Lucas 1938, 199.

16. Geeta and Gharaibeh 2007, 1231.

17. Kuete 2014, 614.

18. Boumba, Mitselou, and Vougiouklakis 2004.

19. Gray 2010.

20. Johnson 2018.

21. Forrest 2014.

22. Mosaic c325-M167, House of the Mysteries of Isis (House 2). See "Raised Mosaic Panel D from Room 3 Central Emblema of the Mors Voluntaria." n.d.

23. Florus 1929, bk. II, section xxi, ch. 12.

24. Pignattari 2018, 105.

25. Pignattari 2018, 104–5.

26. Pignattari 2018, 105.

27. Graffito no. SNM34390. See Callender 1998b, 50; Pignattari 2018, 69, 99, 105.
28. Pignattari 2018, 104.
29. Grimal (1988) 1992, 171.
30. Gardiner (1961) 1976, 141.

CHAPTER 21.
ENEMIES OF SOBEKNEFERU

1. Pignattari 2018, 85–86.

PART 5. FAITH
CHAPTER 22. JOSEPH IN EGYPT

1. Bell 1975, 224, 251, 254.
2. Colavito 2018.
3. Colavito 2018.
4. Genesis 40:1–32.
5. Colavito 2018.
6. Colavito 2018.
7. Colavito 2018.
8. Colavito 2018.
9. Gardiner and Bell 1943, 43.
10. Gardiner and Bell 1943, 42.
11. Brugsch 1879, vol. I, 169; Gardiner and Bell 1943, 39. See Griffiths 1899, 21, where he translates the hieroglyphic text of the coffin of a Thirteenth Dynasty individual named Ankhrui found at Hawara, where the name Ta-she appears on a number of occasions in reference to the region.
12. Gardiner and Bell 1943, 39.
13. The direct relationship between Amenemhat III and Raiyam ibn al-Walid as the pharaoh at the time of Joseph is made clear in Moritz 1927, s.v. "al-Faiyum," 40–43. For Amenemhat III as the king when Joseph was in Egypt see, for example, Kitchen 1956 and Rohl 1995, 332, 334–35, 338, 340–51.
14. Pignattari 2018, 107.
15. Malleson 2019, 150–53, 186.
16. Malleson 2019, 150–53, 186. The work in question was translated into French by Bernard Carra de Vaux and published in 1896 under the title *Maçoudi. Le Livre de l'avertissement et de la révision.* [*Kitáb at-Tanbih Wa-l-išráf*]. It is attributed to Al- Mas'ūdī (Abū-l-Ḥasan b. al-Ḥusayn).

17. Malleson 2019, 163, 255–56.

18. Colavito 2016.

19. Murtada ibn al-'Afif (1672) 2015.

20. Murtada ibn al-'Afif (1672) 2015, 181.

21. Murtada ibn al-'Afif (1672) 2015, 181.

22. Malleson 2019, 187.

23. Exodus 2:3.

24. Murtada ibn al-'Afif (1672) 2015, 181.

25. Murtada ibn al-'Afif (1672) 2015, 182.

26. Murtada ibn al-'Afif (1672) 2015, 183.

27. Murtada ibn al-'Afif (1672) 2015, 183.

28. Herodotus 1920. bk. II, 101, 148–49.

29. Diodorus Siculus 1933, bk. I, ch. 52.

30. Sampsell 2003, 42.

31. Genesis 41:43.

32. Seters (1966) 2010, 92. See also n. 22 of this same page where the author provides evidence and references for this statement.

33. Genesis 41:43. See, for instance, David Rohl's impressive work on Joseph being vizier of Egypt (Rohl 1995, ch. 15).

34. Genesis 11:31, 12:1–6

35. Genesis 37: 25, 28, 36.

36. Genesis 37:36, 39:1.

37. Genesis 39:9–18.

38. Genesis 39: 7–20.

39. Genesis 41:15–32, 34, 36, 37.

40. Genesis 41:43.

41. Genesis 41:47–49, 53–56.

42. Bell 1975, 235, 252,

43. Bell 1975, 229–36, 258; Rohl 1995, 335, 337–38, 340 fig. 363, 340–42.

44. Bell 1975 229–30.

45. Genesis 41:43.

46. Rohl 1995, 342–43.

47. Rohl 1995, 349–52.

48. Weigall 1927, vol. II, 112.

49. Weigall 1927, vol. II, 112.

50. Weigall 1927, vol. II, 113.

51. Weigall 1927, vol. II, 112–13.

52. Pignattari 2018, 107.

CHAPTER 23. THE HELIOPOLITAN CONNECTION

1. 39:1. See also Genesis 37:36 for the same statement, although worded slightly differently.
2. Rivka 2009, 258.
3. Genesis 41:45, 50; 46:20.
4. Rivka 2009, 258.
5. Genesis 41:45.
6. Rohl 1995, 349–52.

CHAPTER 24. WHEN SOBEKNEFERU MET JOSEPH

1. Email communications between the author and Claire J. Malleson, June 5, 2021.
2. Colavito 2018.
3. Murtada ibn al-'Afif (1672) 2015, 181–82.
4. Colavito 2018.
5. Colavito 2018.
6. Mas'ūdī 1863, vol. 2, 397–98. See also Banschikova 2008, 3.
7. Mas'ūdī 1863, vol. 2, 397–98. See also Banschikova 2008, 3.
8. Banschikova 2008, 7–8.
9. Exodus 1:8.
10. Exodus 1–19. See Feinman 2021, 87–92 for the relationship between Kamose and the Exodus; and Feinman 2021, 92–100, for the connections between Ahmose and the Exodus.
11. Rohl 1995, 349–52.
12. Genesis 41:43.
13. Genesis 41:45, 50; 46:20.
14. Genesis 41:45, 50; 46:20.
15. Graffito no. SNM34390. See Callender 1998b, 50; Pignattari 2018, 69, 99.
16. Bell 1975, 266.
17. Bell 1975, 259–60.
18. Bell 1975, 266.
19. Genesis 41:43.

CHAPTER 25.
SOBEKNEFERU—THE ASIATIC CONNECTION

1. See Habachi 1954, 458–70.
2. Habachi 1954, 470.

3. Habachi 1954, 470.

4. Genesis 41: 15–32, 53–57.

5. Genesis 45:8, 47:4–6, 27; 50:8.

6. Genesis 47:11–12.

7. Bietak 2007.

8. Genesis 45:10.

9. Exodus 1: 8–11.

10. Giveon 1978, 62.

11. "Scarab with Hathor-like Canaanite Goddess ca. 1740–1640 B.C."

12. Bietak 2007.

13. Cooney (2018) 2020, 87; Diamond 2020, 6.

14. Hayes 1963, 13.

15. Bell 1975, 258.

16. Montet 1968, 67.

PART 6. TWO LANDS

CHAPTER 26. SOBEKNEFERU THE BUILDER

1. See, for instance, Grajetzki 2006, 63.

2. Callender 1998b, 47.

3. Callender 1998b, 50.

4. See Daressy 1917, 34–35; Habachi 1954, 462; Matzker 1986, 175; Callendar 1998b, 50; Pignattari 2018, 14.

5. Habachi 1954, 469.

6. Mackay 1912, 37–55.

7. Grajetzki 2006, 63.

8. Callender 1998b, 48; Grajetzki 2006, 30.

9. Zecchi 2010, 45.

10. Callender 1998b, 49; Grajetzki 2006, 61, 63; Pignattari 2018, 12, 14.

11. Grimal (1988) 1992, 179.

12. Petrie 1889, 6; Petrie 1890, pl. XI.1; Petrie 1912, 30; Habachi 1954, 466; Lloyd 1970, 92; Callender 1998b, 50.

13. Griffith 1889, 21; Petrie 1889, pl. xvii 12; Habachi 1954, 463, pl. XIIIb.

14. Gardiner (1961) 1976, 141; Callender 1998b, 47; and see Piganattari 2018, 108.

15. Gardiner (1961) 1976, 141; Callender 1998b, 47.

16. Grajetski 2006, 60.

17. Grimal (1988) 1992, 179; Grajetski 2006, 57; Zecchi 2010, 54. See also Arnold 1979 for more on this subject.

18. Petrie 1912, 31, pl. xxvi.1; Zecchi 2010, 55; Pignattari 2018, 88–90.

19. Lloyd 1970, 91; Uphill (2000) 2010, 70, 88.

CHAPTER 27.
THE MAGNIFICENT LABYRINTH

1. Herodotus 1920, bk. II, ch. 148; Strabo 1932, bk. XVII, ch. I, sections 3, 37, 42; Pliny 1855, bk. XXXVI, chs. 16, 19, 22, 26; Diodorus Siculus 1933, bk. I, chs. 61, 66; Pomponius Mela 1998, bk. I, 9, 56.

2. Herodotus 1920, bk. II, ch. 148.

3. Herodotus 1920, bk. II, ch. 148.

4. Petrie 1889, 5; Petrie 1894, vol. 1: 187.

5. Petrie 1889, 5; Petrie 1894, vol. 1: 187.

6. Petrie 1889, 5.

7. Zecchi 2010, 53.

8. Lepsius 1853, 90.

9. Herodotus 1920, bk. II, ch. 148 and bk. II, ch. 151, where the "twelve kings" are detailed. See also Lloyd 1988.

10. Herodotus 1920, bk. II, ch. 148.

11. Pliny 1855, bk. XXXVI, ch. 26.

12. Lepsius 1853, 91.

13. Lepsius (1904) 1970, 15, 19.

14. Lundström 2021c.

15. Lundström 2021a.

16. Petrie 1889, 6; Petrie 1912, 29–32.

17. Manetho, fr. 34, Syncellus p. 110 after Africanus. See Waddell 1940 (1964), 66–69.

18. Strabo 1932 (vol. 2), bk. XVII, ch. I, section 37.

19. Diodorus Siculus 1933, bk. I, ch. 61.

20. Pliny 1855, bk. XXXVI, ch. 19.

21. Pignattari 2018, 107–8; Canhão 2019/2020, 10.

22. Callender 1998b, 49; Pignattari 2018, 28.

CHAPTER 28. AT THE CENTER OF IT ALL

1. Pliny 1855, bk. XXXVI, ch. 19.

2. Pliny 1855, bk. XXXVI, ch. 19.

3. Pliny 1855, bk. XXXVI, ch. 19.

4. Mayer 1892, 191.

5. Herodotus 1920, bk. II, ch. 148.

6. Petrie 1889, 6, 10, 63 n.

7. Petrie 1889, 10.

8. Petrie 1912, 31.

9. Zecchi 2010, 55–56.

10. Petrie 1912, 31, pl. XXVII.4.

11. Petrie 1912, 31–32.

12. Petrie 1912, 31–32.

13. See, for instance, Zecchi 2010, 53–54, 56–60, 85–86, for a full review of this subject.

14. Uphill (2000) 2010, 43; Zecchi 2010, 53–58.

15. Beinlich 1991; Tait 2000; Beinlich 2013.

16. Beinlich 2013, 31–32, 45–47, 49, 55, 59.

17. Beinlich 2013, 65, fig. 43.

18. Beinlich 2013, 48, 61, 65, fig. 43.

19. Beinlich 2013, 65, fig. 43.

20. Tait 2003, 192.

21. Beinlich 2013, 72–73.

22. Herodotus 1920, bk. II, ch. 102, 150–51.

23. Tait 2003, 200.

24. Petrie 1912, 31, pl. XXVII.4.

25. Beinlich 2013, 65, 68.

26. Beinlich 2013, 65.

27. Beinlich 2013, 65.

28. Beinlich 2013, 65.

29. Beinlich 2013, 65.

30. Strabo 1932, bk. XVII, ch. I, section 37.

31. Strabo 1932, bk. XVII, ch. I, section 3.

32. Lempriere 1832, s.v. "Ægyptus" 37–66 (p. 43), cf. "Pliny 5, 9."

33. Strabo 1932, bk. XVII, ch. I, section 37.

34. Pliny, bk. XXXVI, ch. 19.

35. Tait 2003, 200.

36. Pleyte 1886, 18–20, 29.

37. Pleyte 1886, 28.

38. Millmore 2016.

39. Herodotus 1920, bk. II, ch. 148.

40. On the subject of the twelvefold division of nations, countries, assemblies, etc., and their focus around a location seen in terms of a sacred center see Michell and Rhone 1991.

41. Uphill (2000) 2010, 3.
42. Zecchi 2008.
43. Zecchi 2008, 379.
44. Zecchi 2008, 379–80.

CHAPTER 29. NAVEL OF THE WORLD

1. On the subject of *omphali* in the ancient world see Roscher 1918.
2. Clark 1960, 37; Reymond 1969.
3. Clark (1959) 1960, 37–39.
4. Clark (1959) 1960, 39.
5. Zecchi 2008, 379.
6. Beinlich 2013, 41, 43, 44–45, 48, 64, 72, 74.
7. Beinlich 2013, 72–73.
8. Beinlich 2013, 45–47, 50, 53, 54, 61, fig. 28.
9. Beinlich 2013, 54.
10. Beinlich 2013, 32, 49.
11. See Zecchi 2010, ch. 1, for a full breakdown of the evidence for the existence of the cult of Sobek of Shedet from the First Dynasty until the end of the Old Kingdom.
12. Beinlich 2013, 47, 72.
13. Herodotus (1935) 2019, bk. II, ch. 100, trans. Heidel.
14. Herodotus 1920, bk. II, ch. 100.
15. Herodotus 1920, bk. II, ch. 148.
16. Herodotus 1920, bk. II, ch. 148.
17. Grajetzki 2001, 24 entry 3.8; Theis 2009, 318–19; Cooney (2018) 2020, 26.

PART 7. ANCESTORS

CHAPTER 30.
THE MYSTERY OF MAZGHUNA NORTH

1. Mackay 1912, 37–41.
2. Mackay 1912, 41–55.
3. Mackay 1912, 54.
4. Mackay 1912, 54.
5. Mackay 1912, 50.
6. Mackay 1912, 51.
7. Mackay 1912, 51.
8. Mackay 1912, 51.

9. Mackay 1912, 53.

10. Mackay 1912, 54.

11. Mackay 1912, 50.

12. Allen 2005, 21–22.

13. Mackay 1912, 51.

14. Mackay 1912, 42–43.

15. Mackay 1912, 53.

16. Mackay 1912, 54.

17. Mackay 1912, 54.

18. Dungen 2006.

19. See, for example, Hadingham 2010.

20. Lehner 1997, 184; Pignattari 2018, 96.

21. Papyrus Harageh no. 6, UCL 32778. See Grajetzki 2004, 54–56; Grajetzki 2006, 63; Canhão 2019/2020, 9.

22. Pignattari 2018, 95.

23. Grajetzki 2006, 63.

24. Pignattari 2018, 97.

25. Beinlich 2013, 42–43, 45, 47, 50, 54.

26. Beinlich 2013, 41, 53–54, 64, 74.

CHAPTER 31. TEMPLE OF THE CROCODILE

1. The account of Petrie's visit to the Qasr el-Sagha temple in 1888 is from Petrie 1890, 21.

2. Caton-Thompson and Gardner 1934, 154.

3. Caton-Thompson and Gardner 1934, 154.

4. Hamilton 2020, 12.

5. Measurements taken from Brown 1892, pl. XVI and checked using Google Earth software.

6. See Reymond 1969.

7. Shaw 2004, 66.

8. Hamilton 2020, 32.

9. Bown and Kraus 1988, 11–12.

10. Petrie 1890, 21.

11. Petrie 1890, 21.

12. Schweinfurth 1886. See also Caton-Thompson and Gardner 1929, 7.

13. Arnold and Arnold 1979, pl. 13d; Hamilton 2020, 3.

14. Brown 1892, 55.

15. Brown 1892, 52, 54.

16. Brown 1892, 54, quoting Schweinfurth.

17. Arnold and Arnold 1979, 20–21.

18. Arnold and Arnold 1979, 20–21.

19. Arnold and Arnold 1979, 7.

20. Caton-Thompson and Gardner 1929, 43.

21. Caton-Thompson and Gardner 1934, 96.

22. Harrell and Bown 1995; Bloxam and Storemyr 2002.

23. Storemyr et al. 2003.

24. Lucas and Harris 1948, 79.

25. Bloxam and Storemyr 2002, 34.

26. Harrell and Bown 1995, fig. 3.

27. Arnold and Arnold 1979, 22–23; Shaw 2004, 66.

28. Arnold and Arnold 1979, 32, 34, 36, 38.

29. Caton-Thompson and Gardner 1934, 132–33.

30. Caton-Thompson and Gardner 1934, 133.

31. Caton-Thompson and Gardner 1934, 133.

32. Newberry 1943a, 74–75.

33. Beinlich 2013, 48.

34. Dolson et al. 2002, 67.

35. Beinlich 2013, 49.

36. Diodorus Siculus 1933, bk. I, ch. 89.

37. Diodorus Siculus 1933, bk. I, ch. 89.

38. See Zecchi 2010, ch. 1, for a full breakdown of the evidence for the existence of the cult of Sobek of Shedet from the First Dynasty through till the end of the Old Kingdom.

CHAPTER 32. PLACE OF THE ANCESTORS

1. Frias 2020, section 5.1.

2. Caton-Thompson 1927; Caton-Thompson and Gardner 1929; Caton-Thompson and Gardner 1934.

3. Caton-Thompson and Gardner 1934, 54, 80, 159.

4. Caton-Thompson and Gardner 1934, 54, 80.

5. Harrell and Bown 1995, 78.

6. Hoffmeier 1993, 121.

7. Hoffmeier 1993, 121.

8. Hoffmeier 1993, 118; Harrell and Bown 1995, 71.

9. Harrell and Bown 1995.

10. For a full account of the cult of Sobek-Geb at Tebtunis see Rondot 2013, 75–80, 122–27, 241–46.

11. Meurer 2002, 295, 304–5.

12. Reymond 1966, 451, 455–56; Bricault 2009, 131–33.

13. Reymond 1966, 455; Bricault 2009, 131–33.

14. Reymond 1966, 455 cf. Griffith 1909, vol. iii, 301, n. 2; Bricault 2009, 132.

15. Bricault 2009, 131.

16. Bricault 2009, 132.

17. Reymond 1966, 451, 455–57.

18. Reymond 1966, 451; Bricault 2009, 132.

19. Beinlich 2013, 44–45, 54.

20. Reymond 1966, 456–57.

21. Bricault 2009, 131–33.

22. Caton-Thompson and Gardner 1934, 154.

23. Caton-Thompson and Gardner 1934, 154.

CHAPTER 33. THE SEVEN SNAKE GODS

1. Allen 2005, s.v. "Nehebkau," 434.

2. Argyros 2018, 40.

3. Argyros 2018, 40.

4. Clark (1959) 1960, 37–38.

5. For an excellent popular account of Nehebkau's manifestation as the primeval serpent within the waters of Nun see Naydler 1996, 35–38.

6. Shorter 1935, 42, 47–48.

7. Shorter 1935, 42, 47–48.

8. Spell 449. See Allen 2005, 153.

9. Beinlich 2013, 72.

10. Shorter 1935, 47.

11. For a summary of the Book of the Heavenly Cow see Mastaff 2002.

12. Spells CT 85–87. See Faulkner 1973, 89–90. See also Argyros 2018, 40.

13. Spell CT 374. See Faulkner 1977, 10.

14. Spell PT 223 (Allen 2005, 61), 256 and 257 (Allen 2005, 89).

15. Spell CT 612. See Faulkner 1977, 199.

16. Budge (1934) 1988, 59.

17. Dawson 1927, 98.

18. Reymond 1966, 456.

19. Reymond 1966, 456.

20. Reymond 1966, 456.

21. Reymond 1966, 457.

22. Reymond 1966, 457.

23. Beinlich 2013, 61.

24. Beinlich 2013, 51.

25. Beinlich 2013, 51, fig. 24.

26. Beinlich 2013, 51, caption to fig. 24.

27. Beinlich 2013, 27–29.

28. Beinlich 2013, fig. 39a and 39b.

29. Beinlich 2013, 61.

30. Beinlich 2013, 61.

31. Beinlich 2013, 61, citing "Botti A" 2.1,0. See Botti 1959, 72ff.

32. Beinlich 2013, 61, citing "Botti A" 2.1,0. See Botti 1959, 72ff.

33. Jochen 2011, 9 cf. Sauneron 1962, 256–57, which uses the term "sept sorts," or "seven spells."

34. Pinch 2002, s.v. "Neith," 169–70.

35. Pinch 2002, s.v. "Neith," 169–70.

36. Pinch 2002, s.v. "Neith," 169–70.

37. Beinlich 2013, 70.

38. Beinlich 2013, figs. 49a and 49b.

39. Beinlich 2013, 70.

40. "Scarab" British Museum number EA66159. The British Museum website.

41. Kroenke 2011, 21; Mairs 2020, 30–31.

42. "Scarab" British Museum number EA66159. The British Museum website.

43. Arnold and Arnold 1979, 28.

44. Arnold and Arnold 1979, 28.

45. For sign F36 see Gardiner (1927) 2007, 548.

46. For sign S42 see Gardiner (1927) 2007, 509.

47. Shorter 1935, 42, 47–48.

CHAPTER 34.
SOBEKNEFERU'S FINAL RESTING PLACE

1. Lehner (1997) 2001, 168.

2. Petrie 1906, 123–24. Veneration of Sneferu was present in the Sinai also under Eighteenth Dynasty kings including Thutmose I, Thutmose III, and Hatshepsut. See Petrie 1906, 130–31, 137.

3. Magli 2010.

4. Magli 2010.

5. Caton-Thompson and Gardner 1934, 140, pl. lxxxv 15 and 20.

6. Caton-Thompson and Gardner 1934, 140, pl. lxxxv 15 and 20.

7. Caton-Thompson and Gardner 1934, 140.

8. Caton-Thompson and Gardner 1934, pls. cix–cxiv.

9. Gallo 1993.

10. Murtada ibn al-'Afif (1672) 2015, 182.

PART 8. RESURRECTION

CHAPTER 35. GODDESS OF THE SEVEN STARS

1. Stoker 1897.

2. Stoker 1903.

3. Stoker (1912) 1980, 188.

4. Stoker (1912) 1980, 139.

5. Stoker (1912) 1980, 140.

6. Stoker (1912) 1980, 178.

7. Naville, Davis, and Carter 1906; Newberry 1939, 68.

8. Naville, Davis, and Carter 1906, xii.

9. See "The Jewel of Seven Stars." Bram Stoker, 1847–1912. Library of Congress Catalog website.

10. Naville, Davis, and Carter 1906.

11. Macnaughton, 1932, 157.

12. Stoker (1912) 1980, 108.

13. Stoker (1912) 1980, 135.

14. Stoker (1912) 1980, 155.

15. Stoker (1912) 1980, 179.

16. Stoker (1912) 1980, 152.

17. Stoker (1912) 1980, 178.

18. Stoker (1912) 1980, 179.

19. Stoker (1912) 1980, 141.

20. Stoker (1912) 1980, 107, 155.

21. Stoker (1912) 1980, 150.

22. Stoker (1912) 1980, 141.

23. Stoker (1912) 1980, 124, 185.

24. Stoker (1912) 1980, 196.

25. Stoker (1912) 1980, 192.

26. Hughes 2000, 186 n. 47, based on the details of sale SC SOTHERBY 7/7/1913.
27. "The Reading Room" 2020.
28. Hughes 2000, 186 ns. 48, 49, 50, 51, 52.
29. Stoker (1912) 1980, 131.
30. Massey 1881, vol. II, 131.
31. Massey 1881, vol. II, 140–41.
32. Massey 1881, vol. II, 141.
33. Massey 1881, vol. II, 344.
34. For example, Massey 1881, vol. II, 26, 48, 75, 81, 131, 133, 144, 276, 320, 403, 436, 473.
35. Massey 1881, vol. I, 373.
36. Massey 1881, vol. II, 131.
37. Massey 1881, vol. II, 131.
38. Massey 1881, vol. I, 35.
39. For a full rundown on theories regarding the hippo-croc hybrid see Lull and Belmonte 2009, 164–67; and Berio 2014, 39–41, the later of whom identifies it as Ursa Minor.
40. Berio 2014, 39.
41. Clark 1959, 206.
42. Please note there are varying theories on what this sky figure represents. For full details see Lull and Belmonte 2009, 157, 164–67, figs. 6.1, 6.3, 6.4, 6.5, 6.7, and Berio 2914, 39–41.
43. See Lull and Belmonte 2009, 161, 163, 166, fig. 6.3.
44. Mohamed 2017.
45. Massey 1881, vol. II, 344.
46. Massey 1881, vol. II, 344.
47. Massey 1881, vol. I, 241; vol. II, 371.
48. Lempriere 1788, s.v. "Typhoeus, or Typhon," n.p.n.
49. Hill 2010b.
50. Beinlich 2013, 56, fig. 32.
51. PT 317 as quoted by Degreef 2003.
52. Degreef 2003.
53. Tredoux 2016, letter 22. 1881/04/07. Richard Burton to Gerald Massey.
54. Tredoux 2016, letter 25. 1881/04/22. Richard Burton to Gerald Massey.
55. Tredoux 2016, letter 26. 1881/04/28. Richard Burton to Gerald Massey.
56. For a good introduction to Bram Stoker's relationship with Richard Burton see Richardson 2021.
57. Massey 1881, vol. II, 318–19, 445.

CHAPTER 36.
SERVANTS OF SOBEK

1. Massey 1881, vol. I, 43; vol. II, 372.
2. Lempriere 1788, s.v. "Typhoeus, or Typhon," n.p.n.; Massey 1881, vol. II, 372.
3. Massey 1881, vol. I, 43; vol. II, 338, 372, 402, 405, 423.
4. Massey 1881, vol. II, 402.
5. Massey 1881, vol. I, 43.
6. Beinlich 2013, 49, fig. 21.
7. Massey 1881, vol. I, 43–44.
8. Massey 1881, vol. I, 44.
9. Lempriere 1788, s.v. "Typhoeus, or Typhon," n.p.n.
10. Brugsch 1859.
11. Brugsch-Bey 1879, vol. I.
12. Brugsch-Bey 1879, vol. I, 168–69.
13. Brugsch-Bey 1879, vol. I, 186–87.
14. Lundström 2011.
15. Stoker (1912) 1980.
16. Zecchi 2010, 29; Jarus 2018.
17. Beinlich 2013, 32, fig. 4.

CHAPTER 37.
PATH OF THE HEADLESS ONE

1. Personal communication with the author.
2. Clark 1959, 206.
3. Allen 1899, 208.
4. Budge (1934) 1988, 126.
5. Budge (1934) 1988, 127.
6. Allen 1899, s.v. "Draco," 202–12.
7. Allen 1899, s.v. "Draco," 202–12.
8. Budge (1904) 1969, vol. ii, 61.
9. Allen 1899, s.v. "Draco," 202–12.
10. Bible Hub, "Dragon."
11. Allen 1899, s.v. "Draco," 202–12.
12. Beinlich 2013, 61.
13. Reymond 1966, 456.

CHAPTER 38. TYPHONIAN GNOSIS

1. The first installment in Grant's Typhonian Trilogies was *The Magical Revival,* which appeared in 1972. The ninth and final installment was *The Ninth Arch,* published in 2002.
2. Grant 1991.
3. Lempriere 1788, s.v. "Typhoeus, or Typhon," n.p.n.
4. Grant 1975, 58–59. He refers here to the Thirteenth Dynasty, but of course, we know that Sobekneferu was the last ruler of the previous dynasty, the Twelfth, this confusion having first been introduced by Gerald Massey in *A Book of the Beginnings.* See Massey 1881, vol. II, 402.
5. Grant 1975, 59.
6. Grant 1975, 60.
7. Grant 1975, 59 n. 31.
8. Grant's *Cults of the Shadow* cites Massey's 1907 work *Ancient Egypt the Light of the World* (1907) as a principal source behind the construction of the chapter titled "The Draconian Cult in Ancient Khem" (see, for instance, page 45 n. 1, the chapter's opening page). It is possible, therefore, that this was Grant's primary source for his information on Sobekneferu, and not *A Book of the Beginnings.*
9. Grant, in *Cults of the Shadow* (1975), references the 1879 English language edition of Brugsch-Bey's *Histoire d'Egypte* on various occasions. See, for instance, Grant 1975, 48 n. 5 and 62 n. 43.
10. Grant 1992, 2.
11. Grant 1992, 2.
12. Grant 1992, 2.
13. Grant 1992, 3–4.
14. Grant 1992, 4.
15. Grant 1992, 1.
16. Greer 1995, xiv, 5–6.
17. Grant 1973, pl. 4.
18. S.S.D.D. [Farr] 1986.
19. Collins 2020.
20. Grant 1999, 241, states: "The first published reference to the Nu Isiac Current appeared in a story entitled 'The Stellar Lode', written by Grant circa 1956," although I understand that the book was begun in the late 1940s.
21. Grant 1991.
22. Grant 1995 and Grant (1995) 2003.
23. Grant (1995) 2003, 122.

24. Grant 1995, 35–42; Grant (1995) 2003, 151–62.

25. Grant (1995) 2003, 155.

26. Grant (1995) 2003, 156.

27. Grant (1995) 2003, 156.

28. Grant (1995) 2003, 160.

29. Grant (1995) 2003, 159–60.

30. Grant (1995) 2003, 175.

31. Grant (1995) 2003, 175.

32. Grant (1995) 2003, 182.

33. Personal communication with Michael Staley, Kenneth Grant's executor and the proprietor of Starfire Publishing, the publisher of Grant's books for the past 25 years.

34. Grant (1995) 2003, 210.

35. Personal communication with Caroline Wise.

36. Grant 2002, 204.

37. Grant 2002, 386.

38. Grant 2002, 386.

39. See, for instance, "Who was Pharaoh's Daughter—Theory #1" 2012.

40. Miller 2017.

41. De Vere 2004, 16, 20, 21, and the genealogical tree on 399–400. See also De Vere and Hunter 2010 for more on this topic.

42. See, in particular, Collins 1991, ch. 30: "The Star of Egypt" and ch. 31 "Isis Arise."

43. See the website Pacific North Witches, which has a page dedicated to Sobekneferu citing her feast day as July 23.

APPENDIX.
SOBEKNEFERU ON FILM AND TELEVISION

1. *Curse of the Mummy* (1970) 2009.

2. *Blood from the Mummy's Tomb* (1971) 2006.

3. *The Awakening* (1980) 2012 DVD.

4. See, for instance, Crow 2017 and Judge 2018.

5. For a full transcript of "The Adventure of Ersatz Sobekneferu" (series 6, episode 10 of *Elementary*) see "The Adventures of Ersatz Sobekneferu/Transcript" (2018) on Elementary Wiki. I wish to thank Paolo Sammut for pointing out the fact that Sobekneferu features in this episode of the show.

Bibliography

Abbreviations: n.d. = no date given;
n.p.n. = no page number(s) given.

Ælianus, Claudius. (1665) 1670. *His Various History.* Translated by Thomas Stanley. London: Thomas Basset.

Ager, Sheila L. 2006. "The Power of Excess: Royal Incest and the Ptolemaic Dynasty." *Anthropologica* 48, no. 2: 165–86.

Al-Mas'ūdī (Abū-l-Ḥasan b. al-Ḥusayn). See de Vaux, 1896.

Allen, James P. 2005. *The Ancient Egyptian Pyramid Texts.* Atlanta, Ga.: Society of Biblical Literature.

———. 2008. "The Historical Inscription of Khnumhotep at Dahshur: Preliminary Report." *Bulletin of the American School of Oriental Research* 352: 29–39.

Allen, Richard Hinkley. 1899. *Star-Names and Their Meanings.* New York: G. E. Stechert.

Alm, Brian. 2018. "Women of Power and Influence in Ancient Egypt." Em Hotep website.

Argyros, Ariadne. 2018. "Reviving Ophidia: Godly Serpents in Ancient Egyptian Magic and Mythology." UVM Honors College Senior Theses 234. Burlington, Vt.: University of Vermont.

Arnold, Deiter. 1979. "Das Labyrinth und seine Vorbilder." *Mitteilungen des Deutschen Archäologischen Institus Kairo* 35: 1–9.

———. 1987. *Der Pyramidenbezirk des Königs Amenemhet III. in Dahschur, Volume 1.* Mainz-am-Rhein, Germany: Philipp von Zabern.

———. 1992. *The Pyramid Complex of Senwosret I.* New York: Metropolitan Museum of Art.

Arnold, Dieter, and Dorothea Arnold. 1979. *Der Tempel Qasr el-Sagha*. Mainz, Germany: Philipp von Zabern.

Baines, J. R. 1987. "The Stela of Khusobek: Private and Royal Military Narrative and Values." In Fecht, Osing, and Dryer 1987, 43–61.

———. "Kingship, Definition of Culture, and Legitimation." In O'Connor and Silverman 1995, 3–49.

Baker. D. D. 2008. *The Encyclopedia of the Pharaohs: Volume I – Predynastic to the Twentieth Dynasty 3300–1069 BC*. London: Oxbow Books.

Bakker, Egbert J., Irene J. F. de Jong, and Hans van Wees. 2002. *Brill's Companion to Herodotus*. Leiden, The Netherlands: E. J. Brill.

Banshchikova, Anastasia. 2008. "The Topos of Amalecite Supremacy over Egypt in Arab Historical Tradition (I mill. A.D.)." *Buletinul Cercurilor Stiintifice Studentesti* 14, originally 39–45 and 1–8 as PDF on Academia.edu.

Barham, Francis. 1842. *The Political Works of Marcus Tullius Cicero: Comprising his Treatise on the Commonwealth; and his Treatise on the Laws. Translated from the Original, with Dissertations and Notes in Two Volumes* (volume 2). London: Edmund Spettigue.

Bart, Anneke. 2016. "Senusret I Kheperkare." Anneke Bart Ancient Egypt website.

———. 2018. "A list of Queens of Ancient Egypt." Anneke Bart Ancient Egypt website.

Bedrosian, Robert (intro. and trans.). 2008. *Eusebius of Caesarea, Chronicle book 1*. Robert Bedrosian's Armenian History website.

Beinlich, Horst. 1991. *Das Buch vom Fayum. Zum religiösen Eigenverständnis einer ägyptischen Landschaft (Ägyptologische Abhandlungen. volume: 51)*. Wiesbaden, Germany: Harrassowitz.

———. 2013. "The *Book of the Faiyum*." In Beinlich, Schulz, and Wieczorek 2013, 27–77.

Beinlich, Horst, Regine Schulz, and Alfried Wieczorek, eds. 2013. *Egypt's Mysterious Book of the Faiyum*. Dettelbach, Germany: J.H. Röll Verlag.

Bell, Barbara. 1975. "Climate and the History of Egypt: The Middle Kingdom." *American Journal of Archaeology* 79, no. 3 (July): 223–69.

Belmonte, Juan Antonio, and Mosalam Shaltout, eds. 2009. *In Search of Cosmic Order: Selected Essays on Egyptian Archaeoastronomy*. Cairo, Egypt: Supreme Council of Antiquities Press.

Ben-Ami, Doron. 2008. "Monolithic Pillars in Canaan: Reconsidering the Date of the High Place at Gezer." *Levant* 40, no. 1: 17–28.

Berio, Alessandro. 2014. *The Celestial River: Identifying the Ancient Egyptian Constellations* (Sino-Platonic Papers 253, December 2014). Philadelphia, Pa.: University of Pennsylvania.

Bietak, Manfred. 2007. "Tell el-Dabʿa." Tell el-Dabʿa website.

Bloxam, Elizabeth, and Per Storemyr. 2002. "Old Kingdom Basalt Quarrying Activities at Widan El-Faras, Northern Faiyum Desert." *The Journal of Egyptian Archaeology* 88: 23–36.

Botti, Giuseppe. 1959. *La glorificazione di Sobk e del Fayyum in un papiro ieratico da Tebtynis (Analecta Aegyptiaca* 8). Copenhagen: E. Munksgaard.

Boumba, Vassiliki A, Antigony Mitselou, and Theodore Vougiouklakis. 2004. "Fatal Poisoning from Ingestion of Datura Stramonium Seeds." *Veterinary and Human Toxicology* (April) 46, no. 2: 81–82.

Bowman, Alan, and Charles Crowther. 2020. *The Epigraphy of Ptolemaic Egypt.* Oxford, UK: Oxford University Press.

Bown, Thomas M., and Mary J. Kraus. 1988. *Geology and Paleoenvironment of the Oligocene Jebel Qatrani Formation and Adjacent Rocks, Fayum Depression, Egypt* (Professional paper 1452): 1–60. DOI: 10.3133/pp1452.

Breasted, J. H. 1936. *Geschichte Aegyptens.* Zurich, Switzerland: Phaidon.

Bricault, Laurent. 2009. "Un trône pour deux." *Mythos.* Rivista di Storia delle Religioni, Caltanissetta: Salvatore Sciascia Editore 3: 131–42.

Brönn, Johanna Aletta. 2006. *Foreign Rulers on The Nile: A Reassessment of the Cultural Contribution of the Hyksos in Egypt* (doctoral thesis). Western Cape, South Africa: Stellenbosch University.

Brown, Major R. H. 1892. *The Fayûm and Lake Mœris.* London: Edward Stanford.

Brugsch, Heinrich. 1859. *Histoire d'Egypte* ("History of Egypt"). Leipzig, Germany: J. C. Hinrichs.

Brugsch-Bey, Dr. Henry Karl. 1879. *A History of Egypt Under the Pharaohs* (English trans. Philip Smith). London: John Murray.

———. 1881. *A History of Egypt Under the Pharaohs* (English trans. Philip Smith, second edition). London: John Murray.

Budge, E. A. Wallis. (1904) 1969. *The Gods of the Egyptians or Studies in Egyptian Mythology* [2 vols.]. New York: Dover Publications.

———. 1913. *The Book of the Dead: The Papyrus of Ani, Scribe and Treasurer of the Temples of Egypt, About B.C. 1450,* vol. 1. London: The Medici Society/New York: G.P. Putnam's Sons.

———. (1934) 1988. *From Fetish to God in Ancient Egypt.* New York, Dover Publications.

Bull, Christian H. 2018. *The Tradition of Hermes Trismegistus: The Egyptian Priestly Figure as a Teacher of Hellenized Wisdom.* Leiden, The Netherlands: E.J. Brill.

Bunsen, Christian C. J. 1848. *Egypt's Place in Universal History.* Vol. I. Trans. Charles H. Cottrell. London: Longman, Brown, Green, and Longmans.

Burton, James. 1825–1828. *Excerpta Hieroglyphica*. Cairo: privately printed.

Bury, J. B., S. A. Cook, and F. E. Adcock. (1923) 1928. *The Cambridge Ancient History: Volume I: Egypt and Babylonia to 1500 B. C*. Cambridge, UK: Cambridge University Press.

Bury, John Bagnell, Stanley Arthur Cook, Norman Hepburn Baynes, eds. 1954. *The Cambridge Ancient History: Volume III–The Assyrian Empire*. London: Macmillan/Cambridge University Press.

Callender, Vivienne Gae. 1998a. "Materials for the Reign of Sebekneferu." In Eyre 1998: 227–36.

———. 1998b. "What Sex Was King Sobekneferu?" *KMT: A Modern Journal of Ancient Egypt* 9, no. 1 (Spring): 45–56.

———. 2000. "The Middle Kingdom Renaissance." In Shaw 2000: 148–83.

———. 2002. "The Innovations of Hatshepsut's Reign." *Bulletin of the Australian Centre for Egyptology* 13: 29–46.

Caminos, Ricardo A. 1964. "The Nitocris Adoption Stela." *The Journal of Egyptian Archaeology* 50 (December): 71–101.

Canhão, Telo Ferreira. 2019/2020. "The Latter Solution Neferusobek." *Hapi. Revista da Associação Cultural de Amizade Portugal-Egipto* 7: 26–53. This English translation of original Portugese title is available on Academia.edu.

Caton-Thompson, Gertrude. 1927. "Explorations in The Northern Fayum." *Antiquity* 1: 326–40.

Caton-Thompson, Gertrude, and E. W. Gardner. 1929. "Recent Work on the Problem of Lake Moeris." *The Geographical Journal* 73, no. 1 (January): 20–58.

———. 1934. *The Desert Fayum*. London: The Royal Anthropological Institute of Great Britain and Ireland.

Černý, Jaroslav. 1935. "Semites in Egyptian Mining Expeditions to Sinai." *Archiv Orientalni* 7: 384–89.

Černý, Jaroslav, ed. 1955. *The Inscriptions of Sinai from the Manuscripts of Alan H. Gardiner and T. Eric Peet* (Forty-Fifth Memoir of the Egypt Exploration Society: Part II—Translations and Commentary). London: Egypt Exploration Society/Geoffrey Cumberlege.

Chetwynd-Hayes, Ronald. 1980. *The Awakening*. London: Magnum Books.

Cicero. *The Treatise on the Laws*. See Barham 1842.

Clark, R. T. Rundle. (1959) 1960. *Myth and Symbol in Ancient Egypt*. New York: Grove Press.

Colavito, Jason. 2016. "The Egyptian History: Murtada ibn al-ʿAfif c. 1200. Translated by John Davies 1672." Jason Colavito website.

———. 2018. "The Fragments of Ibrāhīm ibn Waṣīf Shāh. Kitāb al-ʿAdjāʾib al-kabīr

('Great Book of Marvels'), before 1209 CE. Translated by Jason Colavito 2018."
Jason Colavito website.

Collins, Andrew. 1991. *The Seventh Sword*. London: Century Publishing.

———. 2006. *The Cygnus Mystery: Unlocking the Ancient Secret of Life's Origins in the Cosmos*. London: Watkins Books.

———. 2020. "Goddess of the Seven Stars: The Rebirth of Sobekneferu." Ancient Origins website.

Collins, Andrew, and Greg L. Little. 2022. *Origins of the Gods*. Rochester, Vt.: Inner Traditions/Bear & Company.

Cooney, Kara. (2018) 2020. *When Women Ruled the World: Six Queens of Egypt*. Washington D.C.: National Geographic Partners.

Crow, David. 2017. "The Mummy: Did Bram Stoker Inspire the Whole Franchise?" Den of Geek website, June 7.

Daressy, Georges. 1917. "Deux grandes statues de Ramsès II d'Héracléopolis." *Annales du Service des Antiquités de l'Égypte* 17: 33–38.

Darnell, John Coleman, Deborah Darnell, Renee Freeman, and Stan Hendrickx. 2002. *Theban Desert Road Survey I: The Rock Inscriptions of Gebel Tjauti in the Theban Western Desert, Part 1, and the Rock Inscriptions of the Wadi el Hôl, Part 1* (Oriental Institute Publication 117). Chicago: The University of Chicago/The Oriental Institute.

Davies, N. de Garis, Alan H. Gardiner, and Nina de G. Davies. 1920. *The Tomb of Antefoker, Vizier of Sesostris I, and of His Wife, Senet (No. 60)*. London: Geo. Allen & Unwin.

Dawson, Warren R. 1927. "The Number 'Seven' in Egyptian Texts." *Aegyptus* 8, no. 1 (July 1): 97–107.

De Vaux, Bernard Carra (attributed to Al-Masʿūdī [Abū-l-Ḥasan b. al-Ḥusayn]). 1896. *Maçoudi. Le Livre de l'avertissement et de la révision. [Kitáb at-Tanbih Wa-l-išrāf]*. Paris, France: Imprimerie nationale.

De Vere, Nicholas. 2004. *The Dragon Legacy: The Secret History of an Ancient Bloodline*. San Diego, Calif.: Book Tree.

De Vere, Nicholas, and H. E. Count Michael Hunter. 2010. *The Dragon Cede: The Holy Grail Descent of the House of Vere—Vampire God-Kings of Eurasia*. San Diego, Calif.: Book Tree.

Degreef, J. D. 2003. "Three Archaic Egyptian Constellations Used as Seasonal Markers?" private website.

Diamond, Kelly-Anne. 2020. "The Reign of King Sobekneferu and her Performance of Gender." *The Birmingham Egyptology Journal* 7, Special Issue (May). 1–18.

Dio, Cassius. 1925. *Roman History, Vol. VIII*. Loeb Classic Library.

Cambridge, Mass.: Harvard University Press/London: William Heinemann.

Diodorus Siculus. 1933. *Library of History: Volume 1 (books 1–2.34).* Translated by C. H. Oldfather. Cambridge: Loeb Classical Library.

——. 1935. *Library of History: Volumes II (books 2.35–4.58).* Translated by C. H. Oldfather. Cambridge: Loeb Classical Library.

Diogenes Laertius. See Long 1964.

Dodson, Aidan. 2015. *Ancient Egyptian Coffins: The Medelhavsmuseet Collection.* Stockholm, Sweden: Medelhavet Museum of Mediterranean and Near Eastern Antiquities.

Dodson, Aidan, and Dyan Hilton. 2004. *The Complete Royal Families of Ancient Egypt.* London: Thames & Hudson.

Dolson, John, Ahmed El-Barkooky, Fred Wehr, Philip D. Gingerich, Nina Prochazka, and Mark Shann. 2002. *The Eocene and Oligocene Paleo-Ecology and Paleo-Geography of Whale Valley and the Fayoum Basins: Implications for Hydrocarbon Exploration in the Nile Delta and Eco-Tourism in the Greater Fayoum Basin (AAPG/EPEX/SEG/EGS/EAGE Field Trip No. 7. Search and Discovery Article #10030).* Cairo, Egypt: American Association of Petroleum Geologists.

Donne, William Bodham. 1854. s.v. "Aegyptus," in Smith (1854) 1873, vol. I.

Doré, Gustave. 1866. *La Grande Bible de Tours.* 2 vols. Tours, France: Mame/ London: Cassell & Company.

Dungen, Wim van den. 2006. "The Book of the Heavenly Cow ca.1323 BCE." MAAT-Sofiatopia website.

Dunham, Dows, and Jozef Marie Antoon Janssen. 1960. *Second Cataract Forts. Vol. I: Semna Kumma: Excavated by George Andrew Reisner.* Boston: Museum of Fine Arts.

Eady, Dorothy. 1968. "Some Miraculous Wells and Springs of Egypt." *Newsletter of the American Research Center in Egypt* 75: 17–22.

Edward, I. E. S. (1947) 1972. *The Pyramids of Egypt.* London: Ebury Press & Michael Joseph.

El-Weshahy, Mofida Hassan, and Samar Mohammed Mosleh. 2004. "The Relationship between the Main Gods of El-Baharyah Province and the Goddess Neith during the Late Period." *Journal of Association of Arab Universities for Tourism and Hospitality* 11, no. 2 (December): 27–42.

Engelbach, R., and Battiscombe Gunn. 1923. *Harageh.* London: British School of Archaeology in Egypt.

Eratosthenes. *Eratosthenis aliorumque Græcorum de temporibus Ægytiorum fragmenta* [circa late 3rd century BCE]. In Bunsen 1848, 667–75.

Evans, J. A. S. 1987. "The Faiyum and the Lake of Moeris." *Ancient History Bulletin* 92: 66–74.

Eyma, A. K., and C. J. Bennett. 2003. *A Delta-man in Yebu.* Irvine, Calif.: Universal-Publishers.

Eyre, Christopher J., ed. 1998. *Proceedings of the Seventh International Congress of Egyptologists: Cambridge, 3–9 September, 1995 (Orientalia Lovaniensia analecta 82).* Leuven: Peeters.

Farag, Nagib, and Zaky Iskander. 1971. *The Discovery of Neferwptah.* Cairo: General Organization for Government Printing Offices.

Faulkner, R. O. 1968. "The Pregnancy of Isis." *The Journal of Egyptian Archaeology* 54 (August): 40–44.

———. 1972. *The Ancient Egyptian Book of the Dead.* New York: Macmillan Publishing Co.

———. 1973. *The Ancient Egyptian Coffin Texts Vol. I, Spells 1–354.* Warminster, Wiltshire: Aris & Phillips.

———. 1977. *The Ancient Egyptian Coffin Texts Vol. II, Spells 355–787.* Warminster, Wiltshire: Aris & Phillips.

Fay, Biri, Rita E. Freed, Thomas Schelper, and Friederike Seyfried. 2015. "The Neferusobek Project, Part 1." In Miniaci and Grajetzki 2015, 89–91.

Fechheimer, Hedwig. (1914) 1920. *Die Plastik der Ägypter.* Berlin, Germany: Bruno Cassirer.

Fecht, Gerhard, Jürgen Osing, and Günter Dreyer, eds. 1987. *Form und Mass: Beiträge zur Literatur, Sprache und Kunst des alten Ägypten: Festschrift für Gerhard Fecht zum 65. Geburtstag am 6. Februar 1987.* Wiesbaden, Germany: Otto Harrassowitz.

Feinman, Peter. *The Exodus: An Exodus Story.* Oxford, UK/Philadelphia, Pa.: Oxbow Books.

Ferguson, Christine, and Andrew Radford, eds. 2018. *In the Occult Imagination in Britain, 1875–1947.* New York: Routledge/London: Taylor & Francis.

Florus, Lucius Annaeus. 1929. *The Epitome of Roman History.* Translated by Edward Seymour Forster. Cambridge, Mass.: Harvard University Press/London: William Heinemann.

Forman, Werner, and Stephen Quirke. 1996. *Hieroglyphs and the Afterlife in Ancient Egypt.* Norman, Okla.: University of Oklahoma Press.

Forrest, M. Isidora. 2014. "The Mysteries of Isis in Antioch." Isiopolis website, August 30.

Fowden, Garth. (1986) 1993. *The Egyptian Hermes: A Historical Approach to the Late Pagan Mind.* Princeton, N.J.: Princeton University Press.

"Fragment of Basalt Standing Statue of Khafre." 2020. Digital Giza website.

Frias, Sara Martinez. 2020. "Gebel Qatrani and the Ancient Quarries, Egypt." Med-O-Med Cultural Landscapes website.

Friedman, Florence Dunn. 2011. "Reading the Menkaure Triads, Part I." In Gundlach and Spence 2011, 23–55.

Fukaya, Masashi. 2019. *The Festivals of Opet, the Valley, and the New Year: Their Socio-religious Functions.* Summertown, Oxford, UK: Archaeopress Publishing.

Gabolde, Marc. 1998. *D'Akhenaton à Toutankhamon: Histoire Monothéisme Egyptologie.* Lyon, France: Université Lumière-Lyon.

Galán, José M., Betsy M. Bryan, and Peter F. Dorman, eds. 2014. *Creativity and Innovation in the Reign of Hatshepsut. Occasional Proceedings of the Theban Workshop 2010.* Vol. 69 of *Studies in Ancient Oriental Civilization.* Chicago: The Oriental Institute of the University of Chicago.

Gallo, Paolo. 1993. "Il Vero Deir Abu Lifa Rivisitato." *Egitto e Vicino Oriente* 16: 57–66.

Gardiner, Alan H. 1916. "The Egyptian Origin of the Semitic Alphabet." *The Journal of Egyptian Archaeology* 3, no. 1: 1–16.

———. 1920. "The Graffiti." In Davies, Gardiner, and Davies 1920, 27–29.

———. (1927) 2007. *Egyptian Grammar Being an Introduction to the Study of Hieroglyphs.* Oxford: Griffith Institute.

———. (1961) 1976. *Egypt of the Pharaohs.* Oxford, UK: Oxford University Press.

Gardiner, Alan H., and T. Eric Peet. 1917. *The Inscriptions of Sinai: Part I—Introduction and Plates.* London: The Egypt Exploration Society.

Geeta, R., and Waleed Gharaibeh. 2007. "Historical Evidence for a Pre-Columbian Presence of Datura in the Old World and Implications for a First Millennium Transfer from the New World." *Journal of Biosciences* 32: 1227–44.

Gillam, Robyn A. 1995. "Priestesses of Hathor: Their Function, Decline and Disappearance." *Journal of the American Research Center in Egypt* 32: 211–37.

Gillam, Robyn A. 2018. "Sobeknefru." Wiley Online Library website.

Giveon, Raphael. 1978. *The Impact of Egypt on Canaan: Iconographical and Related Studies (Orbis Biblicus et Orientalis 20).* Freiburg, Switzerland: Universitätsverlag/ Göttingen, Germany: Vandenhoeck & Ruprech.

Grajetzki, Wolfram. 2001. *Two Treasurers of the Late Middle Kingdom.* BAR International Series 1007. Oxford, UK: BAR Publishing.

———. 2004. *Harageh, an Egyptian Burial Ground for the Rich Around 1800 BCE.* London: Golden House Publications.

———. 2005. "The Coffin of the 'King's Daughter' Neferuptah and the Sarcophagus of the 'Great King's Wife' Hatshepsut." *Göttinger Miszellen: Beitrage zur ägyptologischen Diskussion* 205: 55–66.

———. 2006. *The Middle Kingdom in Ancient Egypt.* London: Duckworth.

———. (2009) 2012. *Court Officials of the Egyptian Middle Kingdom*. Bristol: Bristol Classical Press.

———. 2013. "Late Middle Kingdom." *UCLA Encyclopedia of Egypt* 1, no.1 (July 6): 1–14.

———. 2014. *Tomb Treasures of the Late Middle Kingdom: The Archaeology of Female Burials*. Philadelphia, Penn.: University of Pennsylvania Press.

Grant, Kenneth. 1972. *The Magical Revival*. London: Frederick Muller.

———. 1973. *Aleister Crowley and the Hidden God*. London: Frederick Muller.

———. 1975. *Cults of the Shadow*. London: Frederick Muller.

———. 1991. *Remembering Aleister Crowley*. London: Skoob Books.

———. 1991. "The Stellar Lode [first installment]." *Skoob Occult Review* 5: n.p.n.

———. 1992. *Hecate's Fountain*. London: Skoob Books.

———. 1995. "The Stellar Lode [full version]." In Johnson 1995, 17–73.

———. 1999. *Beyond the Mauve Zone*. London: Starfire Publishing.

———. 2002. *The Ninth Arch*. London: Starfire Publishing.

———. 2003. "The Stellar Lode." In Grant 2003, 117–216.

———. 2003. *The Other Child and Other Tales*. London: Starfire Publishing.

Graves-Brown, Carolyn. 2010. *Dancing for Hathor: Women in Ancient Egypt*. London: Bloomsbury Publishing.

Gray, Melissa. 2010. "Poison, Not snake, Killed Cleopatra, Scholar Says." CNN website, June 30.

Greer, Mary K. 1995. *Women of the Golden Dawn: Rebels and Priestesses*. Rochester, Vt.: Park Street Press.

Grenfell, Bernard P., Arthur S. Hunt, D. G. Hogarth, and J. G. Milne. 1900. *Fayûm Towns and their Papyri*. London, Offices of the Egypt Exploration Fund.

Griffith, F. Ll. 1889. "Chapter IV: The Hieroglyphic Inscriptions." In Petrie 1889, 21–23.

———. 1909. *Catalogue of the Demotic Papyri in the John Rylands Library, Manchester. (P.Ryl.Dem.): Volume III: Key-list, Translations, Commentaries and Indices*. Manchester, UK: Manchester University Press.

Grimal, Nicolas. (1988) 1992. *A History of Ancient Egypt*. Oxford, UK/Cambridge, Mass.: Blackwell.

Grout, James. 2017. "The Death of Cleopatra." Encyclopædia Romana (University of Chicago) website.

Guéraud, O. 1940. "Une stèle gréco-romaine au cartouche d'Amenemhet III." *Annales du Service des Antiquités de l'Égypte* 40: 553–60.

Gundlach, Rolf, and Kate Spence, eds. 2011. *Palace and Temple: Architecture, Decoration, Ritual. Cambridge, July 16th–17th, 2007*. Königtum, Staat und Gesellschaft früher Hochkulturen 4, no. 2. Wiesbaden, Germany: Harrassowitz.

Gurval, Robert A. 2011. "Dying Like a Queen: The Story of Cleopatra and the Asp(s) in Antiquity." In Miles 2011, 54–77.

Gutbub, Adolphe. 1961. "Un emprunt aux Textes des Pyramides dans l'hymne à Hathor, dame de l'ivresse." *Mélanges Maspero 1–Orient Ancien* 4: 37–72.

Habachi, Labib. 1937. "Une 'vaste salle' d'Amenemhat III a Kiman-Fares (Fayoum)." *Annales du Service des Antiquités de l'Égypte* 32: 85–95.

———. 1954. "Khatâ'na-Qantir: Importance, Statues of Sobeknofru and Iamu-Sahornedjheriotef Discovered at Tell ed-Dab'a." *Annales du Service des Antiquités de l'Égypte* 52: 443–562.

———. 1954. "The Gateway of Amenemhêt I and Senusert III in Tell Qirqâfa (Khatà'na)." In Habachi 1954, 448–58.

———. 1954. "Statues of Sobknofru and Iamu-Sahornedjheriotef Discovered at Tell Ed-Dab'a (Khatâ'na)." In Habachi 1954, 458–70.

———. 1955. "A Strange Monument of the Ptolemaic Period from Crocodilopolis." *The Journal of Egyptian Archaeology* 41 (December 1955): 106–11.

Hackley, Laurel Darcy. 2014. "Amethyst, Apotropaia, and the Eye of Re." Ph.D. diss. Cairo, Egypt: The American University in Cairo.

Hadingham, Evan. 2010. "Uncovering Secrets of the Sphinx." *Smithsonian Magazine* website, February.

Hall, H. R. 1904. "Nitokris-Rhodopis." *Journal of Hellenic Studies* 24: 208–13.

———. (1923) 1928. "The Union of Egypt and the Old Kingdom." In Bury, Cook, and Adcock 1904, 257–98.

———. 1928. "A Sphinx of Amenemhet IV." *The British Museum Quarterly* 2, no. 4 (March): 87–88, pl. LVIIa.

Hall, Sidney, and Jehoshaphat Aspin. 1824. *Urania's Mirror.* London: Samuel Leigh.

Hamilton, Keith. 2020. *Qsar el-Sagha Temple: A Layman's Guide* (March 27). Available at Academia.edu.

———. 2020. *The Black Pyramid of Amenemhet III at Dahshur: A Layman's Guide* (October 10). Available at Academia.edu.

Haney, Lisa Saladino. 2020. *Visualizing Coregency: An Exploration of the Link between Royal Image and Co-Rule during the Reign of Senwosret III and Amenemhet III.* Harvard Egyptological Studies, Volume 8. Leiden, The Netherlands: E. J. Brill.

Harrell, J. A., and T. M. Bown. 1995. "An Old Kingdom Basalt Quarry at Widan el-Faras and the Quarry Road to Lake Moeris in the Faiyum." *Journal of the American Research Center in Egypt* 39: 71–91.

Hassan, Selim. 1943. *Excavations at Giza vol. 4 (1932–1933).* Cairo: Faculty of Arts of the Egyptian University.

Hasson, Nir. 2016. "Gold, Silver Offering to the Gods 3,600 Years Ago Found in Canaanite Gezer." Haaretz website, November 15.

Hayes, William C. 1953. *The Scepter of Egypt: A Background for the Study of the Egyptian Antiquities in the Metropolitan Museum of Art · Part 1*. New York: Metropolitan Museum of Art.

———. 1963. *The Cambridge Ancient History. Egypt: From the Death of Ammenemes III to Seqenenre II. Revised edition of volumes I & II*. Cambridge, UK: Cambridge University Press.

"Head from a Sphinx." 2008. Brooklyn Museum.

Hebblethwaite, Kate. 2008. Introduction to Bram Stoker's *The Jewel of Seven Stars*. See Stoker (1903/1912) 2008.

Heidel, William Arthur. (1935) 2019. *Hecataeus and the Egyptian Priests in Herodotus, Book 2: American Academy of Arts and Sciences, Memoirs, V18, Part 2*. Abingdon, Oxfordshire, UK: Routledge.

Hermes Mercurius Trismegistus. (1650) 1884. *The Divine Pymander*. Translated by John Everard. London: G. Redway.

Herodotus. 1920. *The Histories*. Loeb Edition. Translated by A. D. Godley. London/New York: Loeb Classical Library.

Hill, Jenny. 2010a. "Isis and Ra." Ancient Egypt Online.

———. 2010b. "Sobek." Ancient Egypt Online website.

———. 2018. "Book of the Two Ways." Ancient Egypt Online website.

———. 2019. "Queen Nitocris (Neterkare or Nitikrty)." Ancient Egypt Online website.

Hoffmeier, J. K. 1993. "The Use of Basalt in Floors of Old Kingdom Pyramid Temples." *Journal of the American Research Center in Egypt* 30: 117–23.

Hornung, Erik, Rolf Krauss, and David A. Warburton, eds. 2006. *Ancient Egyptian Chronology*. Vol. 83 of *Handbook of Oriental Studies, Section 1: The Near and Middle East*. Leiden, The Netherlands: E. J. Brill.

Horváth, Zoltán. 2009. "Temple(s) and Town at El-Lahun: A Study of Ancient Toponyms in the el-Lahun Papyri." In Silverman, Simpson, and Wegner, 171–203.

Houtsma, M. Th., A. J. Wensinck, T. W. Arnold, W. Heffening, and E. Lévi-Provençal, eds. 1927. *The Encyclopaedia of Islam*. Leyden, The Netherlands: E. J. Brill/London: Luzac & Co.

Hughes, William. 2000. *Beyond Dracula: Bram Stoker's Fiction and Its Cultural Context*. Basingstoke, Hampshire, UK: Palgrave Macmillan/New York: St. Martin's Press.

Hunt, Arthur S. 1911. *The Oxyrhynchus Papyri Part VIII Edited with Translations and Notes*. London: The Egypt Exploration Fund.

Hurtado, Larry W. 2006. *The Freer Biblical Manuscripts: Fresh Studies of an American Treasure Trove.* Atlanta, Ga.: Society of Biblical Literature.

Iskander, Zaky, and Alex Badawy. (1948) 1965. *Brief History of Ancient Egypt.* Cairo, Egypt: Madkour Press.

Jackson, Howard M.1999. "A New Proposal for the Origin of the Hermetic God Poimandres." *Zeitschrift für Papyrologie und Epigraphik Zeitschrift für Papyrologie und Epigraphik* 128: 95–106.

Jarus, Owen. 2018. "Stone Engravings of Famous Warrior Pharaoh Found in Ancient Egyptian Temple." Live Science website, October 3.

Jenkyns, Richard. 2013. *God, Space, and City in the Roman Imagination.* Oxford, UK: Oxford University Press.

Jochen, Hallof. 2011. "Esna." *UCLA Encyclopedia of Egyptology* 1, no. 1: 1–15.

Johnson, Christopher, ed. 1995. *Skoob Esoterica Anthology, Volume 1.* London: Skoob Books Publishing.

Johnson, Cody. 2018. "Psychedelics and Witchcraft—The Truth About Hallucinogenic 'Hexing Herbs' The Sordid History of Deadly Nightshade, Mandrake, and Henbane." Psychedelic Frontiers website.

Jonckheere, Frans. 1954. "L'Eunuque dans l'Égypte pharaonique." *Revue d'Histoire des Sciences* 7, no. 2 (April–June): 139–55.

Josephus, Flavius. 1926. *The Life; Against Apion.* Translated by H. St. J. Thackeray. Cambridge, Mass.: Harvard University Press/London: Wm. Heinemann.

Judge, Kieran. 2018. "Odds and DEAD Ends: Resurrecting the Queen." HorrorAddicts.net website, September 5.

Kaper, Olaf E. 2003. *The Egyptian God Tutu; A Study of the Sphinx-God and Master of Demons with a Corpus of Monuments.* Vol. 119 of *Orientalia Lovaniensia Analecta.* Dudley, Mass.: Leuven, Peeters & Departement Oosterse Studies.

Kassem, Mahmoud Awad Alsayd Alsayd. 2019. *Iconography and Style in the Statuary of Ramesses II.* PhD. diss. Warsaw, Poland: University of Warsaw, Faculty of History Institute of Archaeology.

Kircher, Athanasius. 1679. *Turris Babel, sive archontologia: qua priscorum post diluvium hominum vita, mores, turris fabrica civitatunque extructio describuntur.* Amsterdam, The Netherlands: Janssonio-Waesbergiana.

Kitchen, Kenneth. 1956. "A Recently Published Egyptian Papyrus and Its Bearing on the Joseph Story." *The Tyndale House Bulletin* 2 (winter): 1–2.

Koninklijke Akademie van Wetenschappen. 1886. *Verhandelingen der Koninklijke Akademie van Wetenschappen. Afdeeling Letterkunde,* 16th part. Amsterdam, The Netherlands: Johannes Müller.

Kroenke, Karin R. 2011. "The Artifacts from Petrie's Excavation." In Wilkinson 2011, 11–32.

Kuete, Victor. 2014. *Toxicological Survey of African Medicinal Plants*. London: Elsevier.

Laboury, Dimitri. 2014. "How and Why Did Hatshepsut Invent the Image of Her Royal Power?" In Galán, Bryan, and Dorman 2014, 49–91.

Lainton, Danielle, and Louise Coquio. 2021. *Pashterina's Peacocks: For Storm Constantine*. Stafford, Staffordshire, UK: Immanion Press.

"Large Kneeling Statue of Hatshepsut ca. 1479–1458 B.C." Metropolitan Museum of Art website.

Larson, Jennifer Lynn. 2007. *Ancient Greek Cults: A Guide*. Hove, East Sussex, U.K.: Psychology Press.

Lehner, Mark. (1997) 2001. *The Complete Pyramids: Solving the Ancient Mysteries*. London: Thames & Hudson.

Lempriere, John. 1788. *Bibliotheca Classica or, A Classical Dictionary*. London: T. Cadell.

———. 1832. *Bibliotheca Classica or, A Classical Dictionary*. Re-edited and revised by E. H. Barker with corrections by Charles Anthon. London: Black, Young and Young.

Lepsius, Karl Richard. 1842. *Auswahl der wichtigsten urkunden des Aegyptische Alterthums*. Leipzig, Germany: Georg Wiegand.

———. 1853. *Letters from Egypt, Ethiopia, and the Peninsula of Sinai with Extracts from the Chronology of the Egyptians with reference to the Exodus of the Israelites*. Translated by Leonora and Joanna B. Horner. London: Henry G. Bohn.

———. 1904. *Denkmäler aus Ägypten und Äthiopien: Zweiter Band–Mittelaegypten mit dem Faijum*. Leipzig, Germany: J. C. Hinrich.

———. (1904) 1970. *Denkmaeler aus Aegypten und Aethiopien Text*, vol. 2. Osnabruck, Austria: Biblio Verlag.

Lesko, Barbara S. 1999. *The Great Goddesses of Egypt*. Norman, Okla.: University of Oklahoma Press.

Lichtheim, Miriam. 1976. *Ancient Egyptian Literature, Volume Two: The New Kingdom*. Berkeley, Calif.: University of California Press.

Liotsakis, Vasileios. 2014. "Notes on Herodotus' Sesostris (Hdt. II 102-110)." *Maia* 66, no. 3: 500–17.

Lloyd, Alan B. 1970. "The Egyptian Labyrinth." *The Journal of Egyptian Archaeology* 56 (August): 81–100.

Lloyd, Alan B. 1988. "Herodotus' Account of Pharaonic History." *Historia: Zeitschrift für Alte Geschichte* 37, no. 1: 22–53.

———. (1988) 1993. *Herodotus Book II Commentary 99–182*. Leiden, The Netherlands: E. J. Brill.

——. 2002. "Egypt" In Bakker, de Jong, van Wees 2002, 415–36.

——. 2010. *A Companion to Ancient Egypt.* Chichester, West Sussex, UK: John Wiley & Sons.

Long, H. S., ed. 1964. *Diogenis Laertii vitae philosophorum.* 2 vols. Oxford, UK: Oxford University Press.

"Lower body fragment of a female statue seated on a throne." 2019. Museum of Fine Arts Boston website.

Lucas, A. 1938. "Poisons in Ancient Egypt." *The Journal of Egyptian Archaeology* 24, no. 1 (December 1): 198–99.

Lucas, A., and J. R. Harris. 1948. *Ancient Egyptian Materials and Industries.* 3rd revised ed. London: Edward Arnold and Co.

Lull, José, and Juan Antonio Belmonte. 2009. "The Constellations of Ancient Egypt." In Belmonte and Shaltout 2009, 157–94.

Lundström, Peter. 2011. "Abydos Canon." Pharaoh.se website.

——. 2014a. "Amenemhet IV." Pharaoh.se website.

——. 2014b. "Neferusobek." Pharaoh.se website.

——. 2016. "Comparing the King Lists of Manetho." Pharaoh.se website.

——. 2021a. "Karnak Canon." Pharaoh.se website.

——. 2021b. "Saqqara Canon." Pharaoh.se website.

——. 2021c. "Turin King List: Column 7." Pharaoh.se website.

Mackay, Ernest. 1912. "The Cemeteries of Mazghuneh." In Petrie, Wainwright, and Mackay 1912, 37–55.

Macnaughton, Duncan. 1932. *Scheme of Egyptian Chronology with Notes Thereon.* London: Luzac & Co.

Magli, Giulio. 2010. "A Cognitive Approach to the Topography of the 12th Dynasty Pyramids." Preprint: arXiv:1011.2122.

Maier III, Walter. (1986) 2018. *'Ašerah: Extrabiblical Evidence.* Harvard Semitic Monographs series, no. 37. Leiden, The Netherlands: E. J. Brill.

Mairs, Rachel. 2020. "Beyond Rosetta." In Bowman and Crowther 2020, 20–34.

Málek, Jaromír. 1982. "The Original Version of the Royal Canon of Turin." *The Journal of Egyptian Archaeology* 68, 93–106.

Malleson, Claire. 2019. *The Fayum Landscape: Ten Thousand Years of Archaeology.* New York/Cairo: The American University in Cairo Press.

Manetho. In Waddell (1940) 1964.

Maspero, Gaston. 1890. "Monuments Égyptiens du Musée de Marseille." *Recueil de Travaux Relatifs à la Philologie et à l'Archéologie Égyptiennes et Assyriennes* 13: 113–26.

——. 1903. *History of Egypt, Chaldea, Syria, Babylonia, and Assyria,* vol. 2.

Translated into English by M. L. McClure. London: Grolier Society.

Massey, Gerald. 1881. *The Book of Beginnings: Containing an Attempt to Recover and Reconstitute the Lost Origines of the Myths and Mysteries, Types and Symbols, Religion and Language, with Egypt for the Mouthpiece and Africa as the Birthplace.* London: Williams and Norgate.

———. 1883. *The Natural Genesis, or, Second Part of A Book of the Beginnings: Containing an Attempt to Recover and Reconstitute the Lost Origines of the Myths and Mysteries, Types and Symbols, Religion and Language, with Egypt for the Mouthpiece and Africa as the Birthplace.* London: Williams and Norgate.

———. 1907. *Ancient Egypt the Light of the World: A Work of Reclamation and Restitution in Twelve Books.* London: T. Fisher Unwin.

Mastaff, Roland. 2002. "The Book of the Heavenly (Celestial) Cow." Tour Egypt website.

Master, Daniel, ed. 2013. *The Oxford Encyclopedia of the Bible and Archaeology.* Oxford, UK: Oxford University Press.

Mas'ūdī, 'Alī Ibn al-Ḥusain. 1863. *Les prairies d'or.* Translated into English with commentary by C. Barbier de Meynard and Abel Pavet de Courteillein. Paris, France: Imprimerie impériale.

Matzker, Ingo. 1986. *Die letzten Könige der 12. Dynastie. Europäische Hochschulschriften. Reihe III, Geschichte und ihre Hilfswissenschaften.* Frankfurt, Germany/Bern, Switzerland/New York: Lang.

Mayer, Maximilian. 1892. "Mykenische Beiträge. II. Zur mykenischen Tracht und Kultur." *Jahrbuch des Kaiserlich deutschen archäologischen Instituts* VII: 189–202.

Mead, G. R. S. (1906) 1992. *Thrice Greatest Hermes: Studies in Hellenistic Theosophy and Gnosis Being a Translation of the Extant Sermons and Fragments of the Trismegistic Literature with Prolegomena Commentaries and Notes–Book 1: Prolegomena.* York Beach, Maine: Samuel Weiser.

Meurer, Georg. 2002. *Die Feinde des Königs in den Pyramidentexten (Orbis biblicus et orientalis* 189). Freiburg, Switzerland: Universitätsverlag/Göttingen, Germany: Vandenhoeck & Ruprecht.

Michell, John, and Christine Rhone. 1991. *Twelve-tribe Nations: And the Science of Enchanting the Landscape.* London: Thames and Hudson.

Miles, Margaret M. 2011. *Cleopatra: A Sphinx Revisited.* Berkeley/Los Angeles, Calif.: University of California Press.

Millmore, Mark. 2016. "Finding the City Itjtawy from Space" Discovering Egypt website (Newsletter 54), September 23.

Miniaci, Gianluca, and Wolfram Grajetzki, eds. 2015. *The World of Middle Kingdom Egypt (2000–1550 BC).* Volume 1: *Contributions on Archaeology Art Religion and Written Sources; Middle Kingdom Studies I*. London: Golden House Publications.

Mohamed, Maher Hammam. 2017. "The Celestial Cow Goddess Mehet-Weret." *Journal of the Association of Arab Universities for Tourism and Hospitality* 14, no. 2: 55–66.

Montet, Pierre. 1968. *Lives of the Pharaohs*. The World Publishing Company: Cleveland, Ohio.

Morgan, Jacques de., G. Legrain, and G. Jéquier. 1903. *Fouilles a Dahchour en 1894–1895*. Vienna, Austria: Adolphe Holzhausen.

Moritz 1927, s.v. "al-Faiyum," In Houtsma et al. 1927, 40–43.

Mosshammer, Alden A., ed. 1984. *Georgii Syncelli Ecloga chronographica*. Leipzig, Germany: Teubner.

Murtaḍā ibn al-'Afîf. 1666. *L'Egypte de Murtadi fils du Gaphiphe: où il est traité des pyramides, du débordement du Nil, et des autres merveilles de cette province, selon les opinions et traditions des Arabes*. Translated into French by Pierre Vattier. Paris, France: Lovys Billaine.

Murtada ibn al-'Afîf. 1672/2015. *The Prodigies of Egypt*. Translated by John Davies. Albany, N.Y.: JasonColavito website.

Naville, Édouard Henri. 1887. *Shrine of Saft el Henneh and the Land of Goshen (1885)*. London: Trübner.

Naville, Edouard, Theodore M. Davis, and Howard Carter. 1906. *The Tomb of Hâtshopsîtû*. London: Archibald Constable and Co.

Naydler, Jeremy. 1996. *Temple of the Cosmos: The Ancient Egyptian Experience of the Sacred*. Rochester, Vt.: Inner Traditions International.

Newberry, Percy E. 1893. *Beni Hasan Part 1 (Archaeological Survey of Egypt)*. London: Egypt Exploration Fund/Kegan Paul, Trench, Trübner & Co.

———. 1939. "Howard Carter." *The Journal of Egyptian Archaeology* 25, no. 1 (June), 67–69.

———. 1943a. "Co-regencies of Ammenemes III, IV and Sebknofru." *The Journal of Egyptian Archaeology* 29 (December), 74–75.

———. 1943b. "Queen Nitocris of the Sixth Dynasty." *The Journal of Egyptian Archaeology* 29 (December), 51–54.

O'Connor, David, and Stephen Quirke, eds. 2003. *Mysterious Lands*. London: UCL Press/Institute of Archeology.

———, and David P. Silverman, eds. 1995. *Ancient Egyptian Kingship*. Leiden, The Netherlands. E. J. Brill.

Ortiz, Steven M., 2013, s.v. "Gezer." In Master 2013, 468–74.

Peters, Elizabeth. 1985. *The Mummy Case*. New York: Congdon & Weed, Inc.

Petrie, W. M. Flinders. 1889. *Hawara, Biahmu, and Arsinoe.* Includes chapters by
F. LL. Griffith, A. H. Sayce, and Percy E. Newberry. London: Field & Tuer.

———. 1890. *Kahun, Gurob and Hawara.* Includes chapters by F. LL. Griffith and
Percy E. Newberry. London: Kegan Paul, Trench, Trübner.

———. [1892]. *Ten Years Digging in Egypt 1881–1891.* New York/Chicago: Fleming
H. Revell.

———. 1894. *A History of Egypt: From the Earliest Kings to the XVIth Dynasty.* 2
vols. London: Methuen & Co.

———. 1906. *Researches in Sinai.* London: John Murray.

———. 1909. *Memphis I.* London: School of Archaeology in Egypt/Bernard
Quaritch.

———. 1912. *The Labyrinth, Gerzah and Mazghuneh.* London: British School of
Archaeology in Egypt.

Pignattari, Stefania. 2008. *Due donne per il trono d'Egitto: Neferuptah e Sobekneferu
(Piccola biblioteca di egittologia 10).* Imola, Italy: La Mandragora.

———. 2009–2011. "Il regno di Amenemhat IV e la fine della XII dinastia."
Ph.D. diss. Pisa, Italy: University of Pisa.

———. 2018. *Amenemhet IV and the End of the Twelfth Dynasty Between the End
and the Beginning.* Oxford, UK: BAR Publishing.

Pinch, Geraldine. 2002. *Handbook of Egyptian Mythology.* Santa Barbara, Calif.:
ABC-CLIO.

———. 2004. *Egyptian Mythology: A Guide to the Gods, Goddesses, and Traditions of
Ancient Egypt.* Oxford, UK: Oxford University Press.

Pleyte, Willem. 1886. "Over drie handschriften op papyrus: bekend onder de titels
van Papyrus du Lac Moeris, du Fayoum, et du Labyrinthe." In *Koninklijke
Akademie van Wetenschappen 1886,* 1–50, and plates I–VIII.

Pliny the Elder. 1855. *The Natural History.* Translated by John Bostock and
H. T. Riley. London: Taylor and Francis.

Plutarch. 1906. *Plutarch's Lives: The Translation called Dryden's Corrected from the
Greek and Revised by A. H. Clough.* 5 vols. Boston, Mass.: Little Brown and
Company.

Pomponius Mela. 1998. *Pomponius Mela's Description of the World* [*Chorographia*].
Translated and introduction by F. E. Romer. Ann Arbor, Mich.: University of
Michigan Press.

Porter, The Late Bertha, and Rosalind L. B. Moss. (1934) 1968. *Topographical
Bibliography of Ancient Egyptian Hieroglyphic Texts, Reliefs, and Paintings: IV.
Lower And Middle Egypt (Delta and Cairo to Asyut).* Oxford, UK: Griffith
Institute.

Pritchard, James B., ed. *Ancient Near Eastern Texts Relating to the Old Testament with Supplement.* Princeton, N.J.: Princeton University Press.

Ragheb, Maryan. [n.d.] "The Rise of Sobek in the Middle Kingdom." American Research Center in Egypt (ARCE) website.

"Raised Mosaic Panel D from Room 3 Central Emblema of the Mors Voluntaria." n.d. Research Photographs, Princeton University website.

Reeves, Nicholas. 2005. *Akhenaten: Egypt's False Prophet.* London: Thames & Hudson.

Reisner, G. A. 1929. "Egyptian Forts at Semna and Uronarti." *Bulletin of the Museum of Fine Arts* 27: 64–75.

Reitzenstein, Richard. 1904. *Poimandres: Studien zur Griechisch-Ägyptischen und Frühchristlichen Literatur.* Leipzig, Teubner.

Reymond, E. A. E. 1966. "Studies in Late Egyptian Documents Preserved in the John Rylands Library: II. Dime and its Papyri: An Introduction." *Bulletin of the John Rylands Library Manchester* 48, no. 2: 433–66.

———. 1969. *The Mythical Origin of the Egyptian Temple.* New York: Barnes & Noble/Manchester, U.K.: Manchester University Press.

Riad, Henri. 1958. "Le culte d'Amenemhat III au Fayoum à l'époque ptolémaïque." *Annales du service des antiquités de l'Égypte* 55: 203–6.

Richardson, Deuce. 2021. "The Literary Afterlife and Legacy of Richard F. Burton (Part Three)." DMR Books website.

Ritner, Robert K. 2018. "The Origin of Evil in Egyptian Theological Speculation." In Ritner 2018, 281–90.

Ritner, Robert K., ed. 2018. *Essays for the Library of Seshat: Studies Presented to Janet H. Johnson on the Occasion of Her 70th Birthday.* Vol. 70 of *Studies in Ancient Oriental Civilization.* Chicago: The Oriental Institute of the University of Chicago.

Rohl, David. 1995. *Pharaohs and Kings: A Biblical Quest.* New York: Crown Publishers.

Rondot, Vincent. 2013. *Derniers visages des dieux d'Égypte. Iconographies, panthéons et cultes dans le Fayoum hellénisé des IIe–IIIe siècles de notre ère.* Paris, France: Presses de l'université Paris-Sorbonne; Éditions du Louvre.

Roscher, Wilhelm H. 1918. *Der Omphalosgedanke bei verschiedenen Volkern, besonders den semitischen.* Leipsig, Germany: B. G. Teubner.

Ryholt, K. S. B. 1997. *The Political Situation in Egypt during the Second Intermediate Period, c. 1800–1550 BC.* Vol. 20 of Carsten Niebuhr Institute Publications. Copenhagen, Denmark: Museum Tusculanum Press.

———. 2000. "The Late Old Kingdom in the Turin King-list and the Identity of

Nitocris." *Zeitschrift für Ägyptische Sprache und Altertumskunde* 127, no. 1: 87–119.

———. 2004. "The Turin King-List." *Ägypten und Levante* 14: 135–55.

Saleem, Sahar N., and Zahi Hawass. 2021. "Digital Unwrapping of the Mummy of King Amenhotep I (1525–1504 BC) Using CT." *Frontiers of Medicine,* December 21.

Sampsell, Bonnie M. 2003. *A Traveler's Guide to the Geology of Egypt.* Cairo & New York: The American University of Cairo Press.

Saretta, Phyllis. 2016. *Asiatics in Middle Kingdom Egypt.* London: Bloomsbury.

Sartain, John. 1885. *On the Antique Painting in Encaustic of Cleopatra Discovered in 1818.* Philadelphia: George Gebbie & Co.

Sauneron, Serge. 1962. *Esna: Les fêtes religieuses d'Esna aux derniers siècles du paganisme.* Cairo, Egypt: Institute français d'archéologie orientale.

"Scarab with Hathor-like Canaanite Goddess ca. 1740–1640 B.C." n.d. The Metropolitan Museum website.

Scheits, Matthias. 1710. *Afbeeldzels van 't Oude en Niewe Testament/Tableaux du Vieux et Nouveau Testament.* Amsterdam, The Netherlands: Francois Halma.

Schweinfurth, G. 1886. "Reise in das Depressionsgebiet im Umkreis des Fayum im Januar 1886." *Zeitschrift der Gesellschaft für Erdkunde* 21: 96–149.

Seters, John van. (1966) 2010. *The Hyksos: A New Investigation.* Eugene, Oreg.: Wipf & Stock.

Shanine, Alaa. 2008. "Ancient Egyptians Did It Tough." ABC Science website, March 31.

Sharpe, Samuel. 1846. *The History of Egypt from the Earliest Times till the Conquest by the Arabs A.D. 640.* London: Edward Moxon.

Shaw, Ian, 2004. *Ancient Egypt: A Very Short Introduction.* Oxford, UK: Oxford University Press.

Shaw, Ian, ed. 2000. *The Oxford History of Ancient Egypt.* Oxford, UK: Oxford University Press.

Shorter, Alan W. 1935. "The God Neḥebkau." *The Journal of Egyptian Archaeology* 21, no. 1 (September): 41–48.

Silverman, David P., William Kelly Simpson, and Josef Wegner, eds. 2009. *In Archaism and Innovation: Studies in the Culture of Middle Kingdom Egypt.* Philadelphia, Pa.: University of Pennsylvania Museum of Archaeology and Anthropology/New Haven, Conn.: Department of Near Eastern Languages and Civilizations at Yale University.

S.S.D.D. [Florence Farr]. 1896. *Egyptian Magic.* Vol. VIII of *Collectanea Hermetica,* edited by W. Wynn Westcott. London: Theosophical Publishing Society.

"Statuette of a Late Middle Kingdom Queen, ca. 1825–1750 B.C." 2016. Metropolitan Museum of Art website.

Stern, Ludwig. 1883. "Die XXII. manethonische Dynastie." *Zeitschrift für Ägyptische Sprache* 21: 15–26.

Stevenson, Alice. 2019. *Scattered Finds: Archaeology, Egyptology and Museums.* London: UCL Press.

Storemyr, Per, Tom Heldal, Elizabeth Bloxam, and James A. Harrell. 2003. *Widan el–Faras Ancient Quarry Landscape, Northern Faiyum Desert, Egypt: Site Description, Historical Significance and Current Destruction.* Zurich: Switzerland: Expert–Center for Conservation of Monuments and Sites.

Stoker, Bram. 1897. *Dracula.* London: Archibald Constable and Co.

———. 1903. *The Jewel of Seven Stars.* London: William Heinemann.

———. (1912) 1980. *The Jewel of Seven Stars.* Revised edition. London: Arrow Books.

———. (1903/1912) 2008. *The Jewel of Seven Stars.* Introduction by Kate Hebblethwaite. New York: Penguin Classics.

Strabo. (1917) 1932. *Geography.* Loeb edition. Translated by H. L. Jones; vol. 1: 1917, vol. 2: 1932. Cambridge, Mass.: Harvard University Press/London: Wm. Heinemann.

Syncellus, George. [873–875 CE]. *Ecloga chronographica.* See Mosshammer 1984.

Tait, John. 2003. "The 'Book of the Fayum': Mystery in a Known Landscape." In O'Connor and Quirke 2003, 183–202.

Tallet, Pierre. 2005. *Sésostris III et la fin de la XII dynastie.* Paris, France: Éditions Flammarion.

———. 2013. *12 reines d'Egypte qui ont change l'Histoire.* Paris, France: Pygmalion.

"The Adventures of Ersatz Sobekneferu/Transcript." 2018. (series 6, episode 10 of *Elementary*) *Elementary* Wiki.

"The Pedestals of Biahmu." 2013. Explore Fayoum website.

"The Reading Room" 2020. British Museum website.

Theis, Christoffer. 2009. "Die Pyramiden 13. Dynastie." *Studien zur Altägyptischen Kultur* 38: 311–42.

Tredoux, Gavan, ed. 2016. "Letters & Memoirs of Sir Richard Francis Burton, Volume 3: 1880 to 1924." The Book of Burtoniana website.

"TT60—Antefoqer and Senet." 2011. Osirisnet Tombs of Ancient Egypt website.

Tully, Caroline. 2018. "Egyptosophy in the British Museum: Florence Farr, the Egyptian Adept and the Ka." In Ferguson and Radford 2018, 131–45.

Tyldesley, Joyce. 2006. *Chronicle of the Queens of Egypt.* London: Thames & Hudson.

Ulmer, Rivka. 2009. *Egyptian Cultural Icons in Midrash.* Berlin, Germany: Walter de Gruyter.

Uphill, Eric P. (2000) 2010. *Pharaoh's Gateway to Eternity: The Hawara Labyrinth of King Amenemhat III.* London and New York: Routledge.

Valloggia, M. 1964. "Remarques sur les noms de la reine Sébek–Ka–Rê Neferou–Sebék." *Revue d'Égyptologie* 16: 45–53.

Vanderlip, Vera Frederika. 1972. *The Four Greek Hymns of Isidorus and the Cult of Isis.* Vol. 12 of *American Studies in Papyrology.* Toronto, Canada: A. M. Hakkert.

Vanderzwet, Pete. 2005. "The Queens of Egypt's 4th Dynasty." Tour Egypt website.

Verner, Miroslav. (2001) 2002. *The Pyramids: The Mystery, Culture, and Science of Egypt's Great Monuments.* New York: Grove Press.

Waddell, W.G. (1940) 1964. *The Fragments of Manetho.* Loeb Classical Library edition. Cambridge, Mass.: Harvard University Press/London: Wm. Heinemann.

Warner, Dan, and Eli Yannai. 2016. "A Summer of Surprises: Gezer Excavation Uncovers Exciting Finds and Possible Date for Water System Construction. Can You Dig it?" New Orleans Baptist Theological Seminary website, November 14.

Warren, Louis S. 2002. "Buffalo Bill Meets Dracula: William F. Cody, Bram Stoker, and the Frontiers of Racial Decay." *The American Historical Review* 107, no. 4: 1124–57.

Wasīf Shāh, Ibrāhīm Ibn (a.k.a. al–Wasīfī), *Kitāb al–ʿAdjāʾib al–kabīr* [attributed to author]. See Colavito 2018.

Weigall, Arthur. 1927. *A History of the Pharaohs, vol. II: The Twelfth to the Eighteenth Dynasties.* London: Thornton Butterworth.

Weinstein, James M. 1974. "A Statuette of the Princess Sobeknefru at Tell Gezer." *Bulletin of the American Schools of Oriental Research* 213 (February): 49–57.

Weston, Paul. 2018. *Atargatis: A Magical East–West New Age Psychodrama.* Glastonbury, Somerset: Avalonian Aeon Publications.

"Who was Pharaoh's Daughter—Theory #1." 2012. Heroines of the Faith: Musings for Mothers and Maidens of All Ages website.

Wilcken, Ulrich. 1884. "Der Labyrintherbauer Petesuchos." *Zeitschrift für Ägyptische Sprache und Altertumskunde* 22:136–39.

Wilkinson, J. G. 1830. *Extracts from Several Hieroglyphical Subjects Found at Thebes, and Other Parts of Egypt.* Malta: Government Press.

———. 1837. *The Manners and Customs of the Ancient Egyptians, vol. II.* London: John Murray.

Wilkinson, Richard H., ed. 2011. *The Temple of Tausret: The University of Arizona Egyptian Expedition Tausret Temple Project, 2004–2011.* Tucson, Az.: University of Arizona Egyptian Expedition.

Williams, Tennessee. 1933. "The Vengeance of Nitocris." *Britannia and Eve* (August 1): 41–43.

Wright, Clara. 2019. "Isis and Cleopatra in Rome: How one of History's Most Famous Queens Influenced an Egyptian Cult in the Heart of the Roman Empire." Classics Senior Thesis. Bryn Mawr, Penn.: Bryn Mawr College.

Žabkar, L.V. 1975. "Semna South: The Southern Fortress." *The Journal of Egyptian Archaeology* 61: 42–44.

Žabkar, L. V., and Žabkar, J. J. 1975. "Semna South: A Preliminary Report on the 1966–68 Excavations of the University of Chicago Oriental Institute Expedition to Sudanese Nubia." *Journal of the American Research Center in Egypt* 19: 7–50.

Zecchi, Marco. 2008. "The Monument of Abgig." *Studien zur Altägyptischen Kultur* 37: 373–386.

———. 2010. *Sobek of Shedet: The Crocodile-god in the Fayyum in the Dynastic Period.* Todi, Italy: Tau Editrice.

Zivie-Coche, Christine. 1972. "Nitocris, Rhodopis et la troisième pyramide de Giza." *Bulletin de l'Institut François d'Archéologie Orientale* 72: 115–38.

MOVIE RELEASES

Blood from the Mummy's Tomb. (1971) 2006 DVD. Seth Holt, dir. The Hammer Collection/Studio Canal.

Bram Stoker's Legend of the Mummy. 1997. Lou Gossett, Jr., dir. Jeffrey Obrow/ Goldbar International/Unapax Entertainment/Goldbar Entertainment/ Metrodome Video Entertainment.

Curse of the Mummy. (1970) 2009 DVD. Guy Verney, dir. Mystery and Imagination/ Talkback Thames/Freemantle Media Enterprizes/Optimum/Studio Canal/ Network.

The Awakening (with original ending). (1980) 2007 DVD. Mike Newell, dir. Orion Pictures Company/Studio Canal.

The Awakening (with final scenes deleted). (1980) 2012 DVD. Mike Newell, dir. Warner Brothers Entertainment.

The Mummy. 2017. Alex Kurtzman, dir. Universal Pictures.

Index